鳥 山 明

Time flies, and suddenly I find I've been working on
Dragon Ball for a full decade. Considering that I have
virtually no self-discipline, it's really amazing. Good job,
me. I'm always a slacker when it comes to work, though
not when it comes to hobbies. I feel like I accidentally did
something impressive without realizing what I was doing.
Now I have to make up for these 10 years of work. I'm
falling way behind on my sitting around doing nothing! I
really don't think I'm cut out for these weekly serials…
                    —Akira Toriyama, 1994

Widely known all over the world for his playful, innovative
storytelling and humorous, distinctive art style, **Dragon Ball**
creator Akira Toriyama is also known in his native Japan for
the wildly popular **Dr. Slump**, his previous manga series
about the adventures of a mad scientist and his android
"daughter." His hit series **Dragon Ball** ran from 1984 to
1995 in Shueisha's **Weekly Shonen Jump** magazine. He is
also known for his design work on video games such as
Dragon Warrior, **Chrono Trigger** and **Tobal No. 1**. His
recent manga works include **Cowa!**, **Kajika**, **Sand Land**,
Neko Majin, and a children's book, **Toccio the Angel**. He
lives with his family in Japan.

DRAGON BALL Z VOL.23
SHONEN JUMP Manga Edition

STORY AND ART BY
AKIRA TORIYAMA

English Adaptation/Gerard Jones
Translation/Lillian Olsen
Touch-up Art & Lettering/Wayne Truman
Design/Sean Lee
Editor/Jason Thompson

In the original Japanese edition, DRAGON BALL and DRAGON BALL Z
are known collectively as the 42-volume series DRAGON BALL. The
English DRAGON BALL Z was originally volumes 17–42 of the Japanese
DRAGON BALL.

Printed in the U.S.A.

Published by VIZ Media, LLC
P.O. Box 77010
San Francisco, CA 94107

10
First printing, November 2005
Tenth printing, September 2018

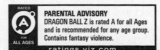

www.viz.com

www.shonenjump.com

SHONEN JUMP MANGA

DRAGON BALL Z

Vol. 23

DB: 39 of 42

STORY AND ART BY
AKIRA TORIYAMA

THE MAIN CHARACTERS

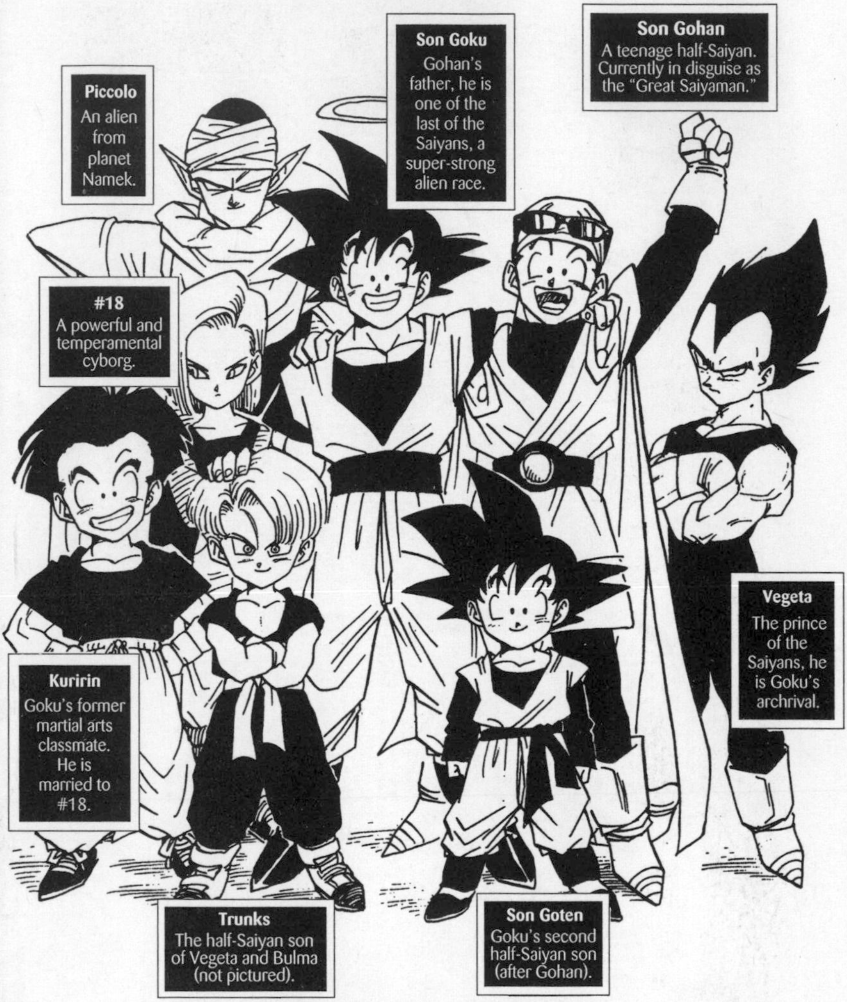
Son Gohan
A teenage half-Saiyan. Currently in disguise as the "Great Saiyaman."
Son Goku
Gohan's father, he is one of the last of the Saiyans, a super-strong alien race.
Piccolo
An alien from planet Namek.
#18
A powerful and temperamental cyborg.
Vegeta
The prince of the Saiyans, he is Goku's archrival.
Kuririn
Goku's former martial arts classmate. He is married to #18.
Son Goten
Goku's second half-Saiyan son (after Gohan).
Trunks
The half-Saiyan son of Vegeta and Bulma (not pictured).

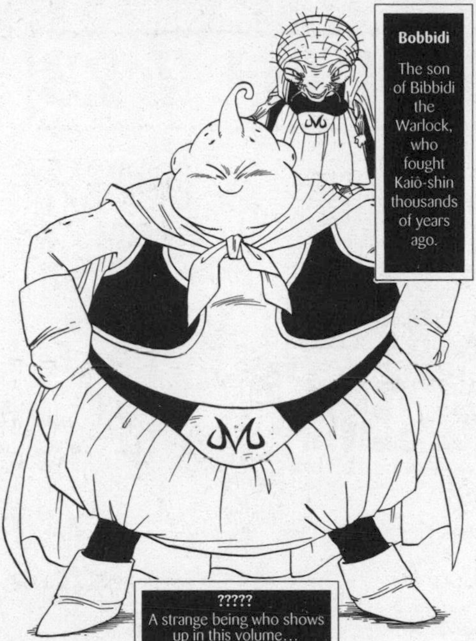

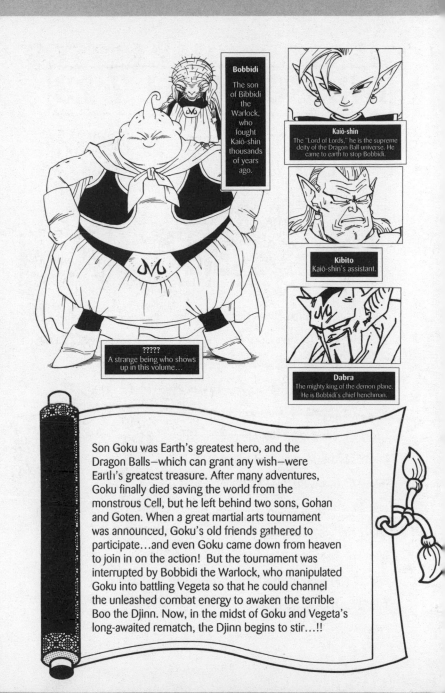

Bobbidi
The son of Bibbidi the Warlock, who fought Kaiô-shin thousands of years ago.

?????
A strange being who shows up in this volume…

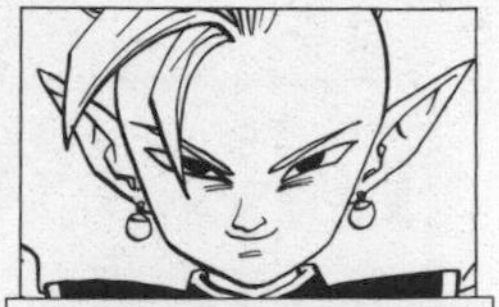

Kaiô-shin
The "Lord of Lords," he is the supreme deity of the Dragon Ball universe. He came to earth to stop Bobbidi.

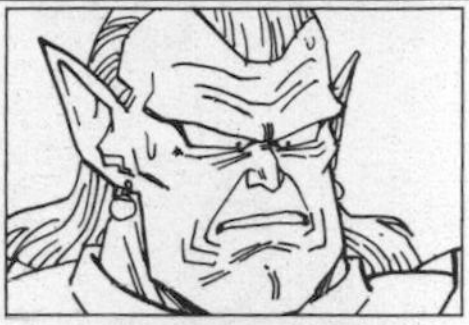

Kibito
Kaiô-shin's assistant.

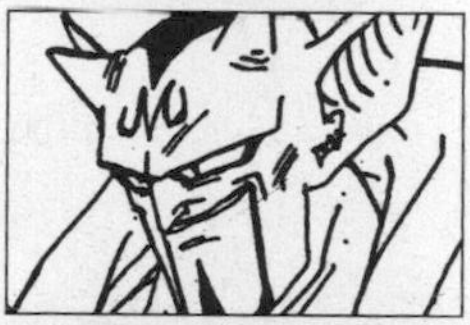

Dabra
The mighty king of the demon plane. He is Bobbidi's chief henchman.

Son Goku was Earth's greatest hero, and the Dragon Balls—which can grant any wish—were Earth's greatest treasure. After many adventures, Goku finally died saving the world from the monstrous Cell, but he left behind two sons, Gohan and Goten. When a great martial arts tournament was announced, Goku's old friends gathered to participate…and even Goku came down from heaven to join in on the action! But the tournament was interrupted by Bobbidi the Warlock, who manipulated Goku into battling Vegeta so that he could channel the unleashed combat energy to awaken the terrible Boo the Djinn. Now, in the midst of Goku and Vegeta's long-awaited rematch, the Djinn begins to stir…!!

DRAGON BALL Z 23

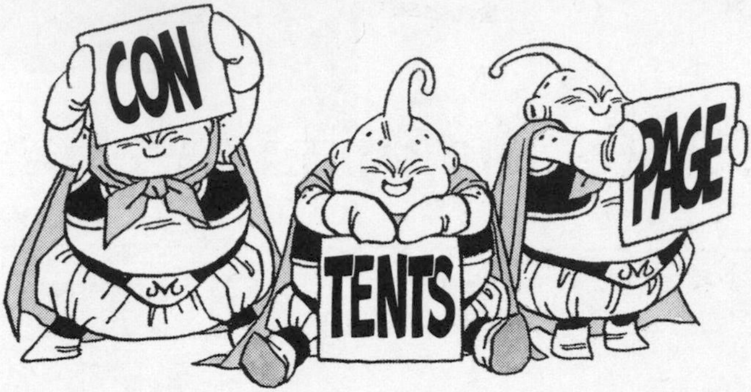
CON
TENTS
PAGE

DRAGON BALL ドラゴンボール

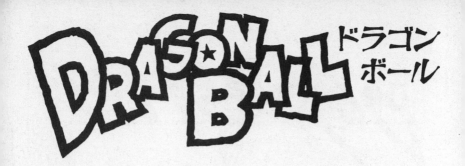

DBZ:266 · The Djinn Awakens?!

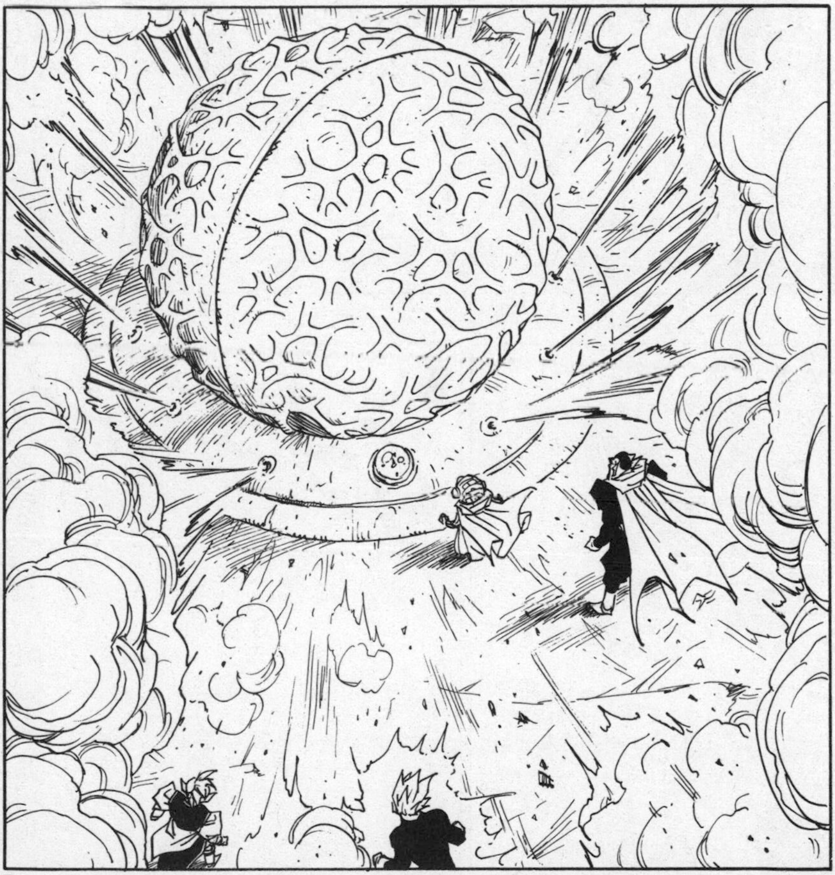

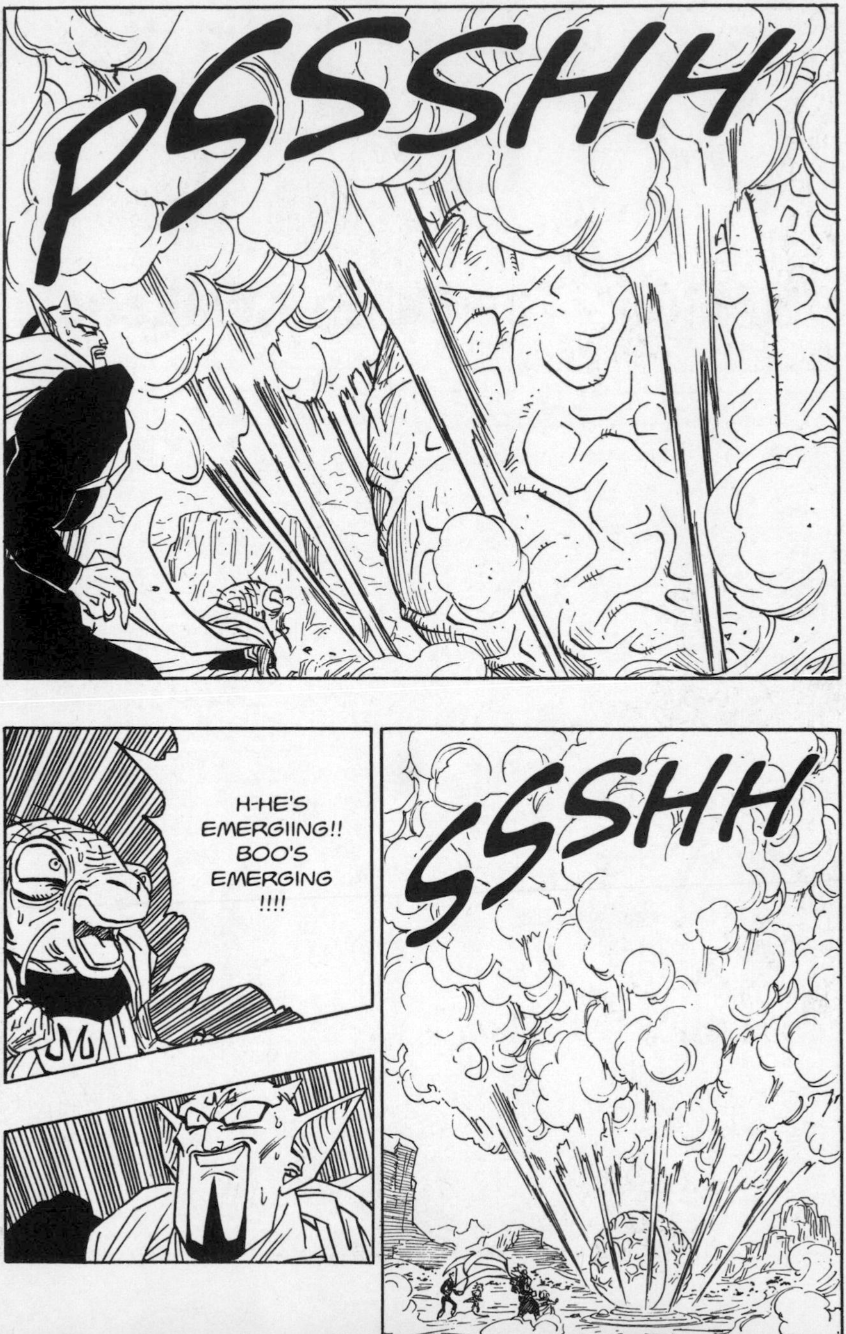
PSSSHH
SSSHH
H-HE'S EMERGIING!! BOO'S EMERGING !!!!

READ THIS WAY

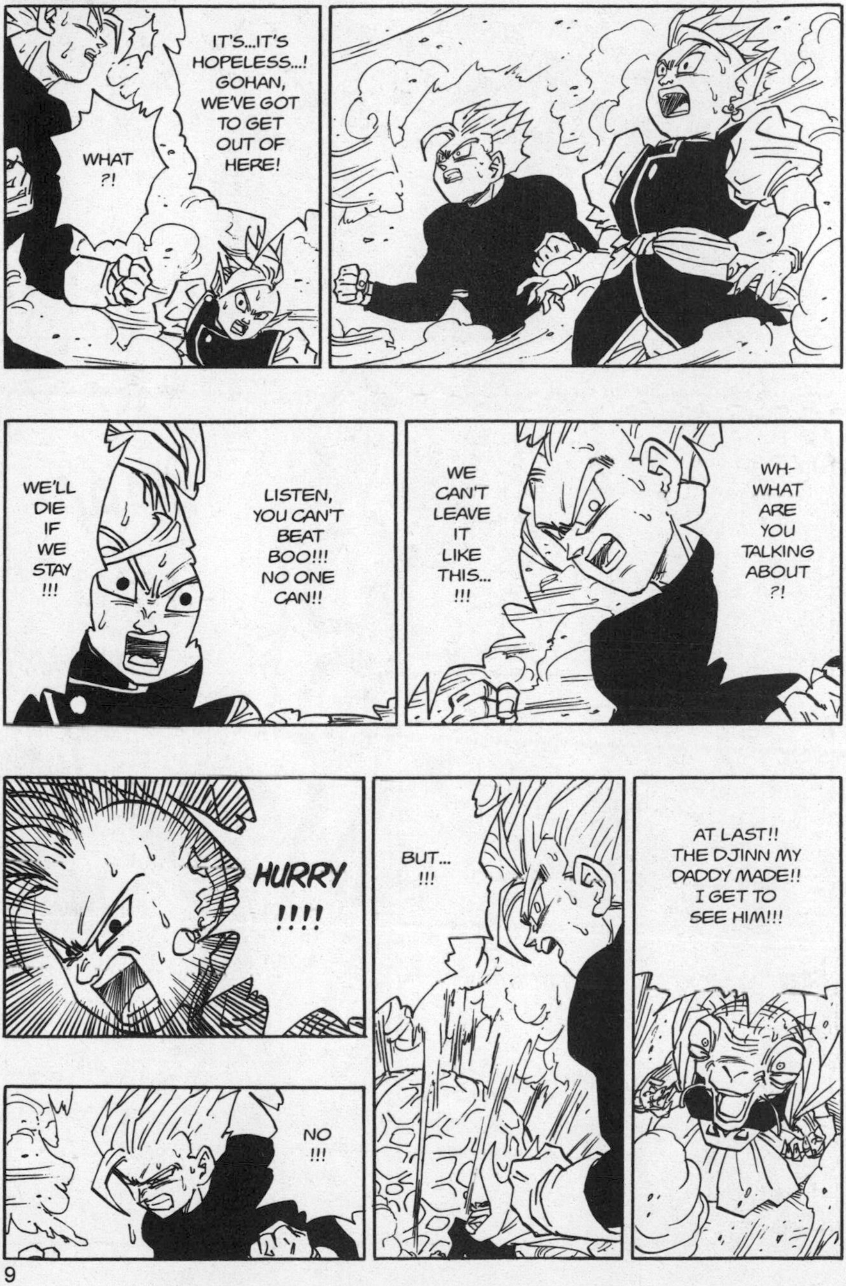
IT'S...IT'S HOPELESS...! GOHAN, WE'VE GOT TO GET OUT OF HERE!
WHAT ?!
WH-WHAT ARE YOU TALKING ABOUT ?!
WE CAN'T LEAVE IT LIKE THIS... !!!
LISTEN, YOU CAN'T BEAT BOO!!! NO ONE CAN!!
WE'LL DIE IF WE STAY !!!
AT LAST!! THE DJINN MY DADDY MADE!! I GET TO SEE HIM!!!
BUT... !!!
HURRY !!!!
NO !!!

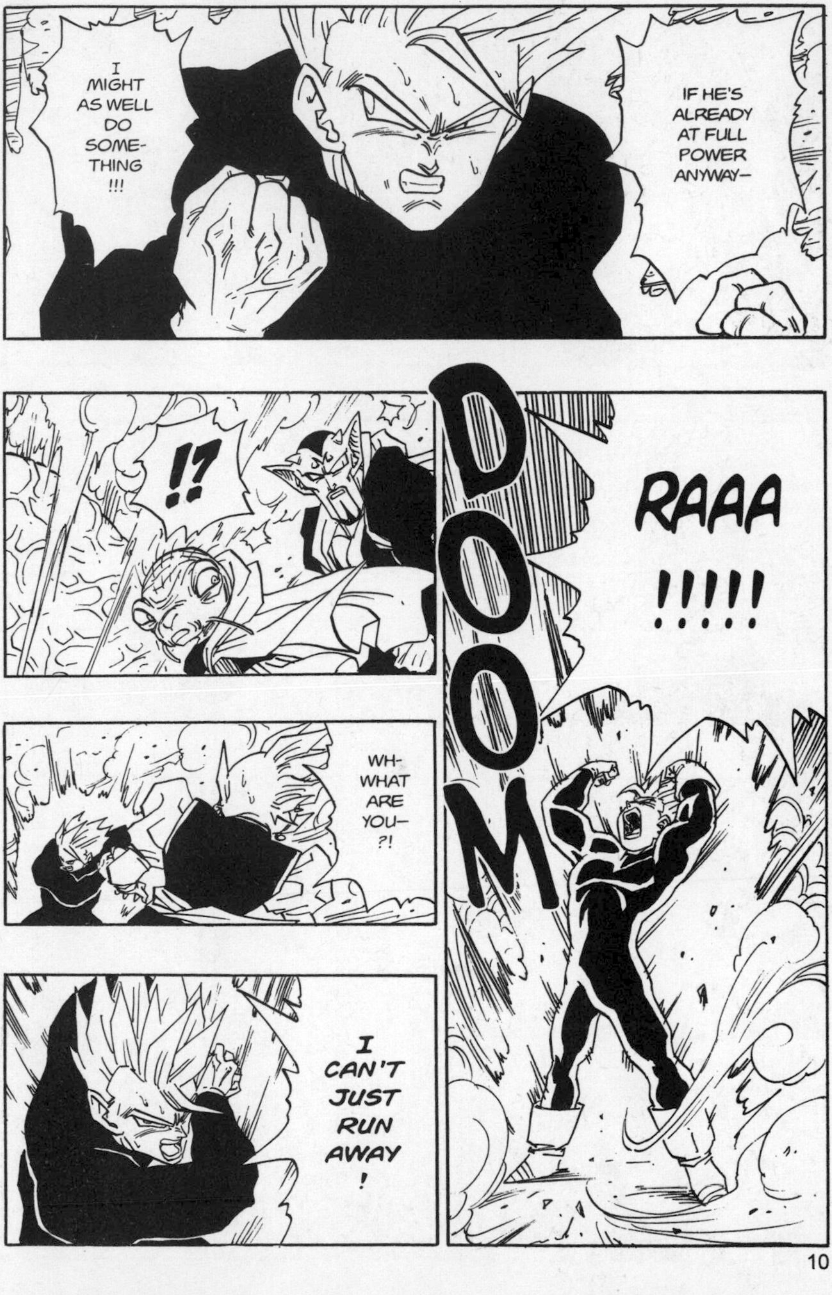
IF HE'S ALREADY AT FULL POWER ANYWAY—
I MIGHT AS WELL DO SOME-THING!!!
RAAA!!!!!
DOOM
!?
WH-WHAT ARE YOU—?!
I CAN'T JUST RUN AWAY!

READ THIS WAY

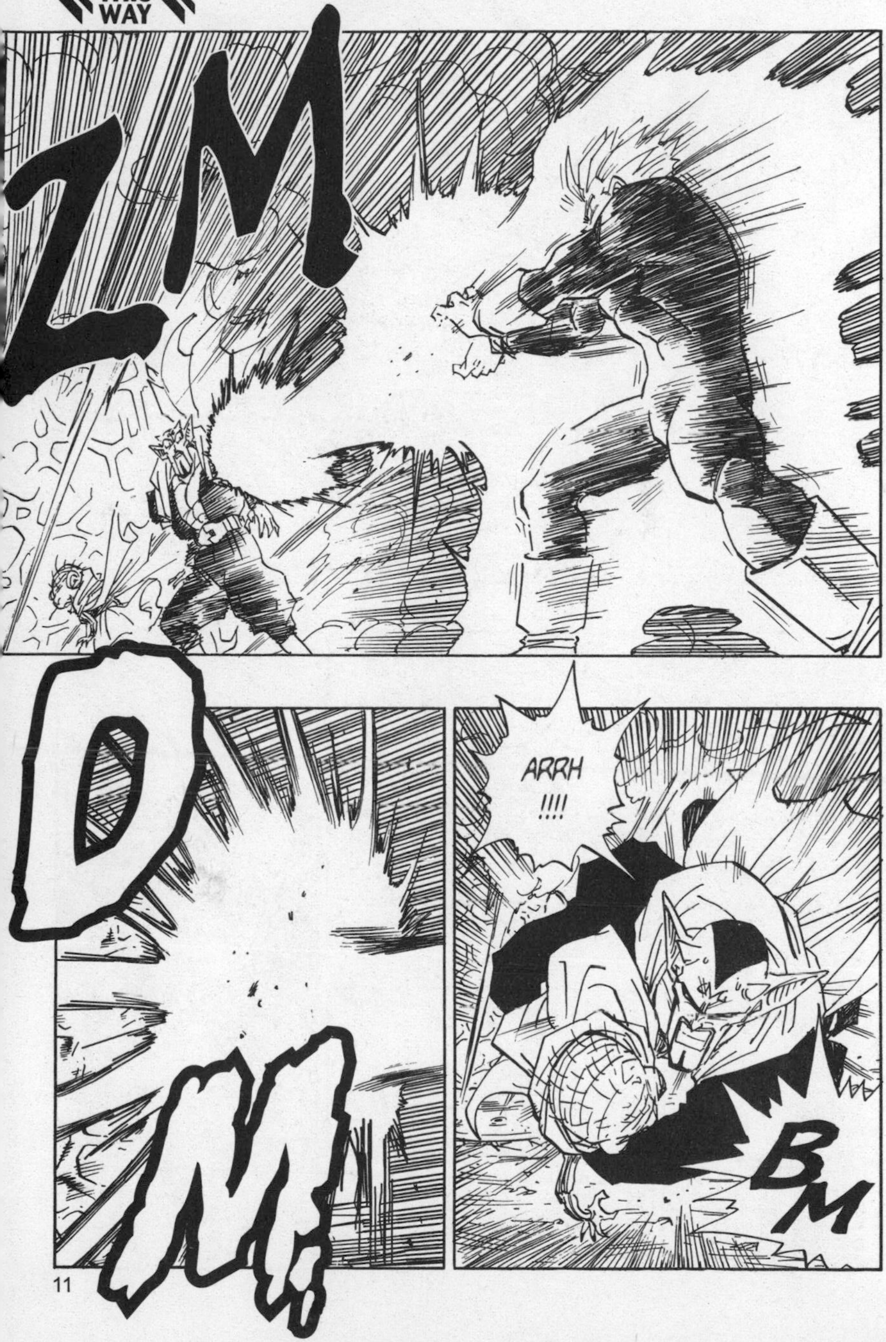

ZM!
ARRH !!!!
BM
DM!

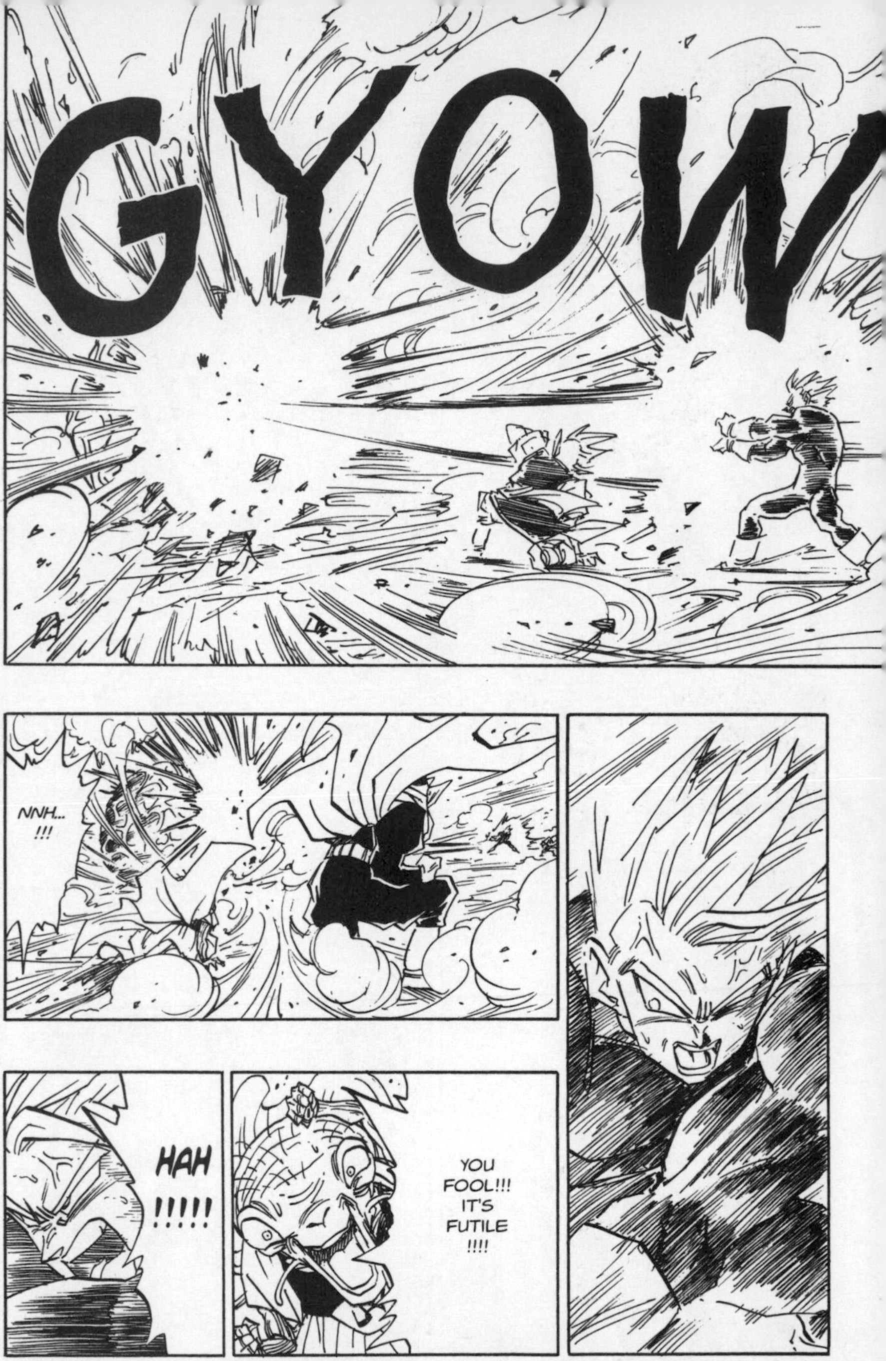
GYOW
NNH... !!!
YOU FOOL!!! IT'S FUTILE !!!!
HAH !!!!!

READ THIS WAY

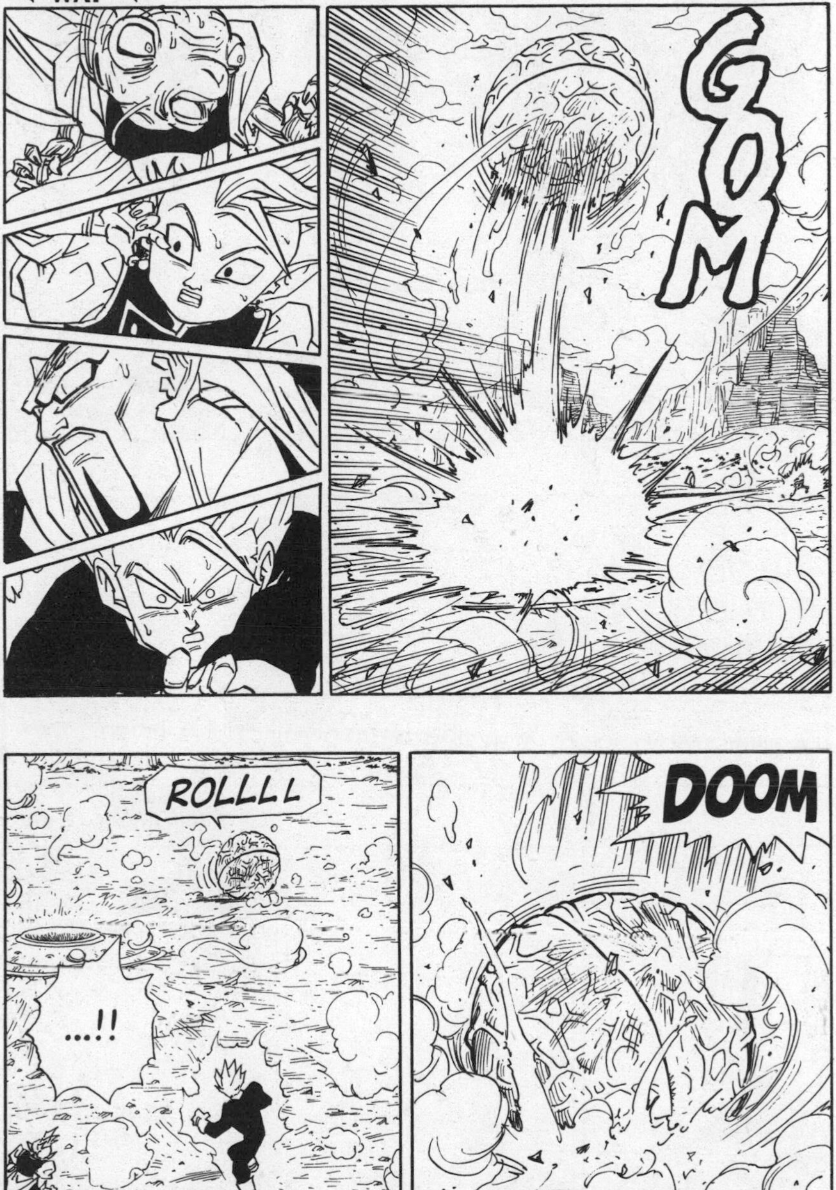

GOM
DOOM
ROLLLL
...!!

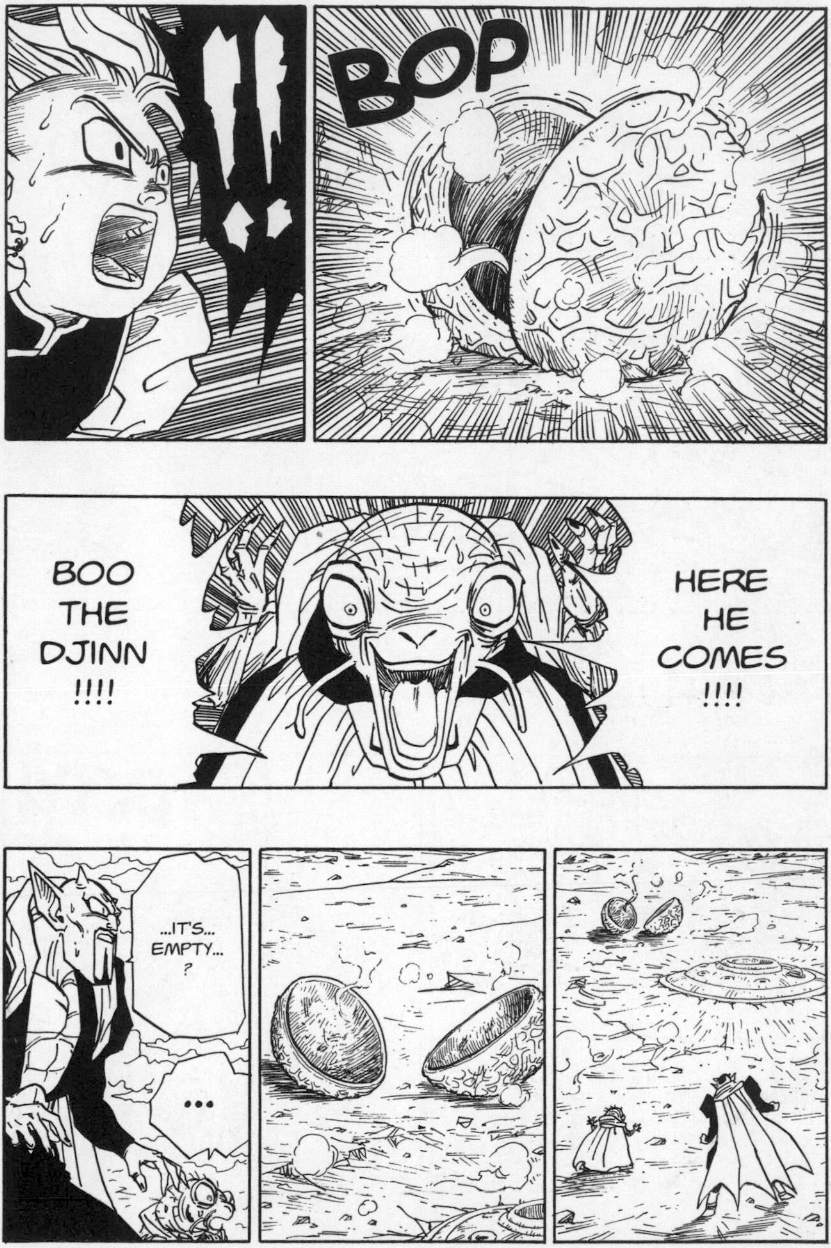
BOP
!!
BOO THE DJINN !!!!
HERE HE COMES !!!!
...IT'S... EMPTY... ?
•••

READ THIS WAY

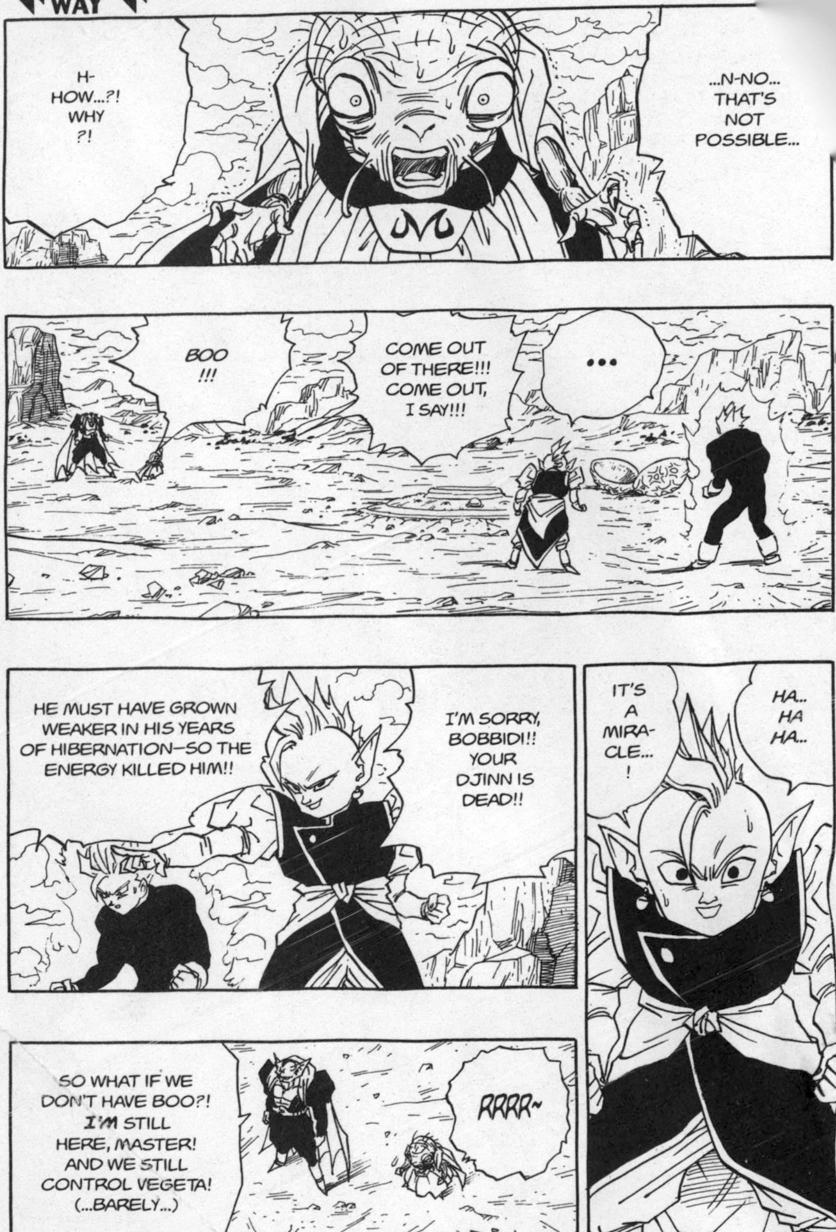
...N-NO... THAT'S NOT POSSIBLE...
H-HOW...?! WHY?!
...
COME OUT OF THERE!!! COME OUT, I SAY!!!
BOO!!!
HA.. HA HA..
IT'S A MIRACLE...!
I'M SORRY, BOBBIDI!! YOUR DJINN IS DEAD!!
HE MUST HAVE GROWN WEAKER IN HIS YEARS OF HIBERNATION—SO THE ENERGY KILLED HIM!!
RRRR~
SO WHAT IF WE DON'T HAVE BOO?! I'M STILL HERE, MASTER! AND WE STILL CONTROL VEGETA! (...BARELY...)

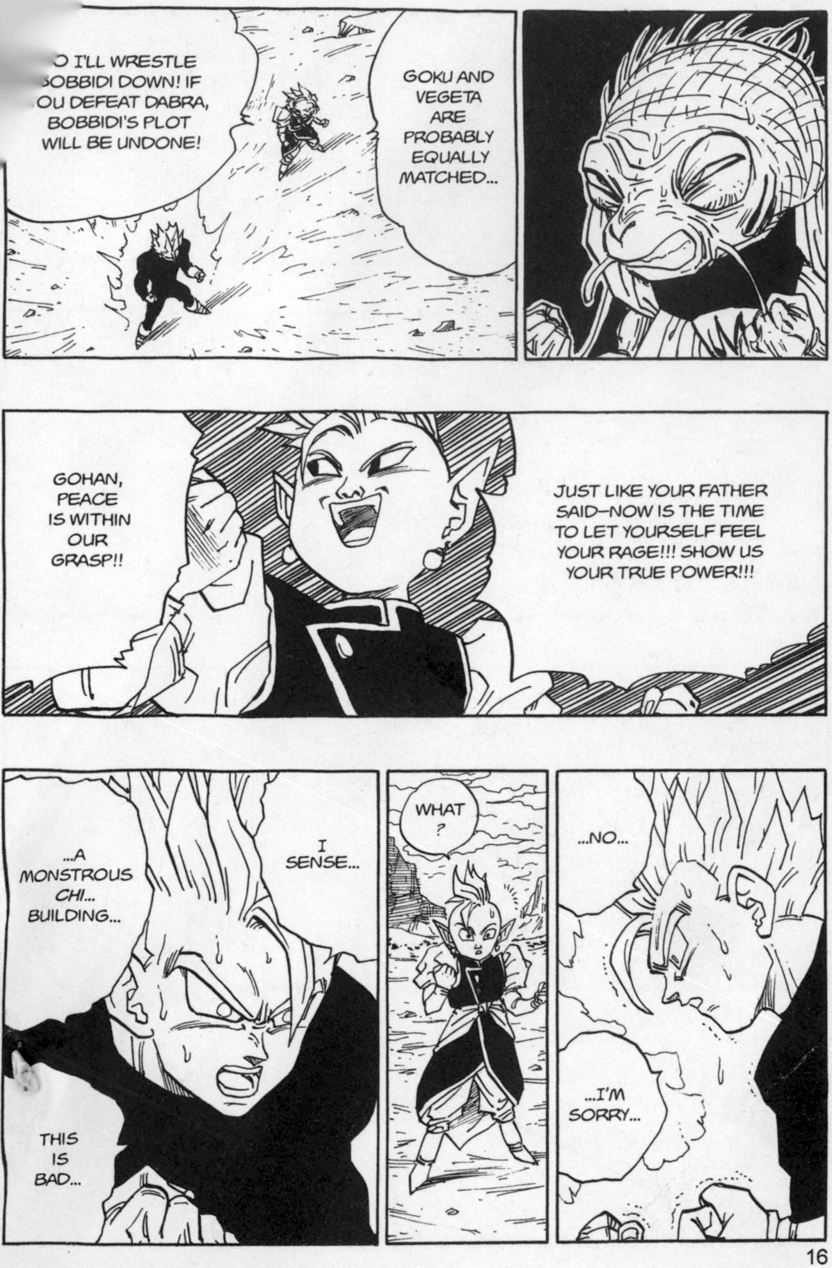
GOKU AND VEGETA ARE PROBABLY EQUALLY MATCHED...
O I'LL WRESTLE BOBBIDI DOWN! IF OU DEFEAT DABRA, BOBBIDI'S PLOT WILL BE UNDONE!
JUST LIKE YOUR FATHER SAID—NOW IS THE TIME TO LET YOURSELF FEEL YOUR RAGE!!! SHOW US YOUR TRUE POWER!!!
GOHAN, PEACE IS WITHIN OUR GRASP!!
...NO...
...I'M SORRY...
WHAT ?
I SENSE...
...A MONSTROUS CHI... BUILDING...
THIS IS BAD...

READ THIS WAY

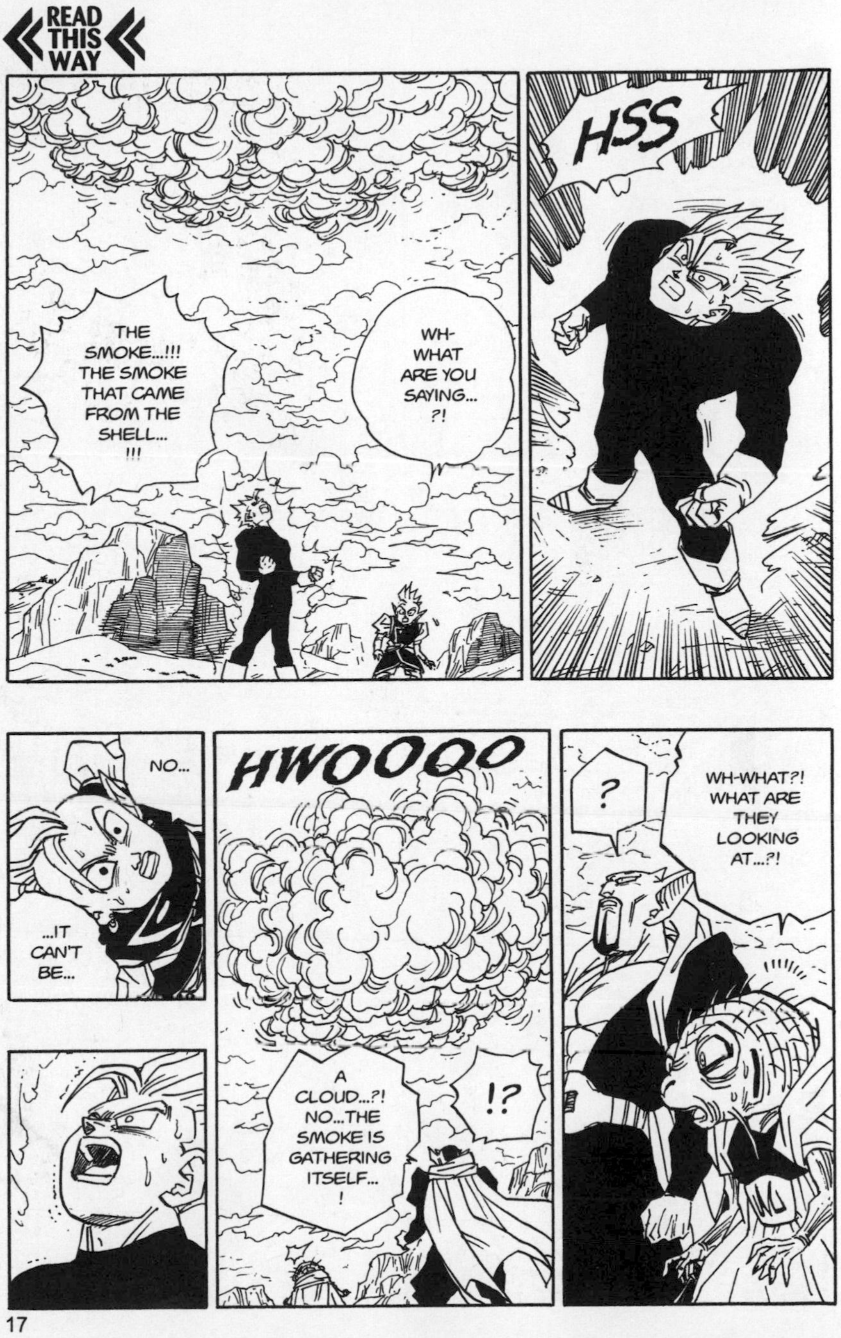
HSS
WH-WHAT ARE YOU SAYING...?!
THE SMOKE...!!! THE SMOKE THAT CAME FROM THE SHELL...!!!
WH-WHAT?! WHAT ARE THEY LOOKING AT...?!
?
HWOOOO
!?
A CLOUD...?! NO...THE SMOKE IS GATHERING ITSELF...!
NO...
...IT CAN'T BE...

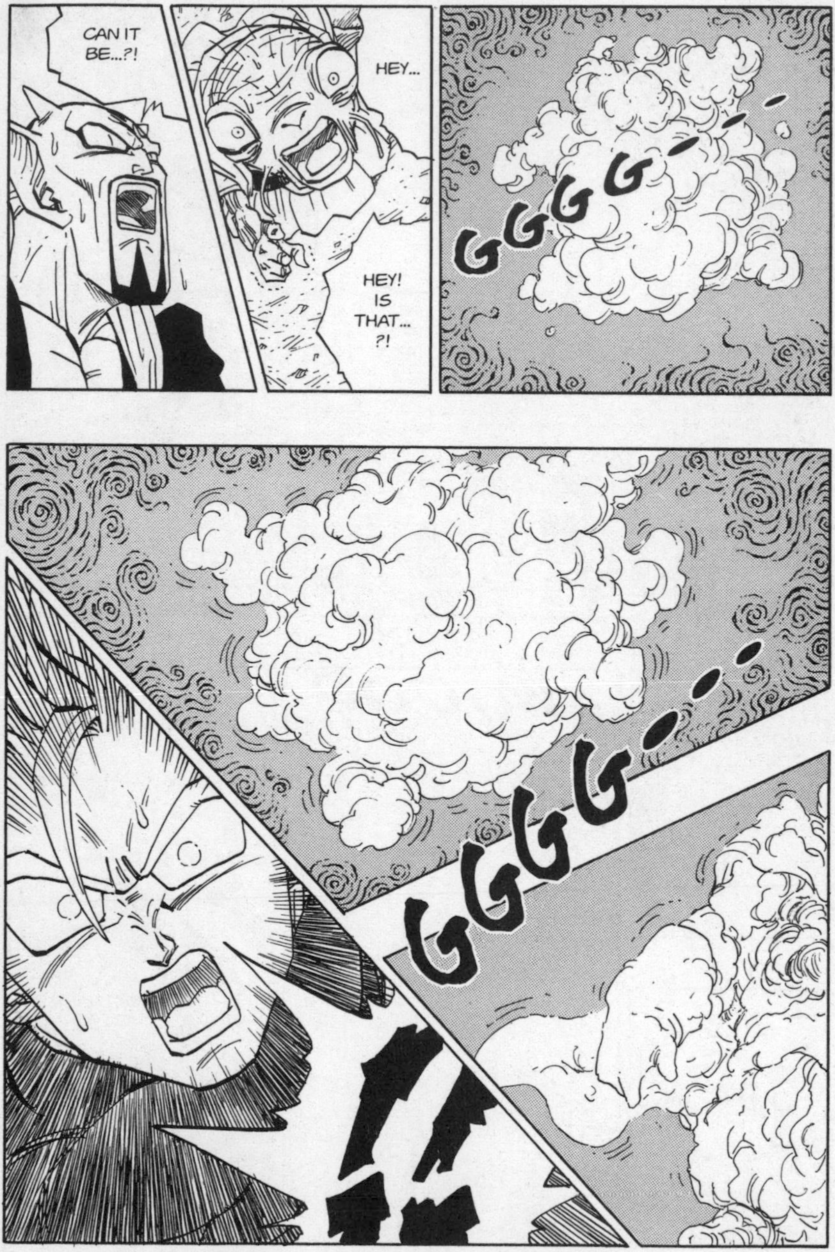
GGGG
HEY...
HEY! IS THAT...?!
CAN IT BE...?!
GGGG

READ THIS WAY

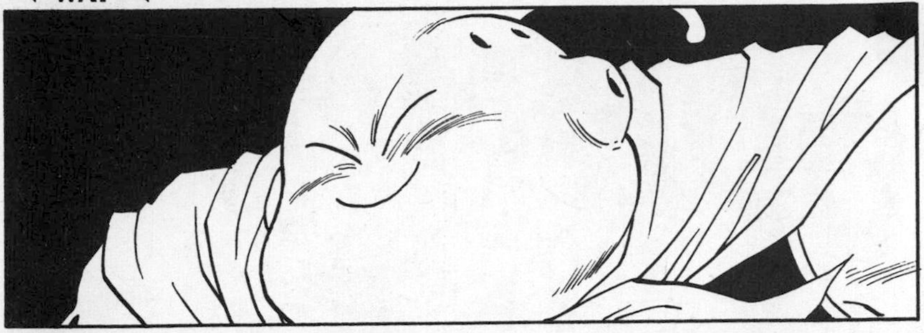

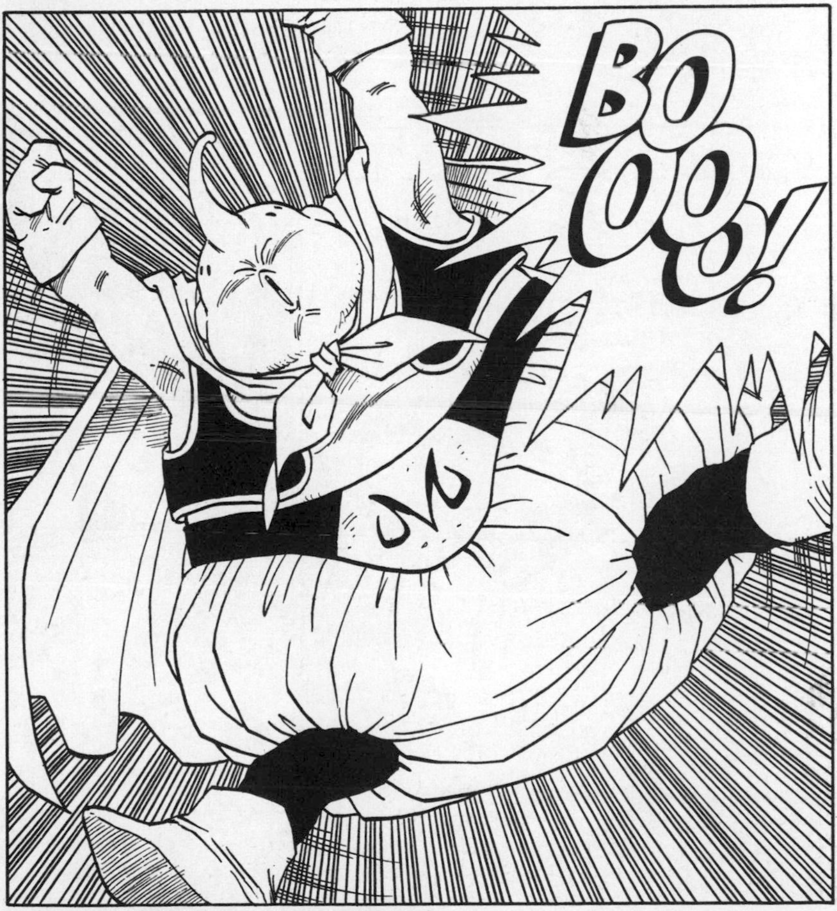
BOOOOO!

NEXT: The Face of Boo!

DBZ:267 · Can This Be Boo?!

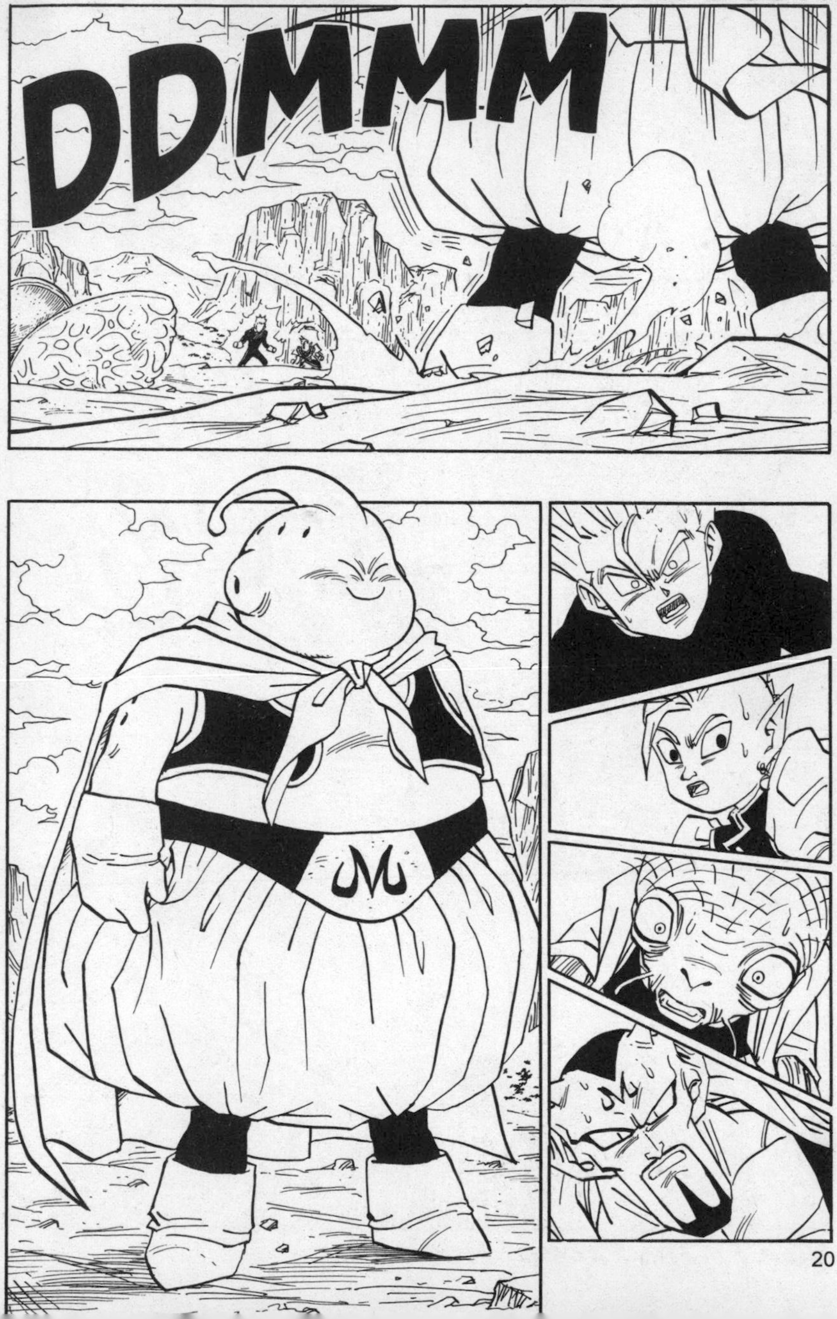
DDMMM

READ THIS WAY

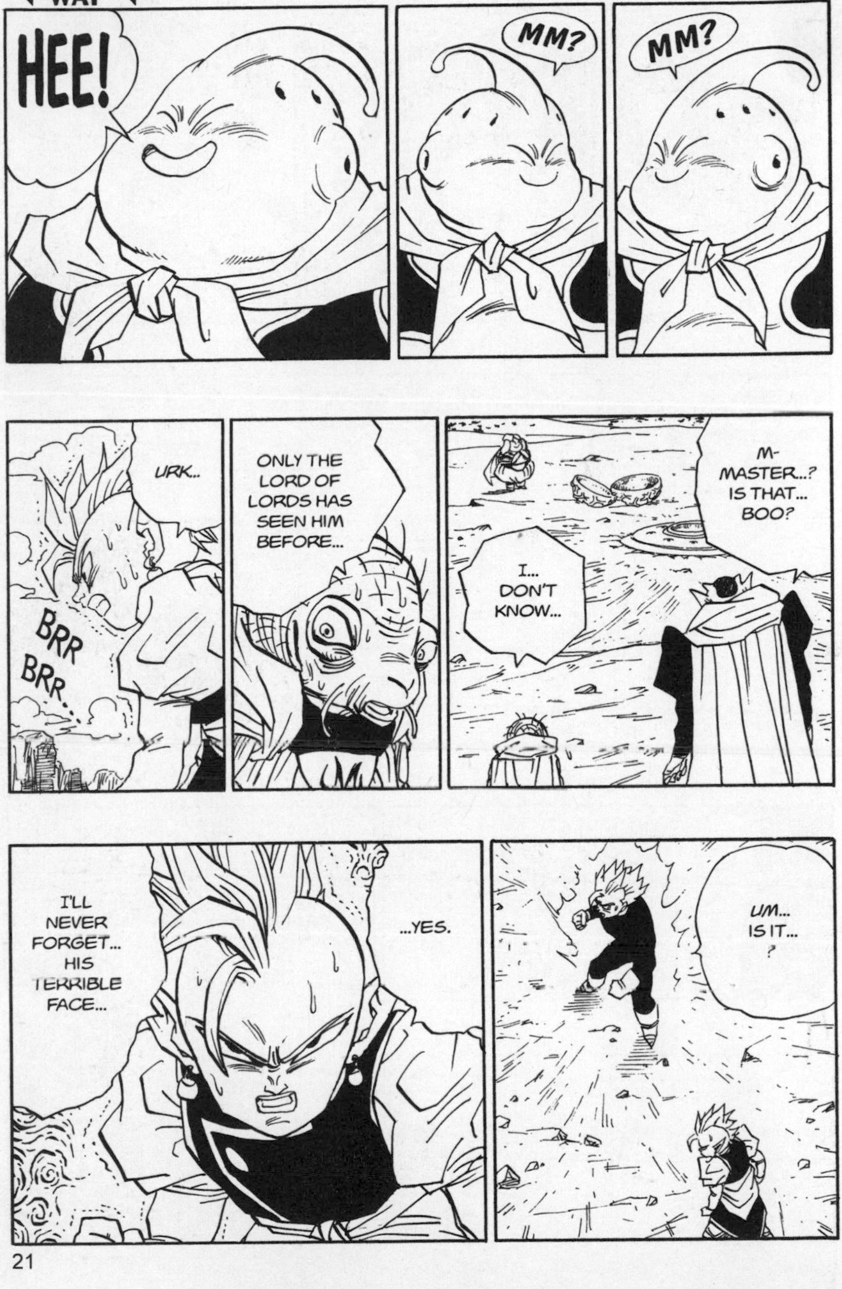
MM?
MM?
HEE!
M-MASTER...? IS THAT... BOO?
I... DON'T KNOW...
ONLY THE LORD OF LORDS HAS SEEN HIM BEFORE...
URK...
BRR BRR
UM... IS IT... ?
...YES.
I'LL NEVER FORGET... HIS TERRIBLE FACE...

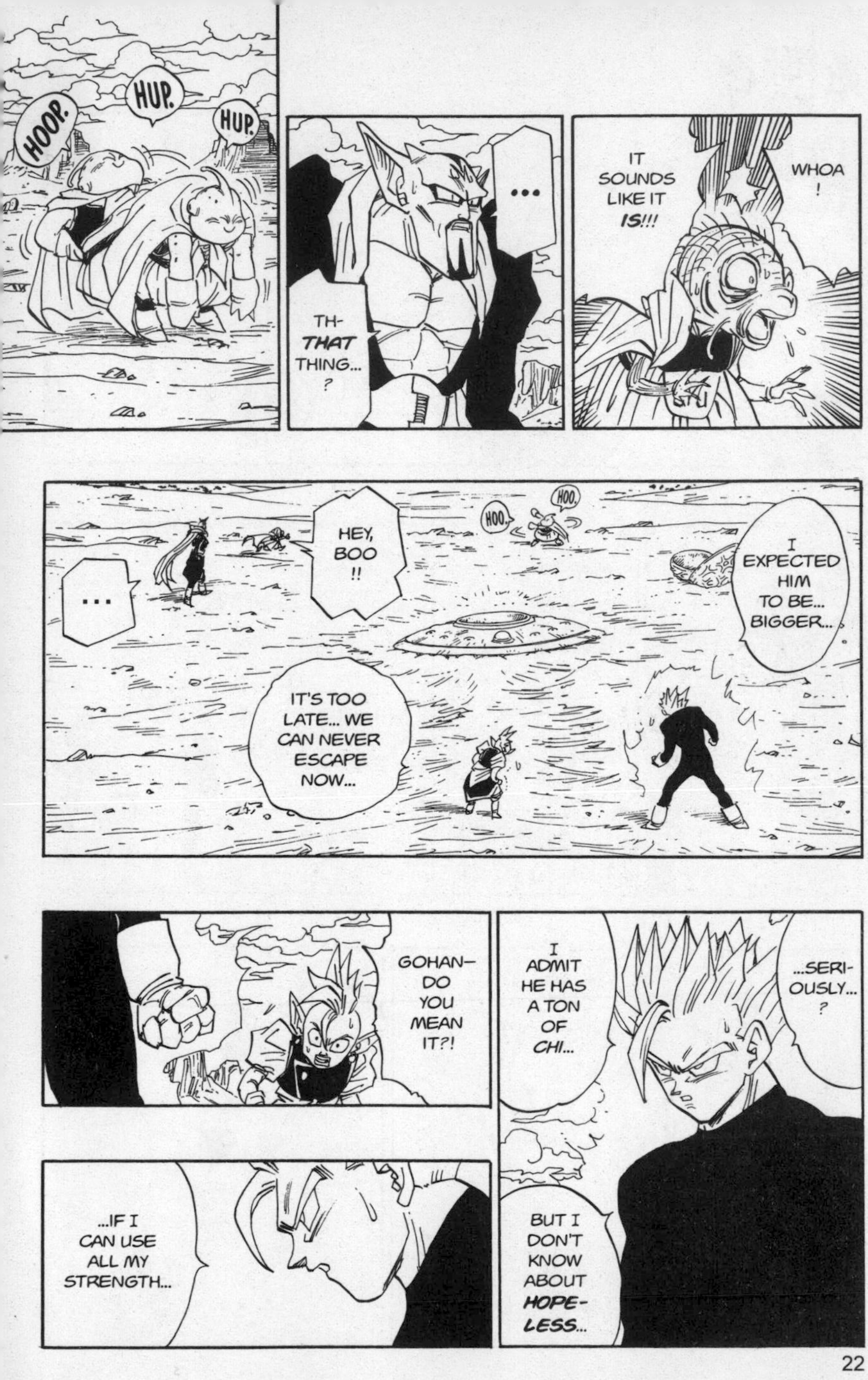

WHOA!
IT SOUNDS LIKE IT *IS*!!!
...
TH-*THAT* THING...?
HUP.
HUP.
HOOP.
I EXPECTED HIM TO BE... BIGGER...
HOO.
HOO.
HEY, BOO!!
...
IT'S TOO LATE... WE CAN NEVER ESCAPE NOW...
...SERIOUSLY...?
I ADMIT HE HAS A TON OF *CHI*...
BUT I DON'T KNOW ABOUT *HOPELESS*...
GOHAN— DO YOU MEAN IT?!
...IF I CAN USE ALL MY STRENGTH...

READ THIS WAY

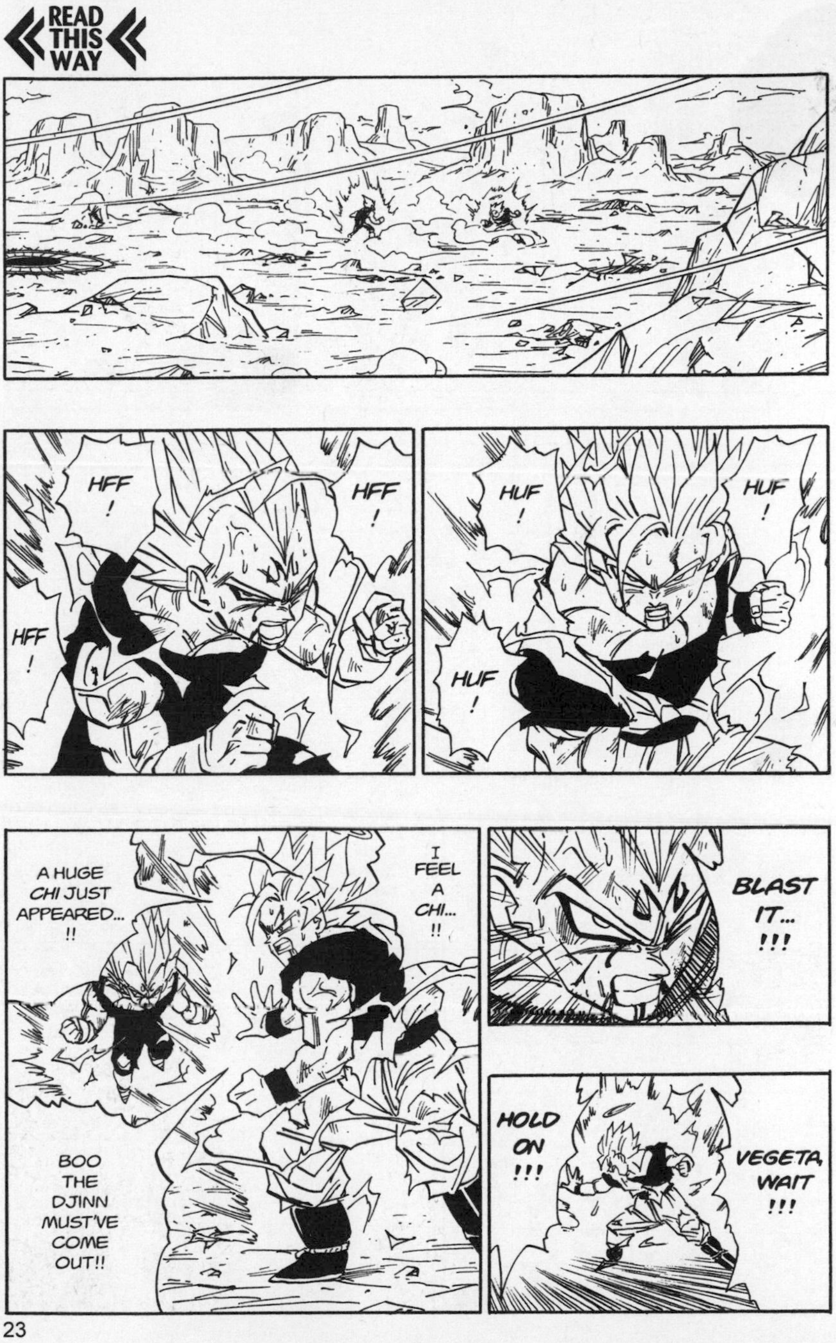
HUF!
HUF!
HUF!
HFF!
HFF!
HFF!
BLAST IT...!!!
VEGETA, WAIT!!!
HOLD ON!!!
I FEEL A CHI...!!
A HUGE CHI JUST APPEARED...!!
BOO THE DJINN MUST'VE COME OUT!!

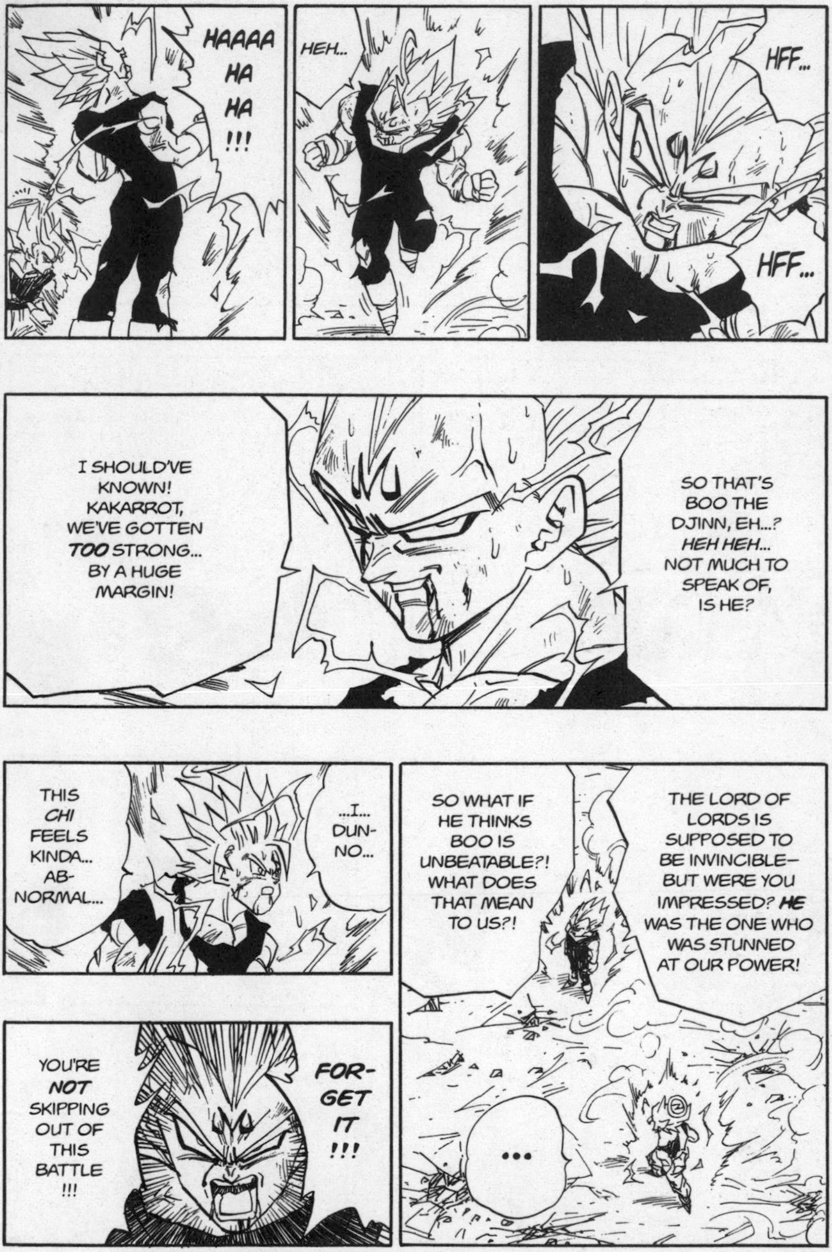
HFF...
HFF...
HEH...
HAAAA HA HA !!!
SO THAT'S BOO THE DJINN, EH...? HEH HEH... NOT MUCH TO SPEAK OF, IS HE?
I SHOULD'VE KNOWN! KAKARROT, WE'VE GOTTEN TOO STRONG... BY A HUGE MARGIN!
THE LORD OF LORDS IS SUPPOSED TO BE INVINCIBLE— BUT WERE YOU IMPRESSED? HE WAS THE ONE WHO WAS STUNNED AT OUR POWER!
SO WHAT IF HE THINKS BOO IS UNBEATABLE?! WHAT DOES THAT MEAN TO US?!
...
...I... DUN-NO...
THIS CHI FEELS KINDA... AB-NORMAL...
FOR-GET IT !!!
YOU'RE NOT SKIPPING OUT OF THIS BATTLE !!!

READ THIS WAY

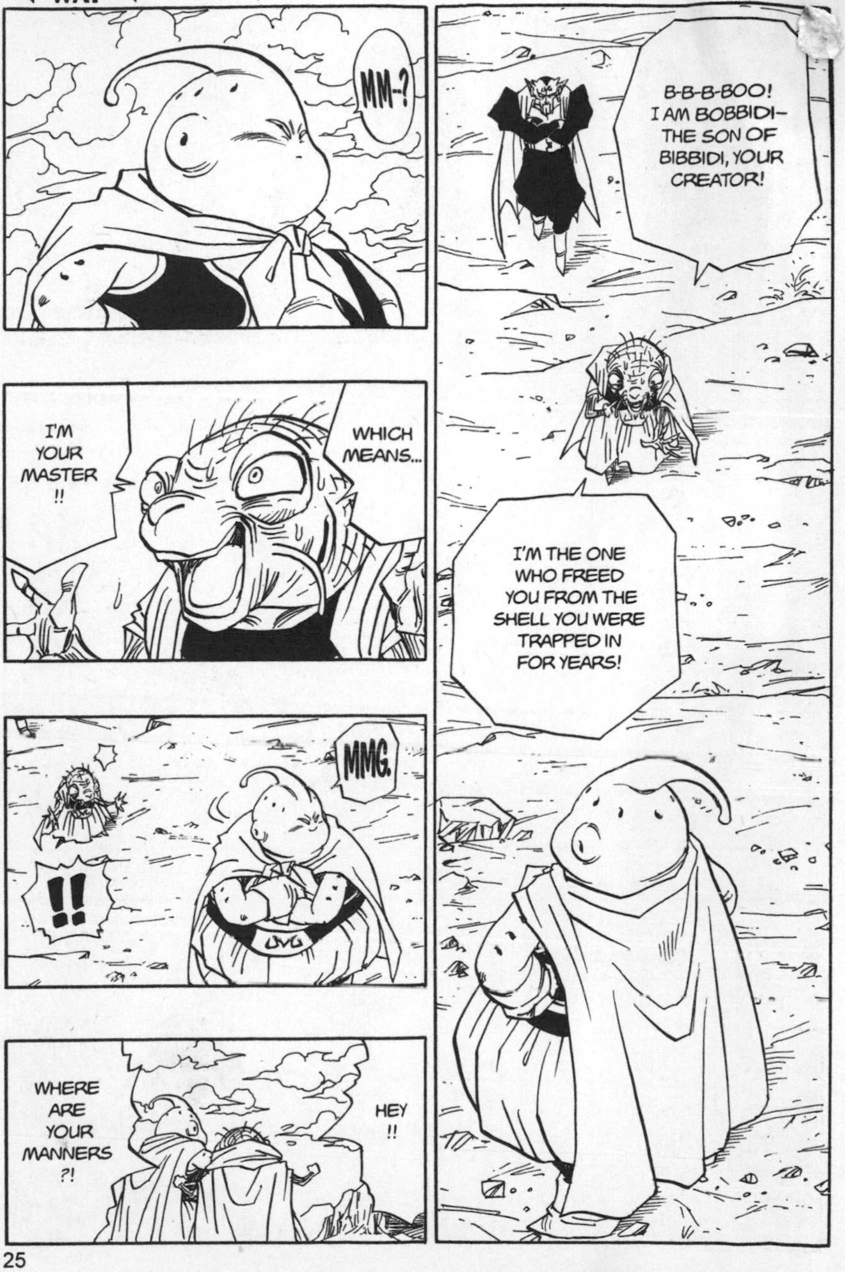

B-B-B-BOO! I AM BOBBIDI— THE SON OF BIBBIDI, YOUR CREATOR!
I'M THE ONE WHO FREED YOU FROM THE SHELL YOU WERE TRAPPED IN FOR YEARS!
MM-?
WHICH MEANS...
I'M YOUR MASTER !!
MMG.
!!
HEY !!
WHERE ARE YOUR MANNERS ?!

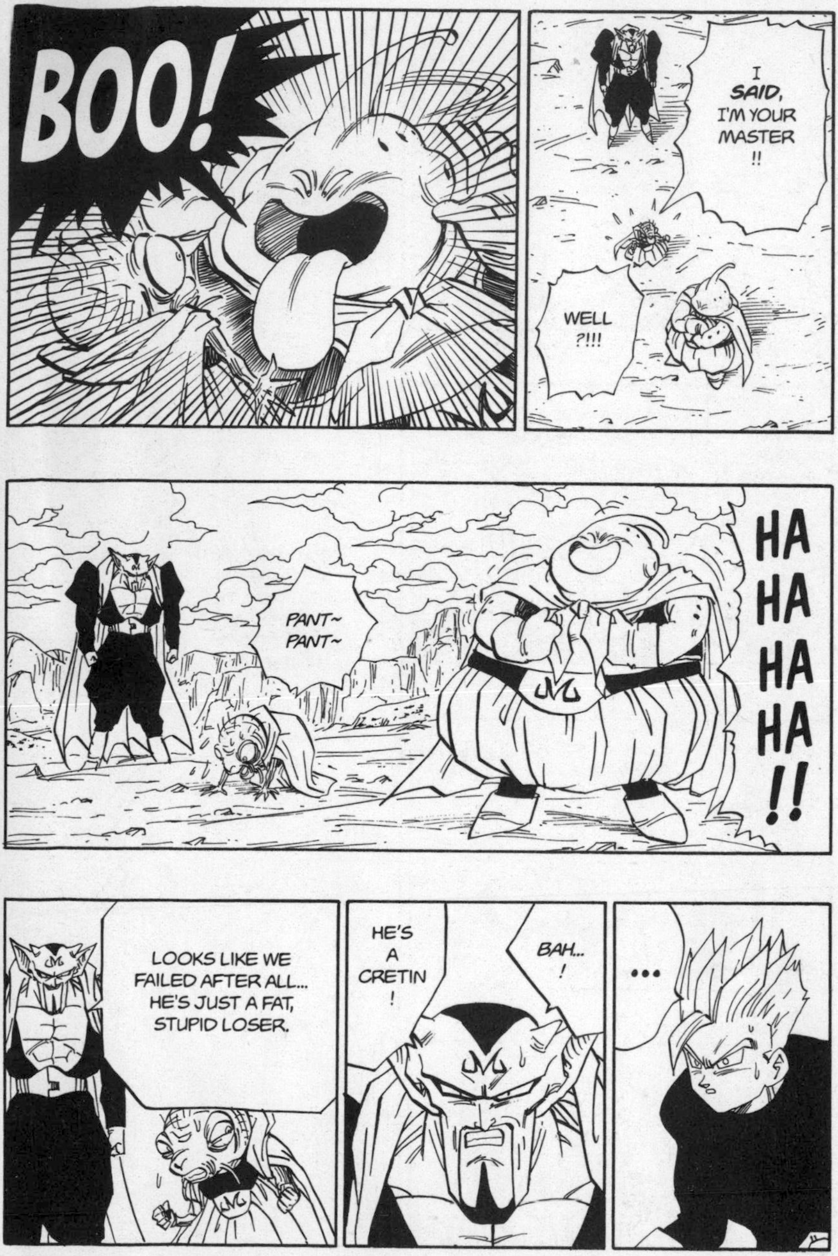
I SAID, I'M YOUR MASTER !!
WELL ?!!!
BOO!
HA HA HA HA HA HA HA!!
PANT~ PANT~
...
BAH... !
HE'S A CRETIN !
LOOKS LIKE WE FAILED AFTER ALL... HE'S JUST A FAT, STUPID LOSER.

READ THIS WAY

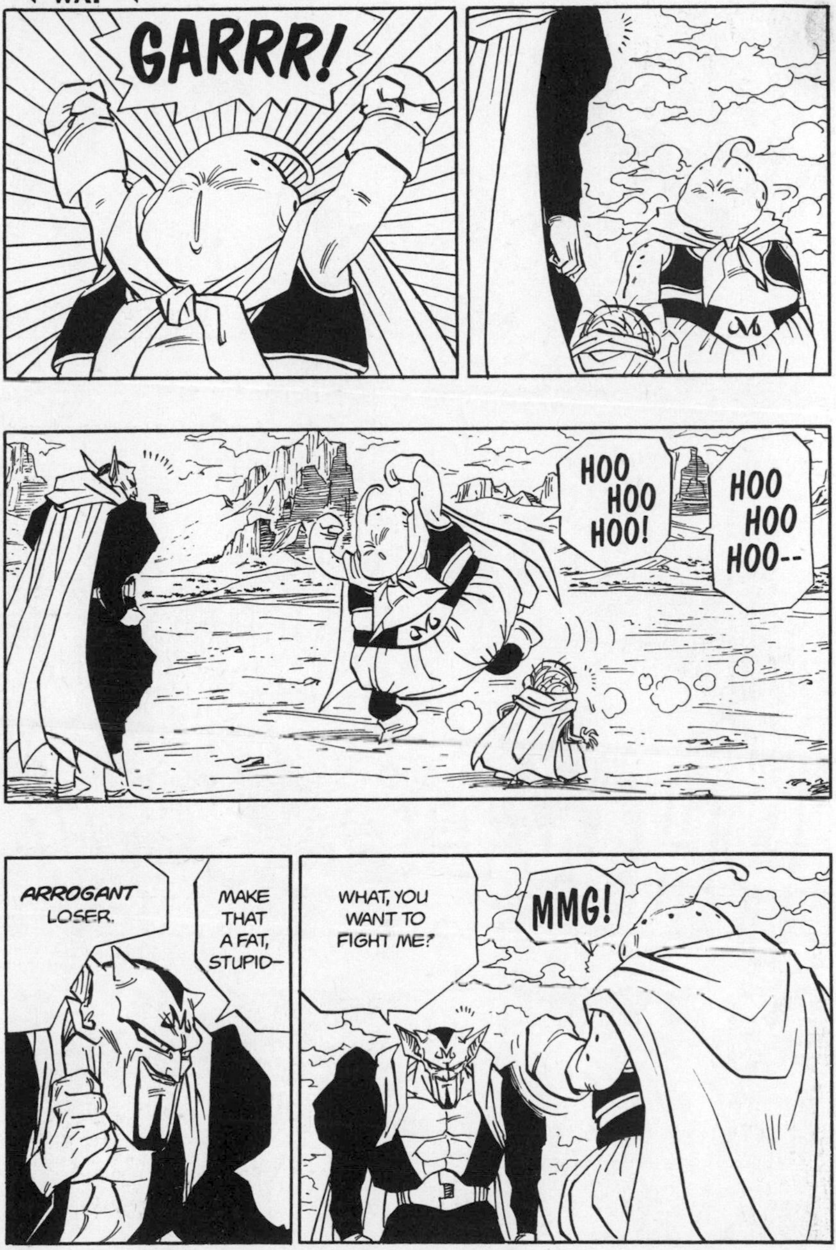

GARRR!
HOO HOO HOO--
HOO HOO HOO!
MMG!
WHAT, YOU WANT TO FIGHT ME?
MAKE THAT A FAT, STUPID—
ARROGANT LOSER.

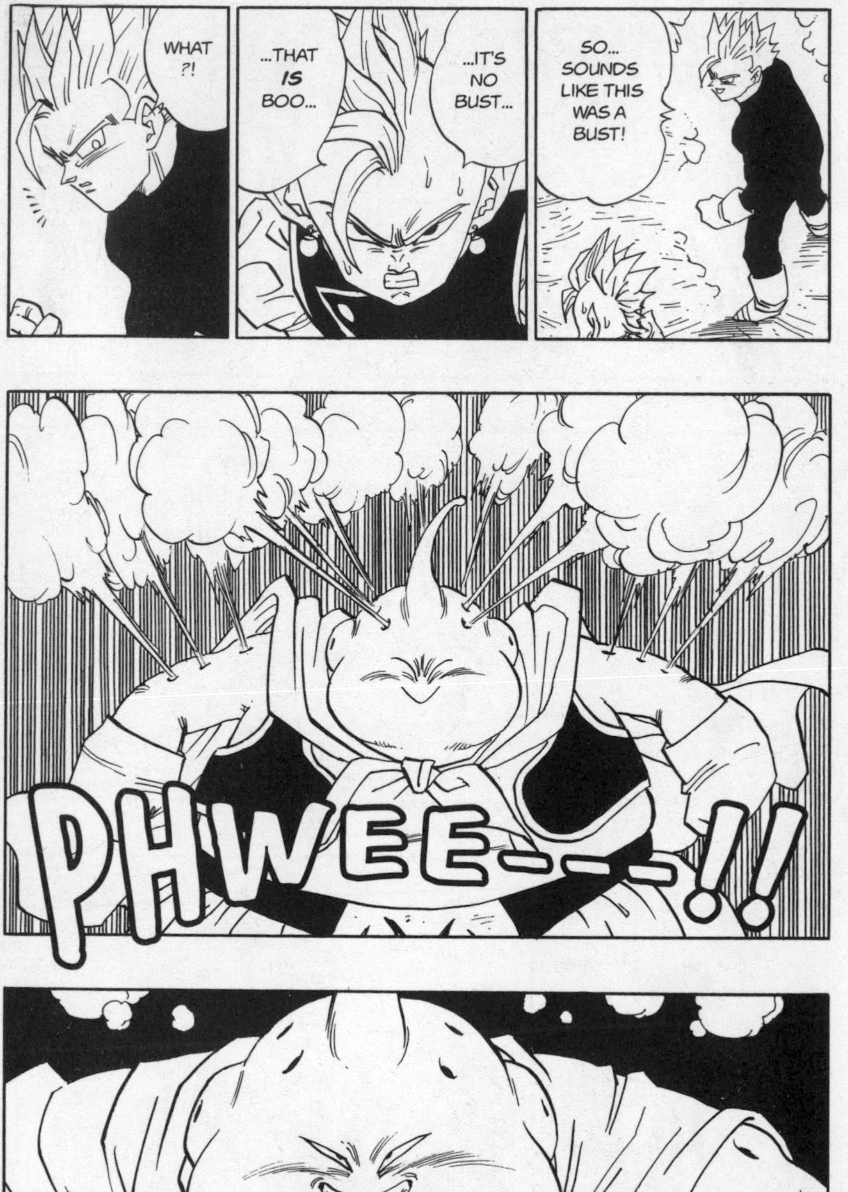
SO... SOUNDS LIKE THIS WAS A BUST!
...IT'S NO BUST...
...THAT IS BOO...
WHAT ?!
PHWEE--!!

READ THIS WAY

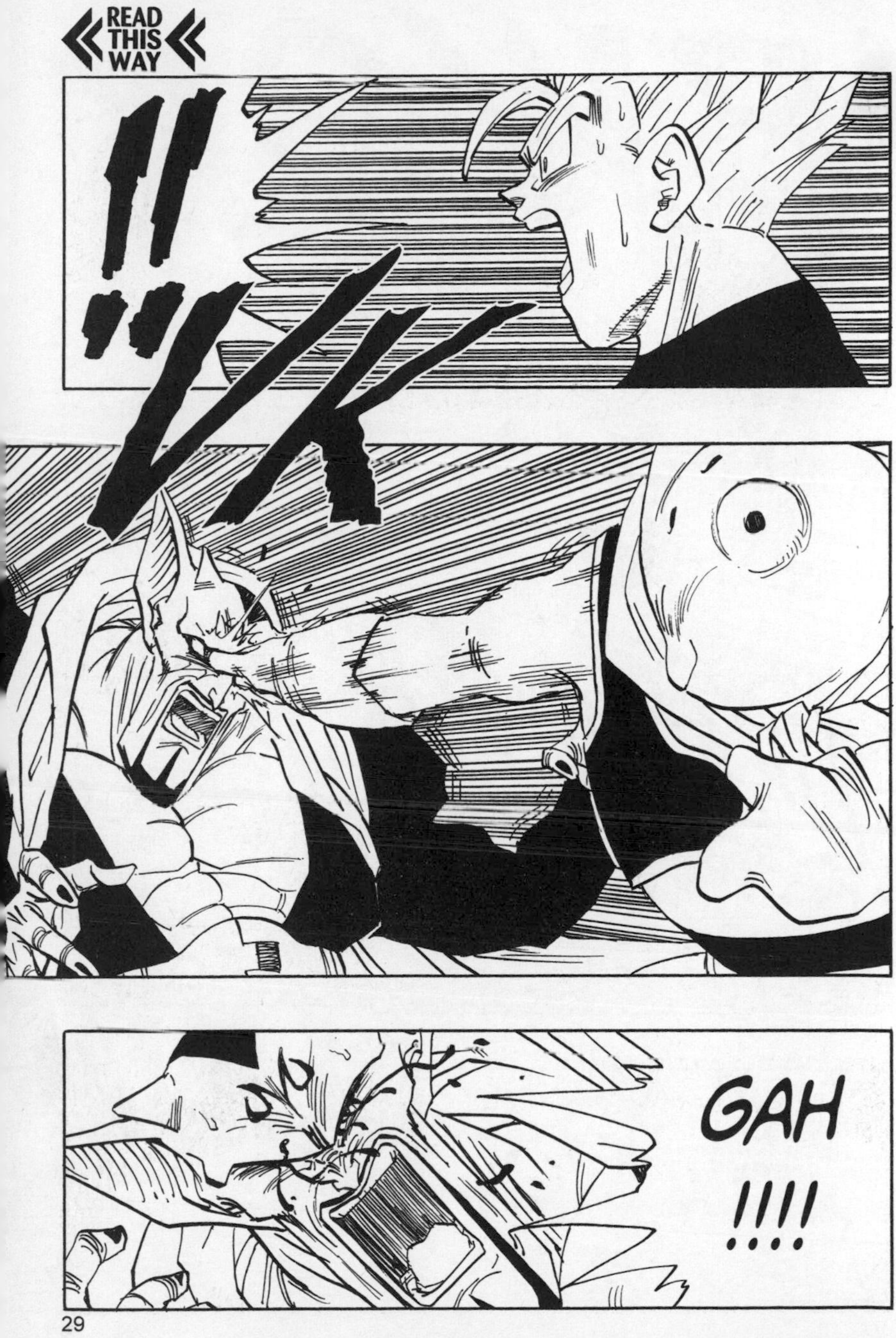
GAH
!!!!

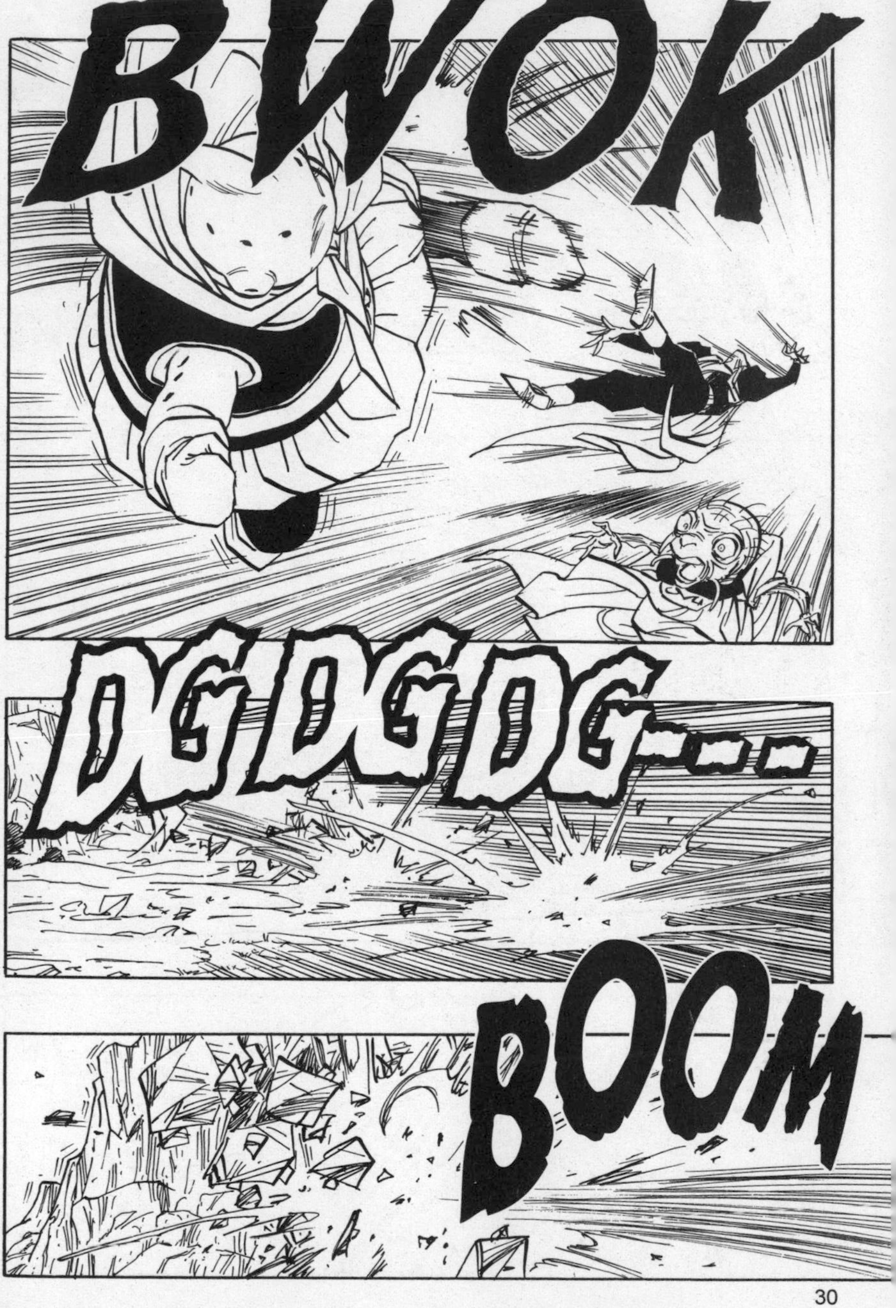
BWOK
DGDGDG...
BOOM

READ THIS WAY

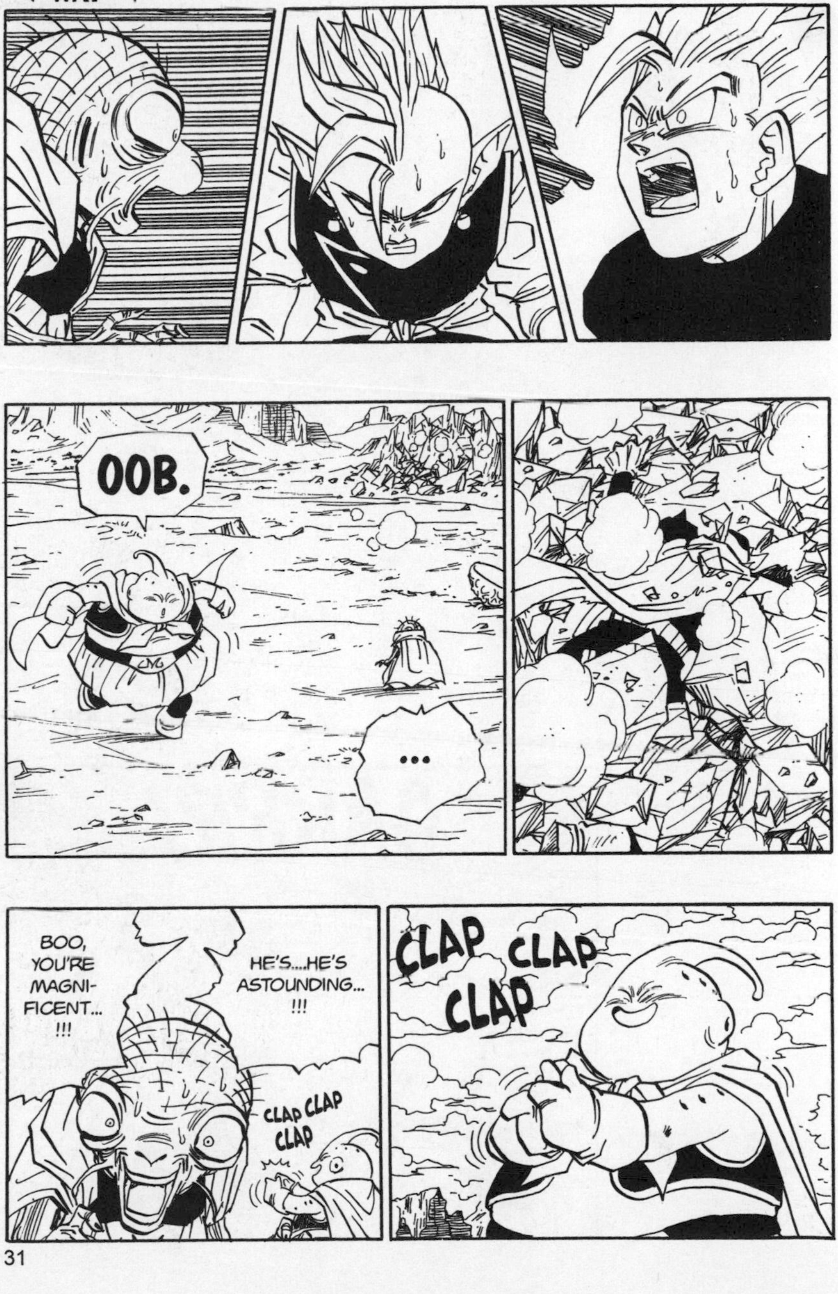
OOB.
...
CLAP CLAP
CLAP
HE'S....HE'S ASTOUNDING... !!!
BOO, YOU'RE MAGNIFICENT... !!!
CLAP CLAP
CLAP

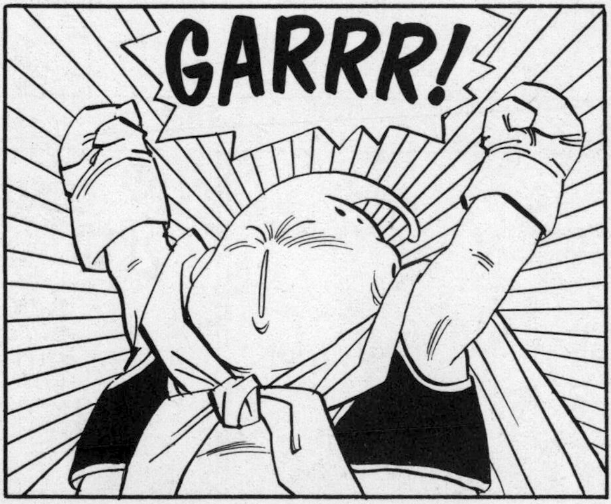
GARRR!

DBZ:268 · The Menace of Boo

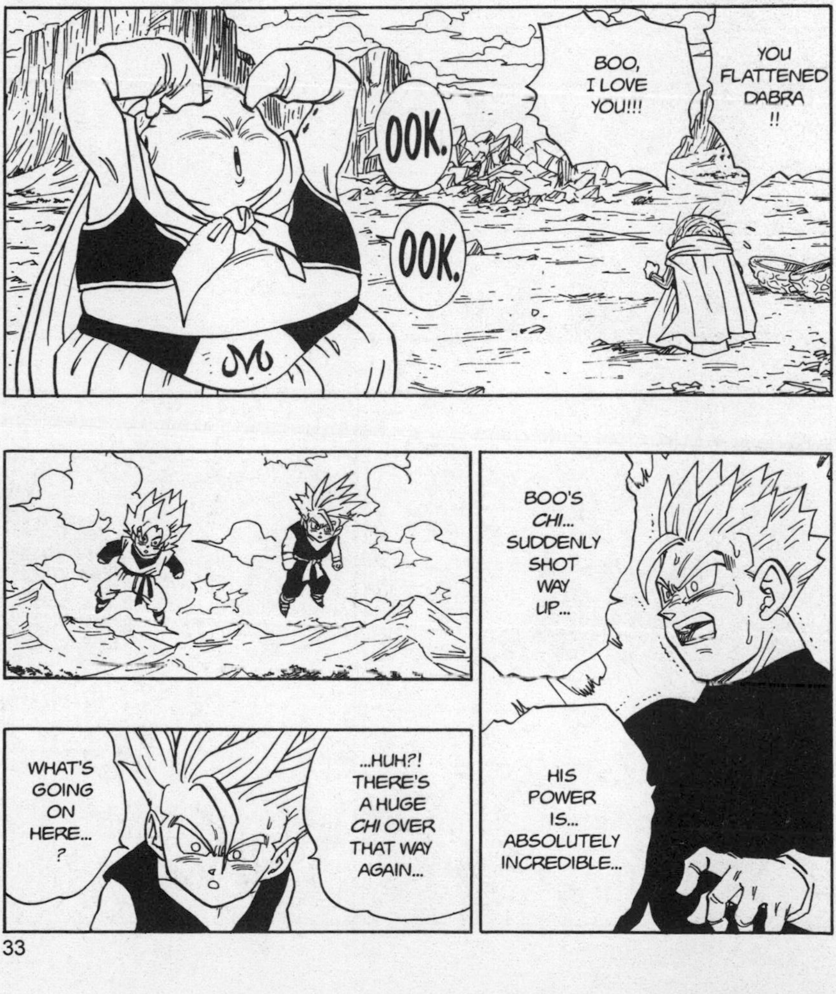
YOU FLATTENED DABRA !!
BOO, I LOVE YOU!!!
OOK.
OOK.
BOO'S *CHI*... SUDDENLY SHOT WAY UP...
HIS POWER IS... ABSOLUTELY INCREDIBLE...
...HUH?! THERE'S A HUGE *CHI* OVER THAT WAY AGAIN...
WHAT'S GOING ON HERE... ?

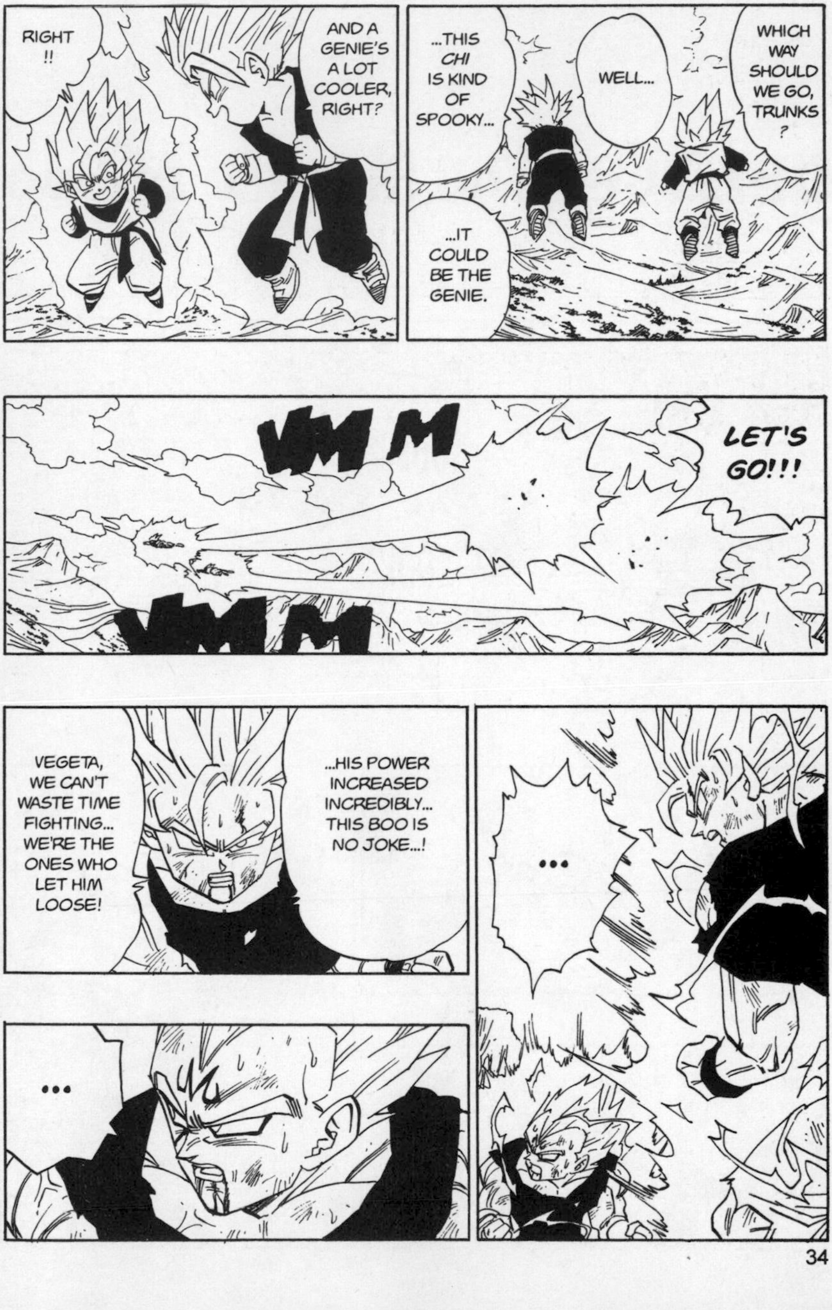
WHICH WAY SHOULD WE GO, TRUNKS?
WELL...
...THIS *CHI* IS KIND OF SPOOKY...
...IT COULD BE THE GENIE.
AND A GENIE'S A LOT COOLER, RIGHT?
RIGHT!!
LET'S GO!!!
VMM
VMM
...
...HIS POWER INCREASED INCREDIBLY... THIS BOO IS NO JOKE...!
VEGETA, WE CAN'T WASTE TIME FIGHTING... WE'RE THE ONES WHO LET HIM LOOSE!
...

READ THIS WAY

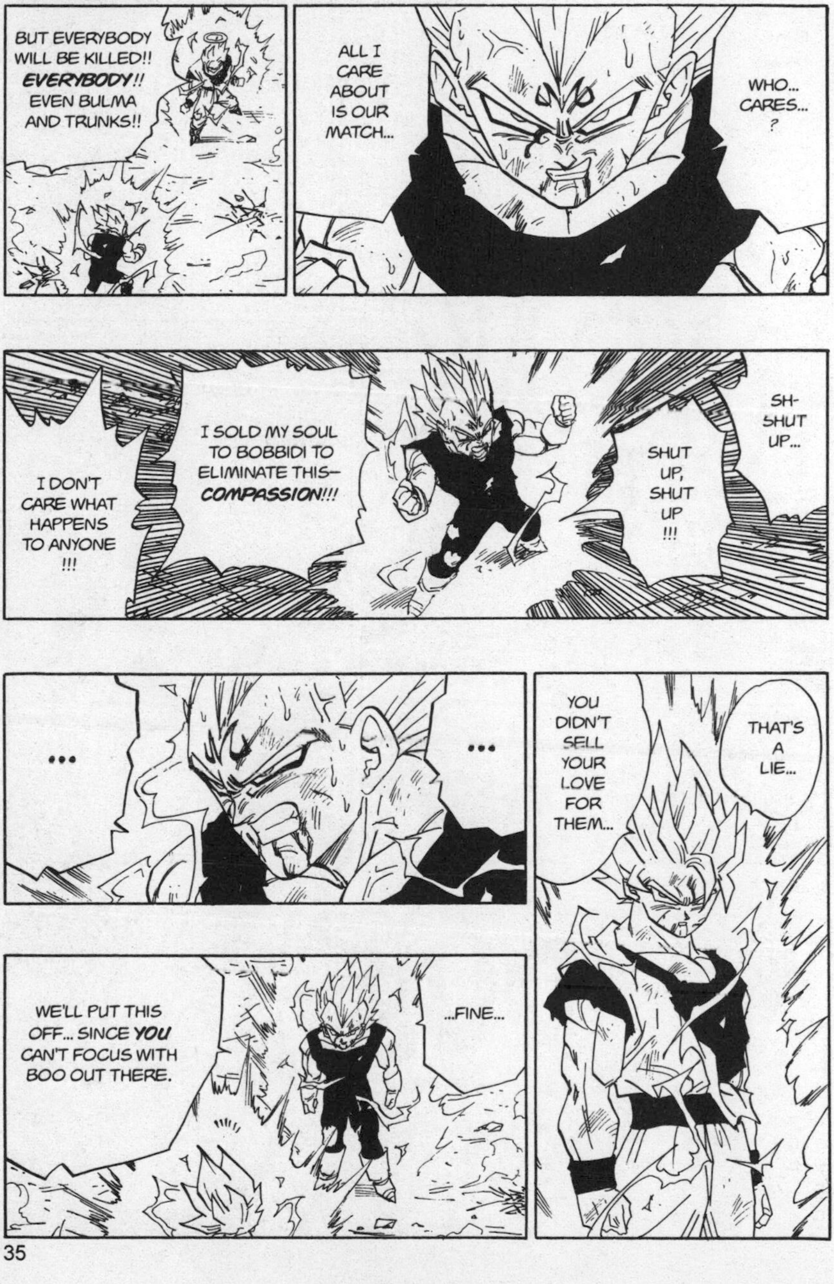

WHO... CARES... ?
ALL I CARE ABOUT IS OUR MATCH...
BUT EVERYBODY WILL BE KILLED!! EVERYBODY!! EVEN BULMA AND TRUNKS!!
SH- SHUT UP...
SHUT UP, SHUT UP !!!
I SOLD MY SOUL TO BOBBIDI TO ELIMINATE THIS— COMPASSION!!!
I DON'T CARE WHAT HAPPENS TO ANYONE !!!
THAT'S A LIE...
YOU DIDN'T SELL YOUR LOVE FOR THEM...
...
...
...FINE...
WE'LL PUT THIS OFF... SINCE YOU CAN'T FOCUS WITH BOO OUT THERE.

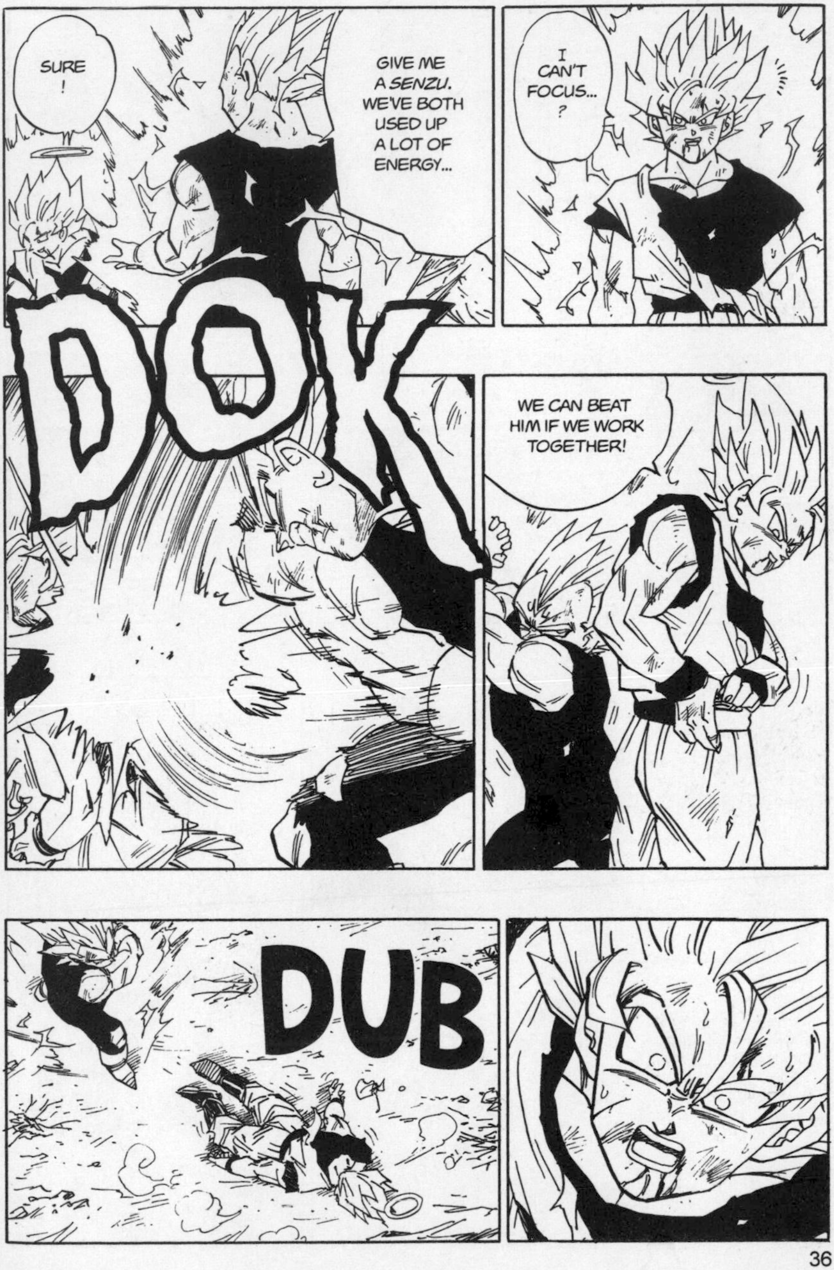
I CAN'T FOCUS...?
GIVE ME A SENZU. WE'VE BOTH USED UP A LOT OF ENERGY...
SURE!
WE CAN BEAT HIM IF WE WORK TOGETHER!
DOK
DUB

READ THIS WAY

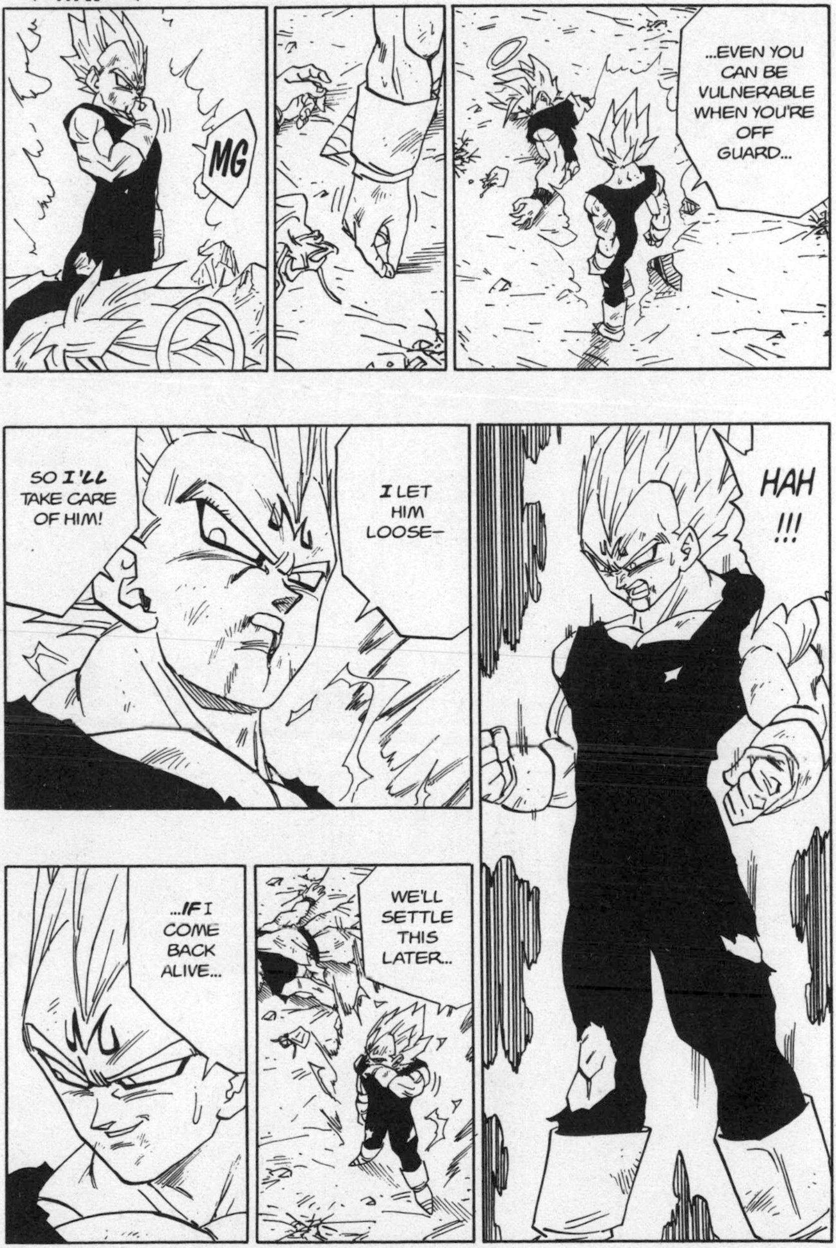

...EVEN YOU CAN BE VULNERABLE WHEN YOU'RE OFF GUARD...
MG
HAH !!!
I LET HIM LOOSE—
SO I'LL TAKE CARE OF HIM!
WE'LL SETTLE THIS LATER...
...IF I COME BACK ALIVE...

READ THIS WAY

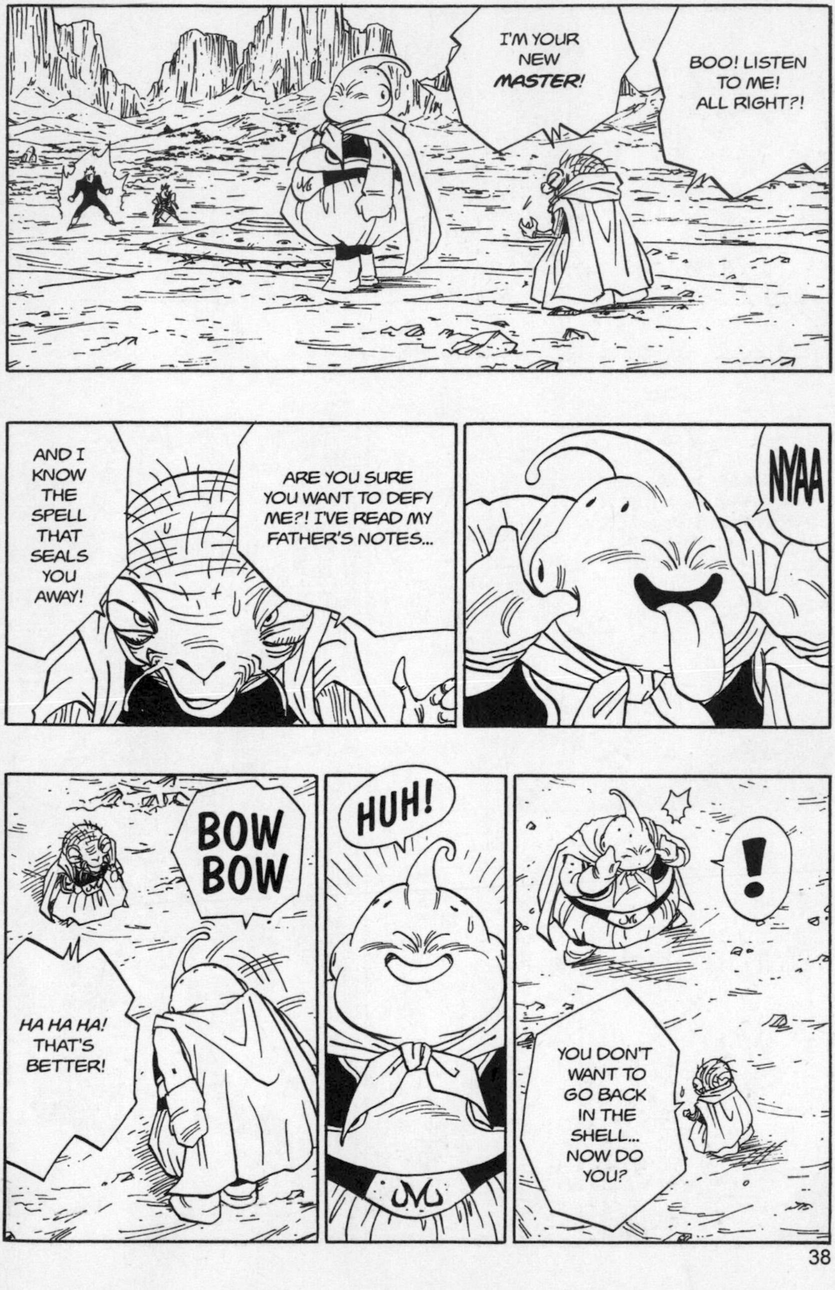

BOO! LISTEN TO ME! ALL RIGHT?!
I'M YOUR NEW *MASTER!*
NYAA
ARE YOU SURE YOU WANT TO DEFY ME?! I'VE READ MY FATHER'S NOTES...
AND I KNOW THE SPELL THAT SEALS YOU AWAY!
!
YOU DON'T WANT TO GO BACK IN THE SHELL... NOW DO YOU?
HUH!
BOW BOW
HA HA HA! THAT'S BETTER!

READ THIS WAY

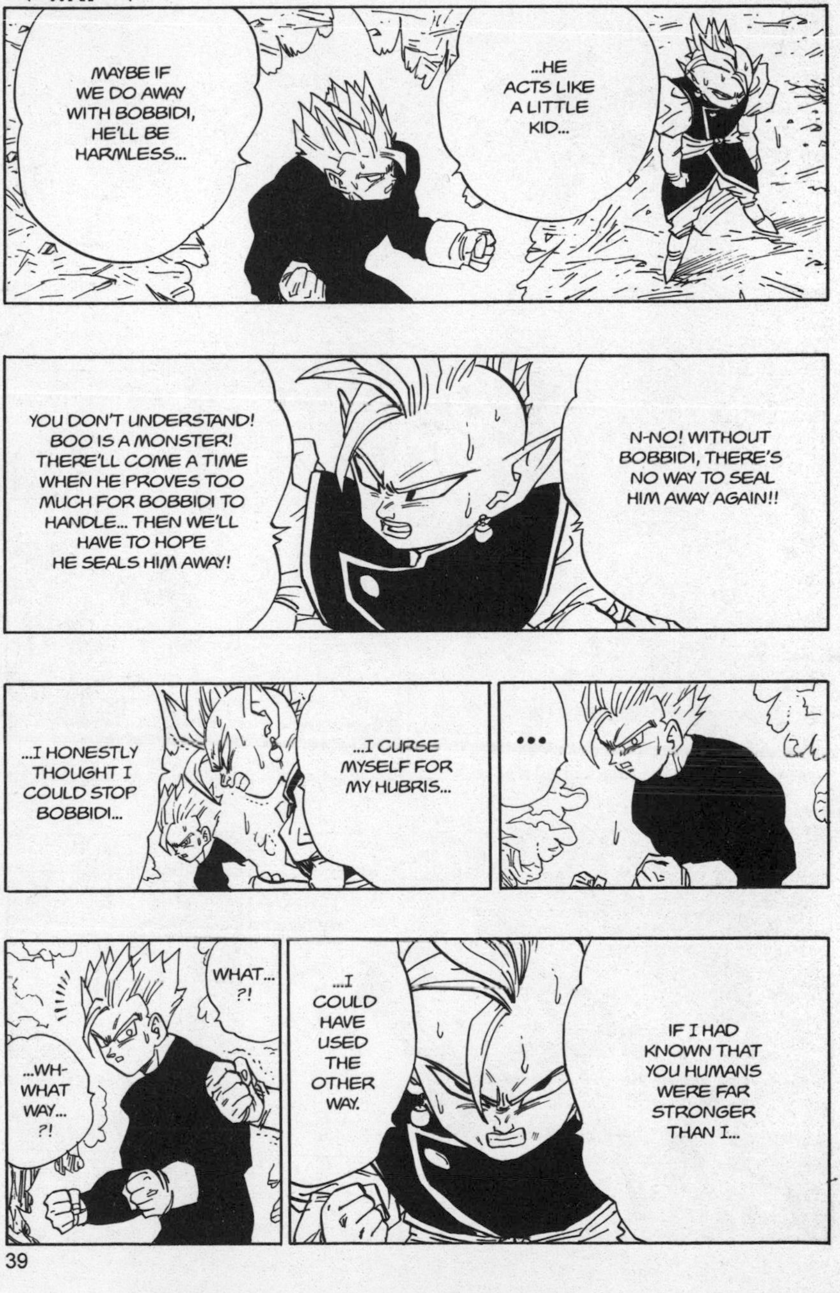
...HE ACTS LIKE A LITTLE KID...
MAYBE IF WE DO AWAY WITH BOBBIDI, HE'LL BE HARMLESS...
N-NO! WITHOUT BOBBIDI, THERE'S NO WAY TO SEAL HIM AWAY AGAIN!!
YOU DON'T UNDERSTAND! BOO IS A MONSTER! THERE'LL COME A TIME WHEN HE PROVES TOO MUCH FOR BOBBIDI TO HANDLE... THEN WE'LL HAVE TO HOPE HE SEALS HIM AWAY!
...
...I CURSE MYSELF FOR MY HUBRIS...
...I HONESTLY THOUGHT I COULD STOP BOBBIDI...
IF I HAD KNOWN THAT YOU HUMANS WERE FAR STRONGER THAN I...
...I COULD HAVE USED THE OTHER WAY.
WHAT...?!
...WH-WHAT WAY...?!

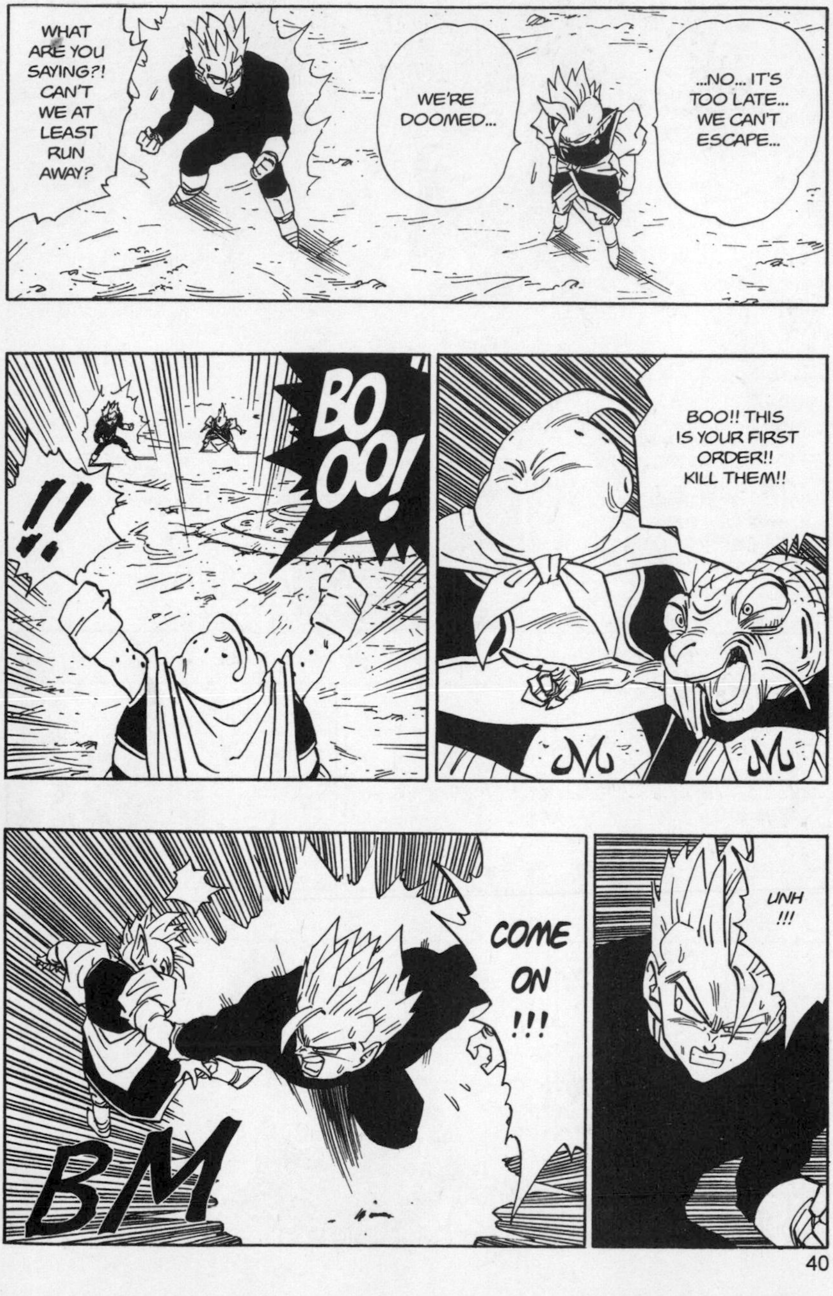
...NO... IT'S TOO LATE... WE CAN'T ESCAPE...
WE'RE DOOMED...
WHAT ARE YOU SAYING?! CAN'T WE AT LEAST RUN AWAY?
BOO!! THIS IS YOUR FIRST ORDER!! KILL THEM!!
BOOO!
!!
UNH !!!
COME ON !!!
BM

READ THIS WAY

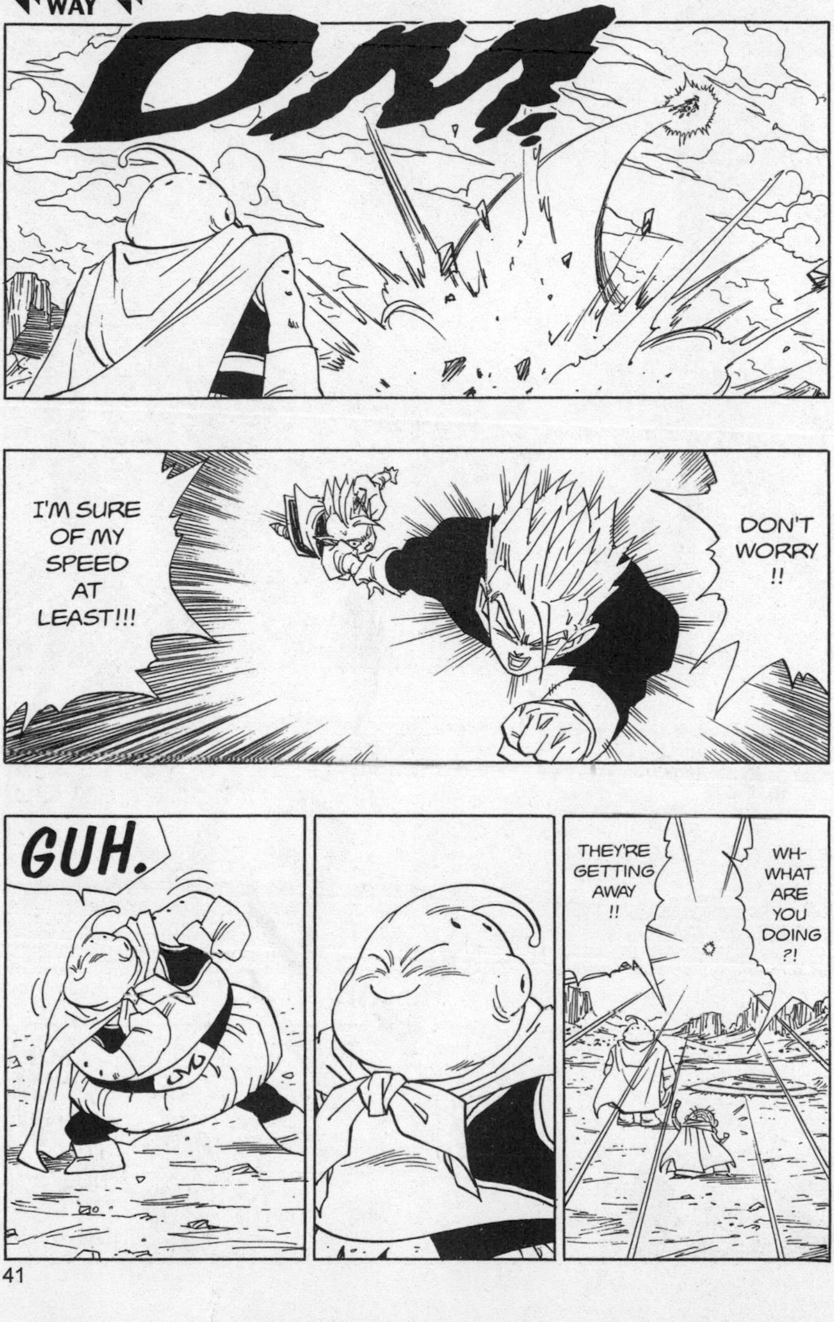
DM!
DON'T WORRY !!
I'M SURE OF MY SPEED AT LEAST!!!
WH- WHAT ARE YOU DOING ?!
THEY'RE GETTING AWAY !!
GUH.

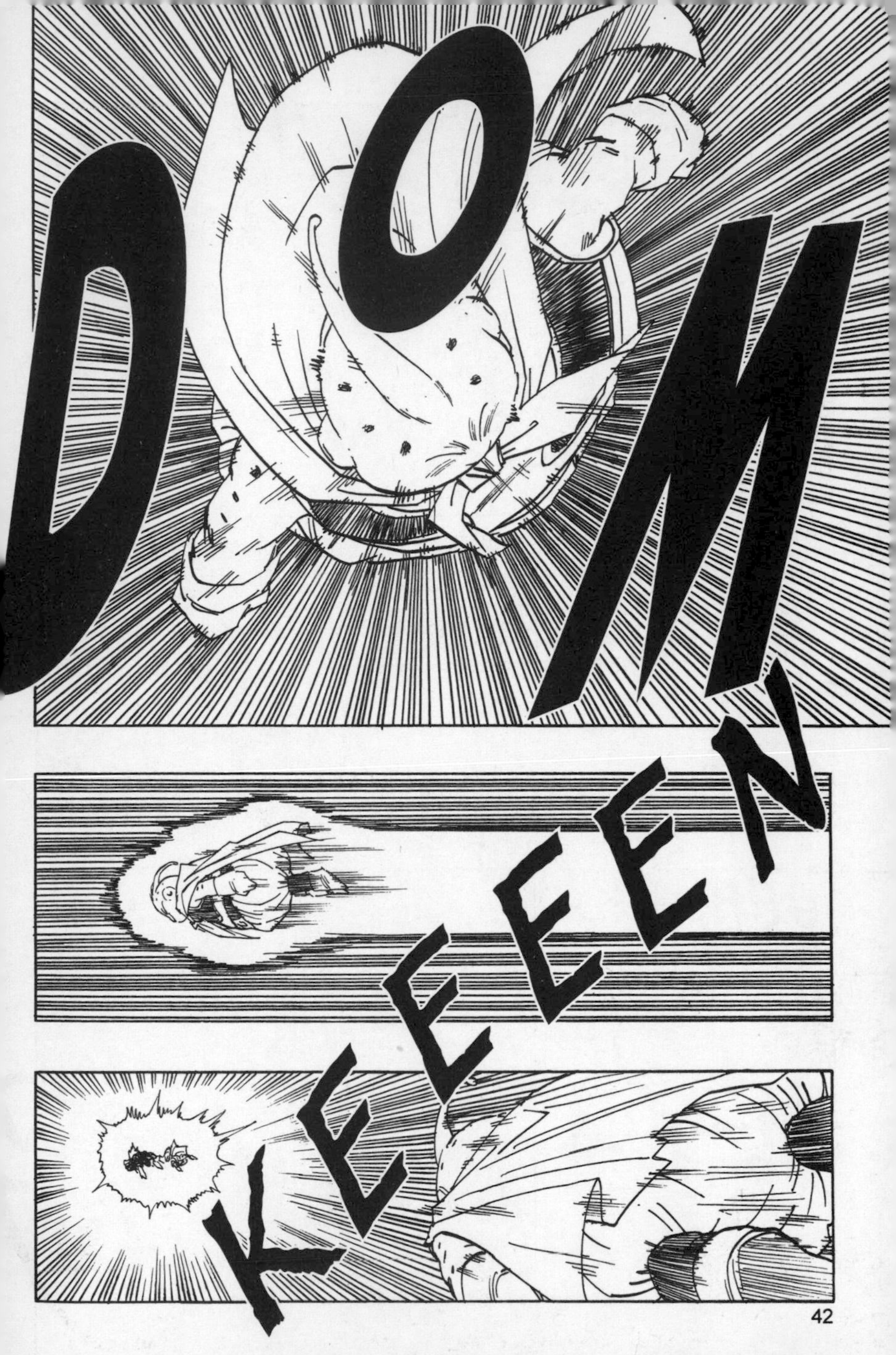
DOOM
KEEEEN

READ THIS WAY

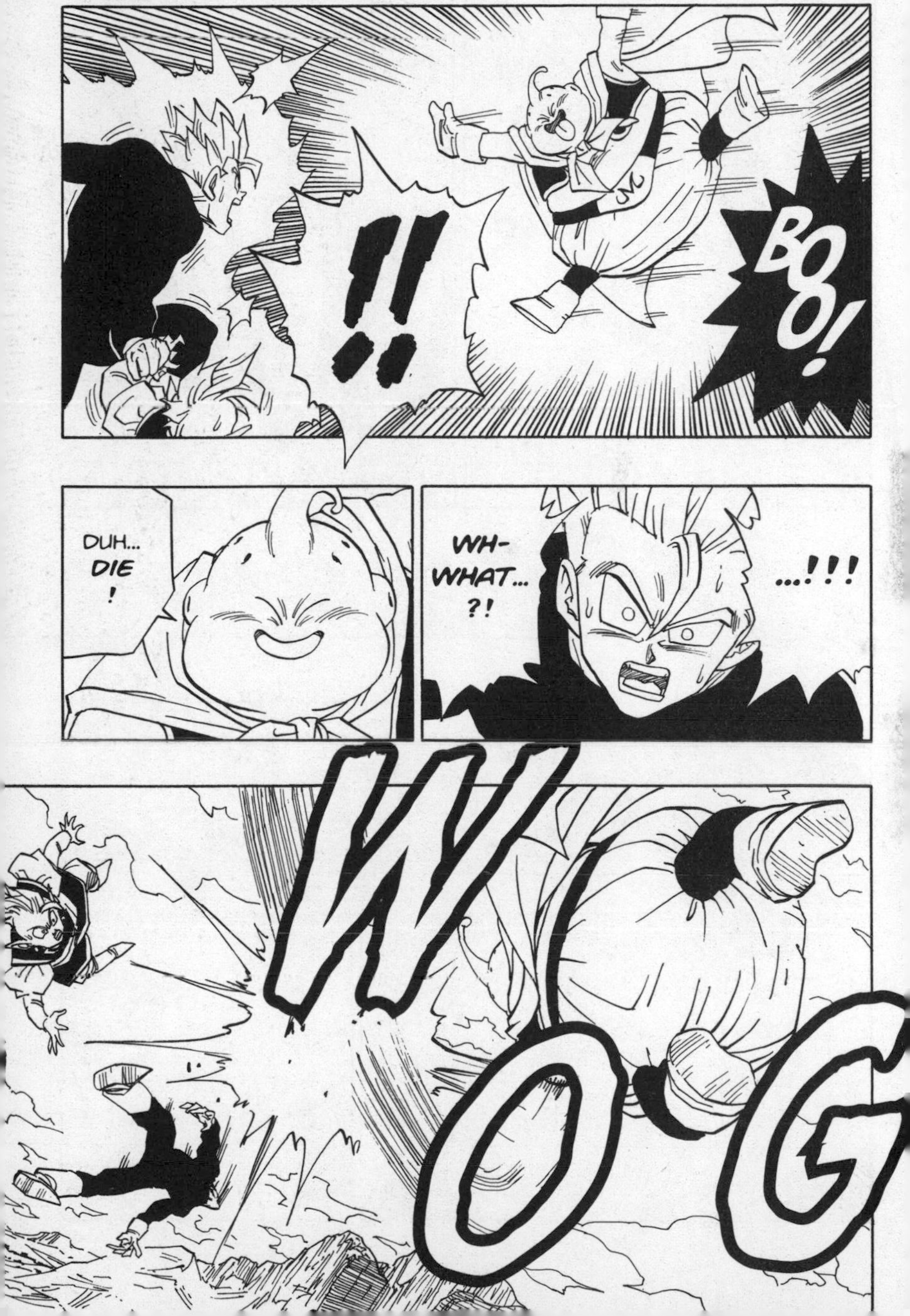

BOO!
!!
...!!!
WH- WHAT... ?!
DUH... DIE !
WOG

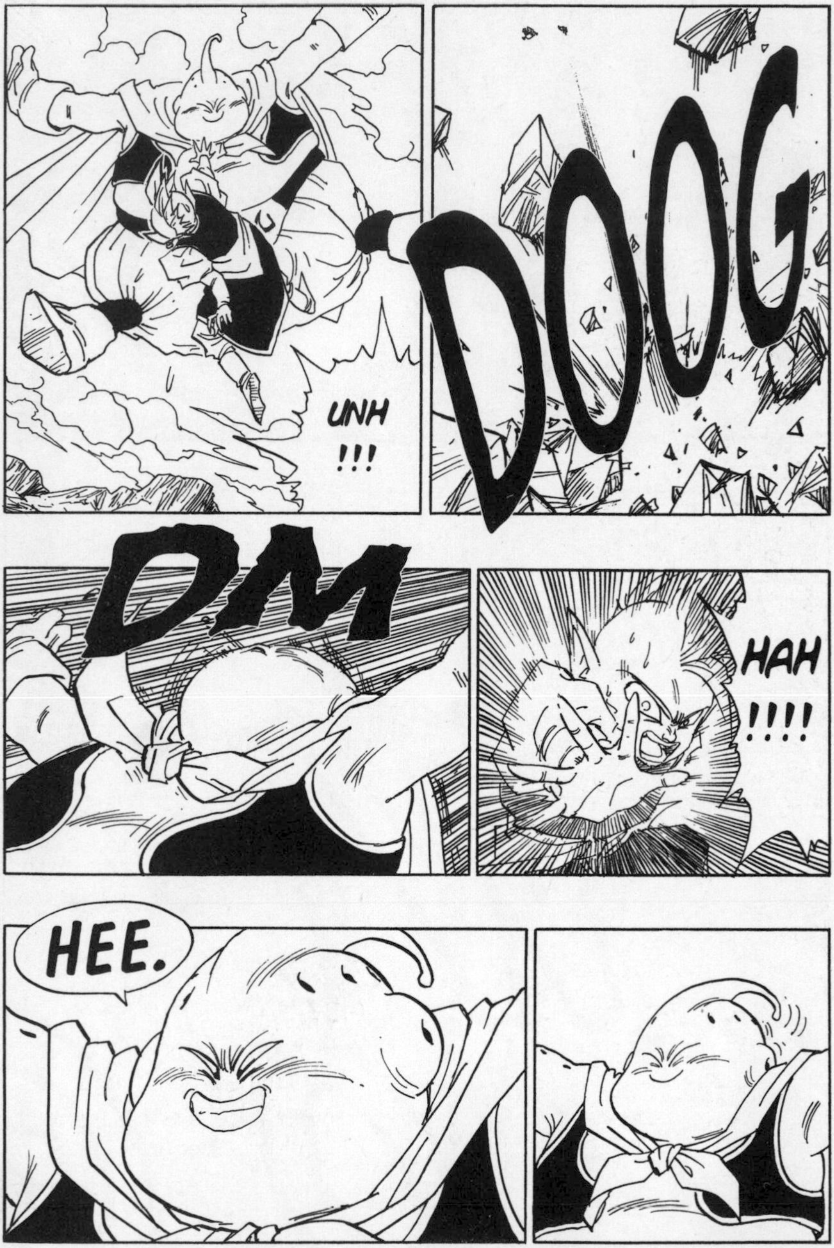
DOOG
UNH !!!
HAH !!!!
DM
HEE.

« READ THIS WAY «

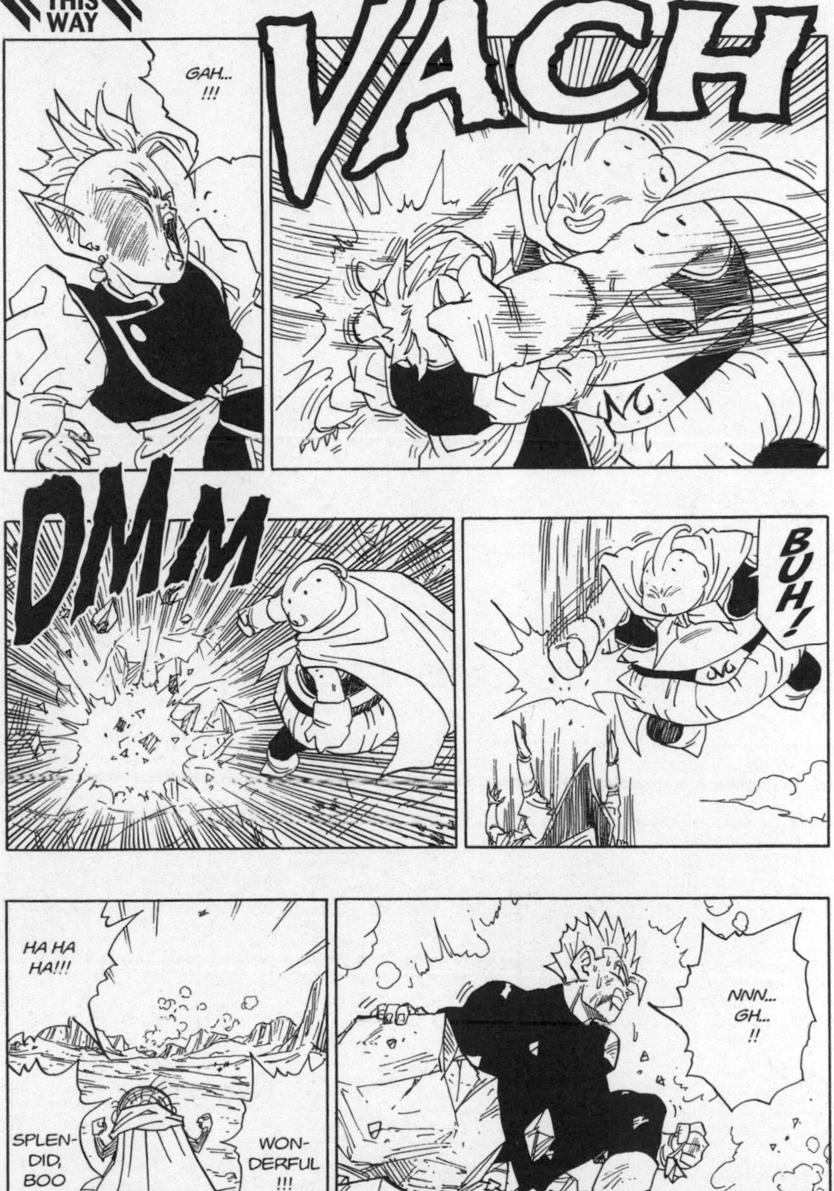
VACH
GAH... !!!
BUH!
DMM
NNN... GH... !!
HA HA HA!!!
WON-DERFUL !!!
SPLEN-DID, BOO !!!

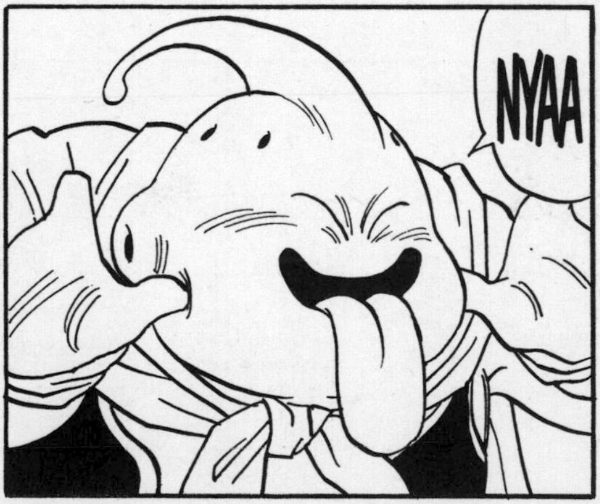
NYAA

DBZ:269 · Terrifying Power

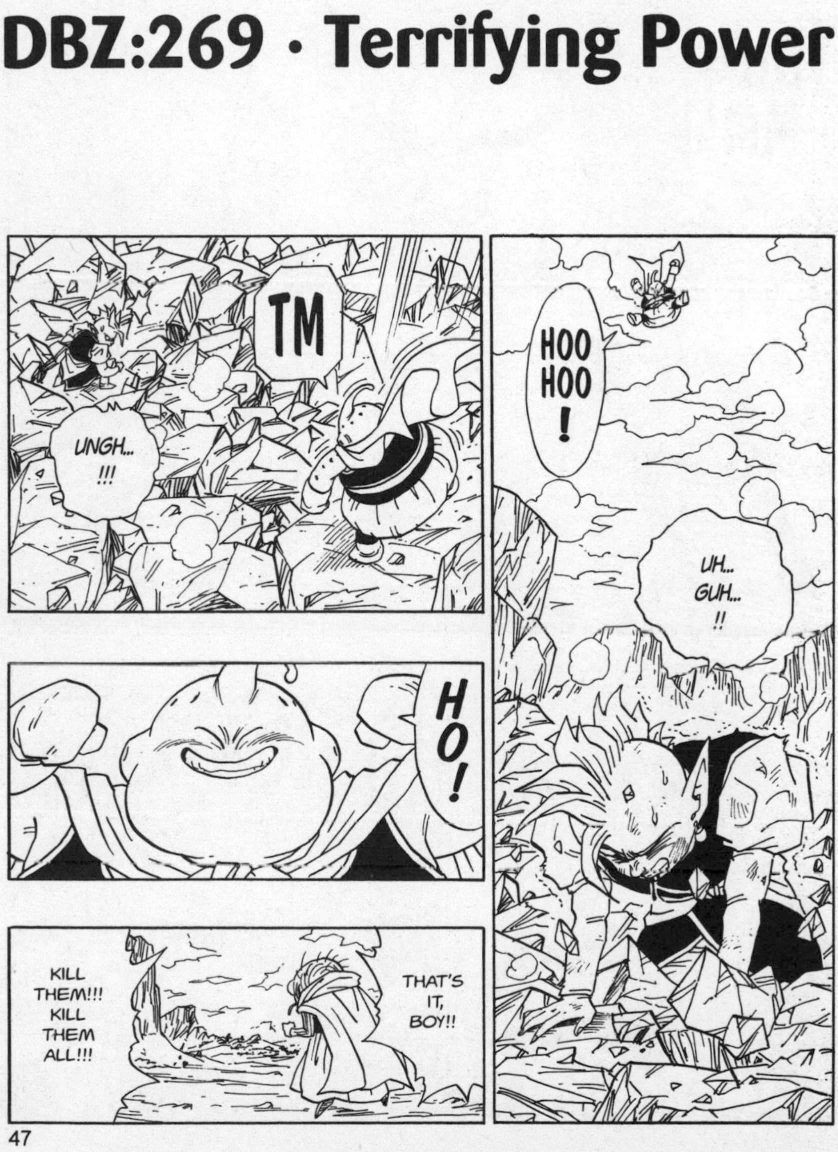
HOO HOO !
UH... GUH... !!
TM
UNGH... !!!
HO HO!
THAT'S IT, BOY!!
KILL THEM!!! KILL THEM ALL!!!

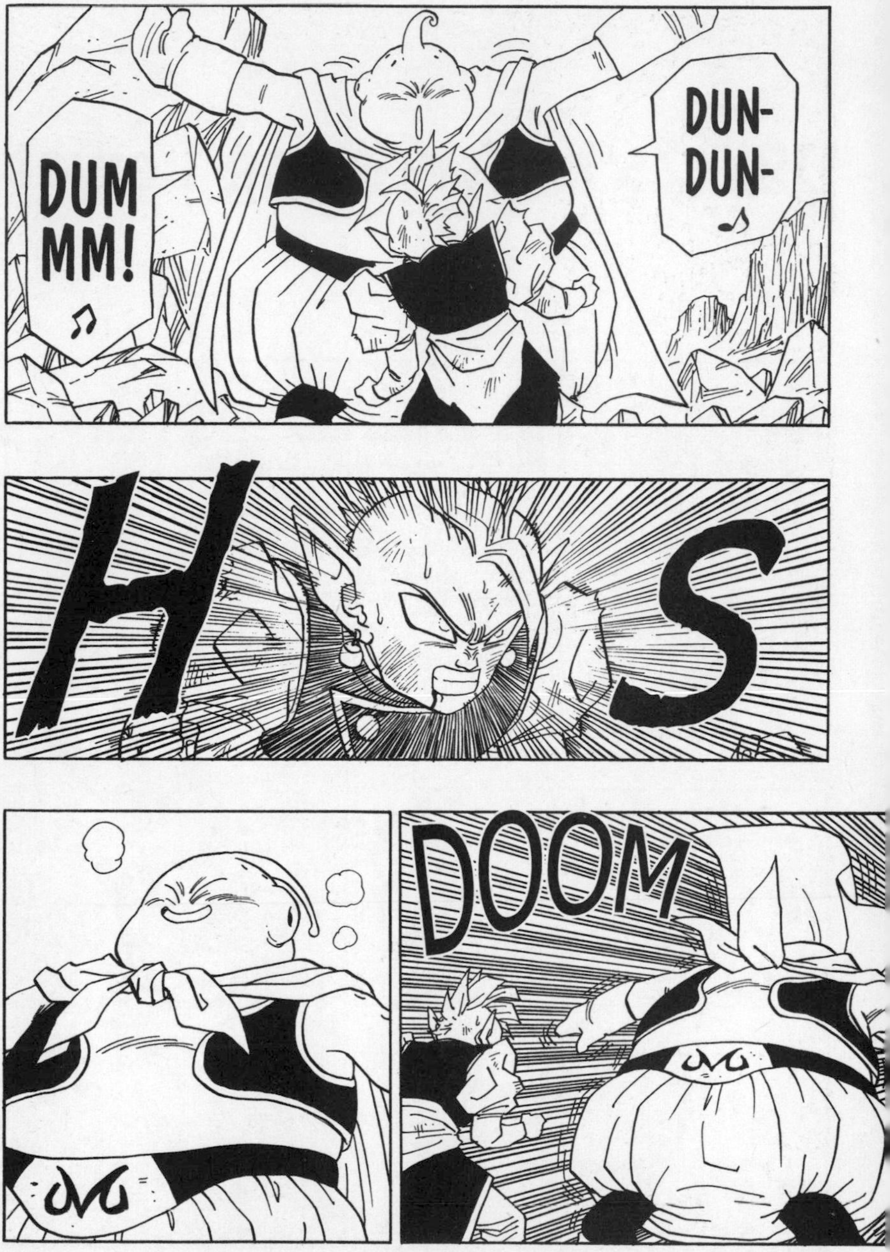
DUN- DUN- ♪
DUMM MM! ♪
H S
DOOM

READ THIS WAY

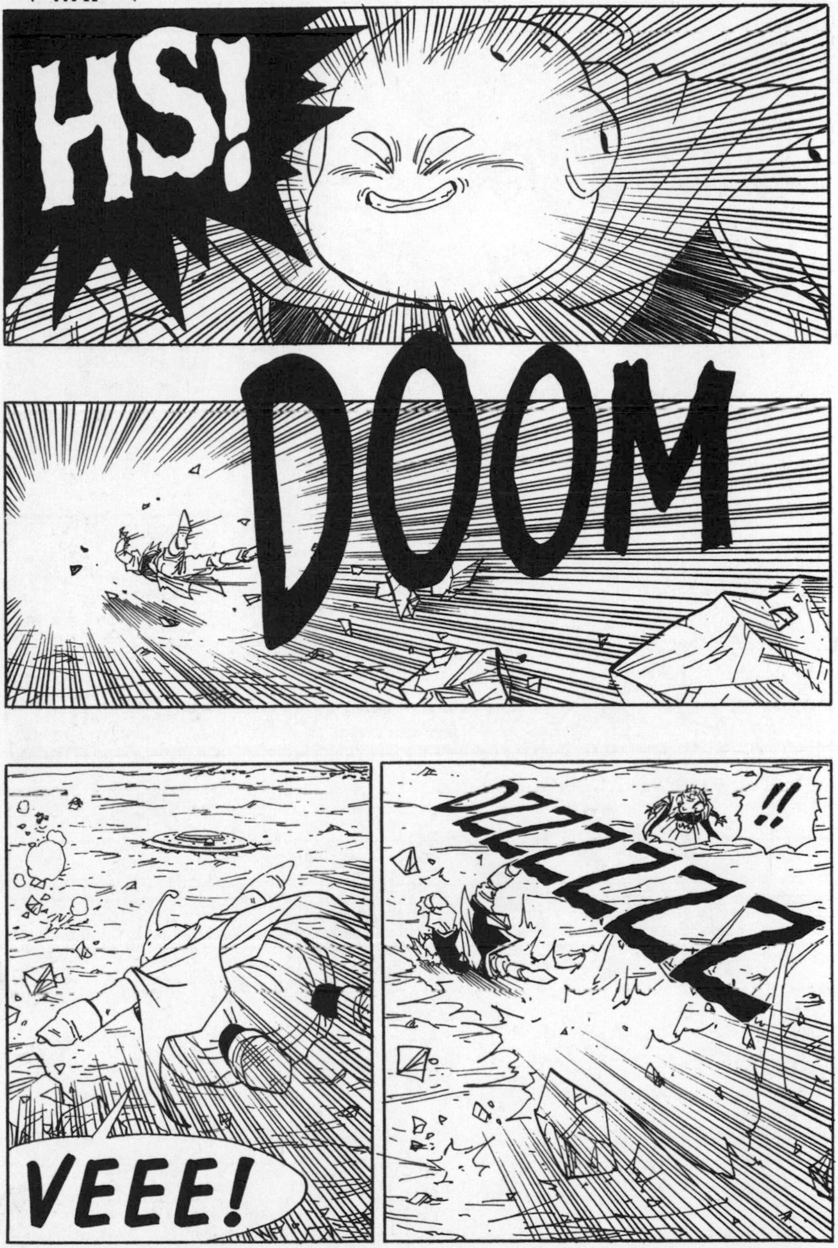
HS!
DOOM
!!
VEEE!

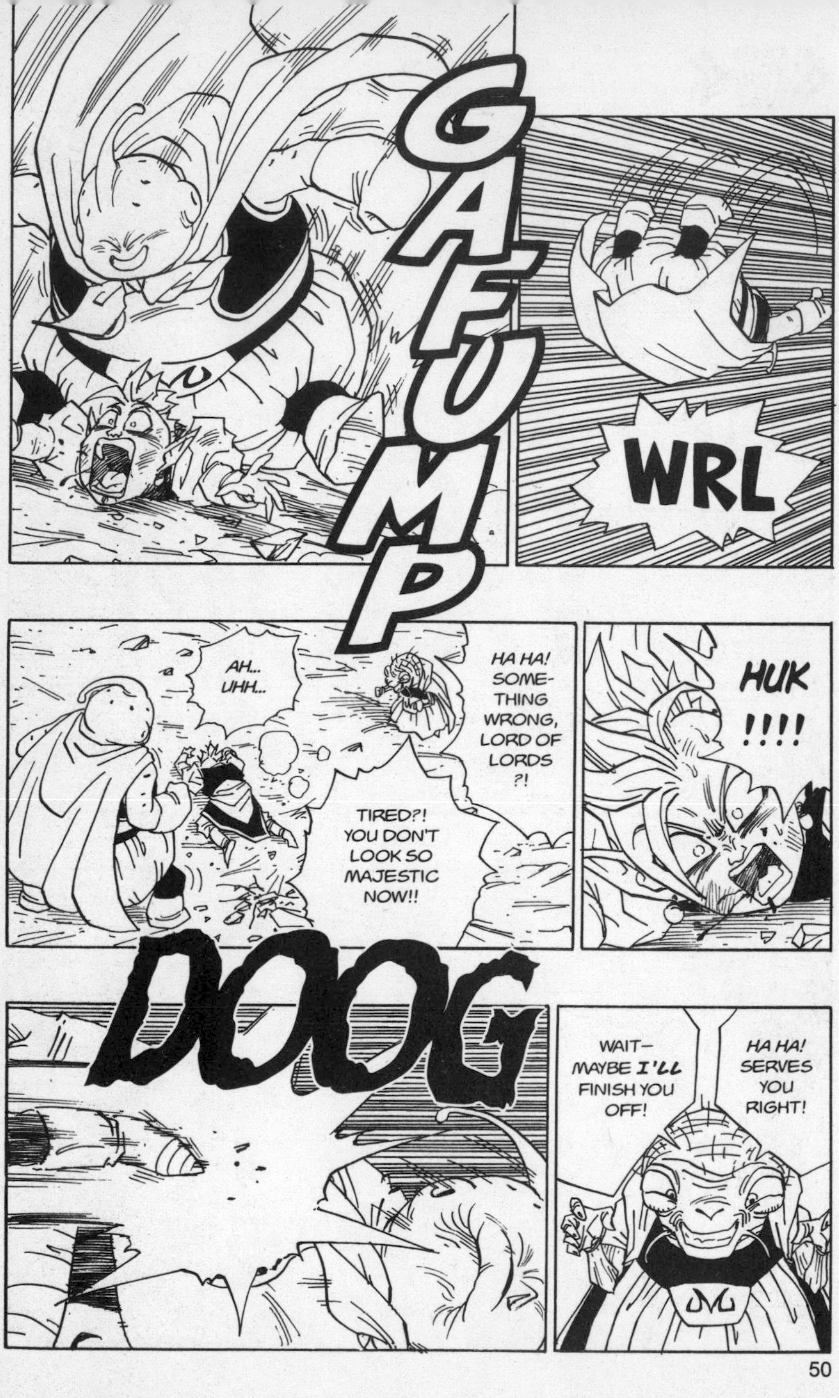
WRL
GAFUMP
HUK
!!!!
HA HA! SOME-THING WRONG, LORD OF LORDS ?!
AH... UHH...
TIRED?! YOU DON'T LOOK SO MAJESTIC NOW!!
HA HA! SERVES YOU RIGHT!
WAIT— MAYBE I'LL FINISH YOU OFF!
DOOG

READ THIS WAY

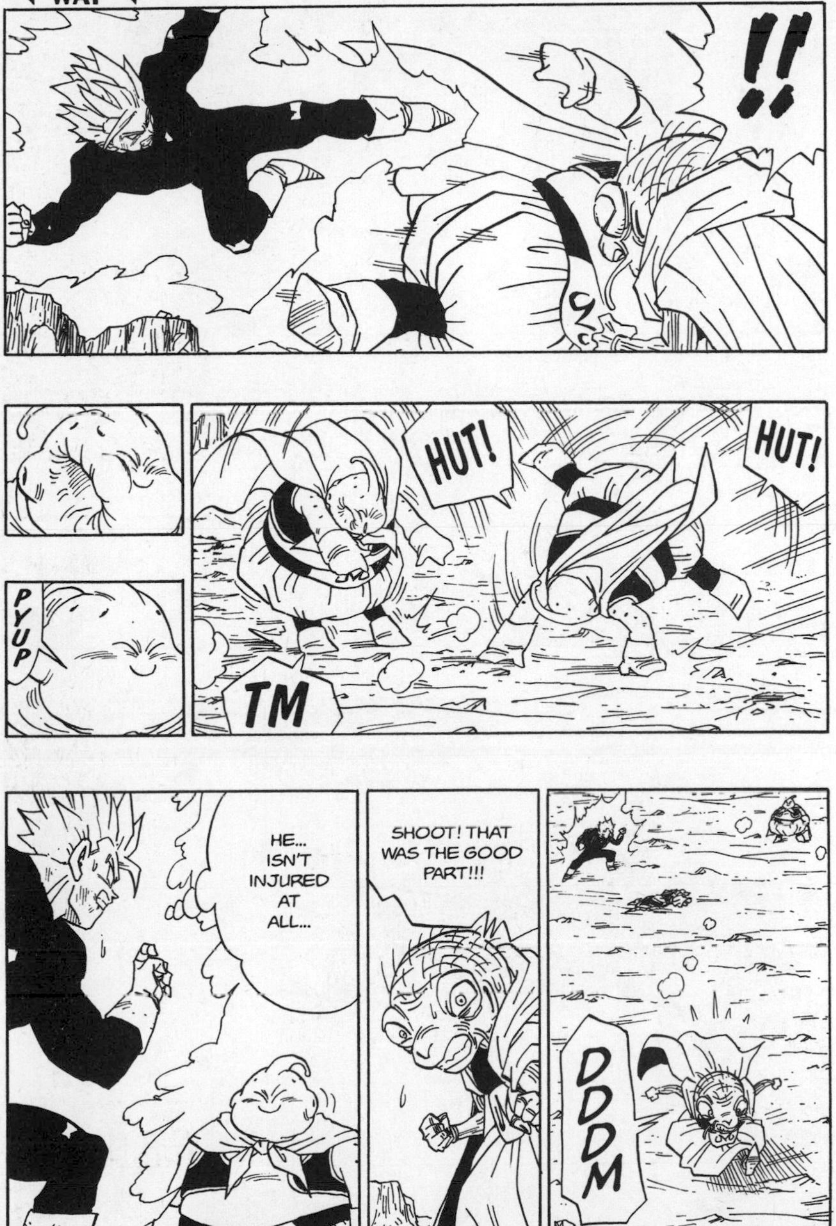

!!
HUT!
HUT!
TM
PYUP
DDDM
SHOOT! THAT WAS THE GOOD PART!!!
HE... ISN'T INJURED AT ALL...

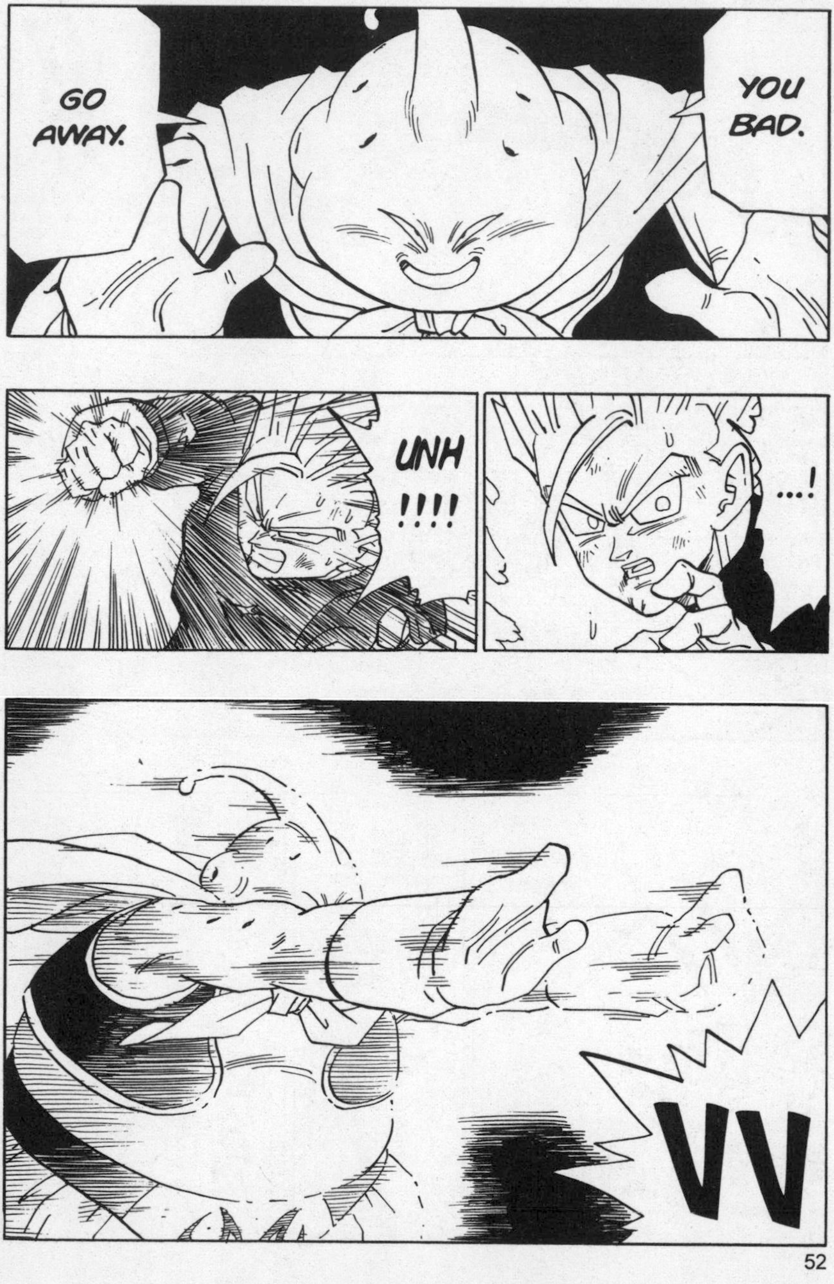
YOU BAD.
GO AWAY.
...!
UNH !!!!
VV

READ THIS WAY

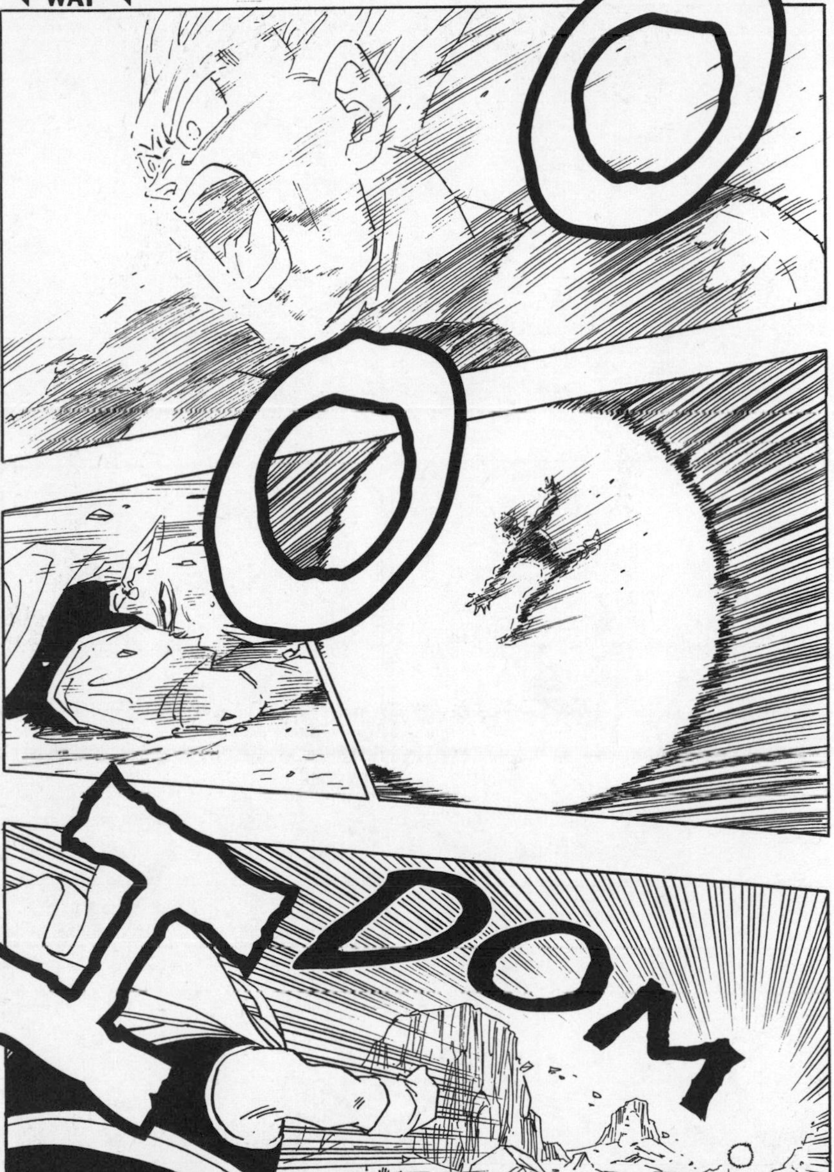
O
O
DOM

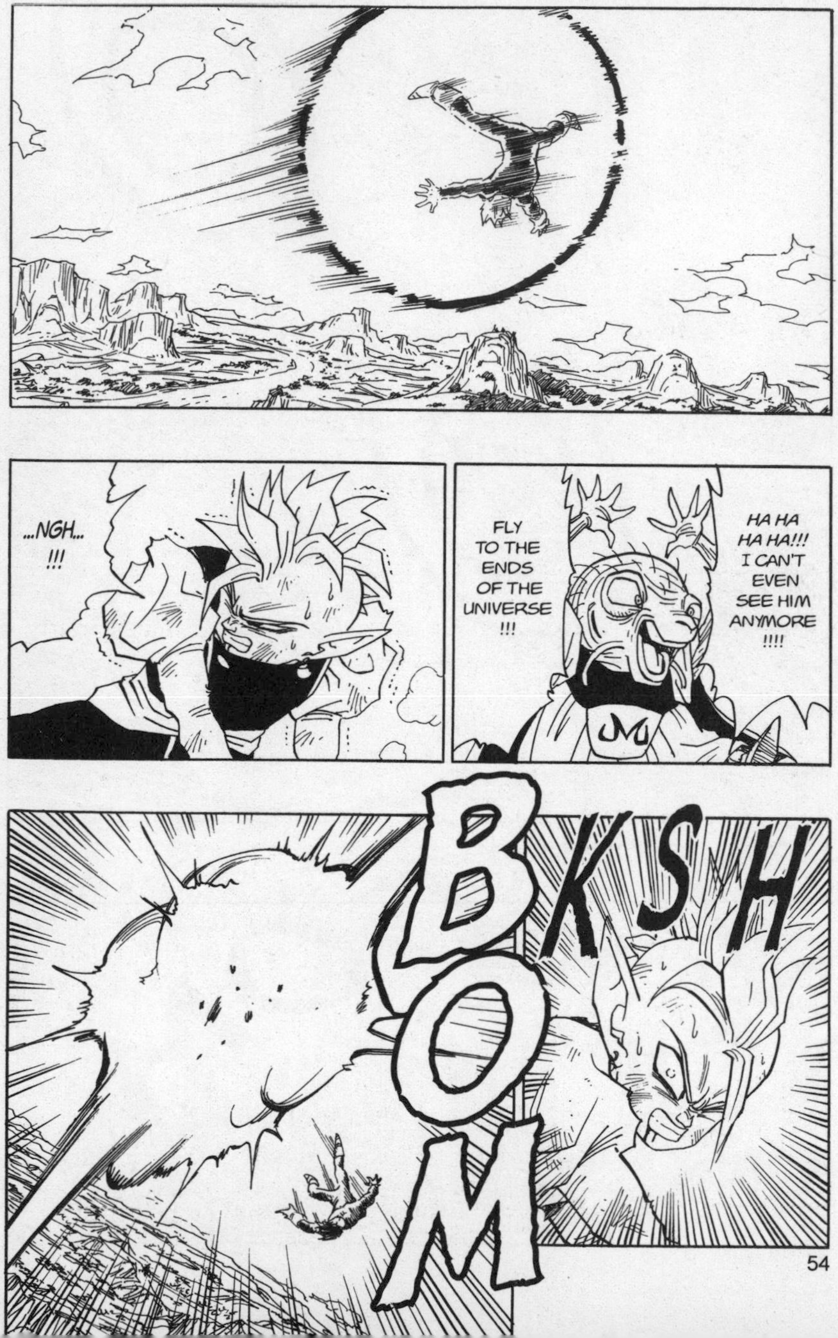
HA HA HA HA!!! I CAN'T EVEN SEE HIM ANYMORE!!!!
FLY TO THE ENDS OF THE UNIVERSE!!!
...NGH... !!!
BKSH
BOOM

READ THIS WAY

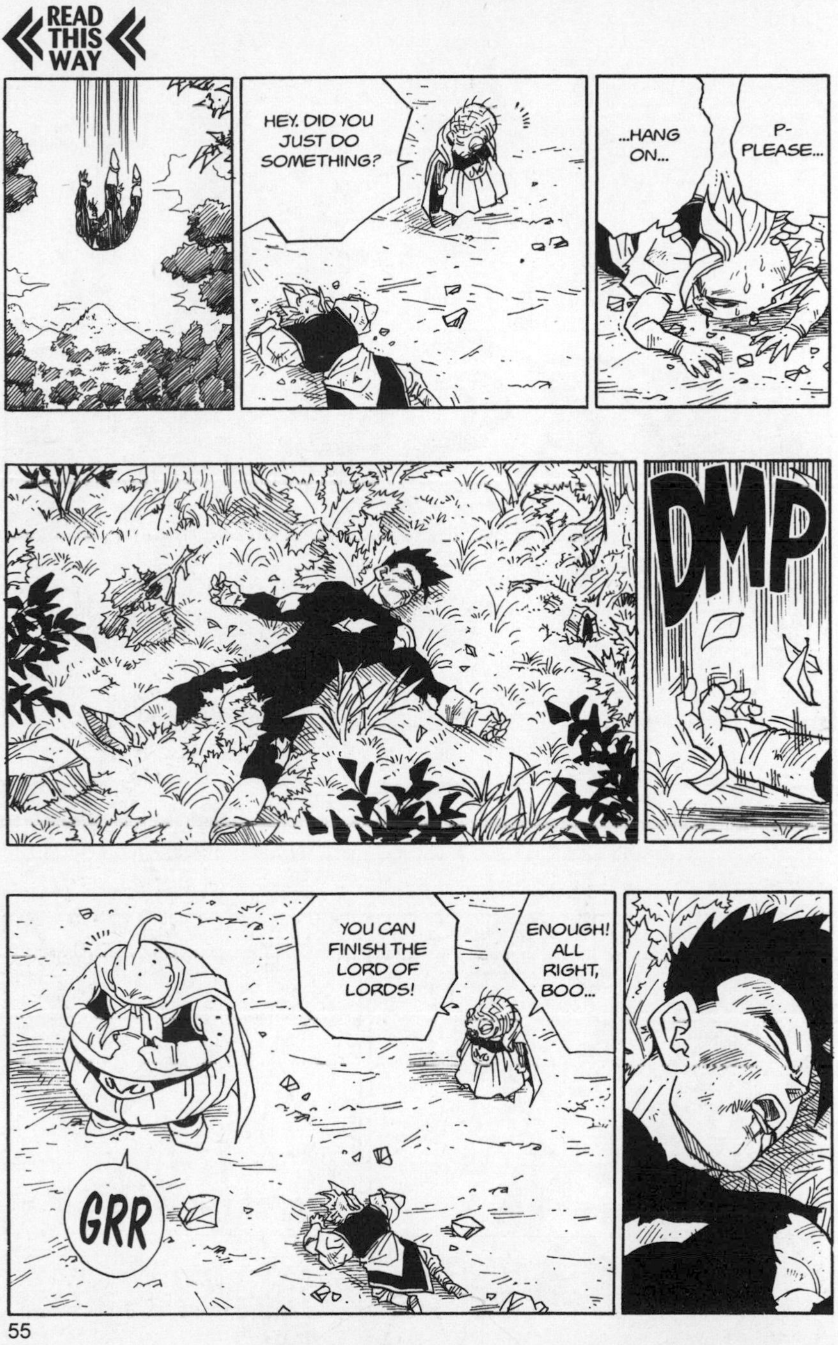

P- PLEASE...
...HANG ON...
HEY. DID YOU JUST DO SOMETHING?
DMP
ENOUGH! ALL RIGHT, BOO...
YOU CAN FINISH THE LORD OF LORDS!
GRR

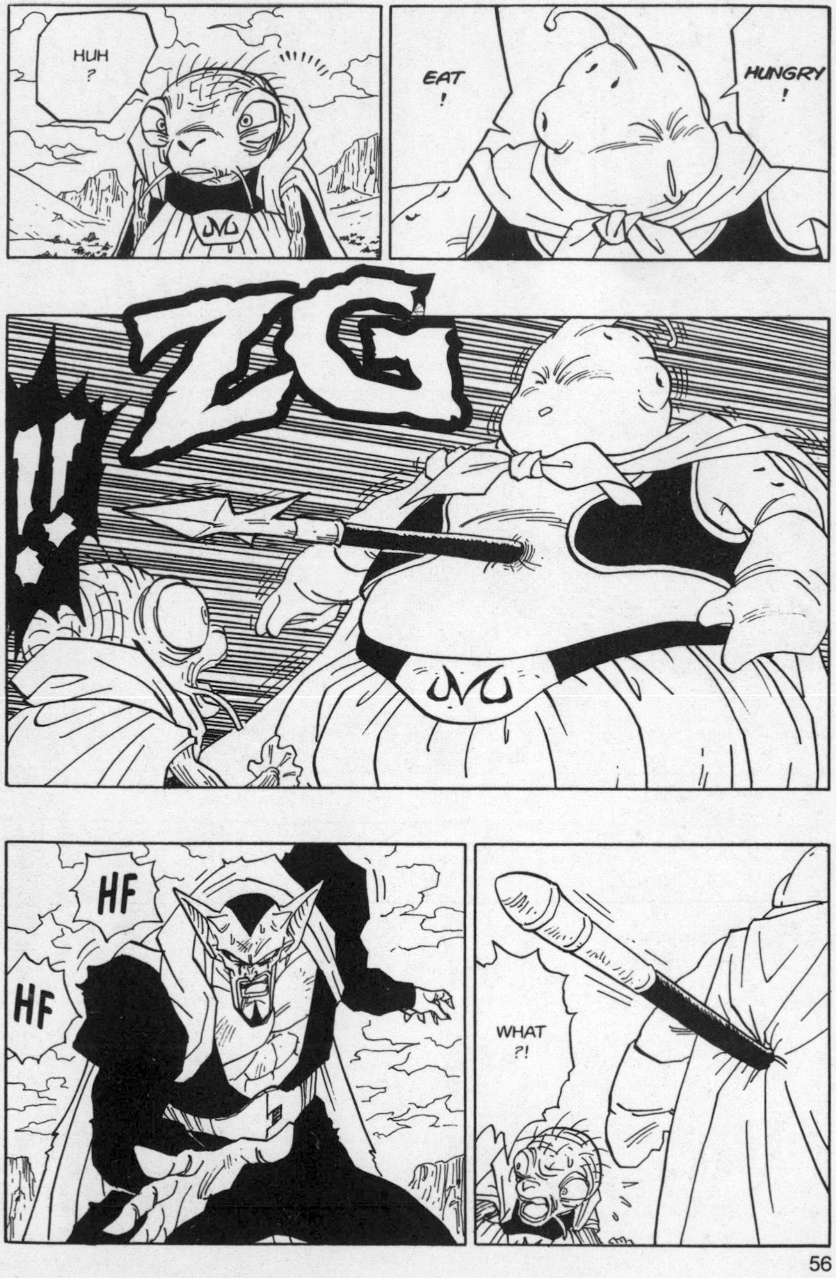
HUNGRY!
EAT!
HUH?
ZG
!!
WHAT?!
HF
HF

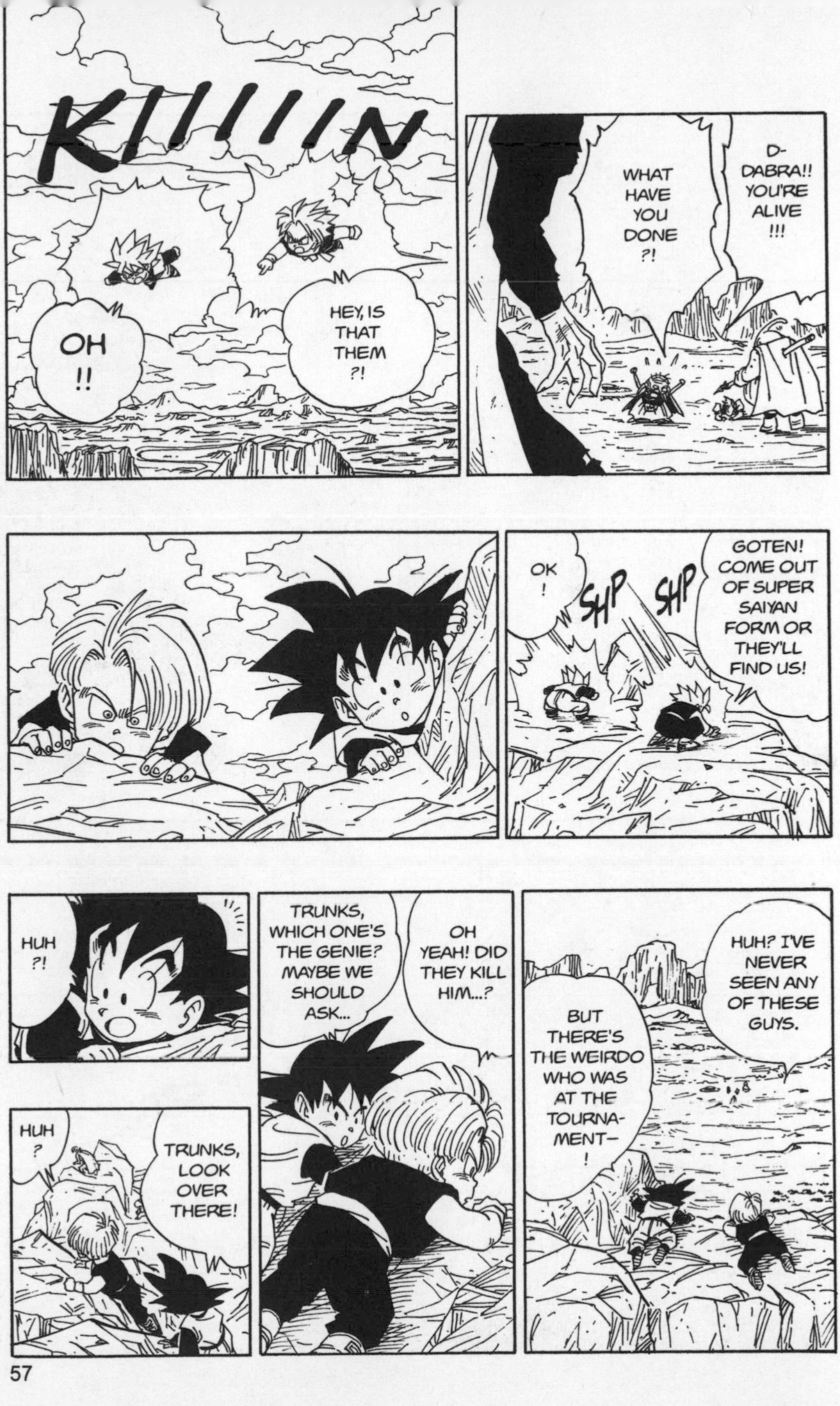
D-DABRA!! YOU'RE ALIVE!!!
WHAT HAVE YOU DONE?!
KIIIIIN
HEY, IS THAT THEM?!
OH!!
GOTEN! COME OUT OF SUPER SAIYAN FORM OR THEY'LL FIND US!
SHP
SHP
OK!
HUH? I'VE NEVER SEEN ANY OF THESE GUYS.
BUT THERE'S THE WEIRDO WHO WAS AT THE TOURNA-MENT-!
OH YEAH! DID THEY KILL HIM...?
TRUNKS, WHICH ONE'S THE GENIE? MAYBE WE SHOULD ASK...
HUH?!
TRUNKS, LOOK OVER THERE!
HUH?

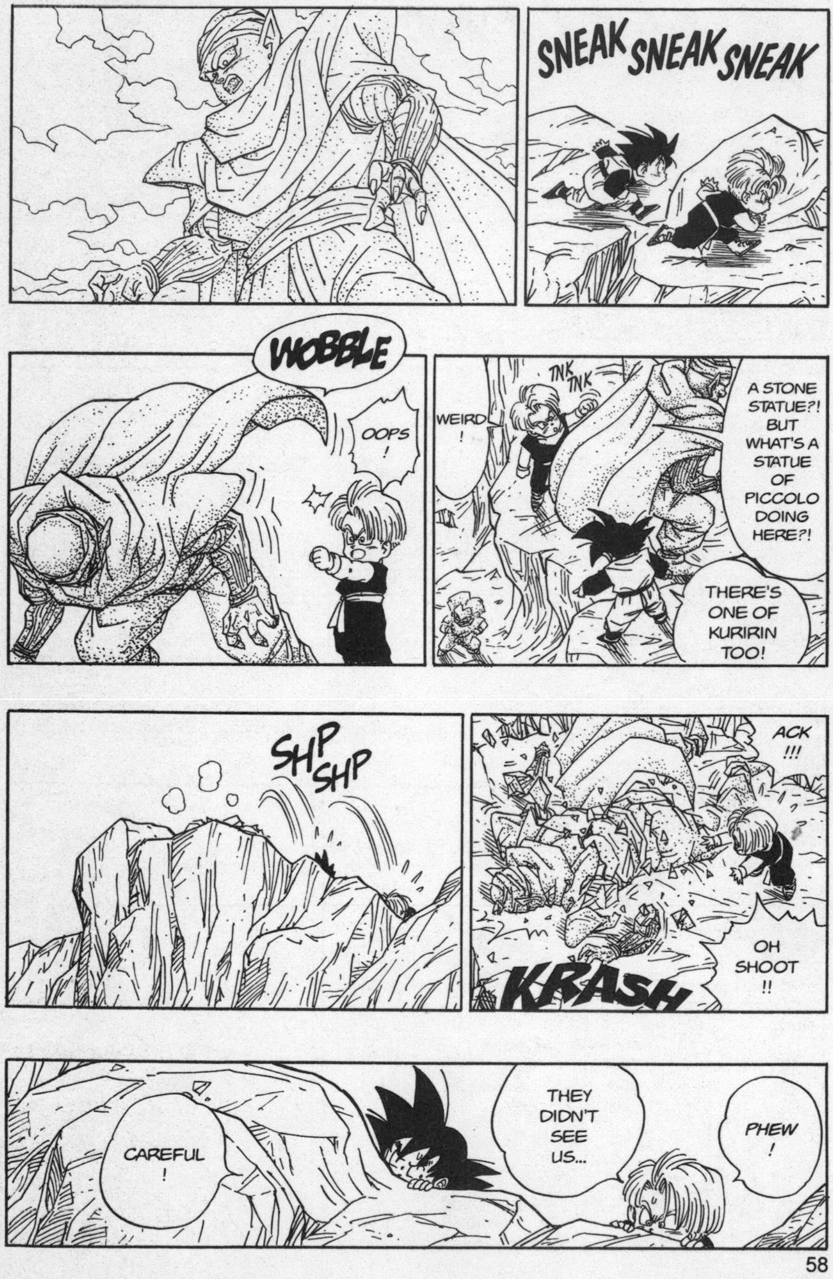
SNEAK SNEAK SNEAK
A STONE STATUE?! BUT WHAT'S A STATUE OF PICCOLO DOING HERE?!
TNK TNK
WEIRD !
THERE'S ONE OF KURIRIN TOO!
WOBBLE
OOPS !
ACK !!!
OH SHOOT !!
KRASH
SHP SHP
PHEW !
THEY DIDN'T SEE US...
CAREFUL !

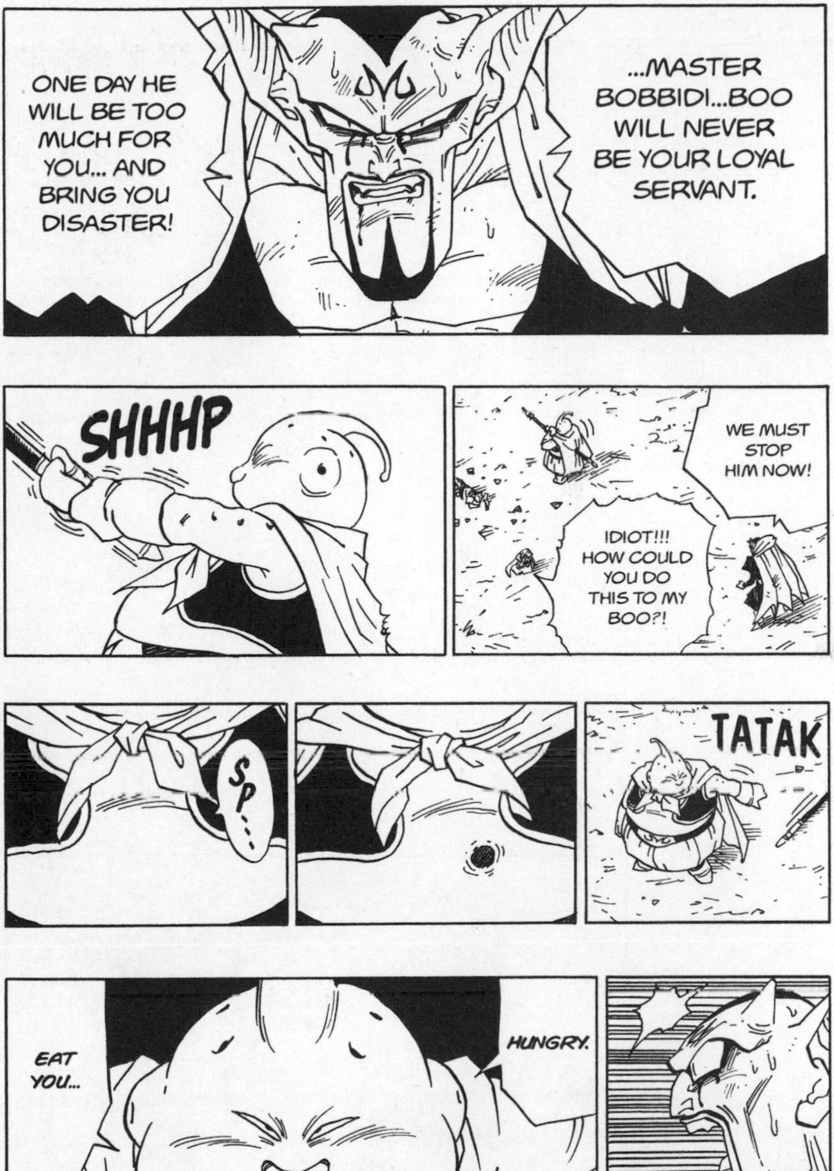
...MASTER BOBBIDI...BOO WILL NEVER BE YOUR LOYAL SERVANT.
ONE DAY HE WILL BE TOO MUCH FOR YOU... AND BRING YOU DISASTER!
WE MUST STOP HIM NOW!
IDIOT!!! HOW COULD YOU DO THIS TO MY BOO?!
SHHHP
TATAK
SP...
HUNGRY.
EAT YOU...

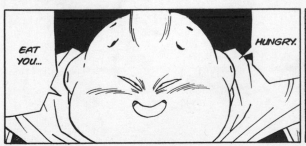

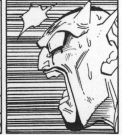

DBZ:270 · Vegeta vs. Boo

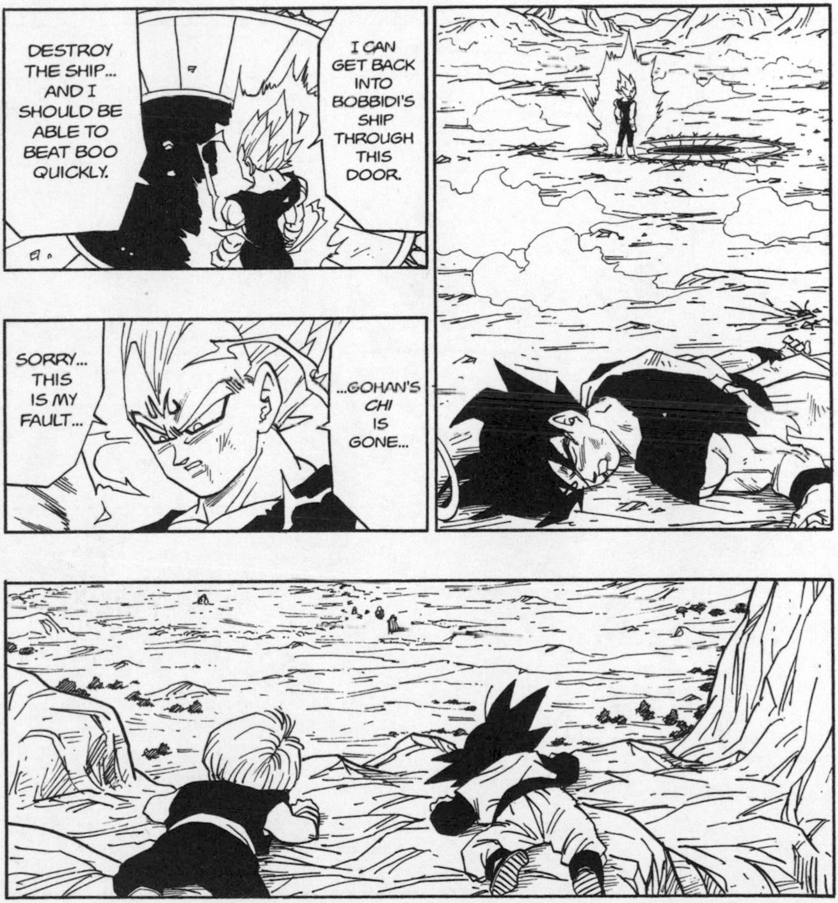
I CAN GET BACK INTO BOBBIDI'S SHIP THROUGH THIS DOOR.
DESTROY THE SHIP... AND I SHOULD BE ABLE TO BEAT BOO QUICKLY.
...GOHAN'S CHI IS GONE...
SORRY... THIS IS MY FAULT...

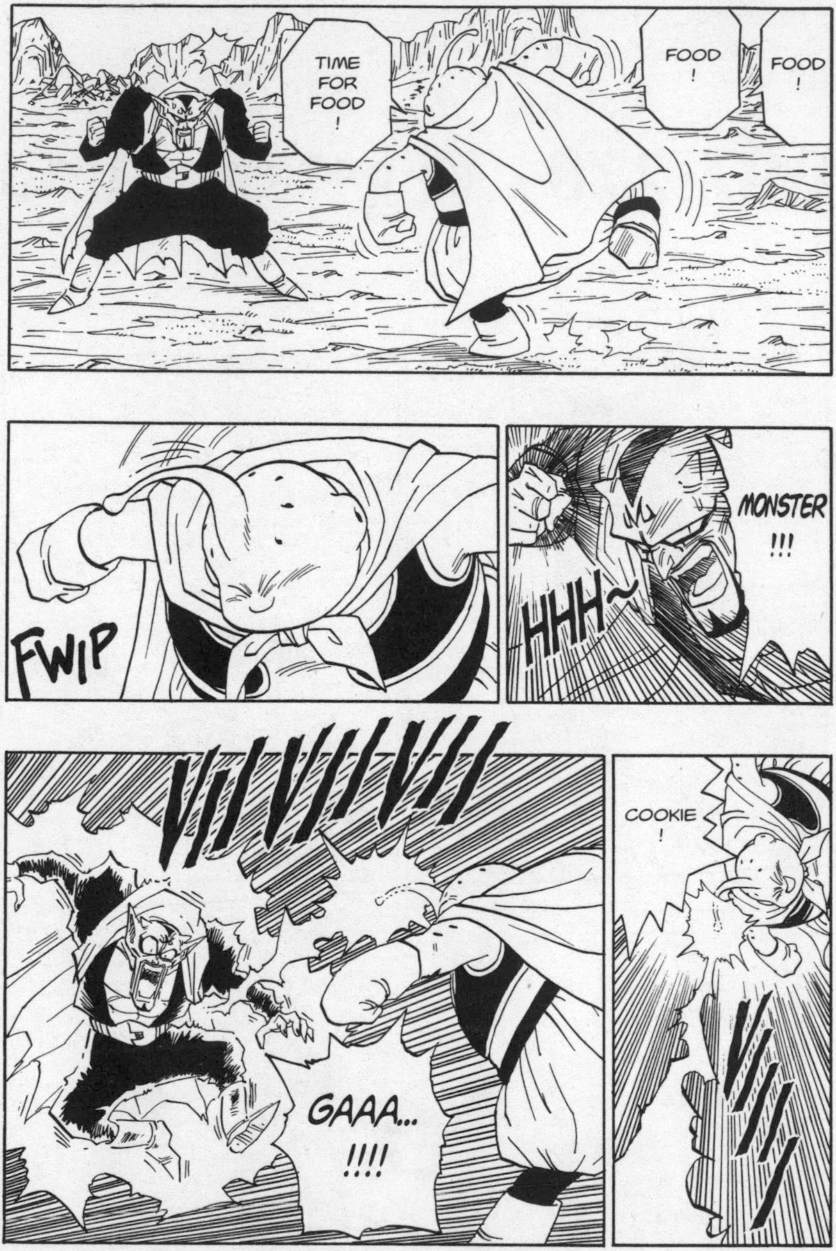
FOOD !
FOOD !
TIME FOR FOOD !
MONSTER !!!
HHH~
FWIP
COOKIE !
GAAA... !!!!

READ THIS WAY

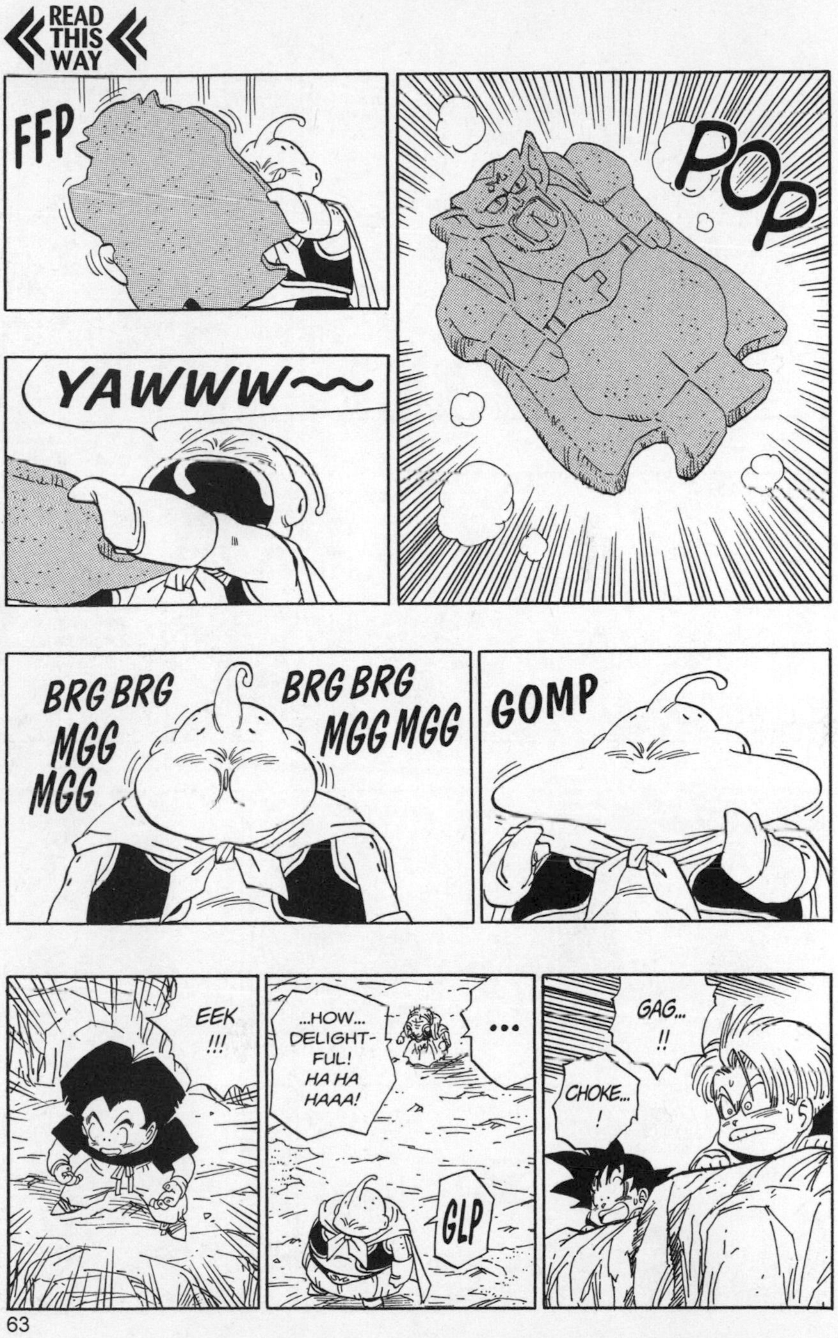
POP
FFP
YAWWW~~
GOMP
BRG BRG
MGG MGG
BRG BRG
MGG
MGG
GAG... !!
CHOKE... !
...
...HOW... DELIGHT-FUL! HA HA HAAA!
GLP
EEK !!!

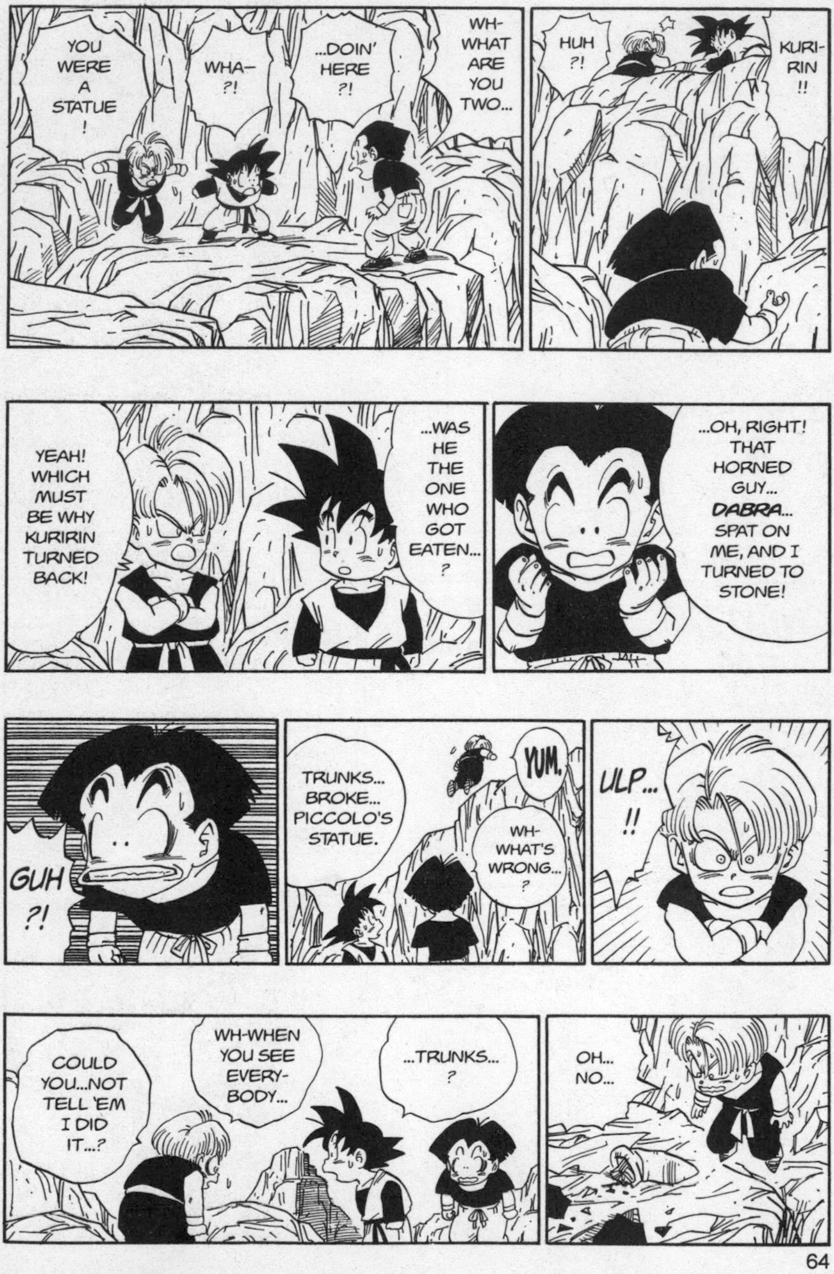
KURI-RIN!!
HUH?!
WH-WHAT ARE YOU TWO...
...DOIN' HERE?!
WHA-?!
YOU WERE A STATUE!
...OH, RIGHT! THAT HORNED GUY... DABRA... SPAT ON ME, AND I TURNED TO STONE!
...WAS HE THE ONE WHO GOT EATEN...?
YEAH! WHICH MUST BE WHY KURIRIN TURNED BACK!
ULP... !!
YUM.
WH-WHAT'S WRONG...?
TRUNKS... BROKE... PICCOLO'S STATUE.
GUH?!
OH... NO...
...TRUNKS...?
WH-WHEN YOU SEE EVERYBODY...
COULD YOU...NOT TELL 'EM I DID IT...?

READ THIS WAY

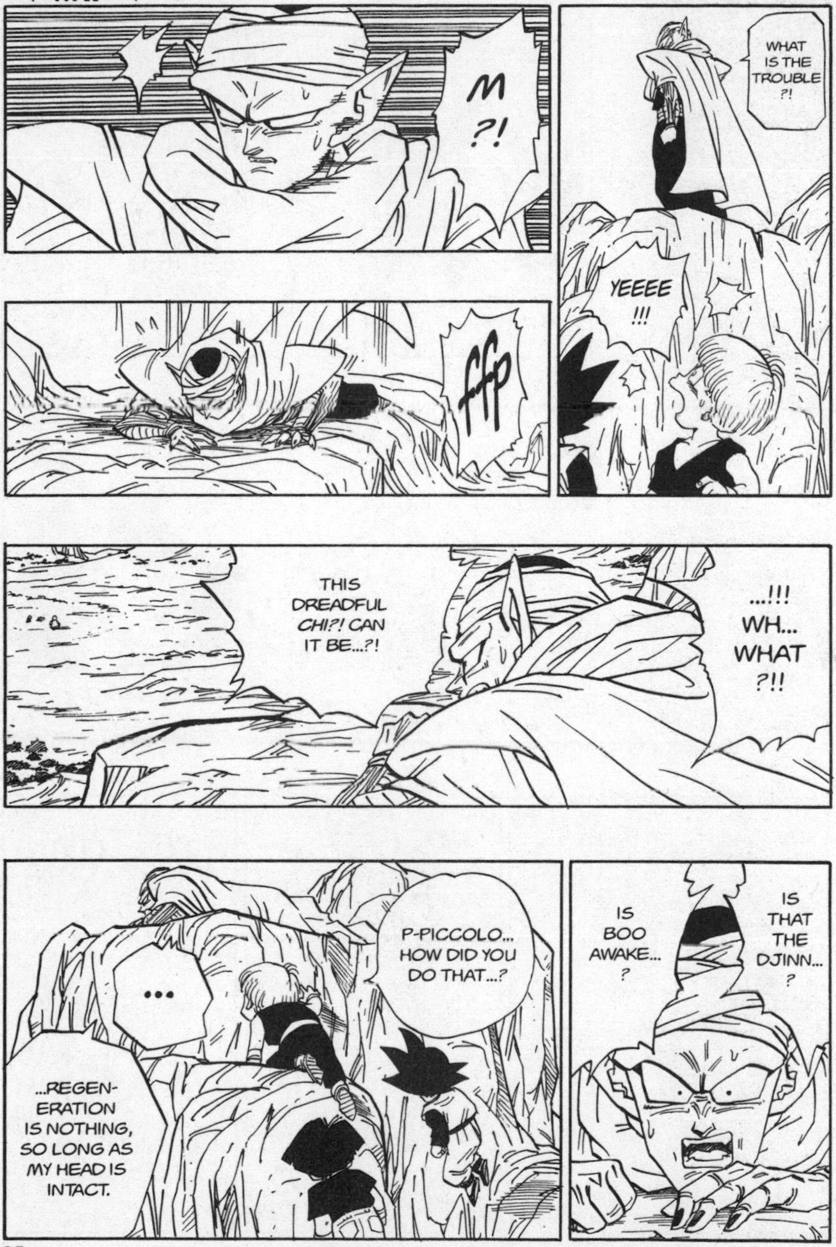
WHAT IS THE TROUBLE ?!
YEEEE !!!
M ?!
ffp
...!!! WH... WHAT ?!!
THIS DREADFUL CHI?! CAN IT BE...?!
IS THAT THE DJINN... ?
IS BOO AWAKE... ?
P-PICCOLO... HOW DID YOU DO THAT...?
...
...REGEN-ERATION IS NOTHING, SO LONG AS MY HEAD IS INTACT.

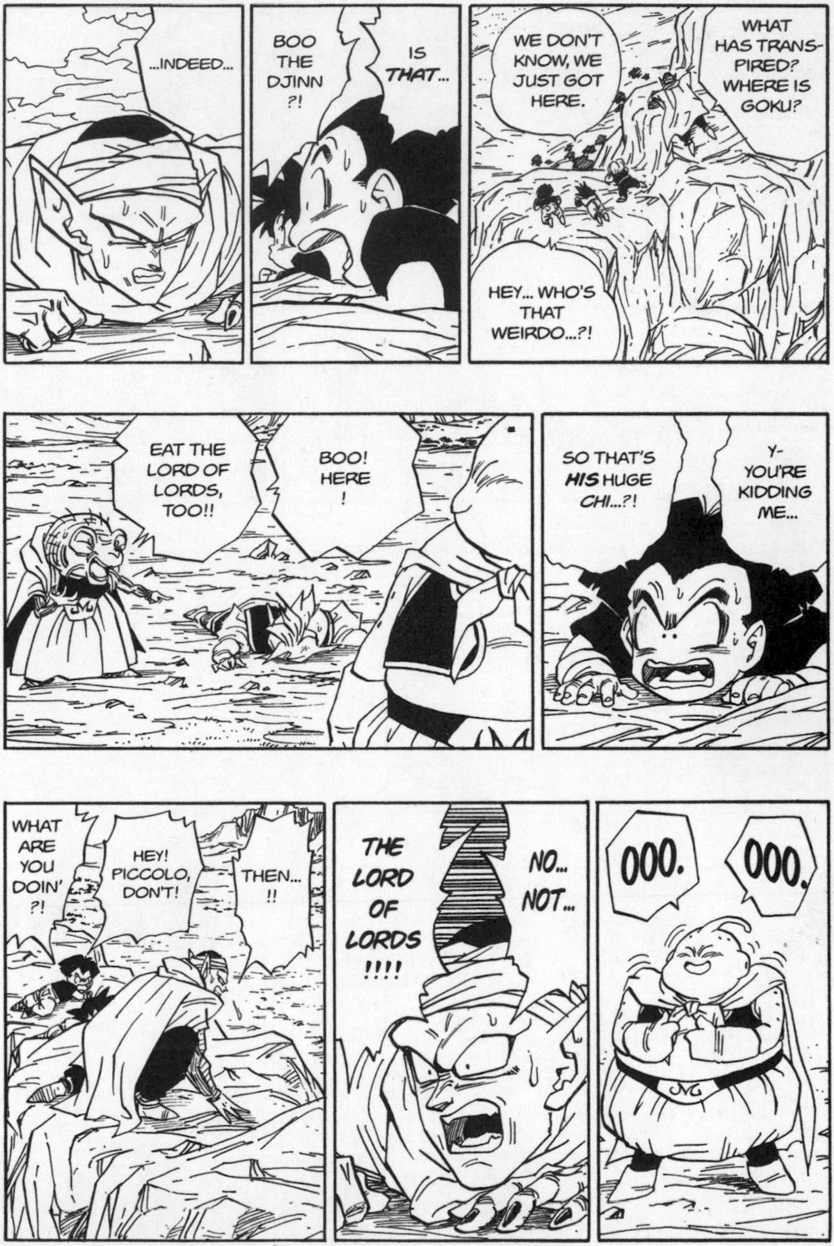
WHAT HAS TRANS-PIRED? WHERE IS GOKU?
WE DON'T KNOW, WE JUST GOT HERE.
HEY... WHO'S THAT WEIRDO...?!
IS *THAT*...
BOO THE DJINN ?!
...INDEED...
Y- YOU'RE KIDDING ME...
SO THAT'S *HIS* HUGE *CHI*...?!
BOO! HERE !
EAT THE LORD OF LORDS, TOO!!
OOO.
OOO.
NO... NOT...
THE LORD OF LORDS !!!!
THEN... !!
HEY! PICCOLO, DON'T!
WHAT ARE YOU DOIN' ?!

READ THIS WAY

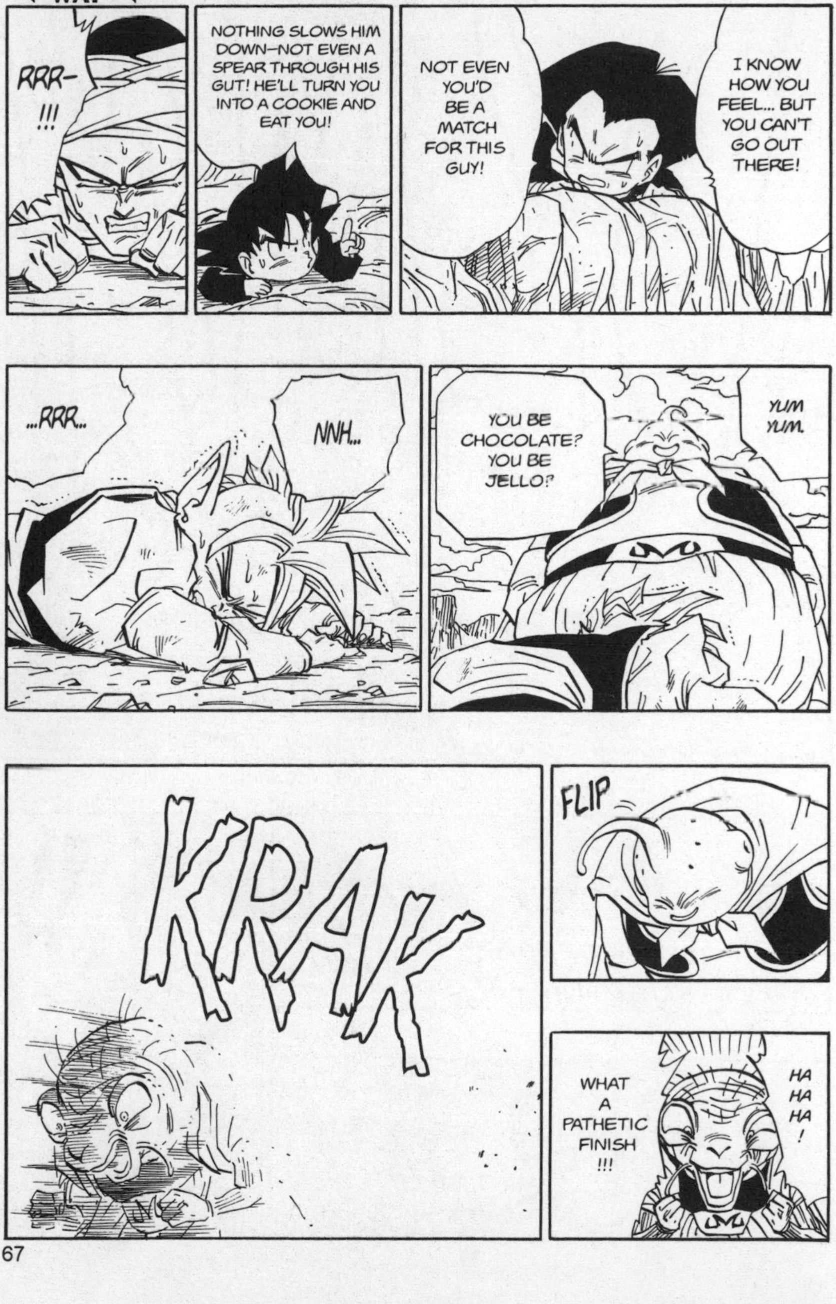
I KNOW HOW YOU FEEL... BUT YOU CAN'T GO OUT THERE!
NOT EVEN YOU'D BE A MATCH FOR THIS GUY!
NOTHING SLOWS HIM DOWN—NOT EVEN A SPEAR THROUGH HIS GUT! HE'LL TURN YOU INTO A COOKIE AND EAT YOU!
RRR- !!!
YUM YUM.
YOU BE CHOCOLATE? YOU BE JELLO?
NNH...
...RRR...
FLIP
HA HA HA!
WHAT A PATHETIC FINISH !!!
KRAK

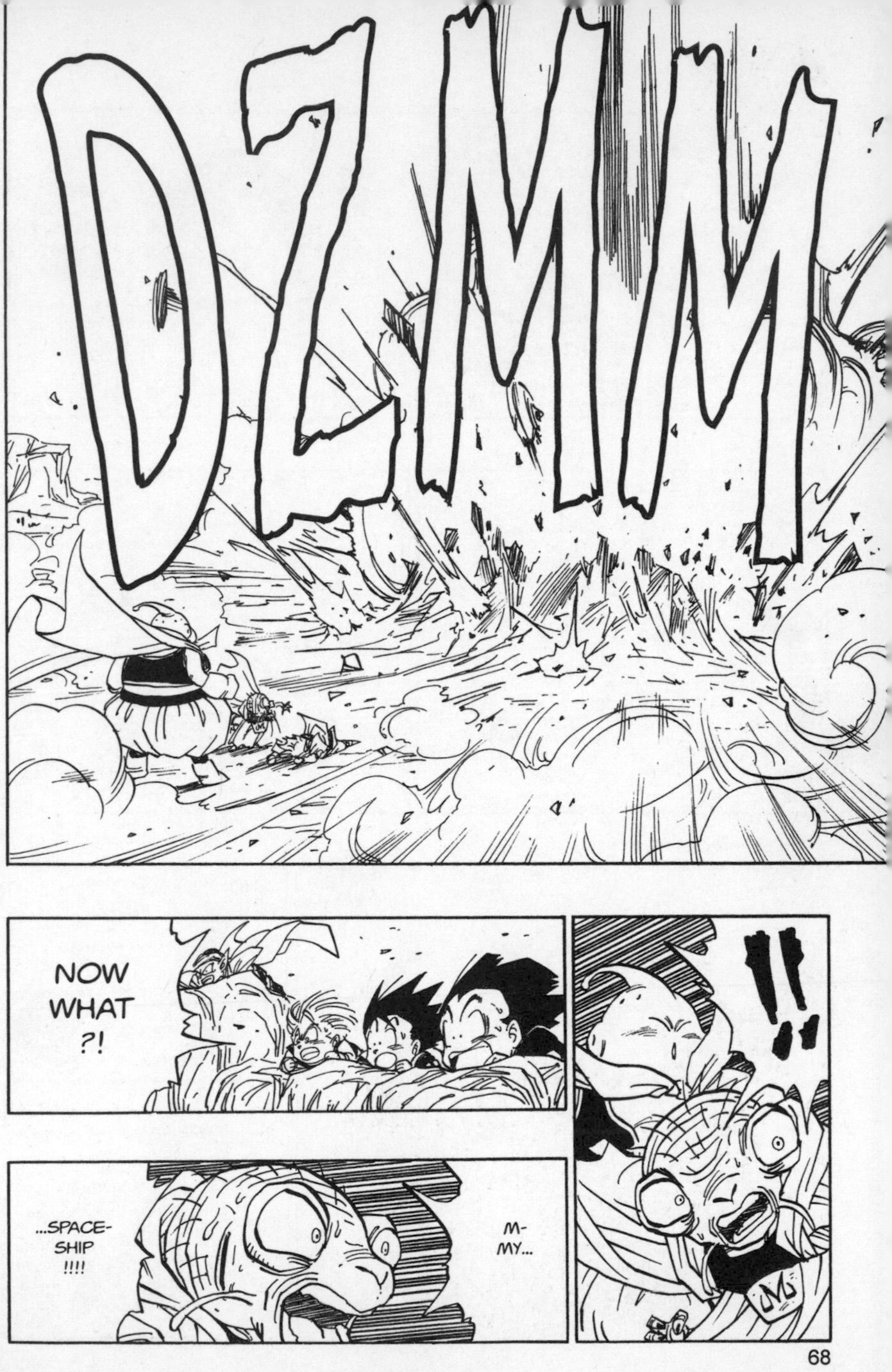
DZMM
!!
NOW WHAT?!
M-MY...
...SPACE-SHIP!!!!

READ THIS WAY

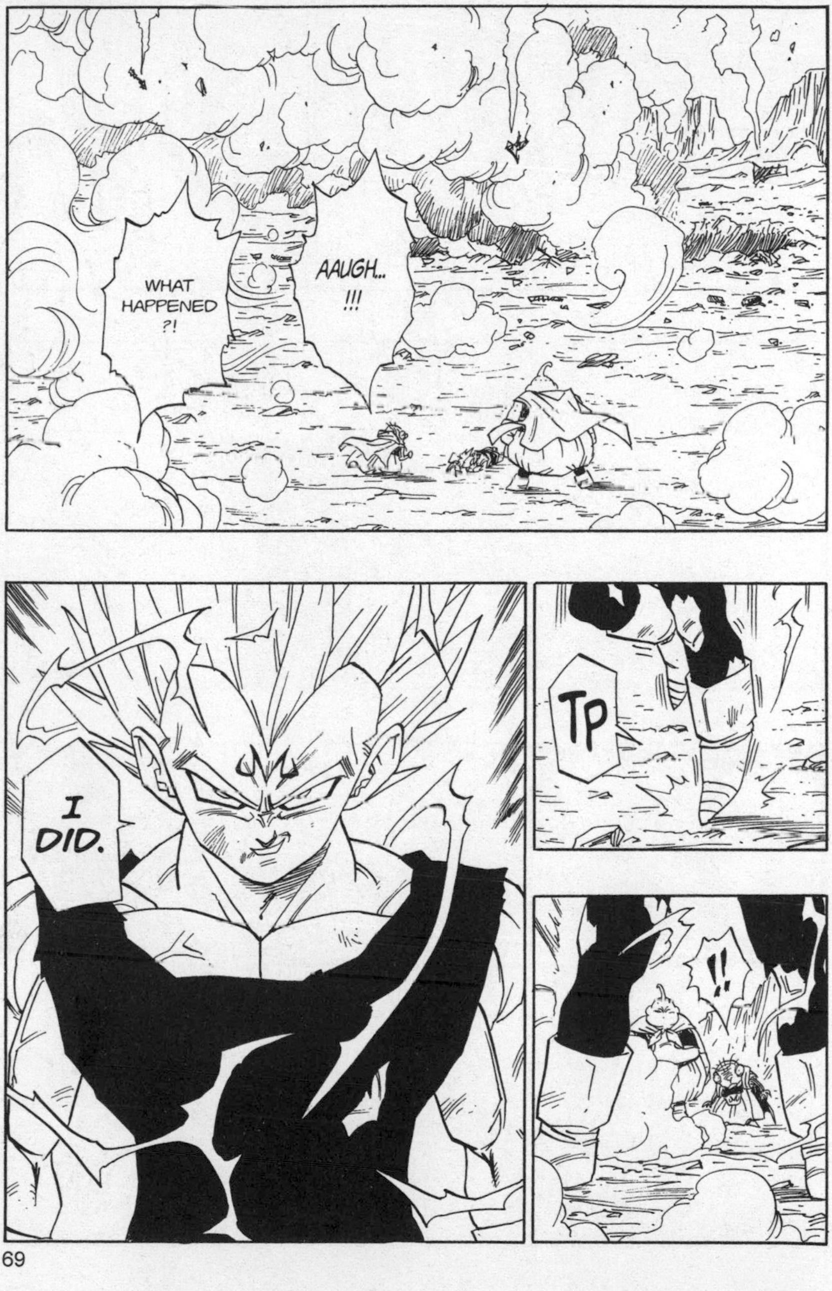
AAUGH... !!!
WHAT HAPPENED ?!
TP
!!
I DID.

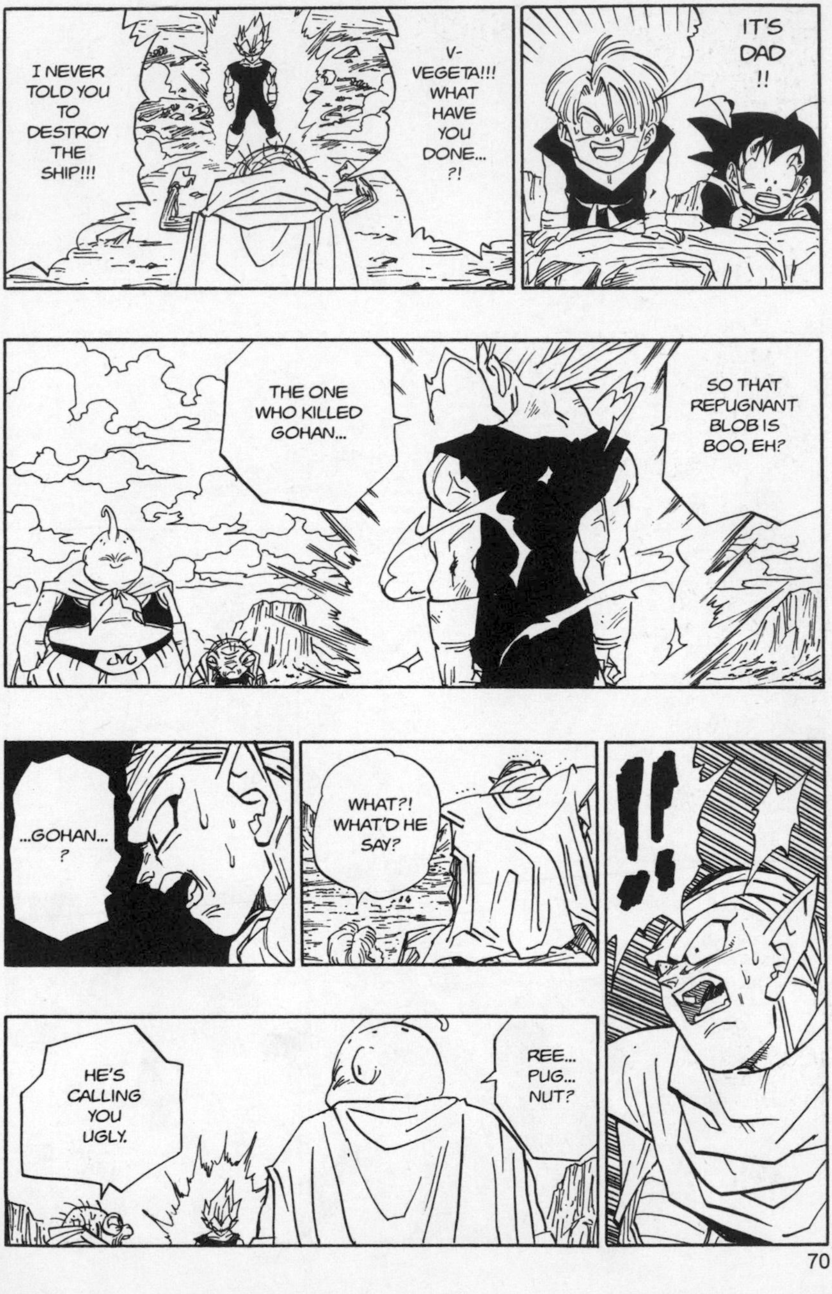
IT'S DAD !!
V-VEGETA!!! WHAT HAVE YOU DONE...?!
I NEVER TOLD YOU TO DESTROY THE SHIP!!!
SO THAT REPUGNANT BLOB IS BOO, EH?
THE ONE WHO KILLED GOHAN...
!!
WHAT?! WHAT'D HE SAY?
...GOHAN...?
REE... PUG... NUT?
HE'S CALLING YOU UGLY.

READ THIS WAY

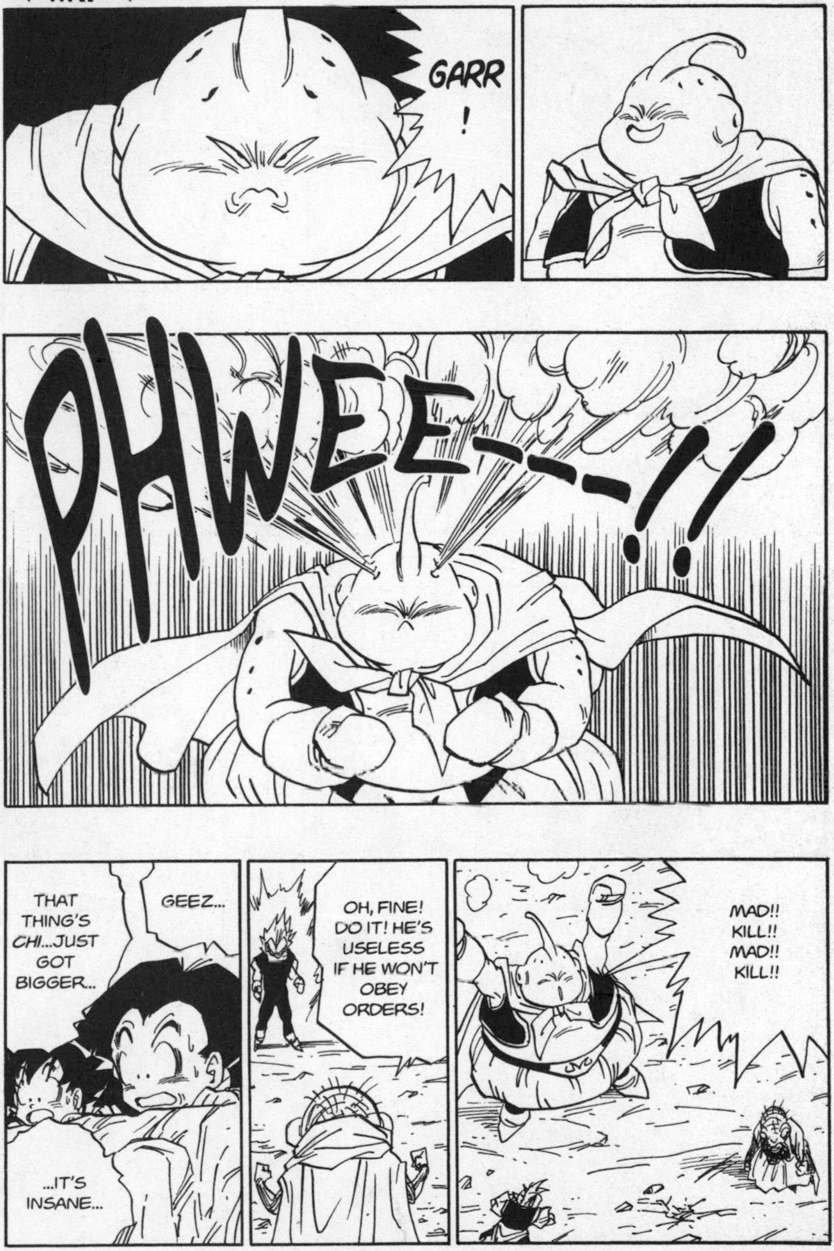
GARR
!
PHWEE---!!
MAD!! KILL!! MAD!! KILL!!
OH, FINE! DO IT! HE'S USELESS IF HE WON'T OBEY ORDERS!
GEEZ...
THAT THING'S *CHI*...JUST GOT BIGGER...
...IT'S INSANE...

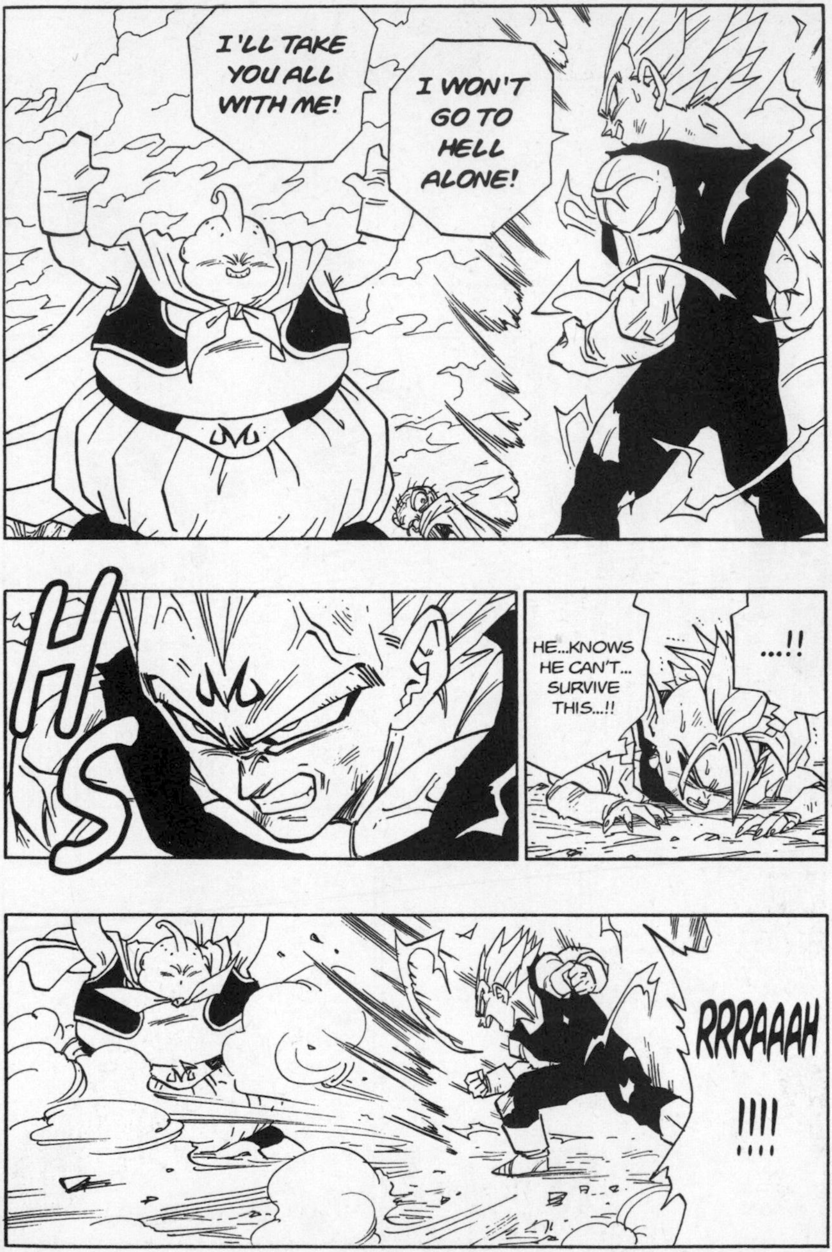
I WON'T GO TO HELL ALONE!
I'LL TAKE YOU ALL WITH ME!
...!!
HE...KNOWS HE CAN'T... SURVIVE THIS...!!
HS
RRRAAAH !!!!

READ THIS WAY

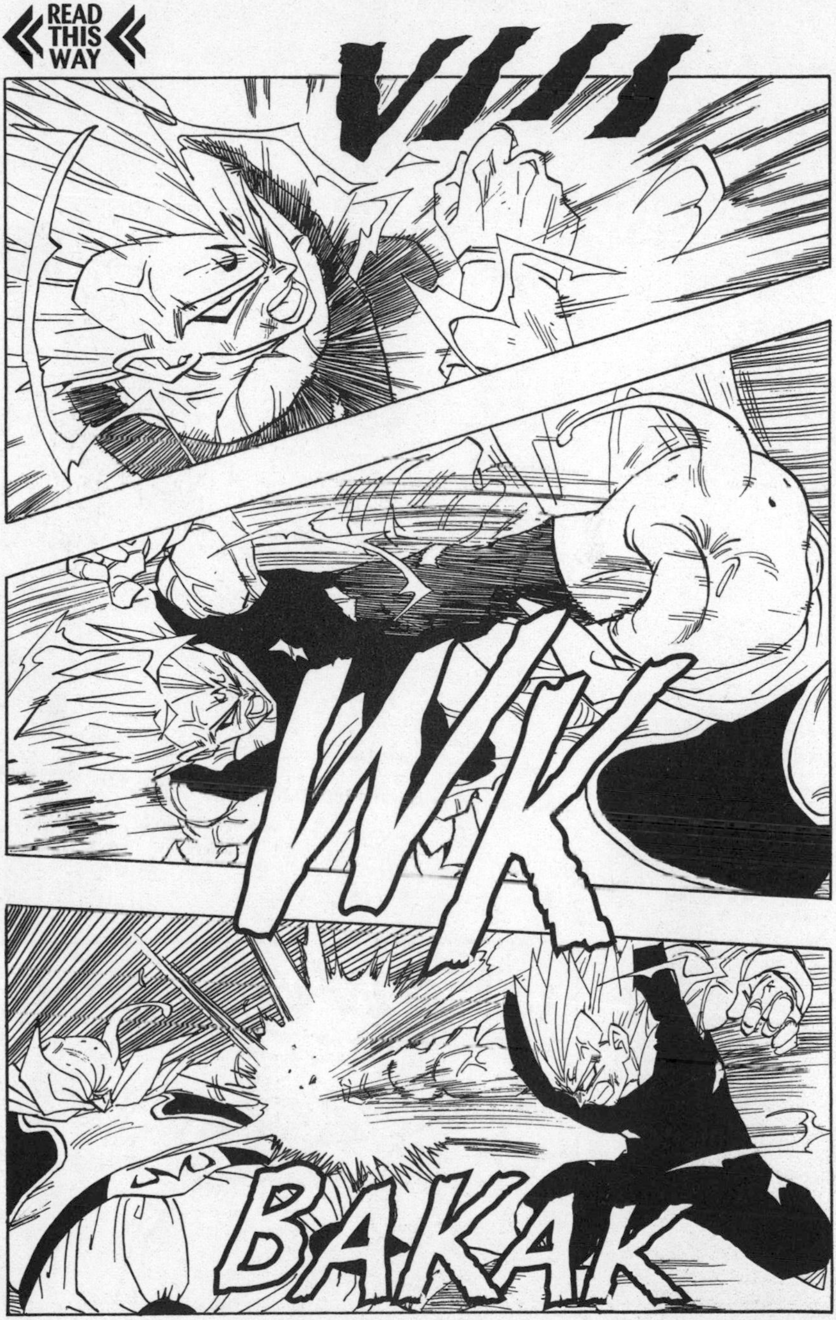
VIII
WK
BAKAK

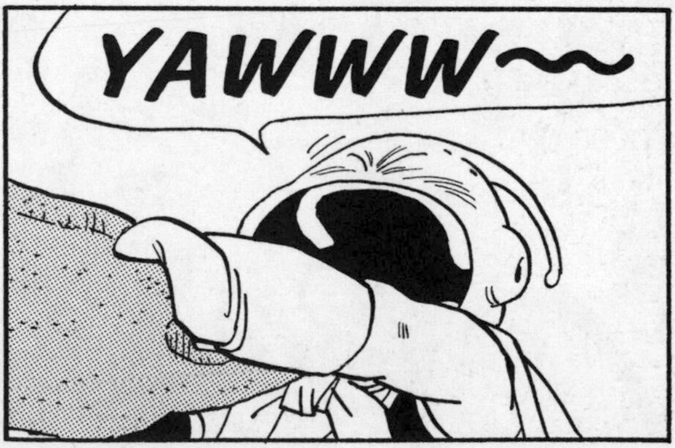
YAWWW~~

DBZ:271 · Boo Gets Mad

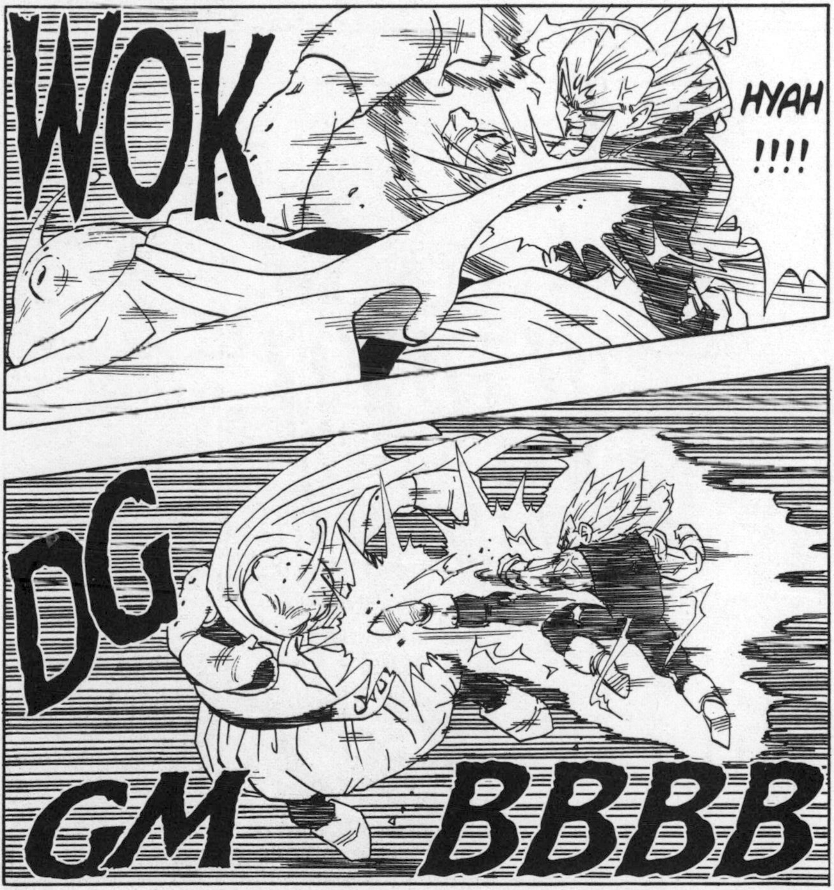
HYAH
!!!!
WOK
DG
BBBB
GM

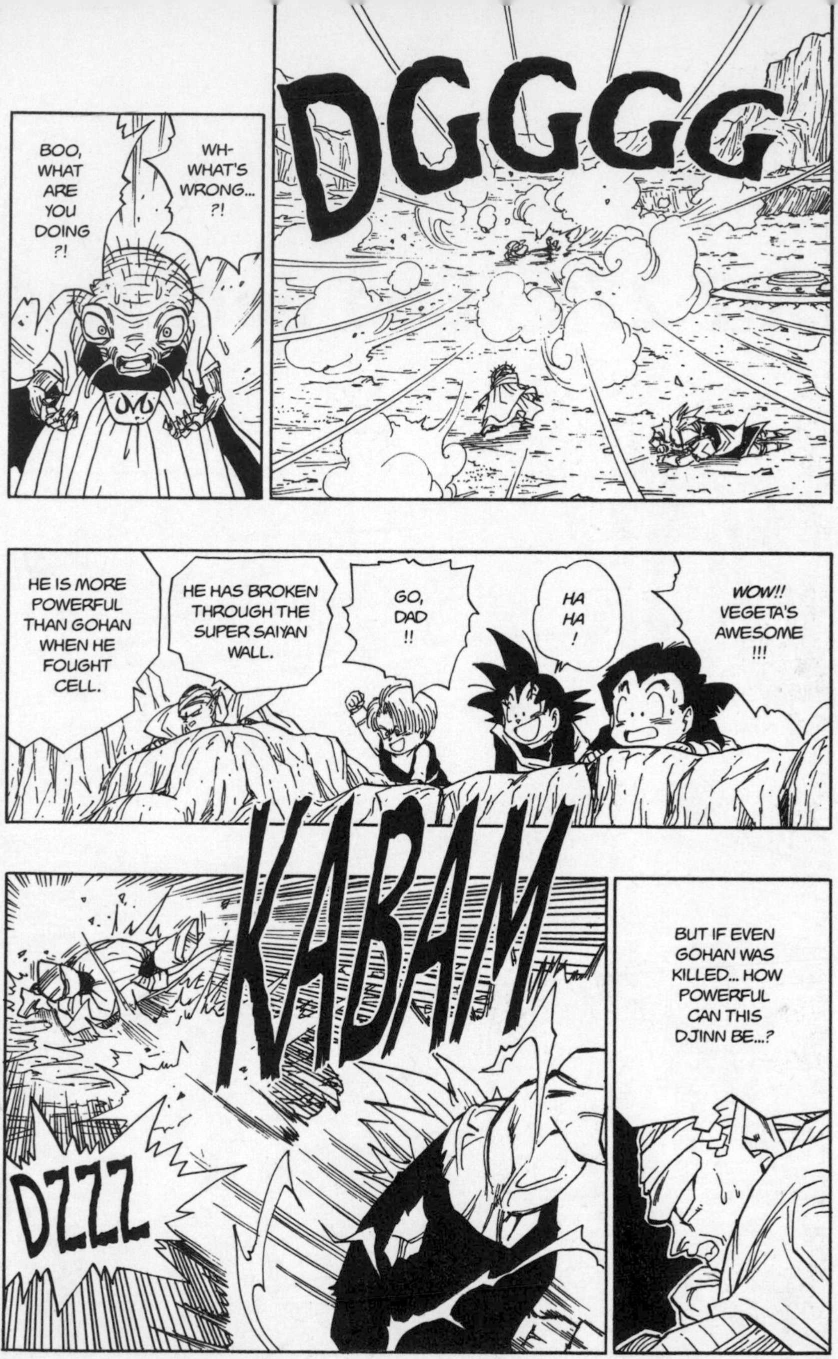
DGGGG
WH- WHAT'S WRONG... ?!
BOO, WHAT ARE YOU DOING ?!
WOW!! VEGETA'S AWESOME !!!
HA HA !
GO, DAD !!
HE HAS BROKEN THROUGH THE SUPER SAIYAN WALL.
HE IS MORE POWERFUL THAN GOHAN WHEN HE FOUGHT CELL.
BUT IF EVEN GOHAN WAS KILLED... HOW POWERFUL CAN THIS DJINN BE...?
KABAM
DZZZ

READ THIS WAY

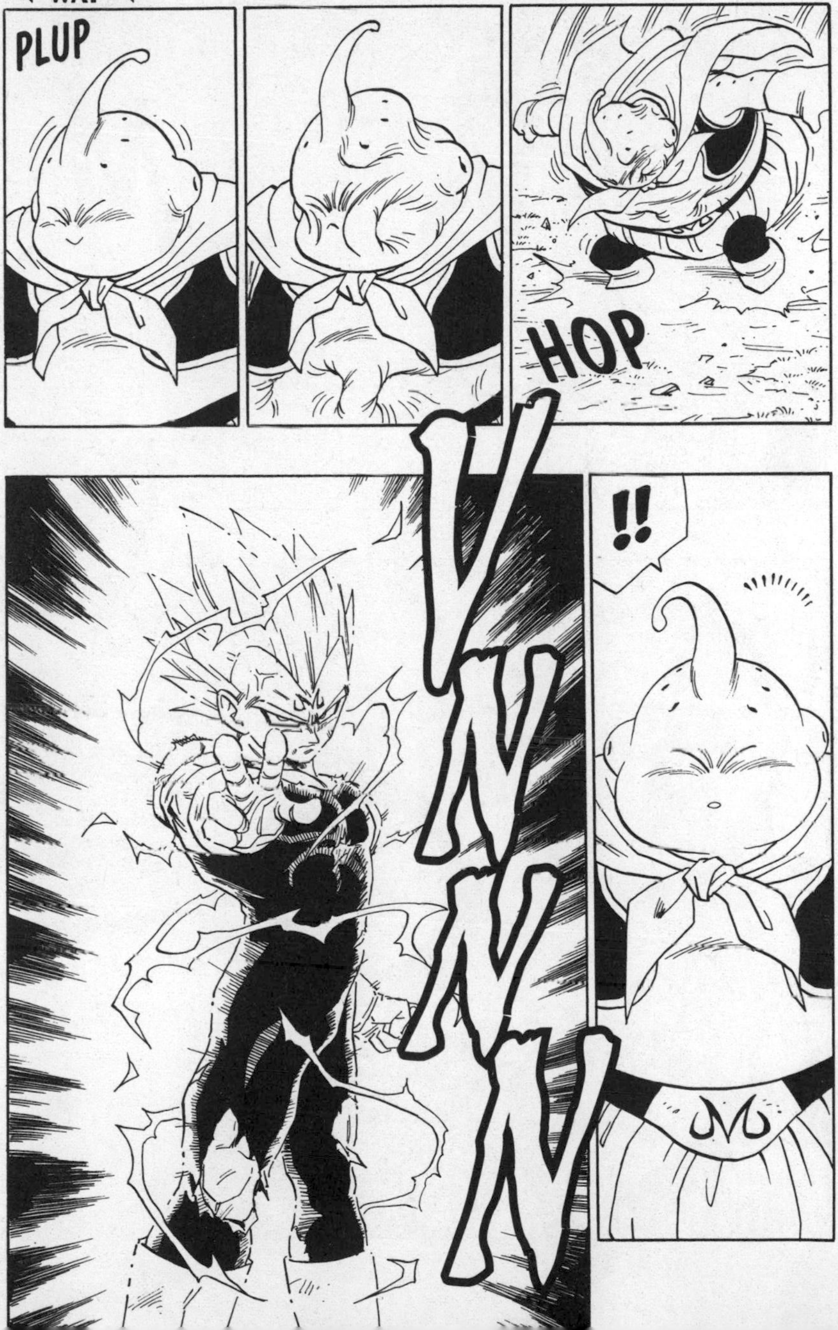
HOP
PLUP
!!
VNNN

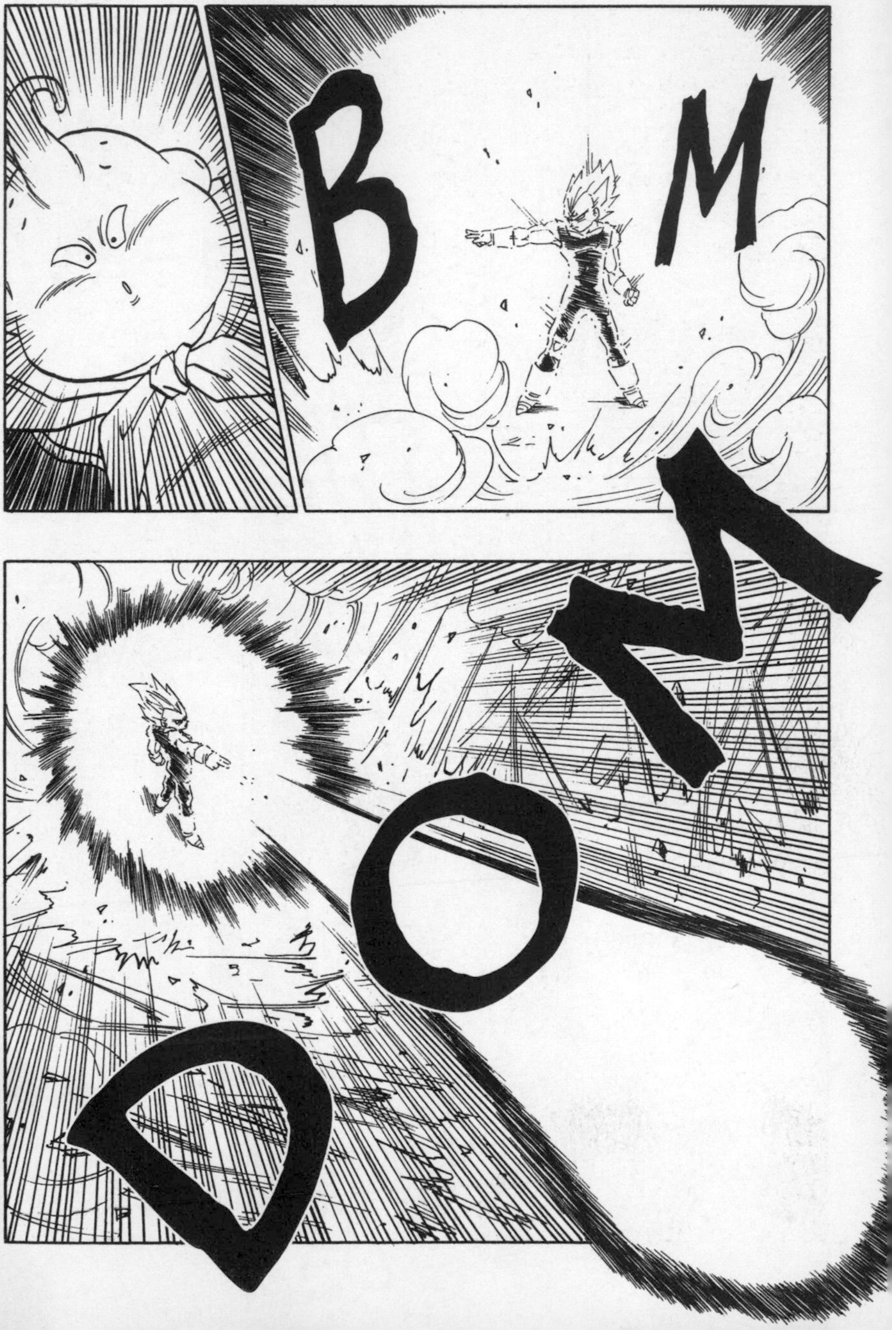
B M
D O M

READ THIS WAY

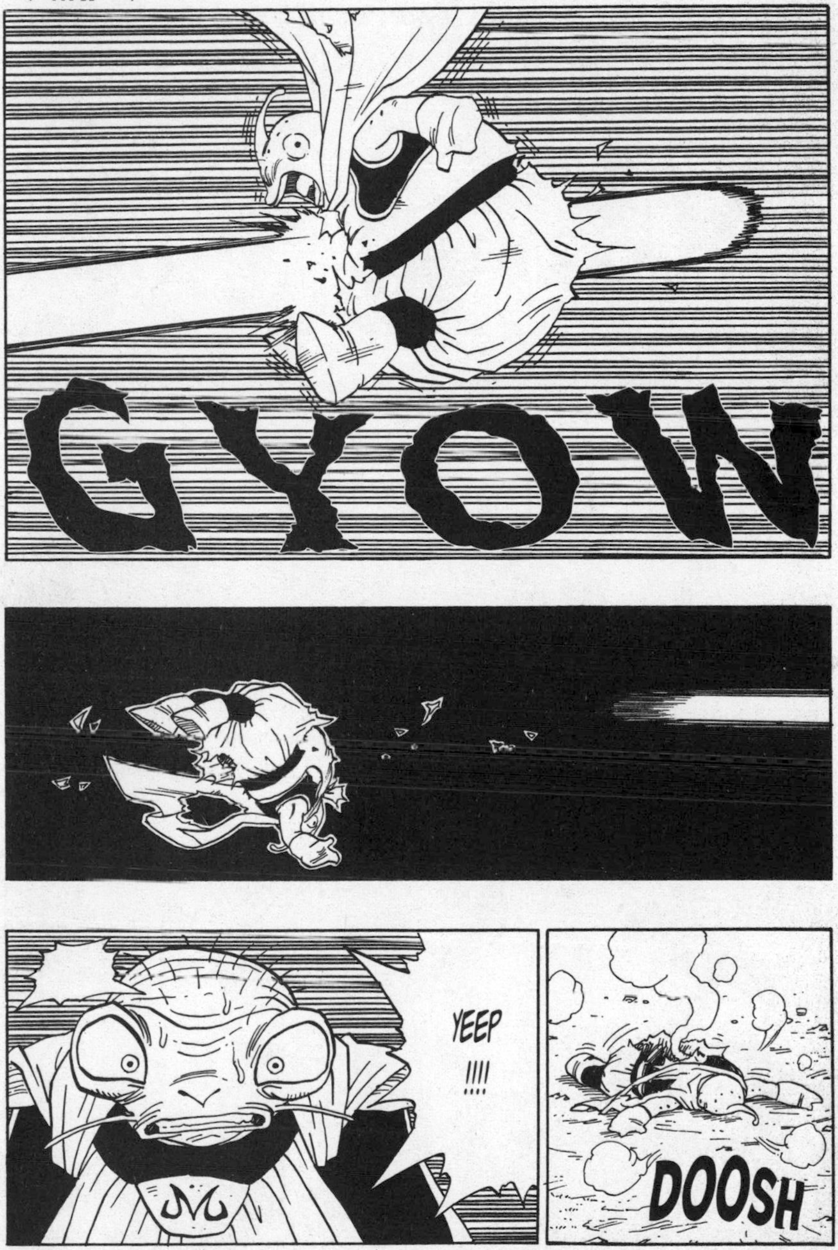
GYOW
DOOSH
YEEP !!!!

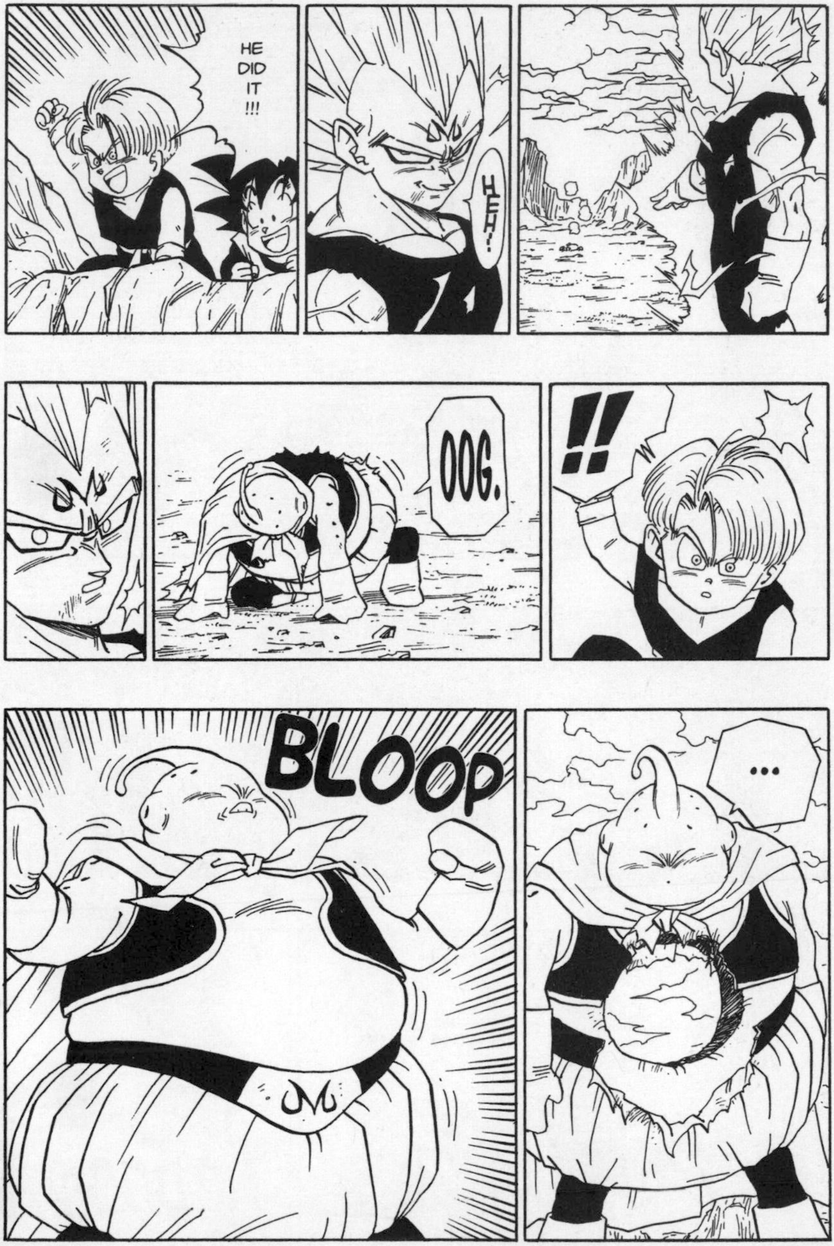
HEH!
HE DID IT !!!
!!
OOG.
...
BLOOP

READ THIS WAY

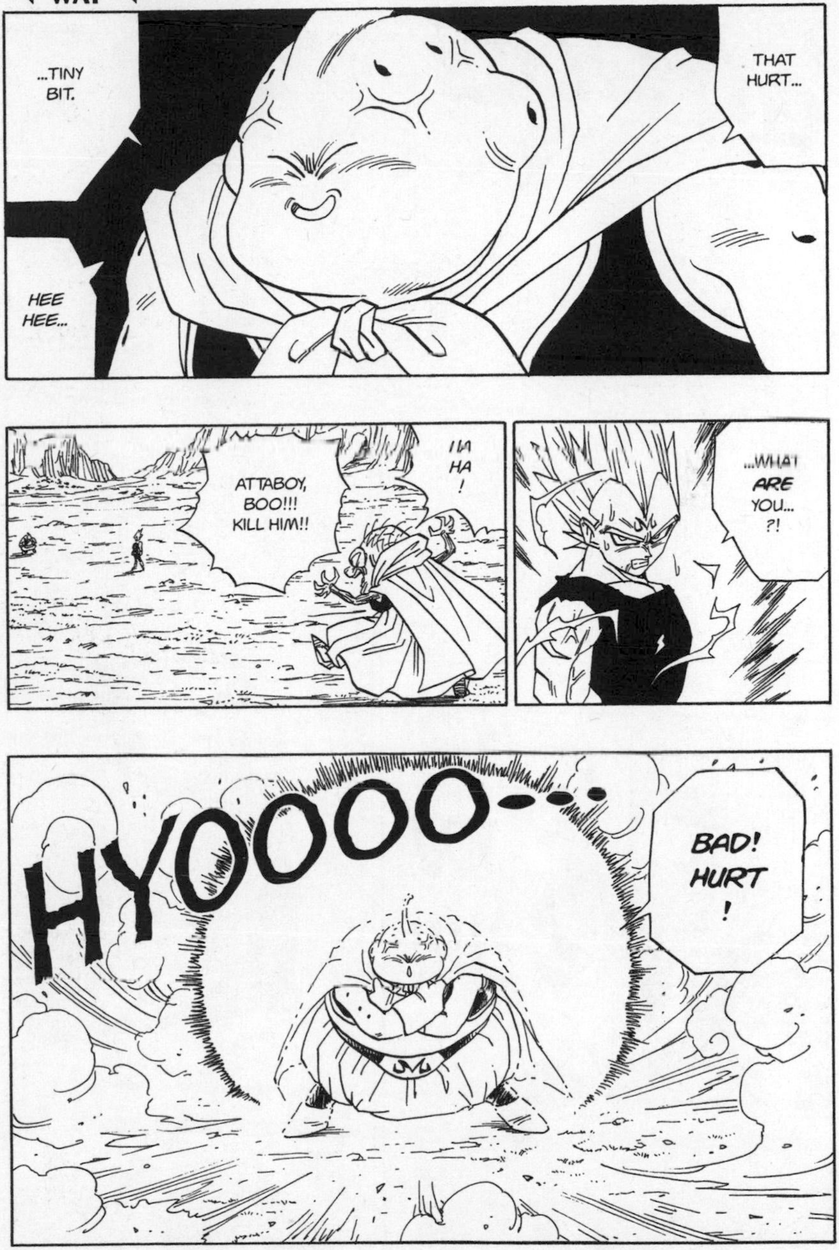
THAT HURT...
...TINY BIT.
HEE HEE...
...WHAT ARE YOU...?!
HA HA!
ATTABOY, BOO!!! KILL HIM!!
BAD! HURT!
HYOOOO-..

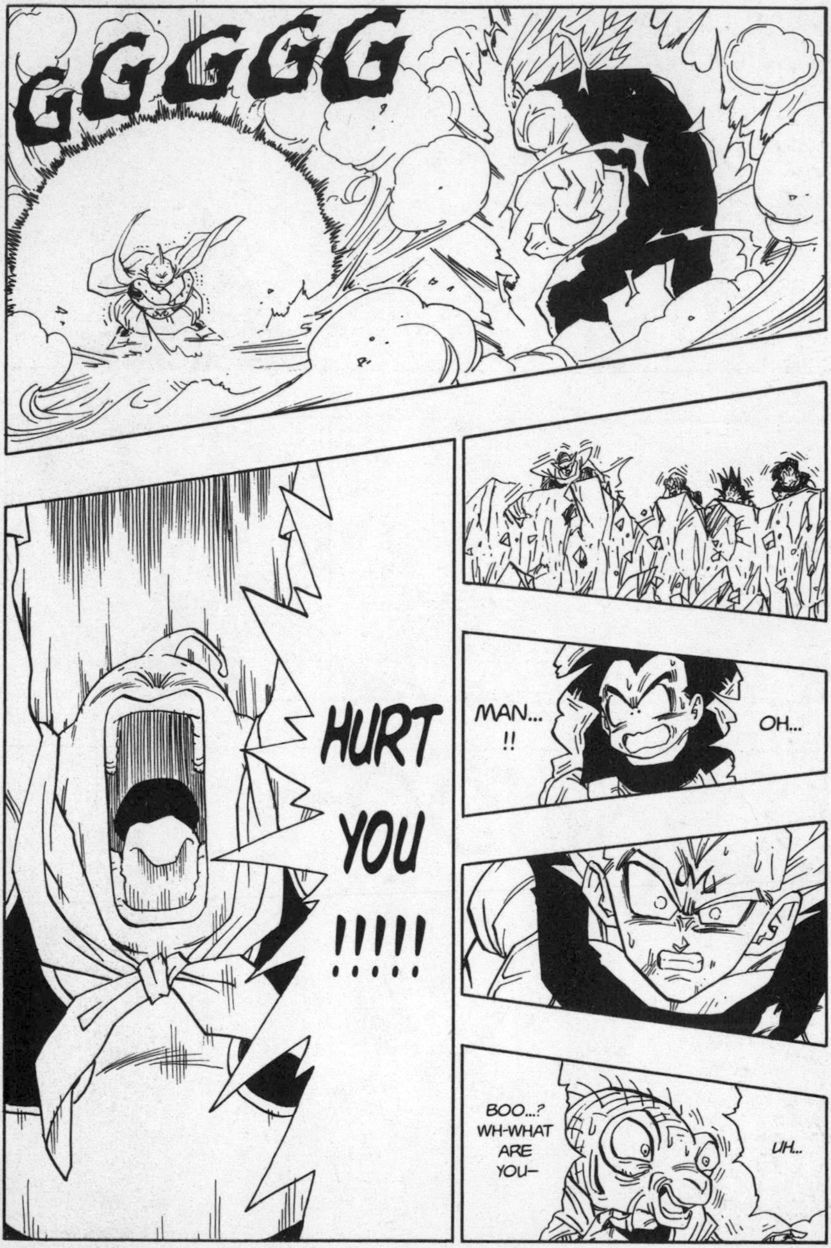
GGGGG
OH...
MAN... !!
UH...
BOO...? WH-WHAT ARE YOU—
HURT YOU !!!!!

READ THIS WAY

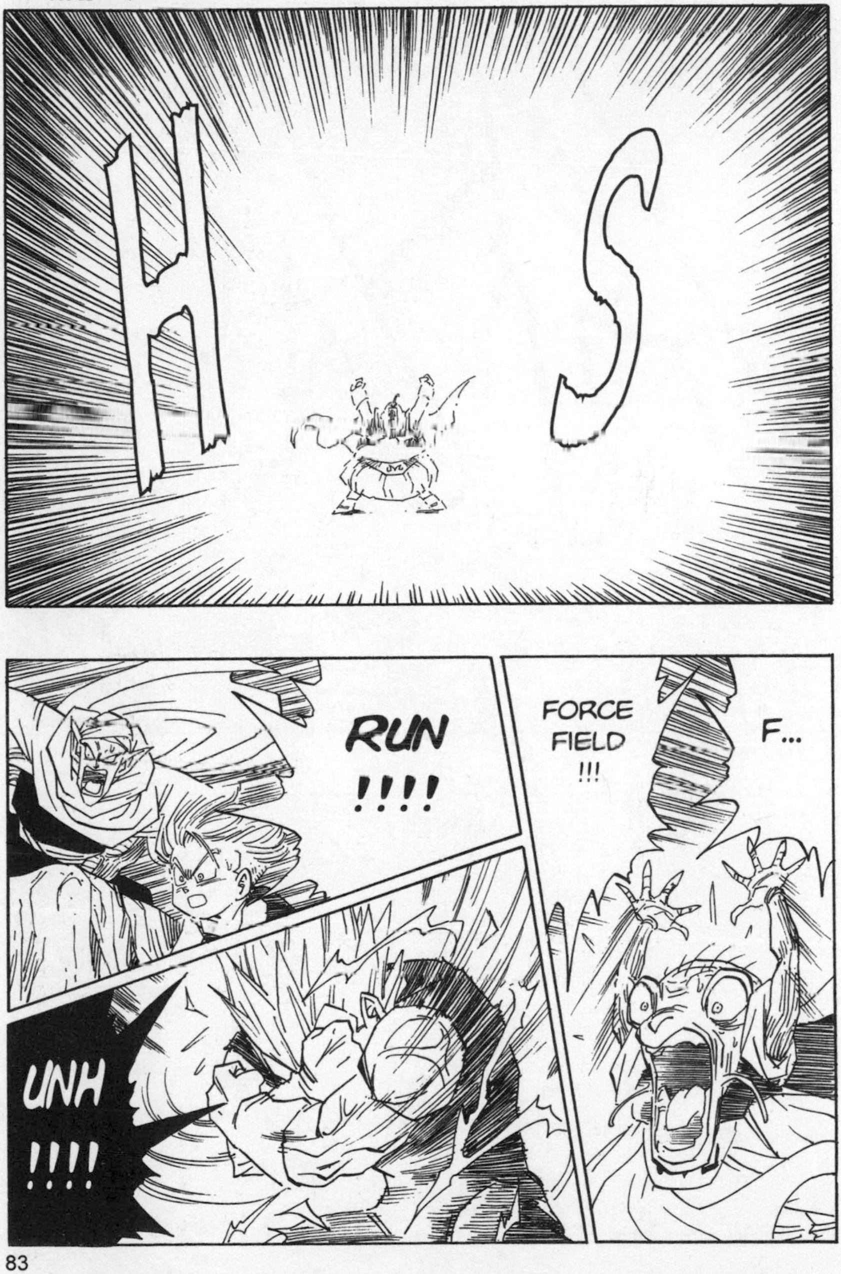
H
S
F...
FORCE FIELD !!!
RUN !!!!
UNH !!!!

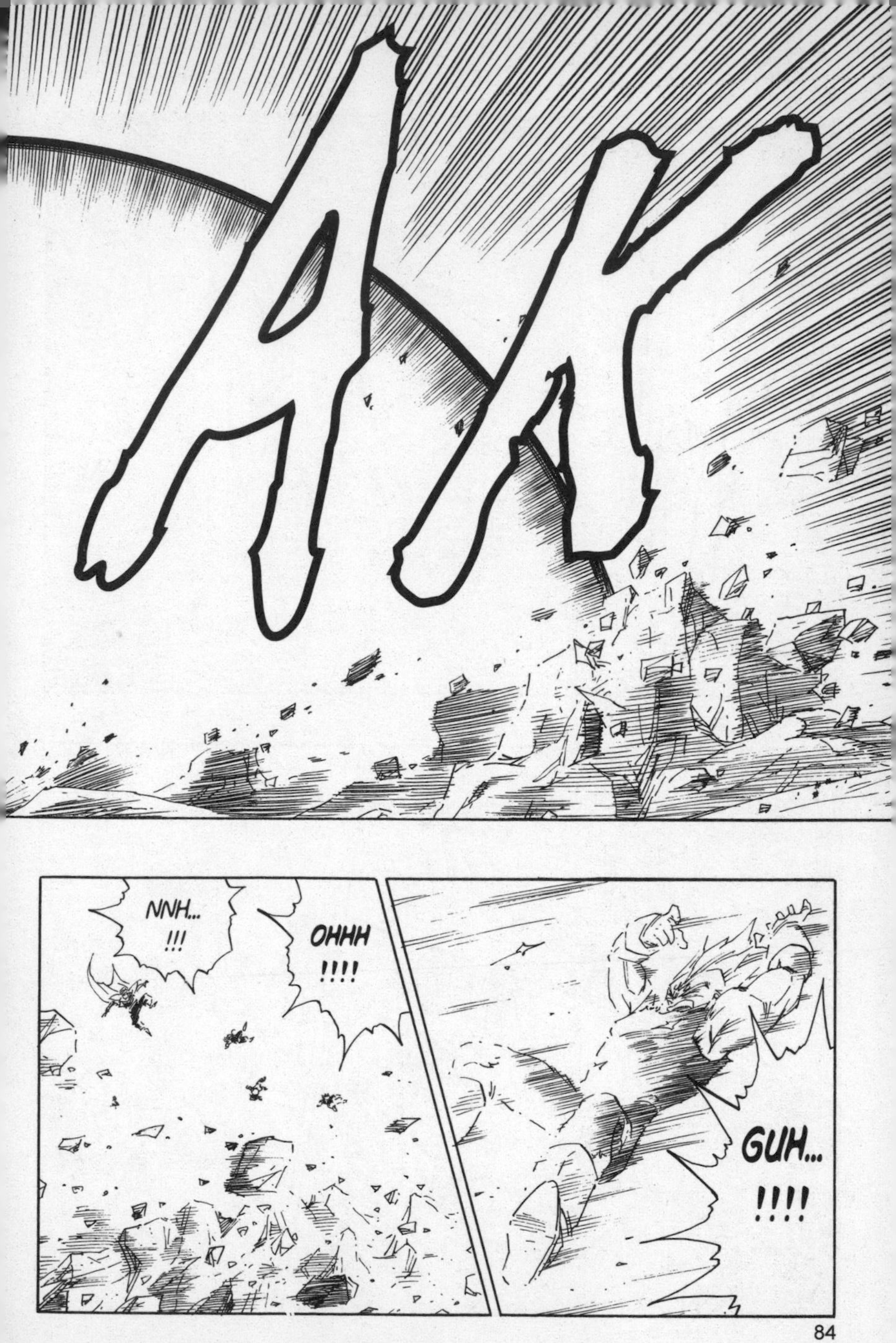
AK
GUH... !!!!
OHHH !!!!
NNH... !!!

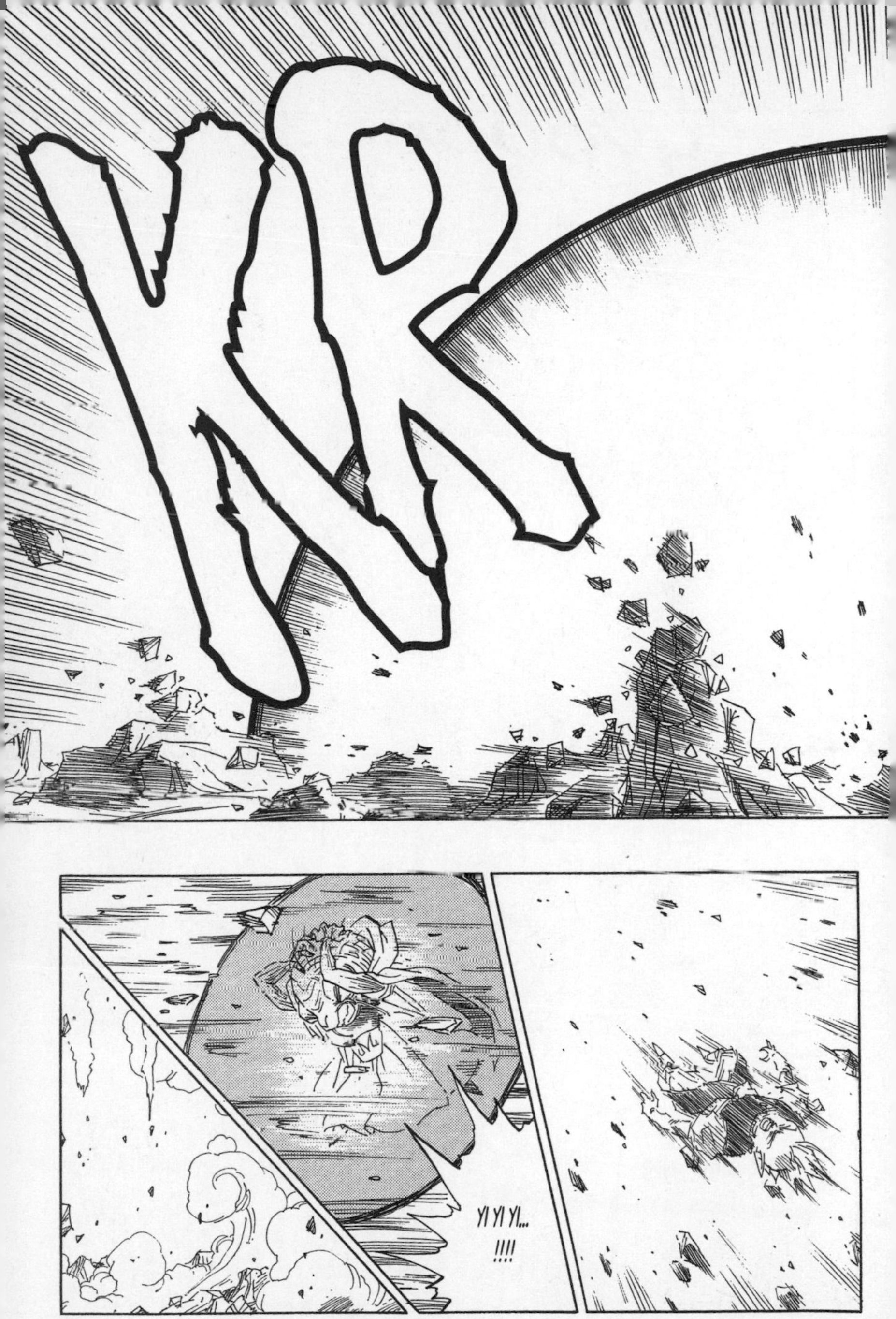
YI YI YI...
!!!!

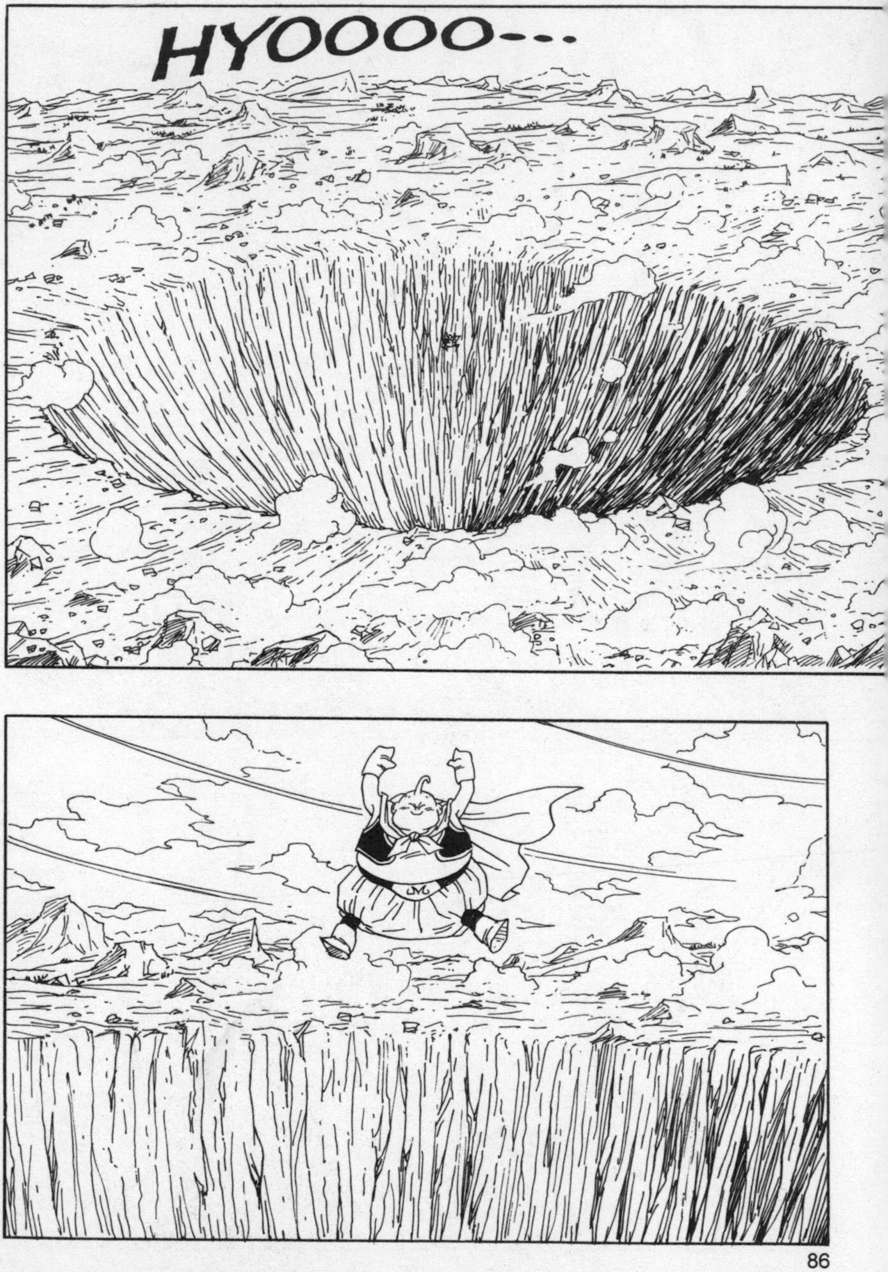
HYOOOO···

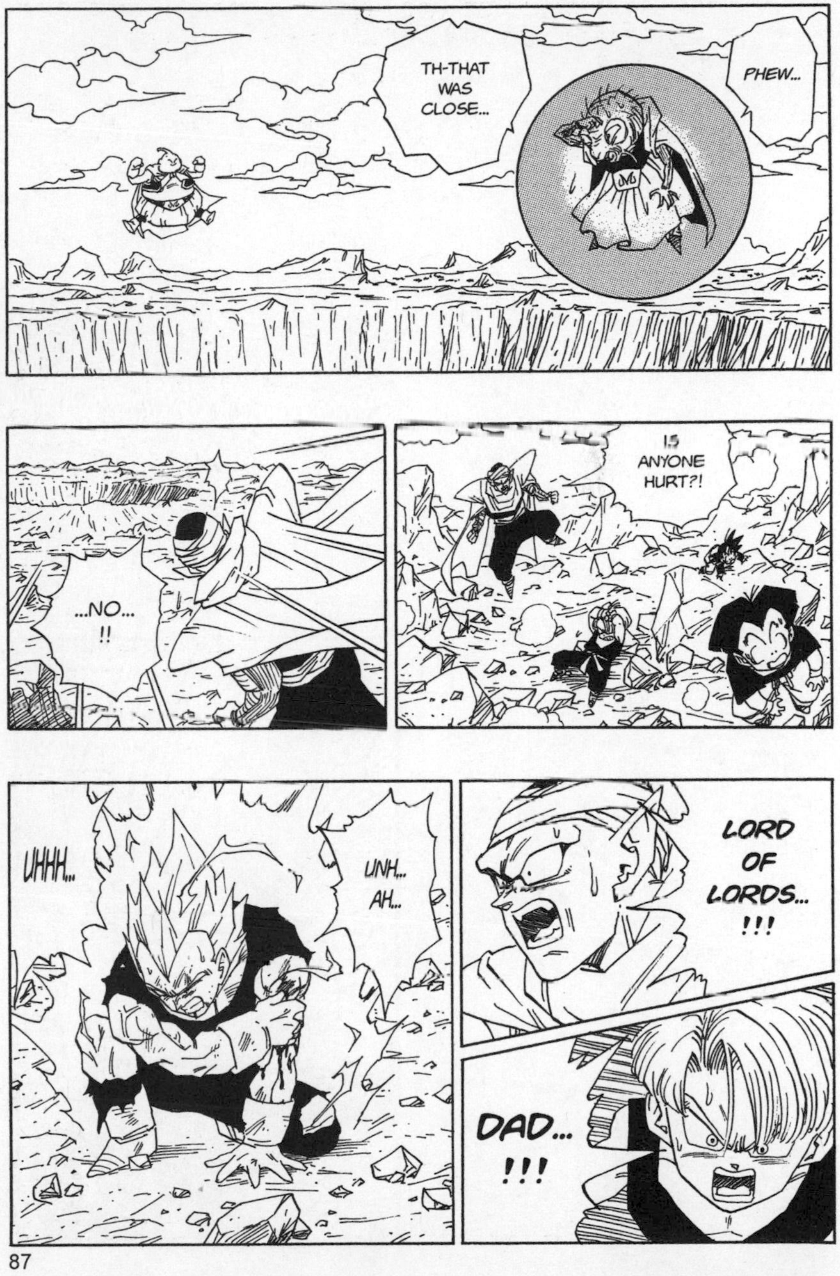
PHEW...
TH-THAT WAS CLOSE...
IS ANYONE HURT?!
...NO... !!
LORD OF LORDS... !!!
DAD... !!!
UNH... AH...
UHHH...

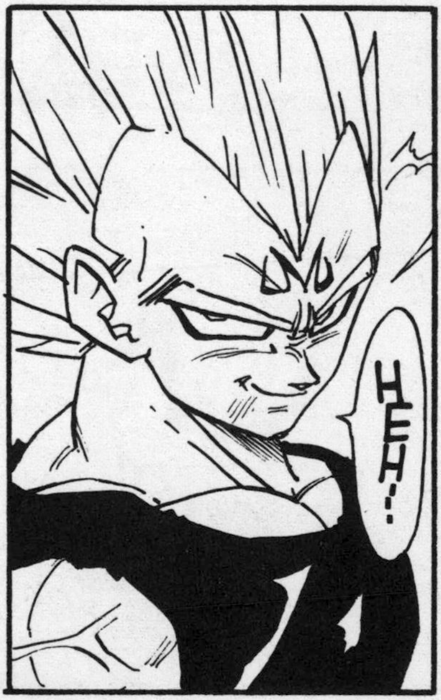
HEH!!

DBZ:272 · The Mastermind's Demise

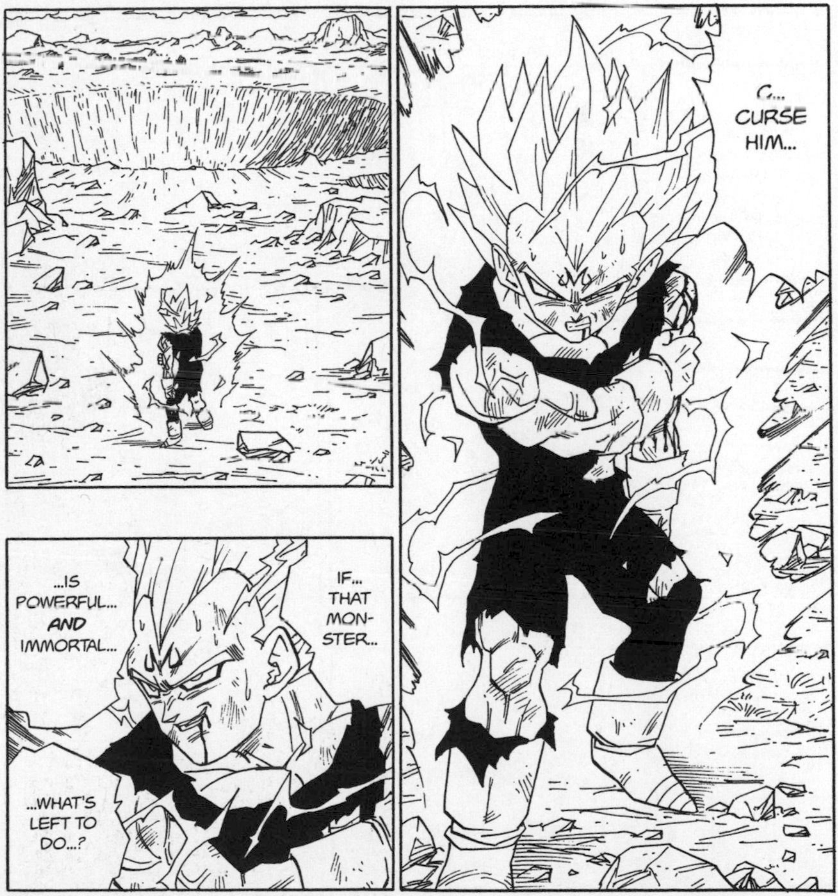
C... CURSE HIM...
IF... THAT MONSTER...
...IS POWERFUL... AND IMMORTAL...
...WHAT'S LEFT TO DO...?

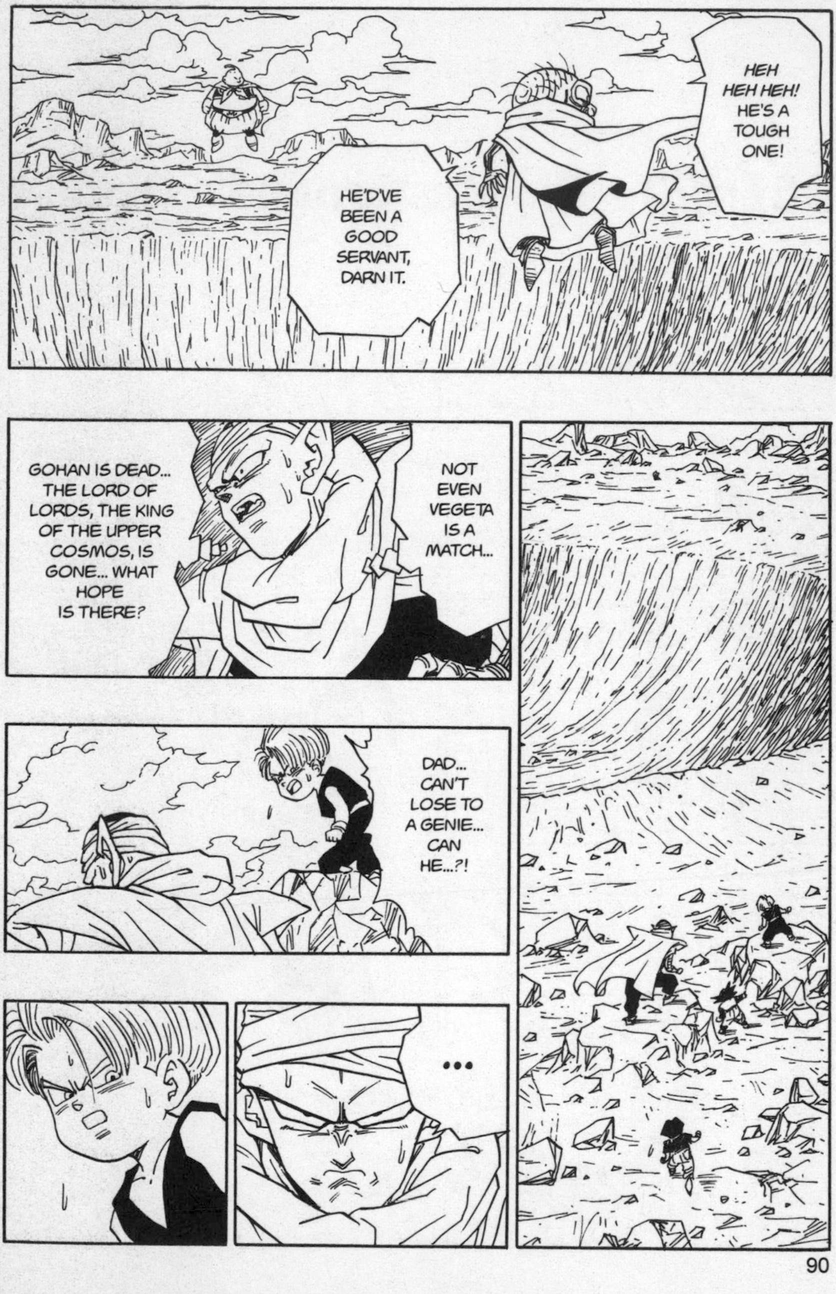
HEH HEH HEH! HE'S A TOUGH ONE!
HE'D'VE BEEN A GOOD SERVANT, DARN IT.
NOT EVEN VEGETA IS A MATCH...
GOHAN IS DEAD... THE LORD OF LORDS, THE KING OF THE UPPER COSMOS, IS GONE... WHAT HOPE IS THERE?
DAD... CAN'T LOSE TO A GENIE... CAN HE...?!
...

READ THIS WAY

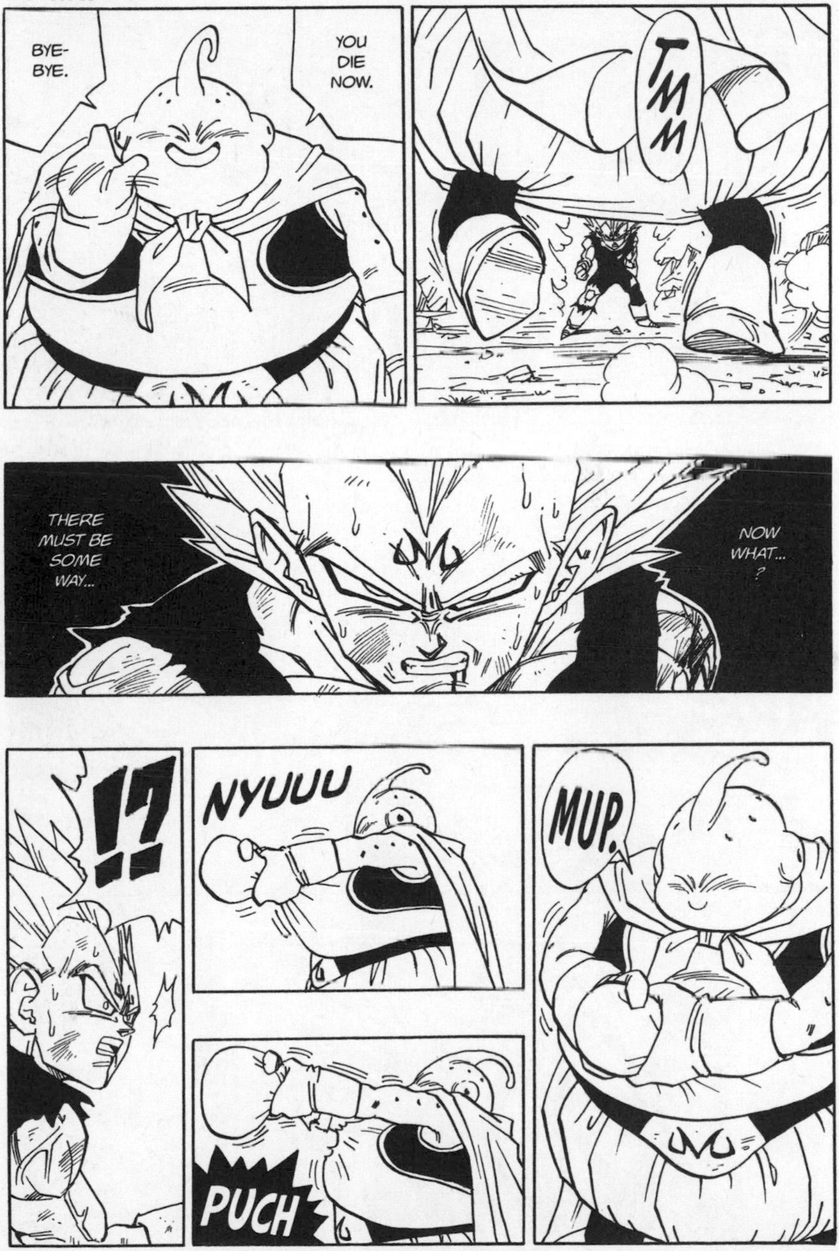

TMM
YOU DIE NOW.
BYE-BYE.
NOW WHAT...?
THERE MUST BE SOME WAY...
MUP.
NYUUU
PUCH
!?

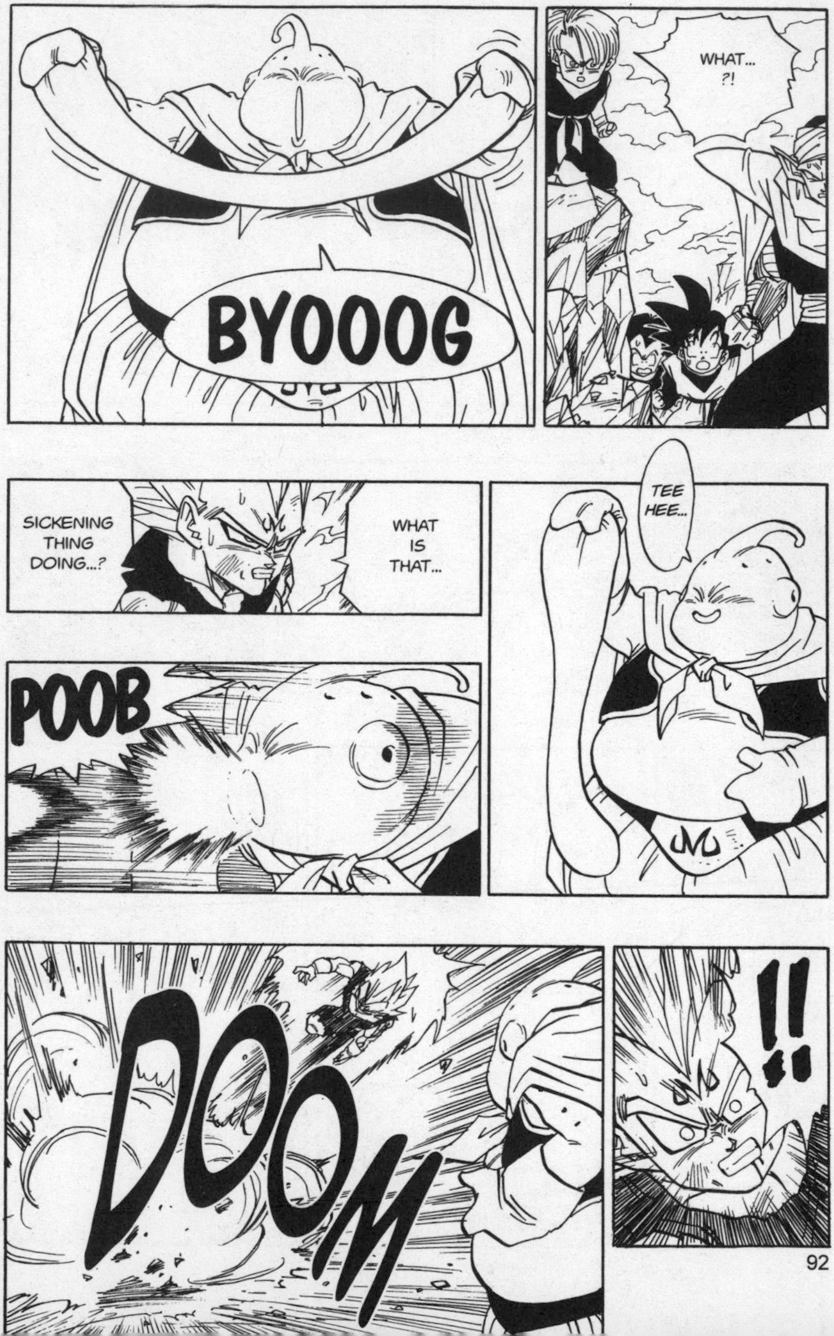
WHAT... ?!
BYOOOG
TEE HEE...
WHAT IS THAT...
SICKENING THING DOING...?
POOB
!!
DOOM

READ THIS WAY

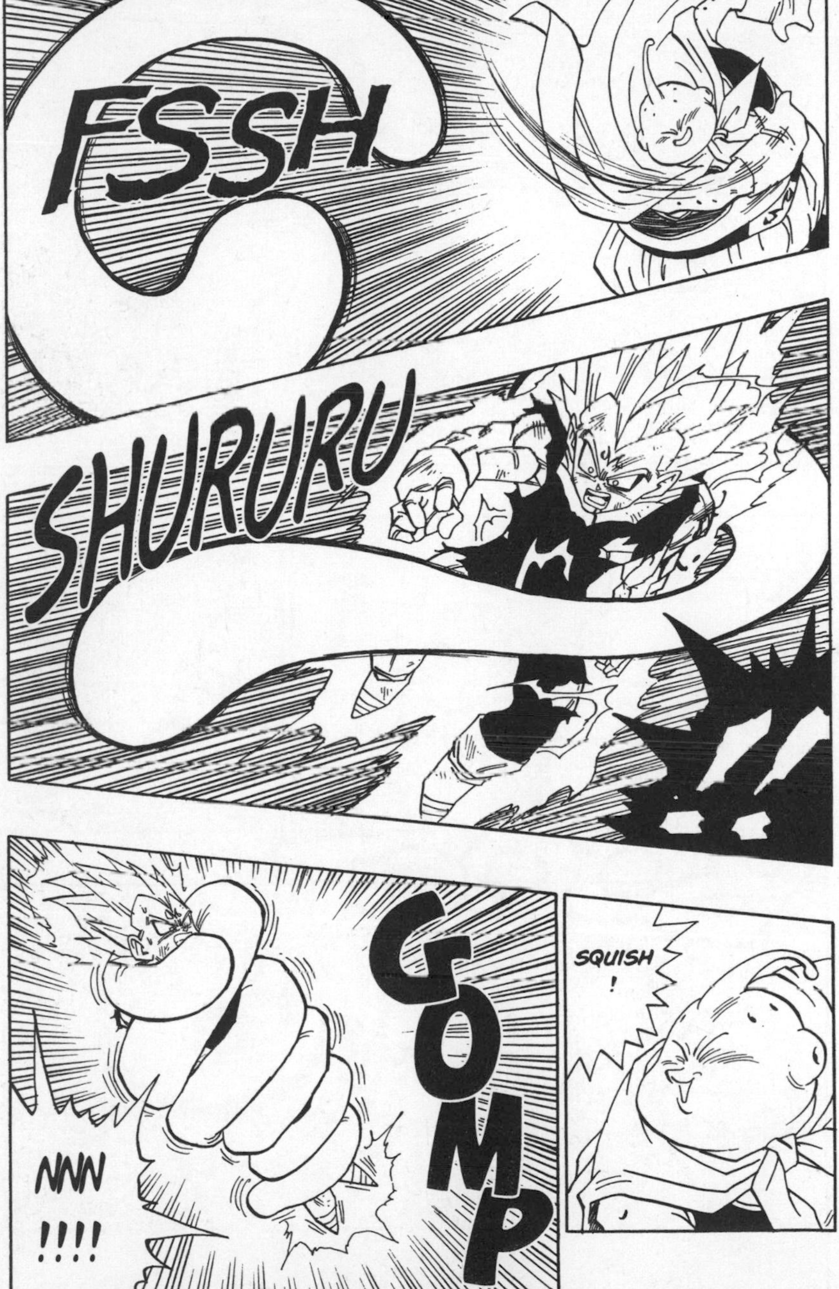
FSSH
SHURURU
SQUISH
!
GOMP
NNN
!!!!

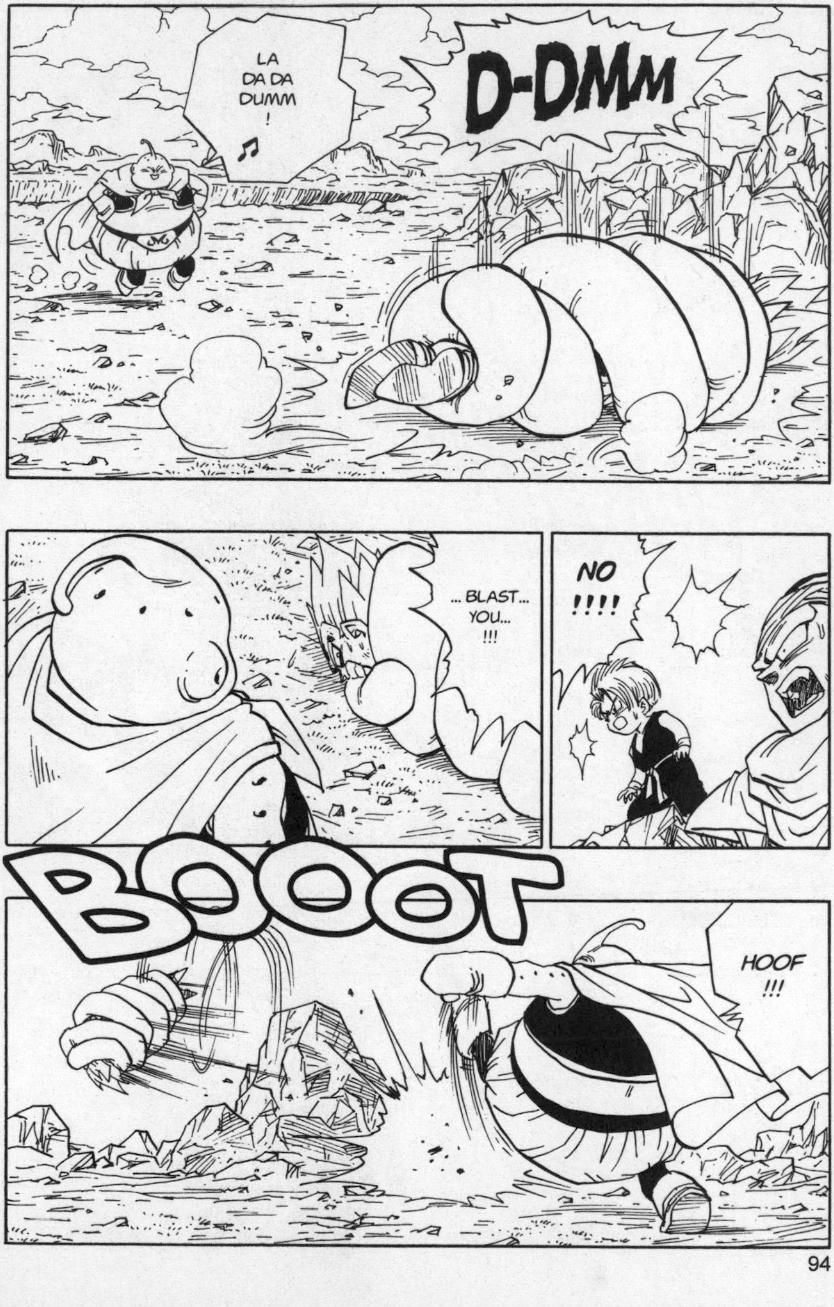
D-DMM
LA DA DA DUMM !
NO !!!!
... BLAST... YOU... !!!
BOOOT
HOOF !!!

READ THIS WAY

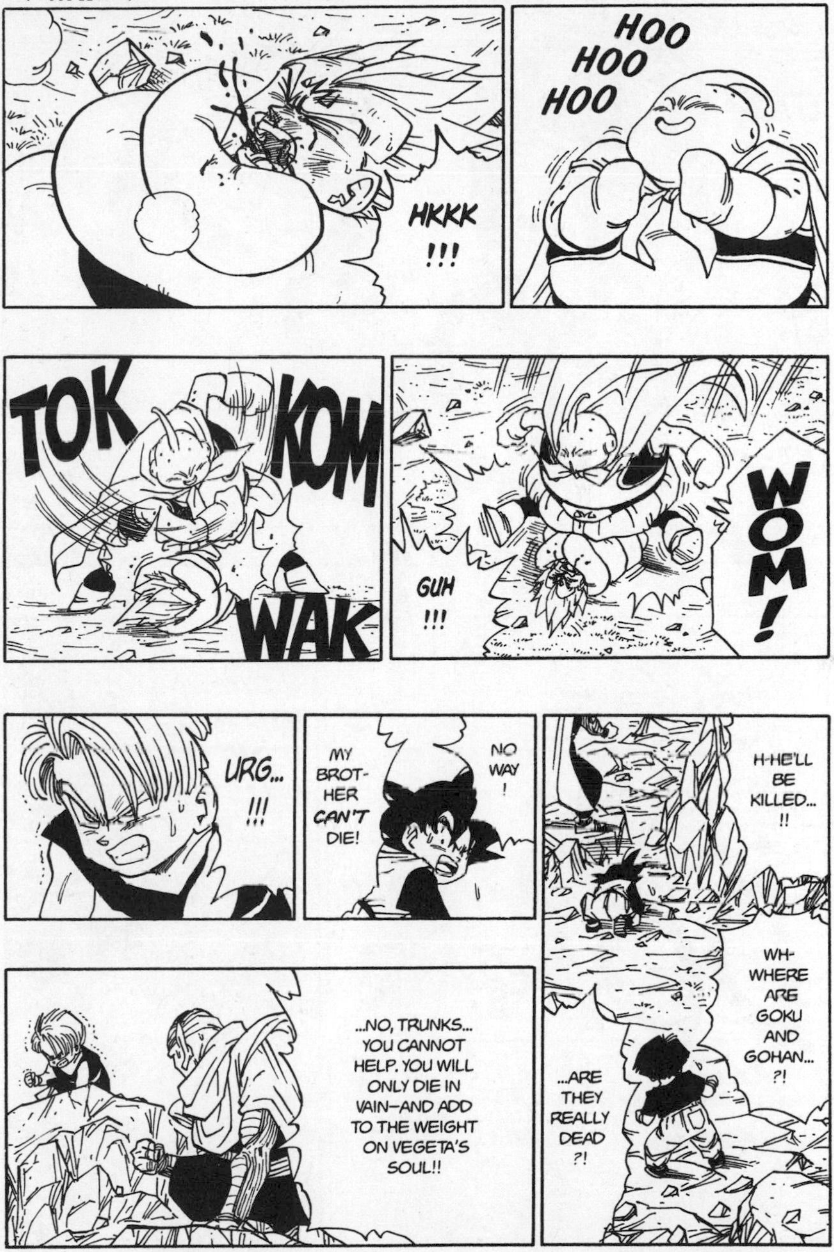
HOO HOO HOO
HKKK!!!
WOM!
GUH!!!
KOM
TOK
WAK
H-HE'LL BE KILLED...!!
WH-WHERE ARE GOKU AND GOHAN...?!
...ARE THEY REALLY DEAD?!
NO WAY!
MY BROTHER CAN'T DIE!
URG...!!!
...NO, TRUNKS... YOU CANNOT HELP. YOU WILL ONLY DIE IN VAIN—AND ADD TO THE WEIGHT ON VEGETA'S SOUL!!

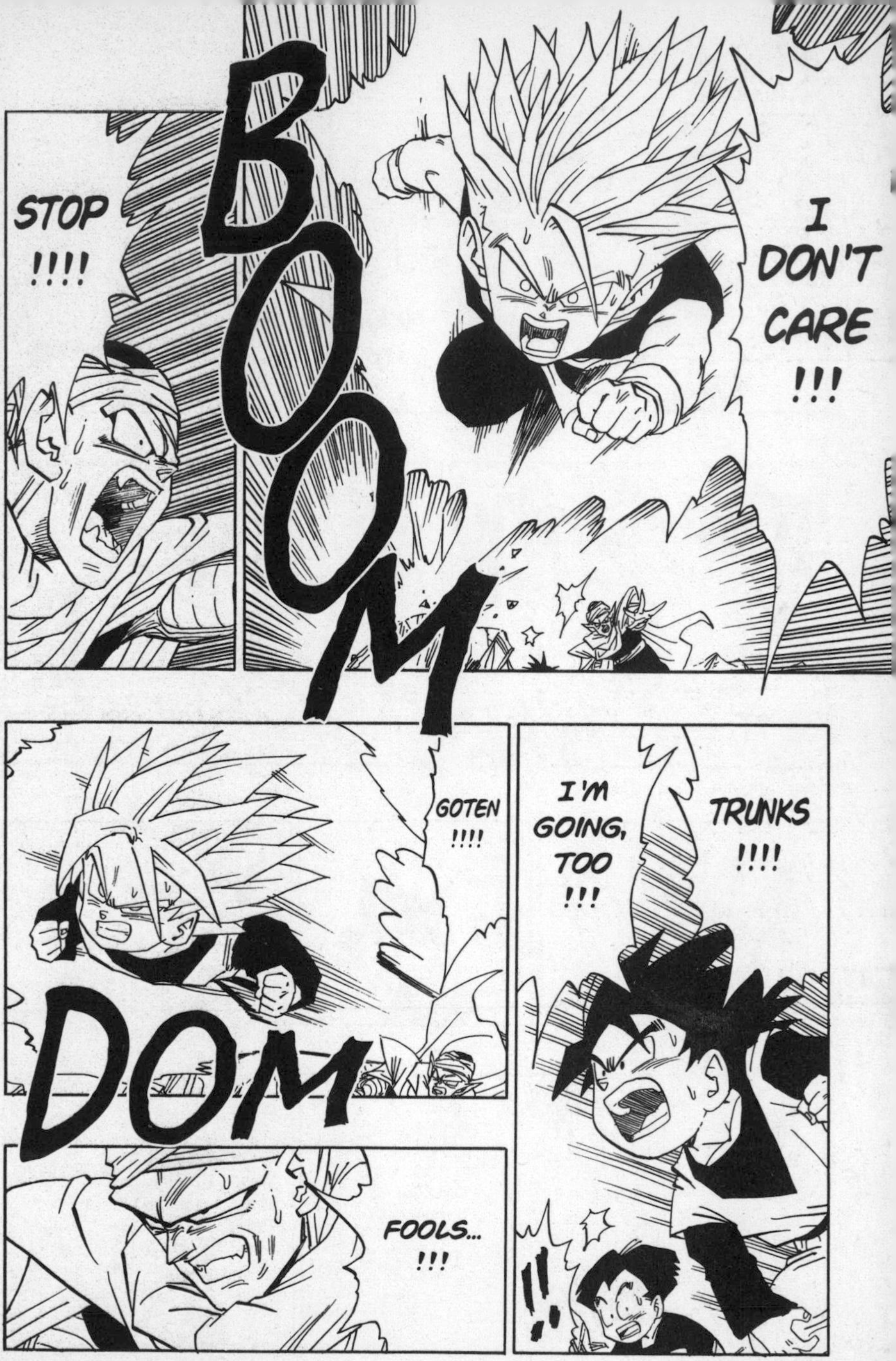
I DON'T CARE !!!
BOOM
STOP !!!!
TRUNKS !!!!
I'M GOING, TOO !!!
!!
GOTEN !!!!
DOM
FOOLS... !!!

READ THIS WAY

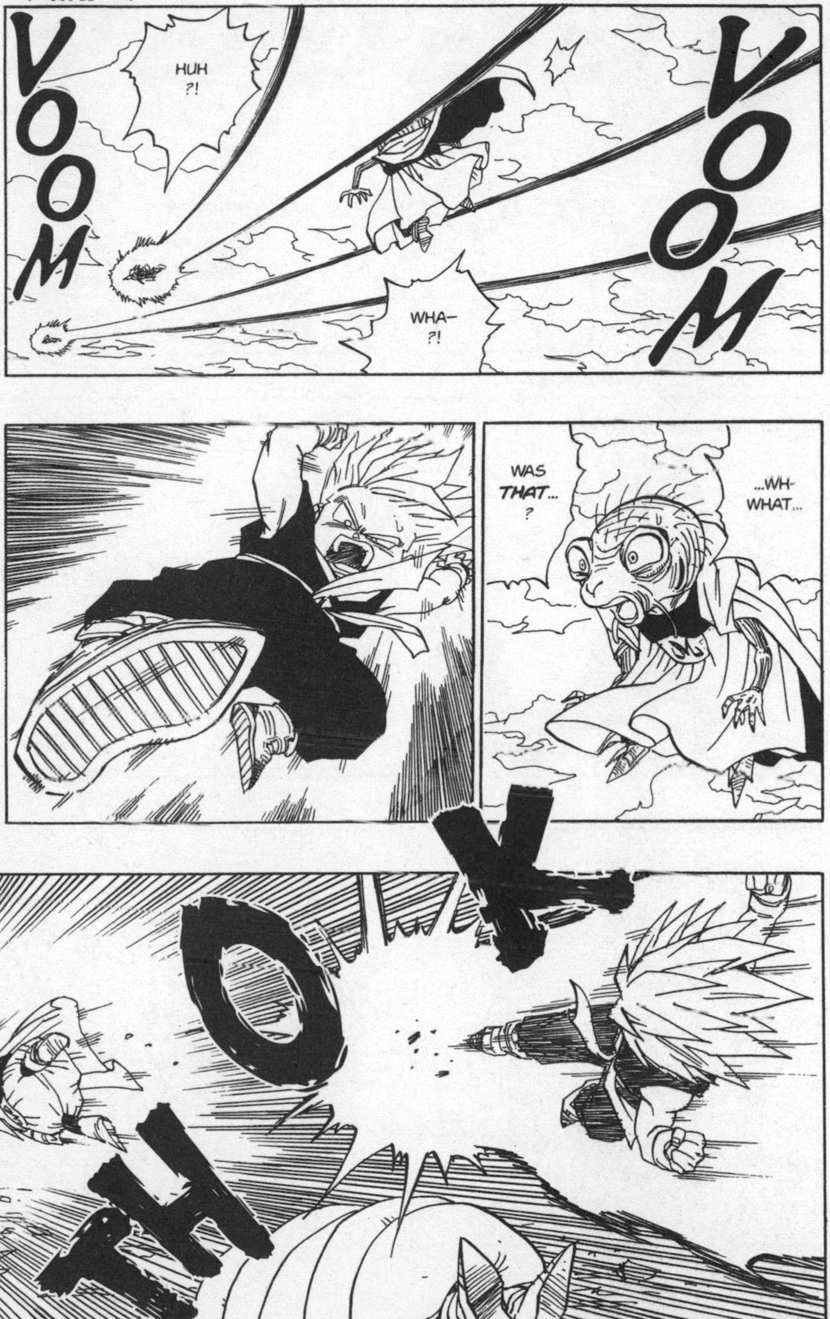
VOOM
HUH ?!
WHA- ?!
VOOM
...WH- WHAT...
WAS THAT... ?
THOK

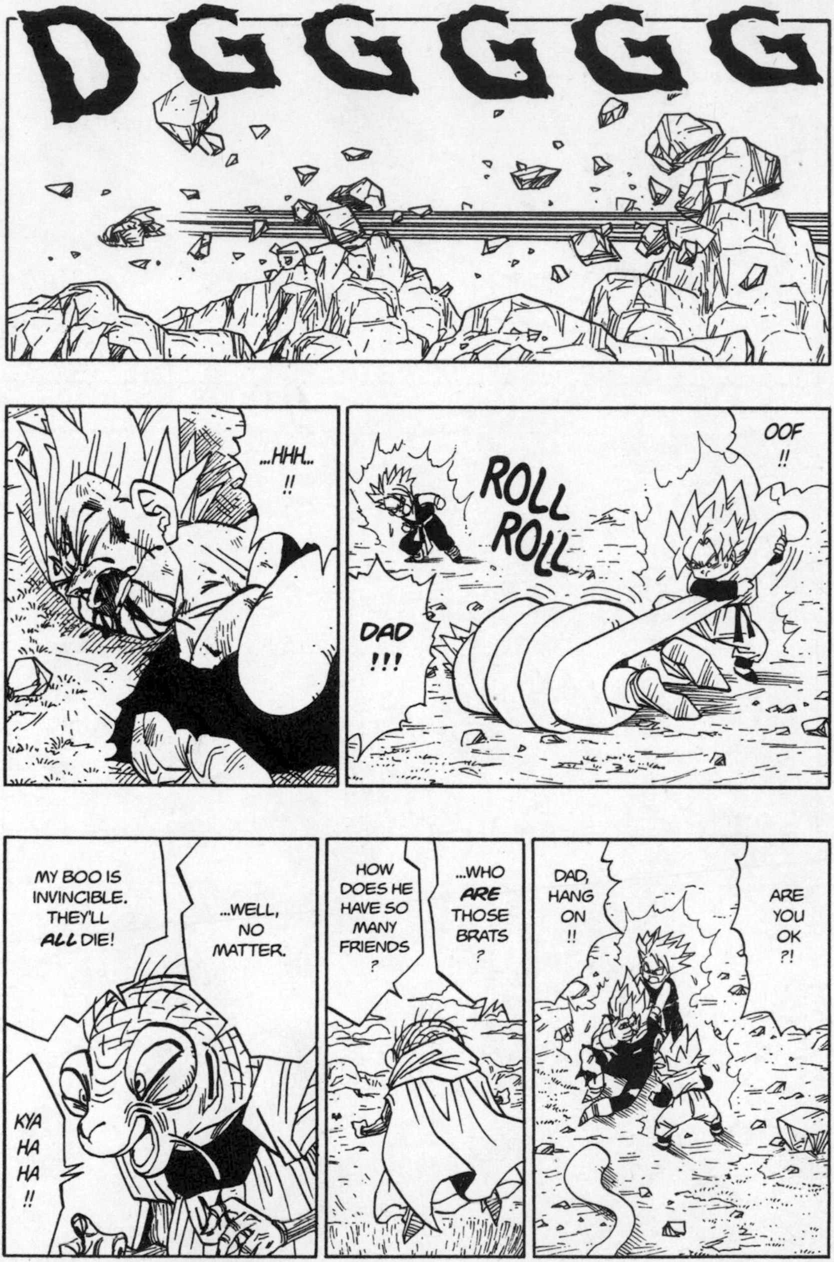
DGGGGG
OOF !!
ROLL ROLL
DAD !!!
...HHH... !!
ARE YOU OK ?!
DAD, HANG ON !!
...WHO ARE THOSE BRATS ?
HOW DOES HE HAVE SO MANY FRIENDS ?
...WELL, NO MATTER.
MY BOO IS INVINCIBLE. THEY'LL ALL DIE!
KYA HA HA !!

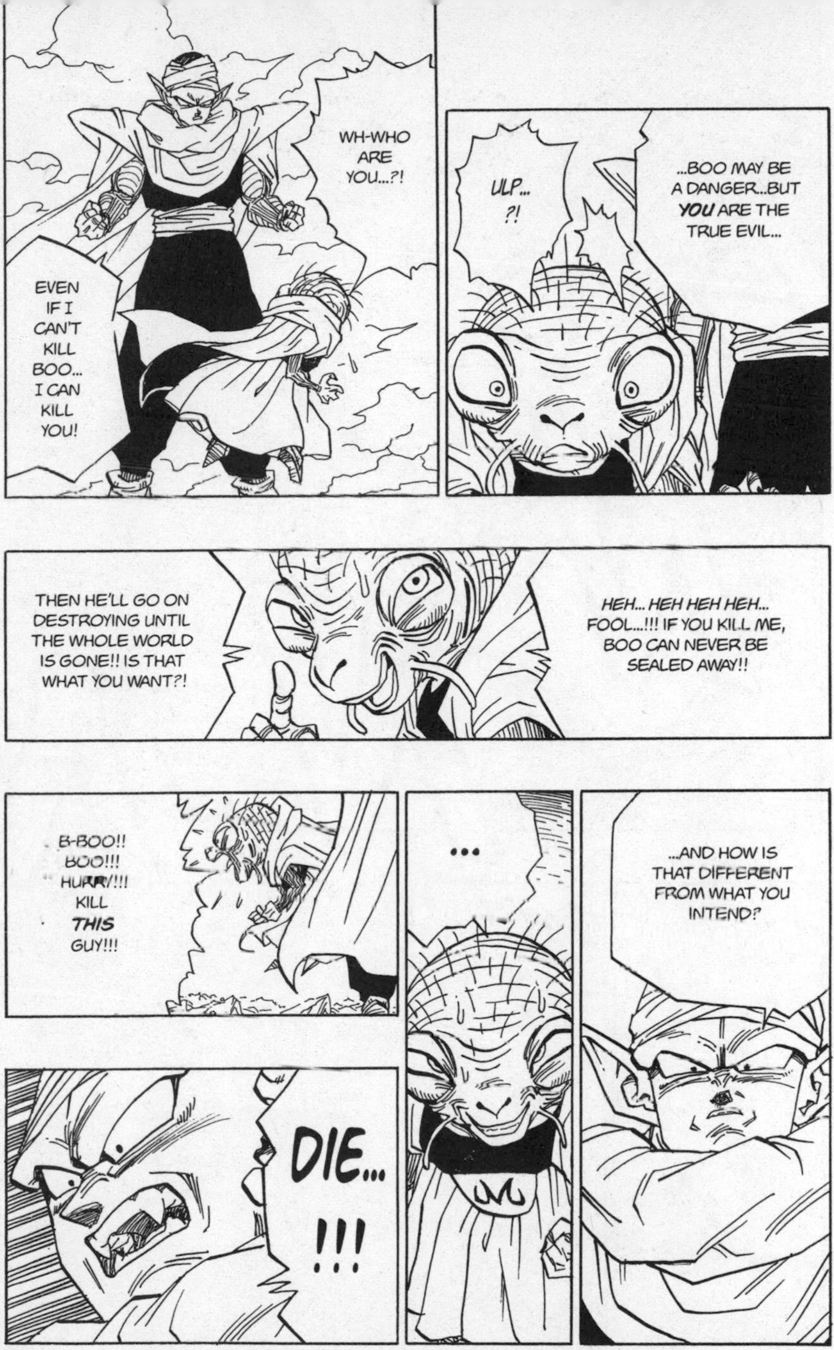
...BOO MAY BE A DANGER...BUT YOU ARE THE TRUE EVIL...
ULP... ?!
WH-WHO ARE YOU...?!
EVEN IF I CAN'T KILL BOO... I CAN KILL YOU!
HEH... HEH HEH HEH... FOOL...!!! IF YOU KILL ME, BOO CAN NEVER BE SEALED AWAY!!
THEN HE'LL GO ON DESTROYING UNTIL THE WHOLE WORLD IS GONE!! IS THAT WHAT YOU WANT?!
...AND HOW IS THAT DIFFERENT FROM WHAT YOU INTEND?
...
B-BOO!! BOO!!! HURRY!!! KILL THIS GUY!!!
DIE... !!!

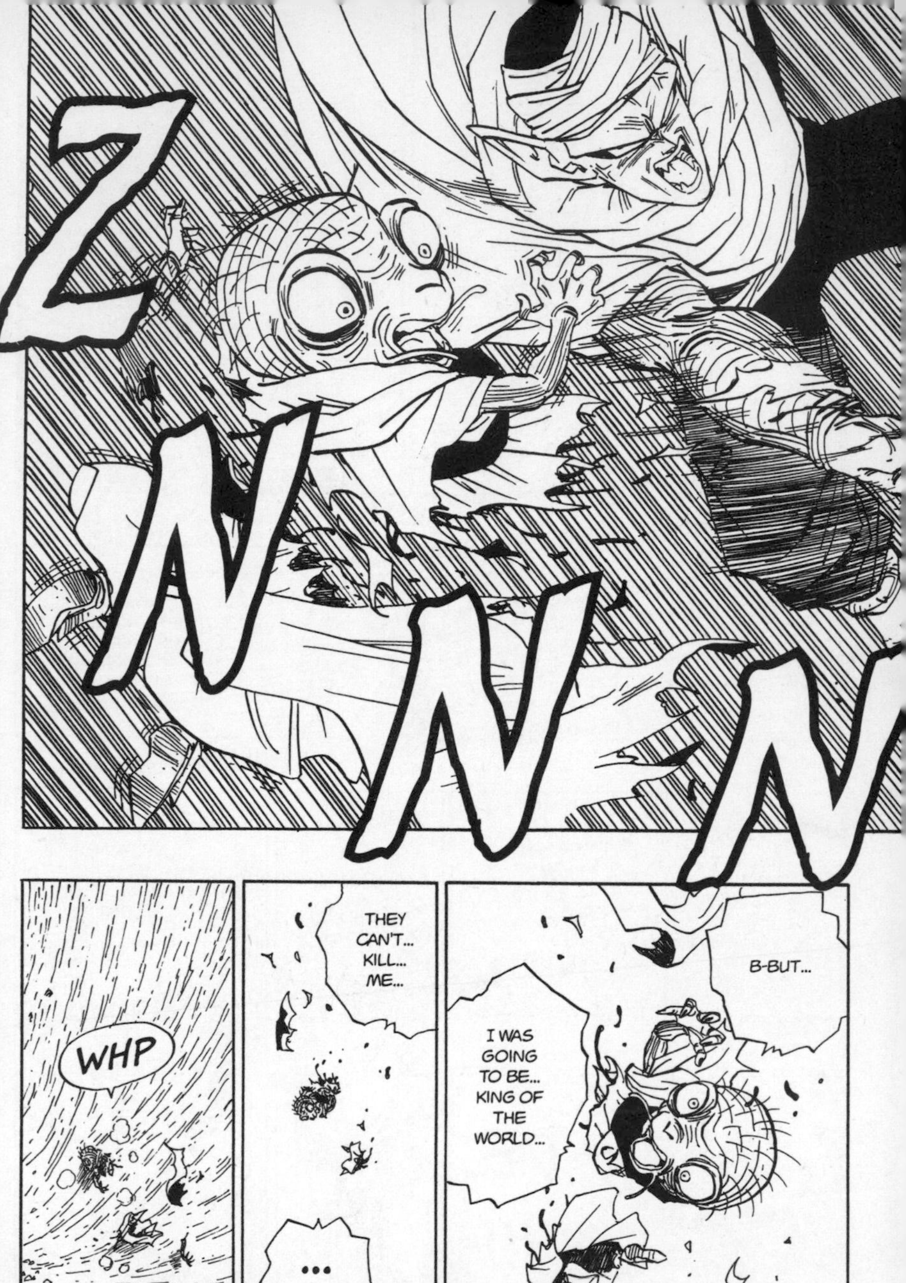
ZNNN
B-BUT...
I WAS GOING TO BE... KING OF THE WORLD...
THEY CAN'T... KILL... ME...
...
WHP

READ THIS WAY

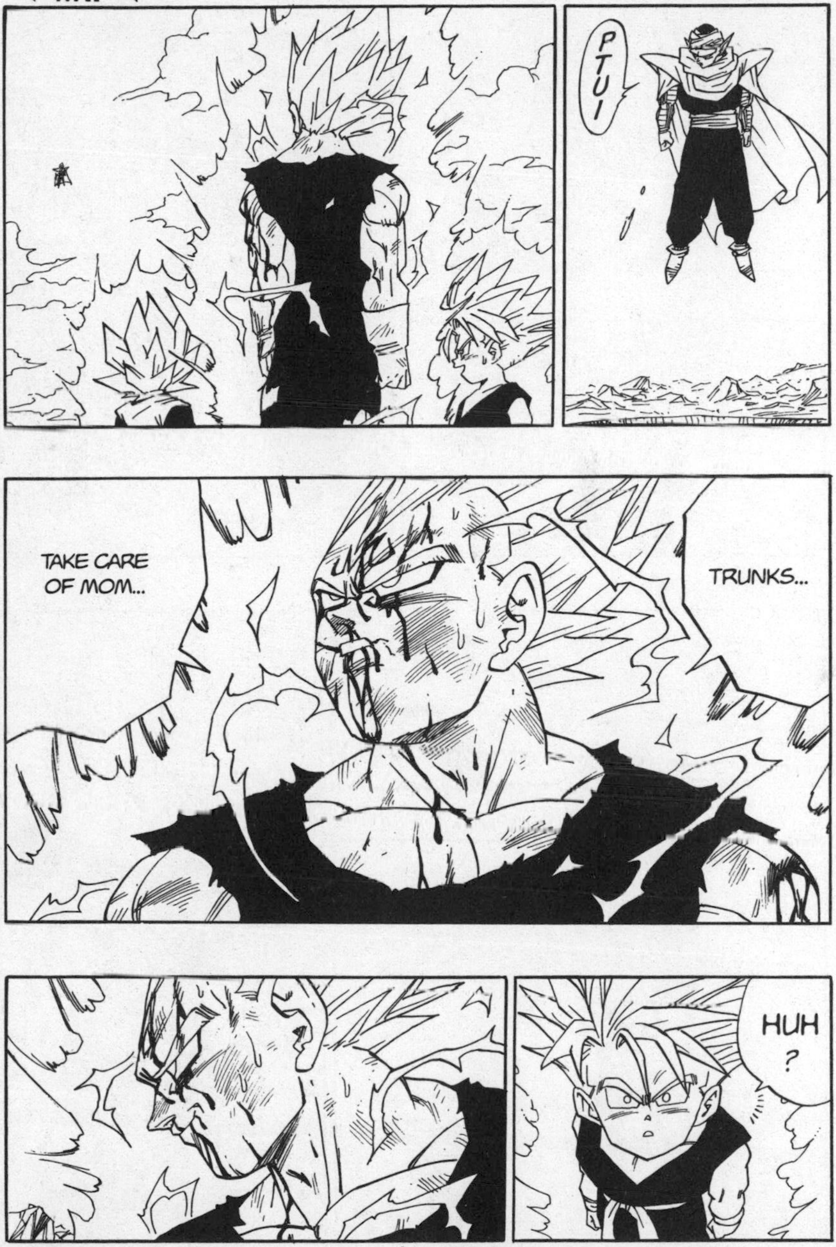
PTUI
TRUNKS...
TAKE CARE OF MOM...
HUH?

NEXT: Is This the End of Vegeta?

DBZ:273 • Farewell, Proud Warrior

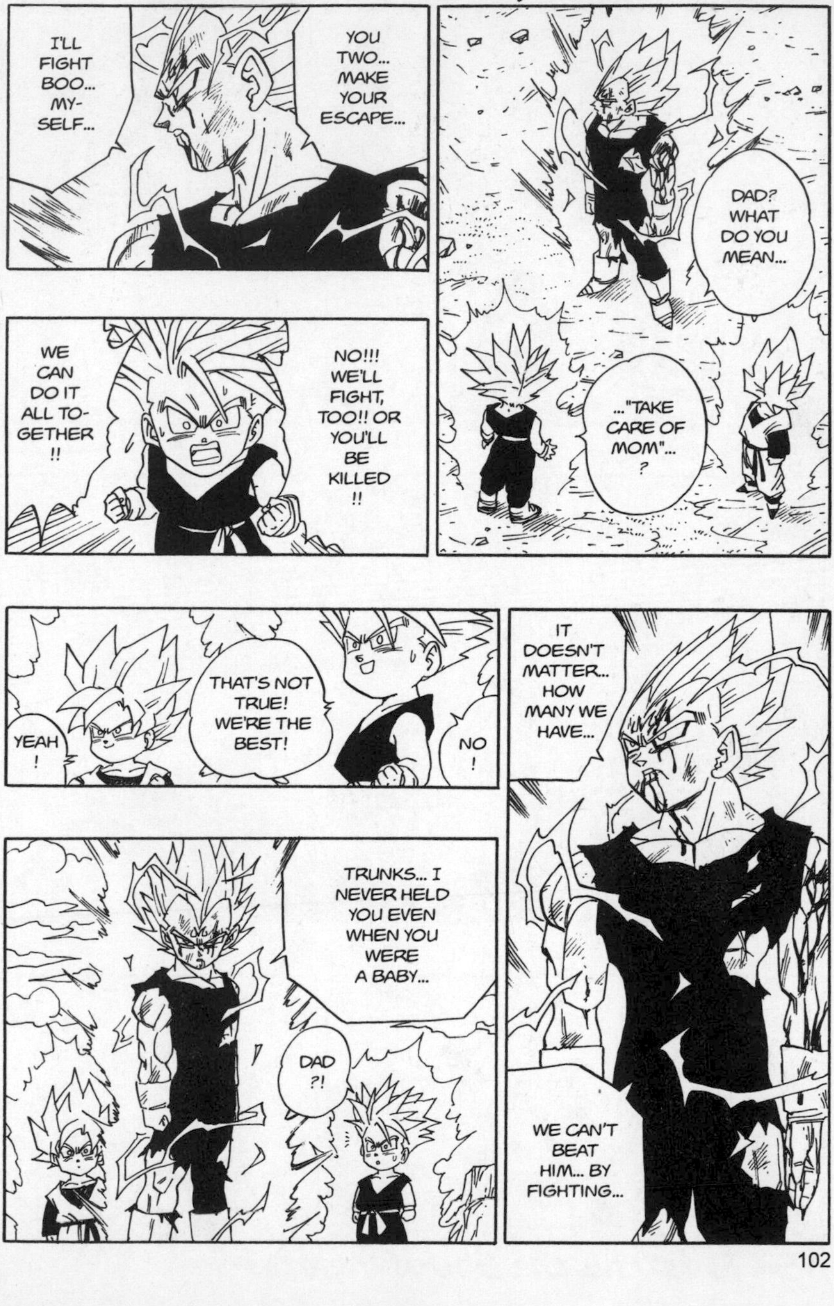
DAD? WHAT DO YOU MEAN...
..."TAKE CARE OF MOM"... ?
YOU TWO... MAKE YOUR ESCAPE...
I'LL FIGHT BOO... MY-SELF...
NO!!! WE'LL FIGHT, TOO!! OR YOU'LL BE KILLED !!
WE CAN DO IT ALL TO-GETHER !!
IT DOESN'T MATTER... HOW MANY WE HAVE...
WE CAN'T BEAT HIM... BY FIGHTING...
NO !
THAT'S NOT TRUE! WE'RE THE BEST!
YEAH !
TRUNKS... I NEVER HELD YOU EVEN WHEN YOU WERE A BABY...
DAD ?!

READ THIS WAY

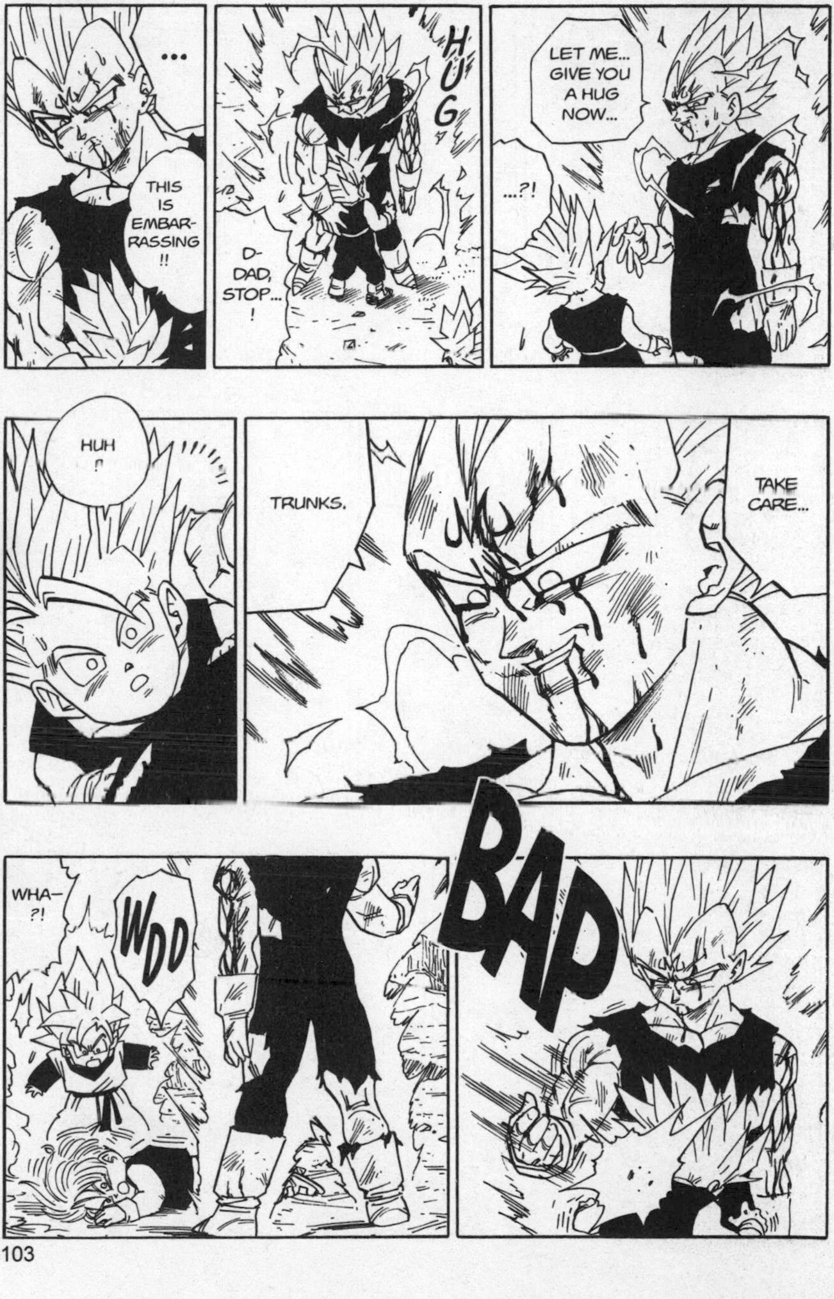
LET ME... GIVE YOU A HUG NOW...
...?!
HUG
D-DAD, STOP...!
...
THIS IS EMBARRASSING!!
TAKE CARE...
TRUNKS.
HUH!
BAP
WDD
WHA-?!

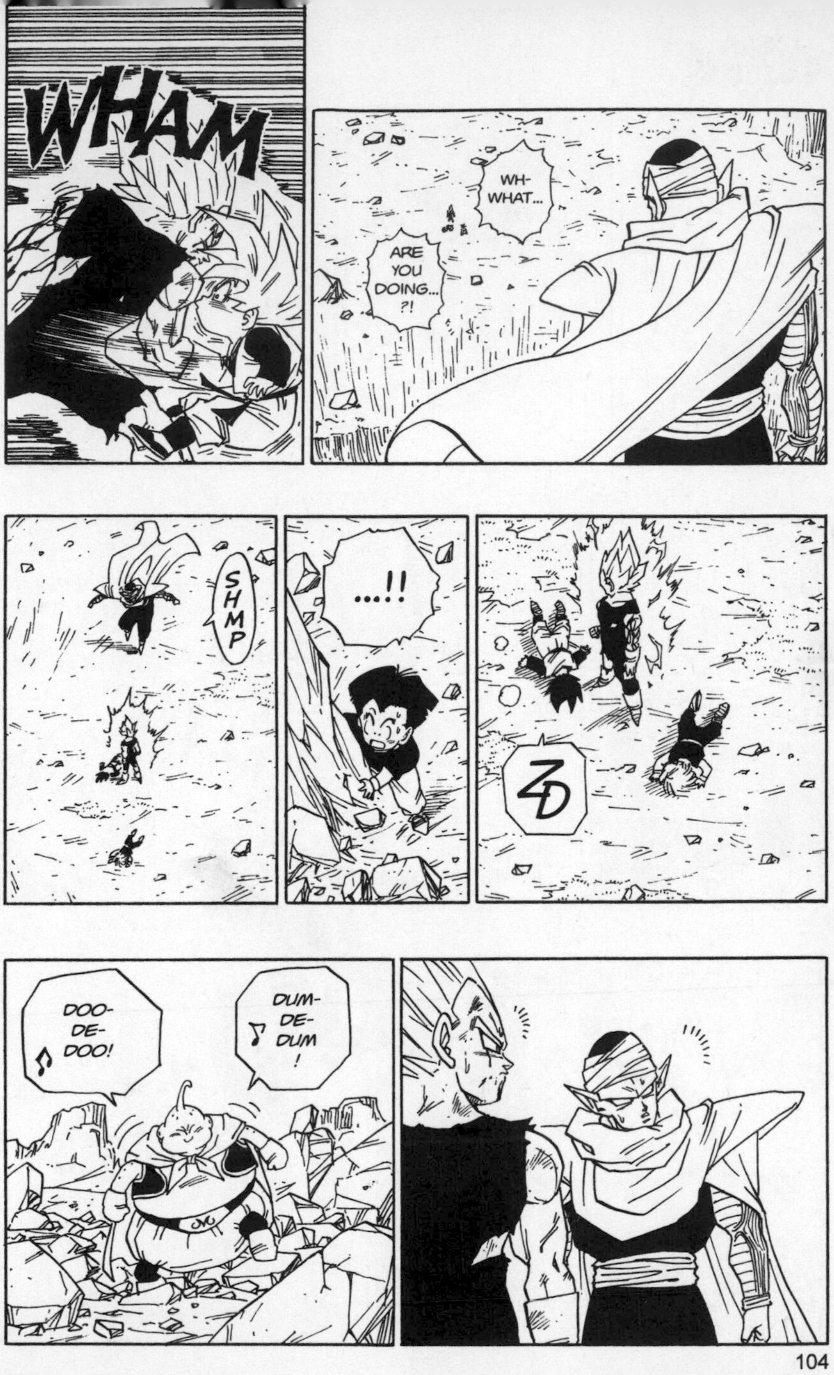
WH- WHAT...
ARE YOU DOING...?!
WHAM
ZD
....!!
SHMP
DUM-DE-DUM!
DOO-DE-DOO!

READ THIS WAY

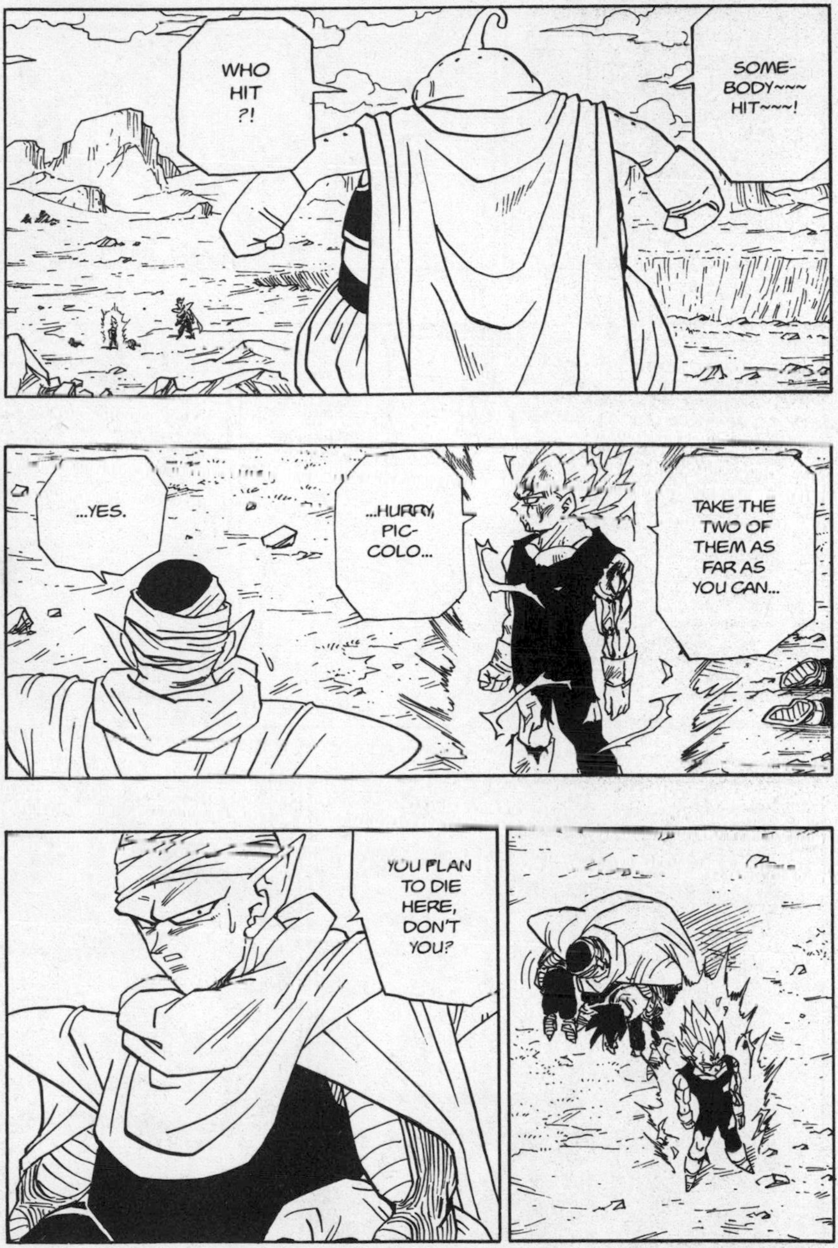
SOME-BODY~~~ HIT~~~!
WHO HIT ?!
TAKE THE TWO OF THEM AS FAR AS YOU CAN...
...HURRY, PIC-COLO...
...YES.
YOU PLAN TO DIE HERE, DON'T YOU?

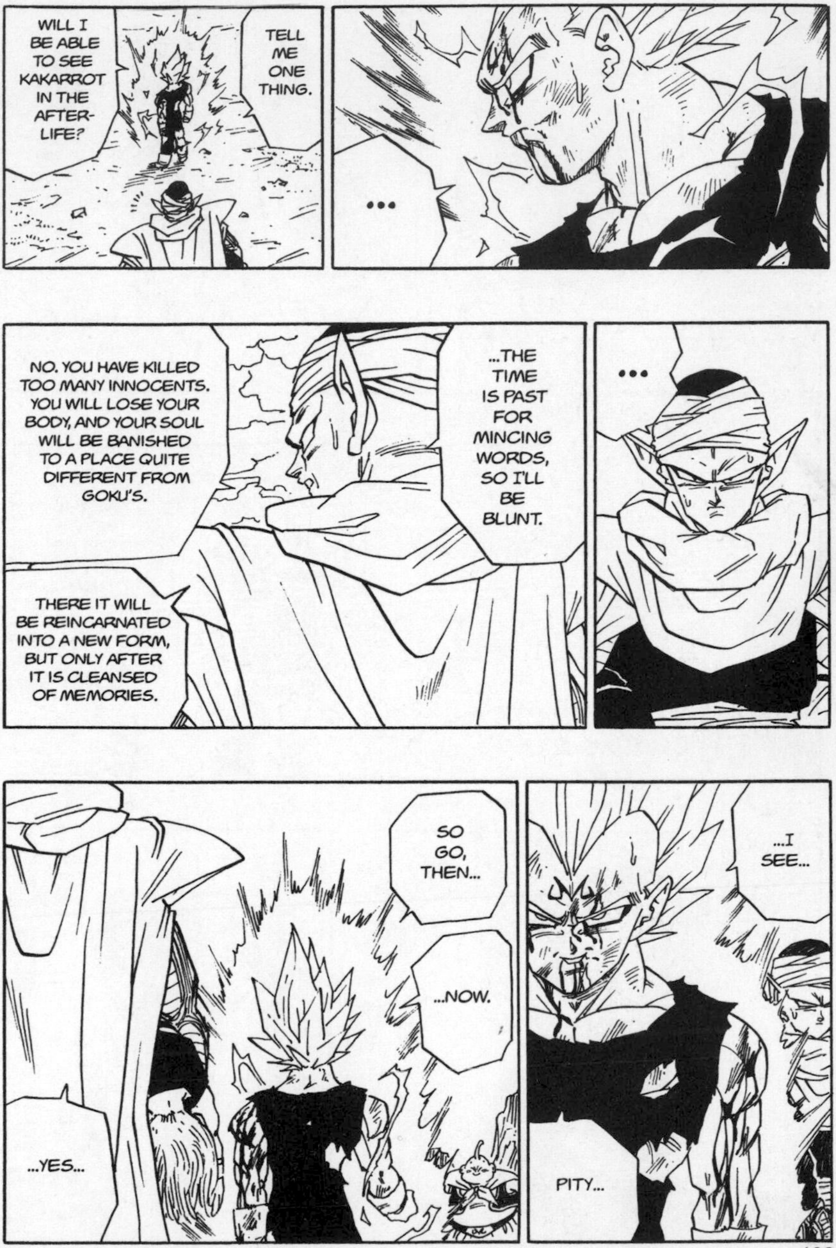

...
TELL ME ONE THING.
WILL I BE ABLE TO SEE KAKARROT IN THE AFTER-LIFE?
...
...THE TIME IS PAST FOR MINCING WORDS, SO I'LL BE BLUNT.
NO. YOU HAVE KILLED TOO MANY INNOCENTS. YOU WILL LOSE YOUR BODY, AND YOUR SOUL WILL BE BANISHED TO A PLACE QUITE DIFFERENT FROM GOKU'S.
THERE IT WILL BE REINCARNATED INTO A NEW FORM, BUT ONLY AFTER IT IS CLEANSED OF MEMORIES.
...I SEE...
PITY...
SO GO, THEN...
...NOW.
...YES...

READ THIS WAY

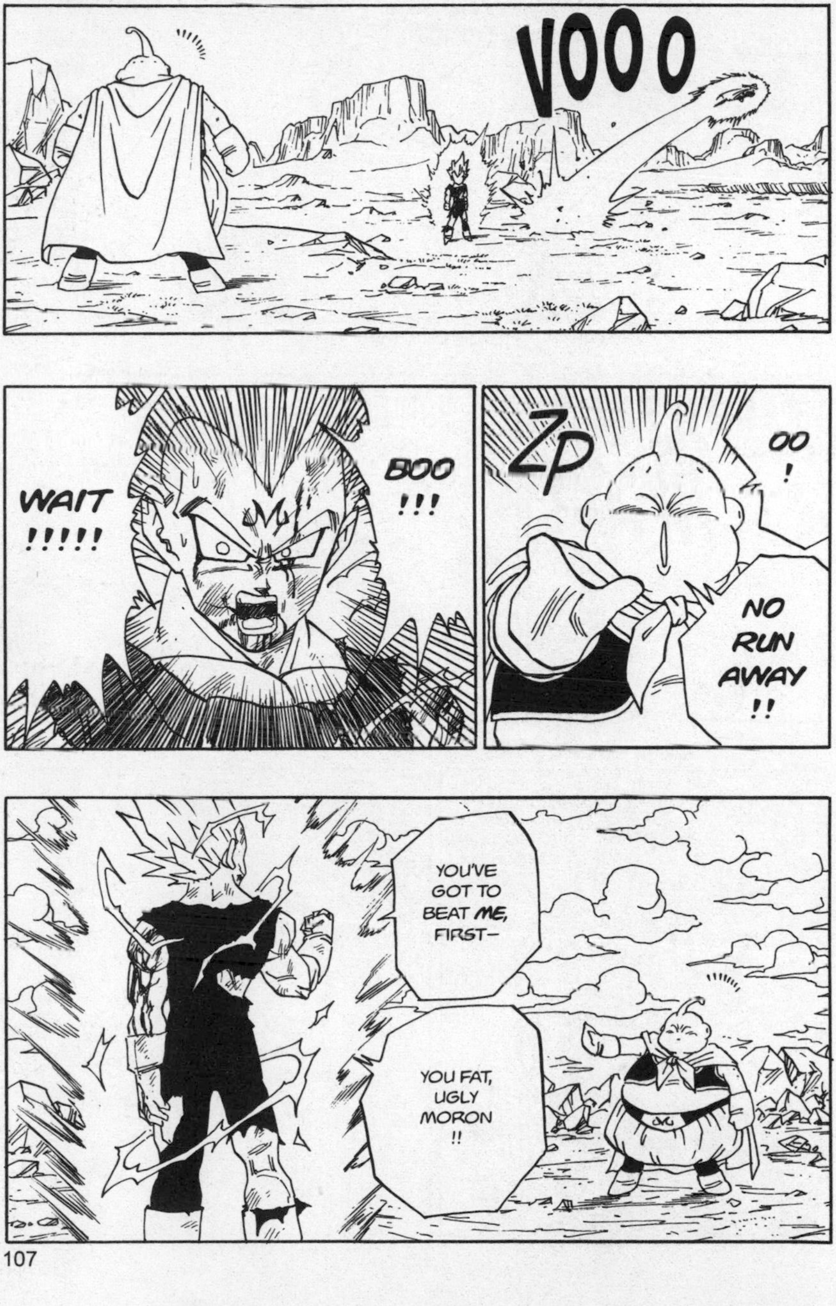
VOOO
ZP
OO!
NO RUN AWAY!!
BOO!!!
WAIT!!!!!
YOU'VE GOT TO BEAT *ME*, FIRST—
YOU FAT, UGLY MORON!!

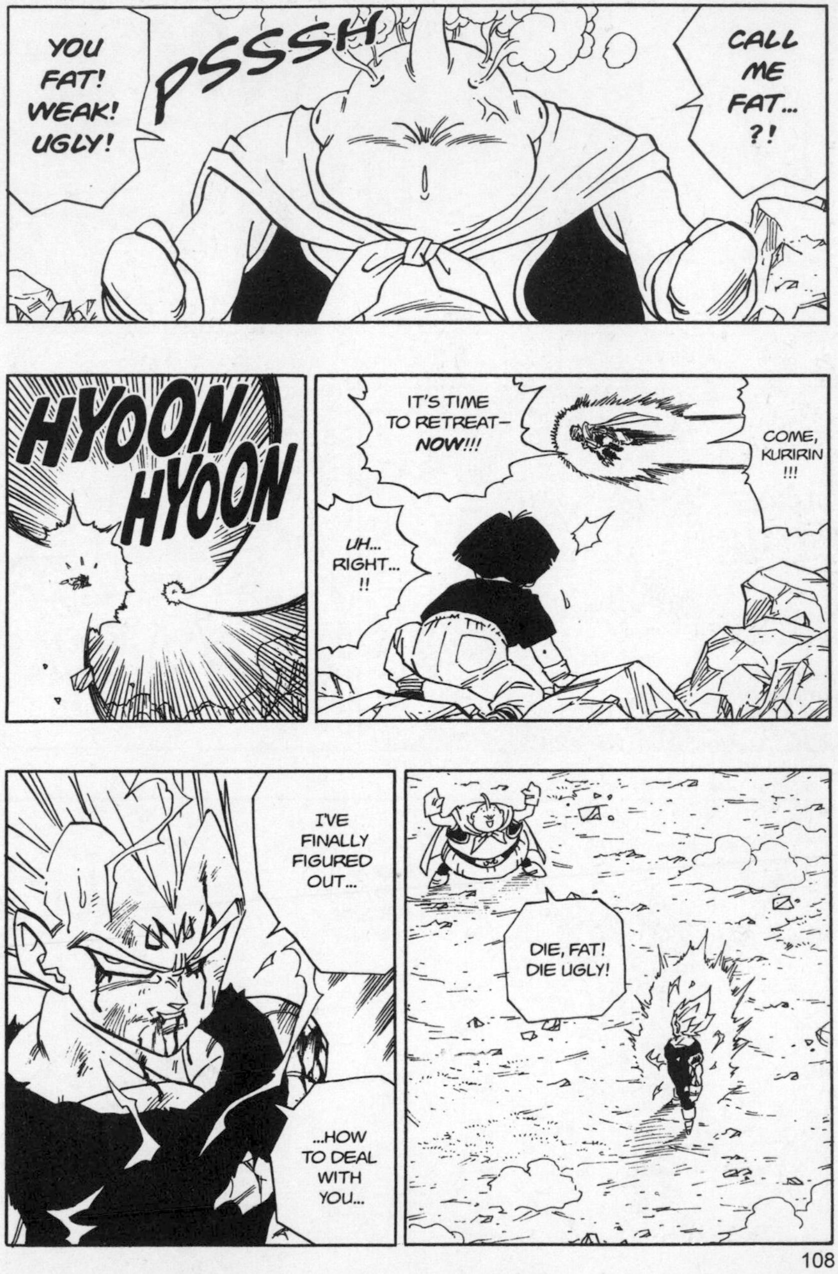
CALL ME FAT... ?!
PSSSH
YOU FAT! WEAK! UGLY!
COME, KURIRIN !!!
IT'S TIME TO RETREAT— NOW!!!
UH... RIGHT... !!
HYOON HYOON
DIE, FAT! DIE UGLY!
I'VE FINALLY FIGURED OUT...
...HOW TO DEAL WITH YOU...

READ THIS WAY

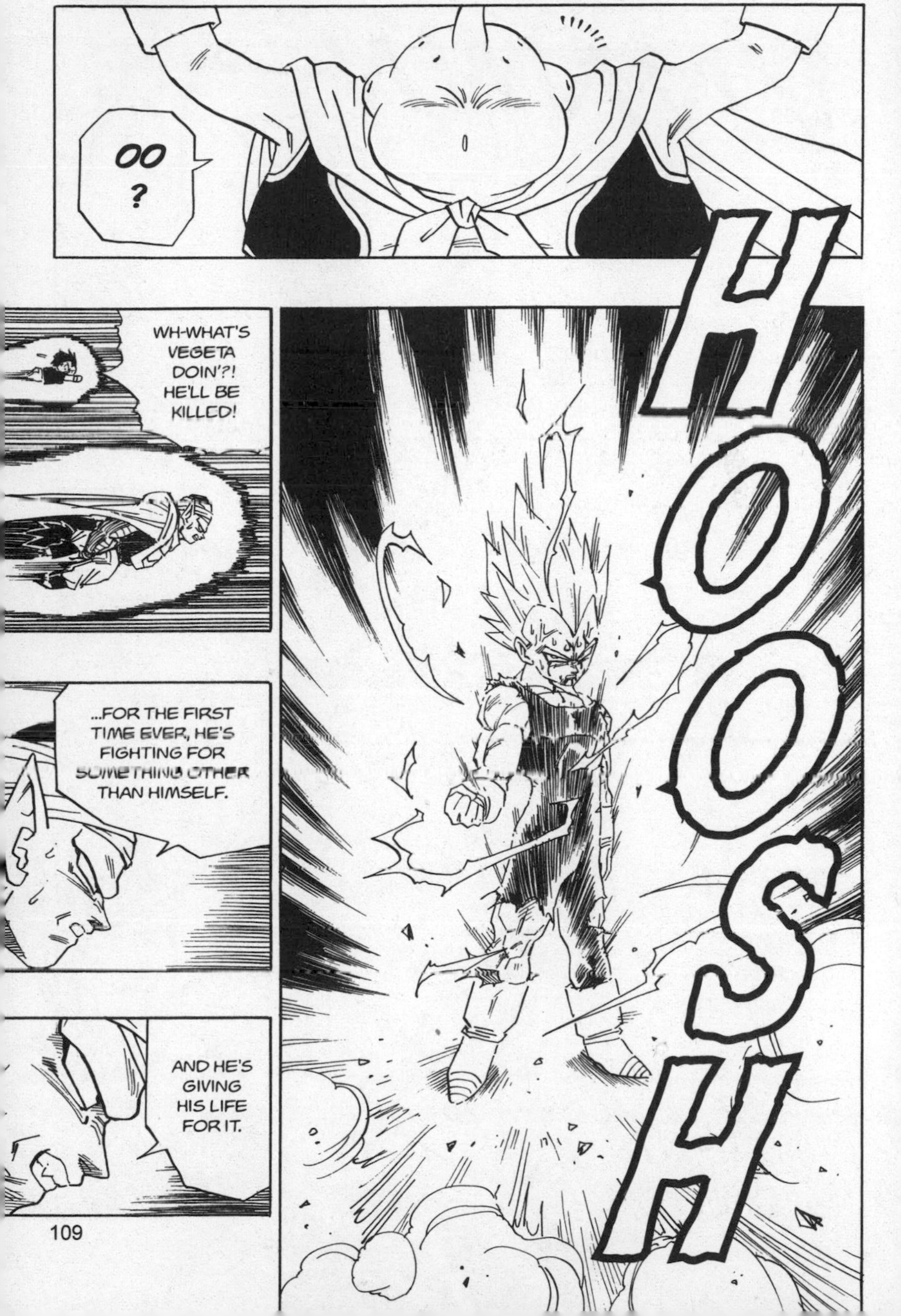
OO ?
HOOSH
WH-WHAT'S VEGETA DOIN'?! HE'LL BE KILLED!
...FOR THE FIRST TIME EVER, HE'S FIGHTING FOR SOMETHING OTHER THAN HIMSELF.
AND HE'S GIVING HIS LIFE FOR IT.

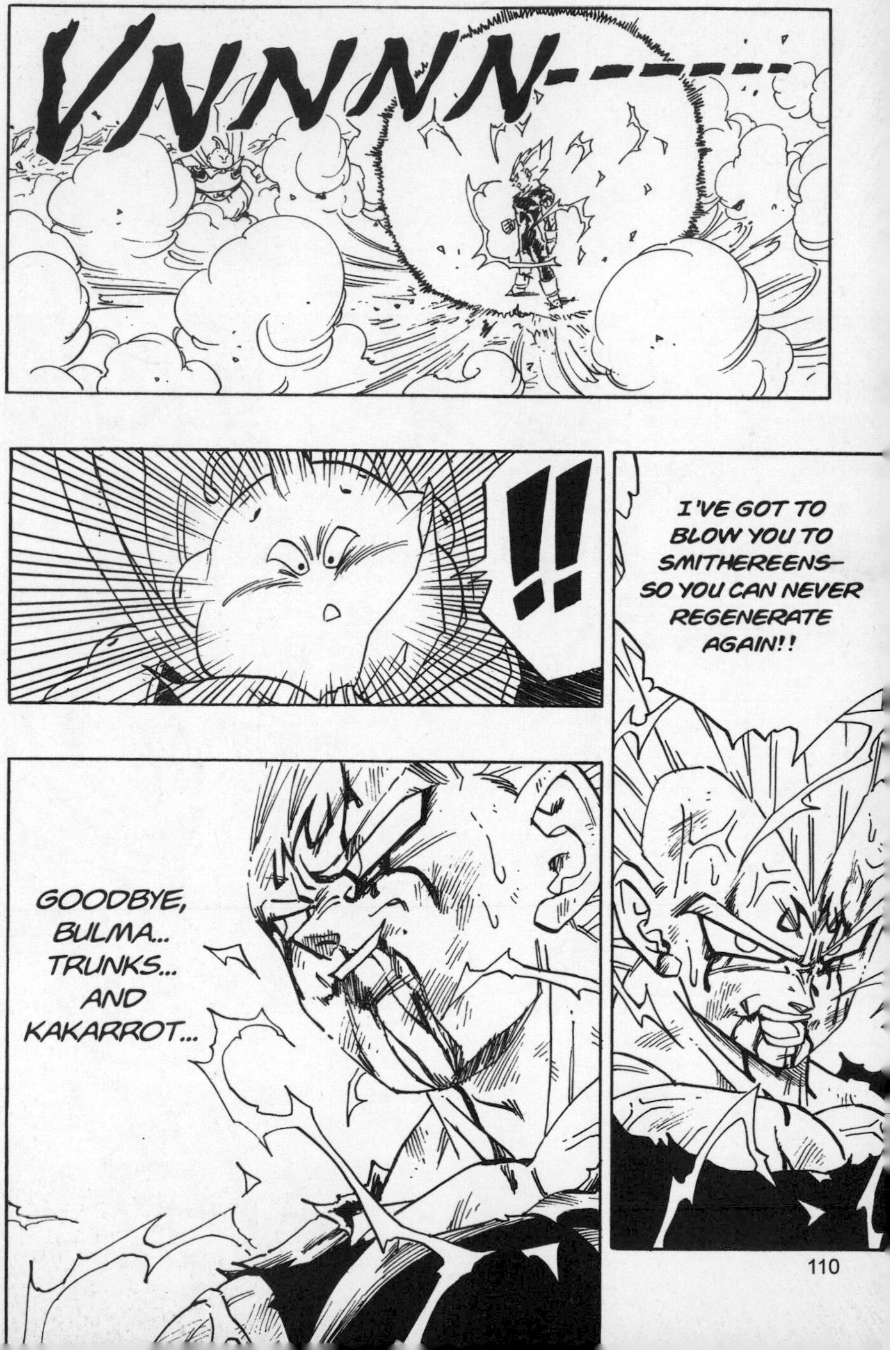
VNNNN-----
I'VE GOT TO BLOW YOU TO SMITHEREENS-- SO YOU CAN NEVER REGENERATE AGAIN!!
!!
GOODBYE, BULMA... TRUNKS... AND KAKARROT...

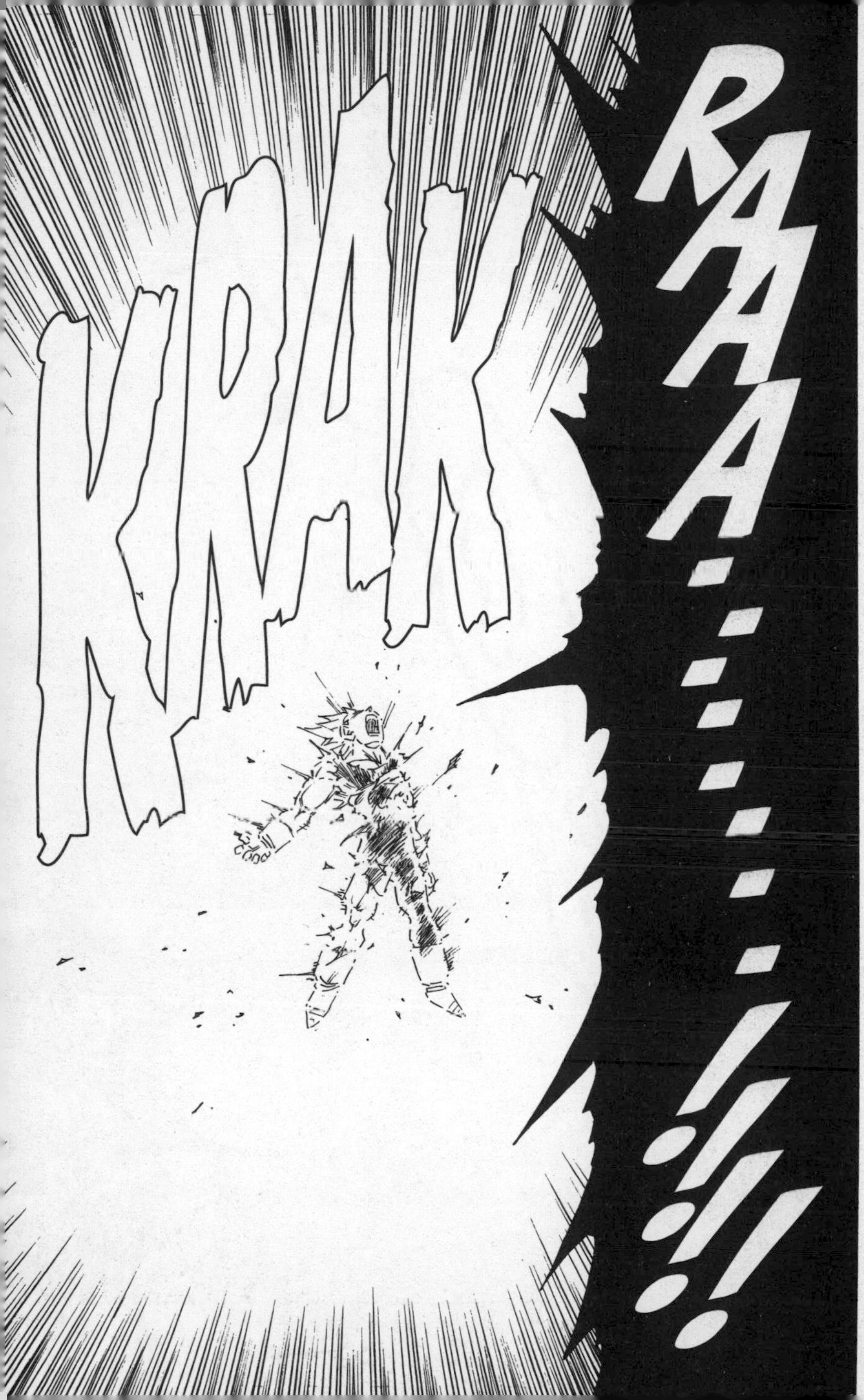
RAAA......!!!
KRAK

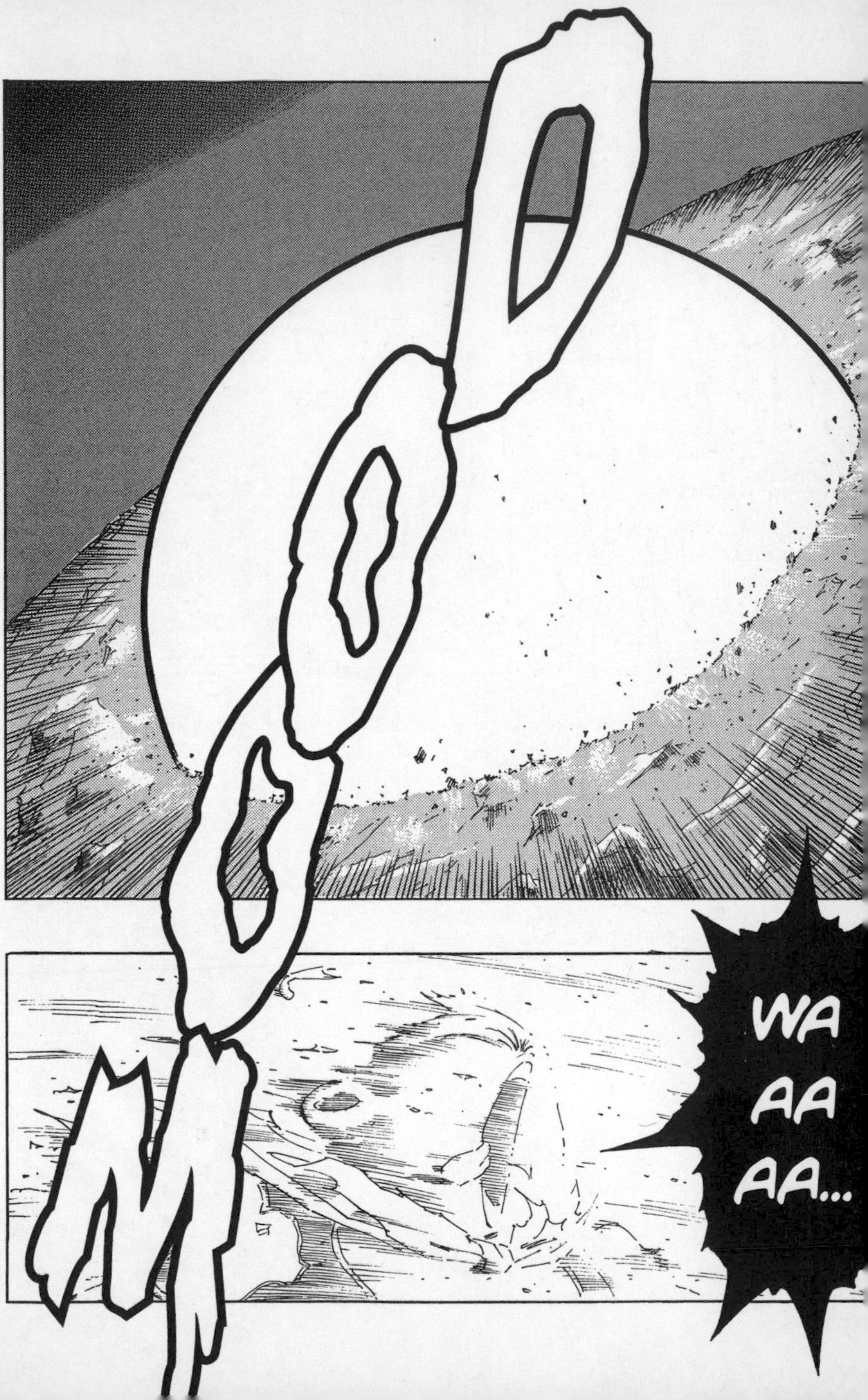
WA
AA
AA...

ZSSH
V... VEGETA...
VEGETA !!!!!
...NNH...

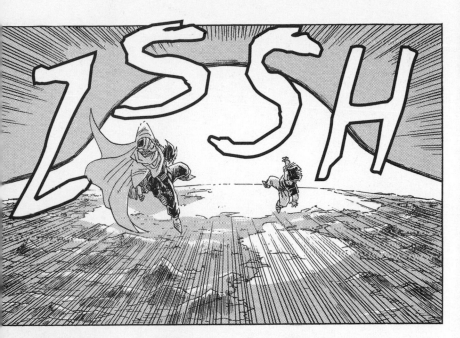

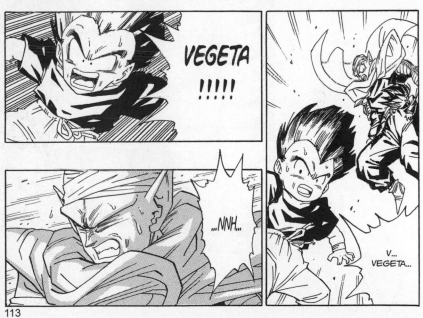

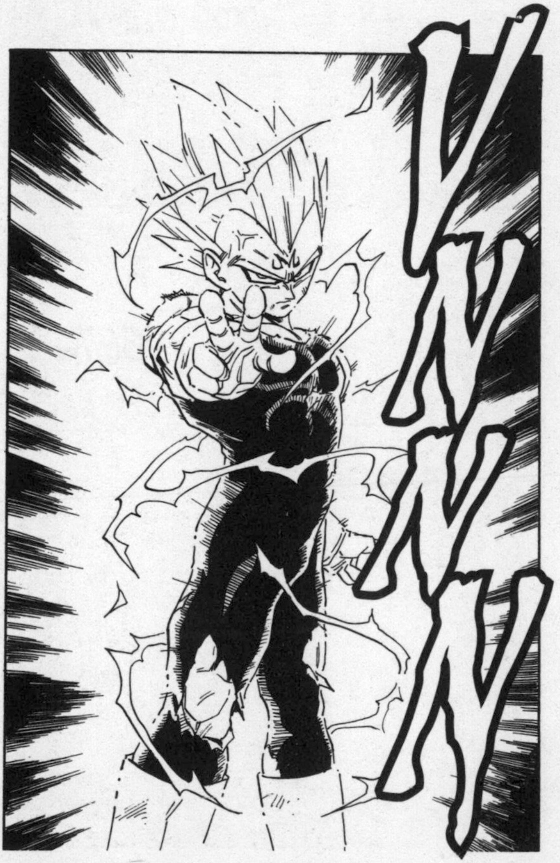
VNNN

DBZ:274 • Back to the Nightmare

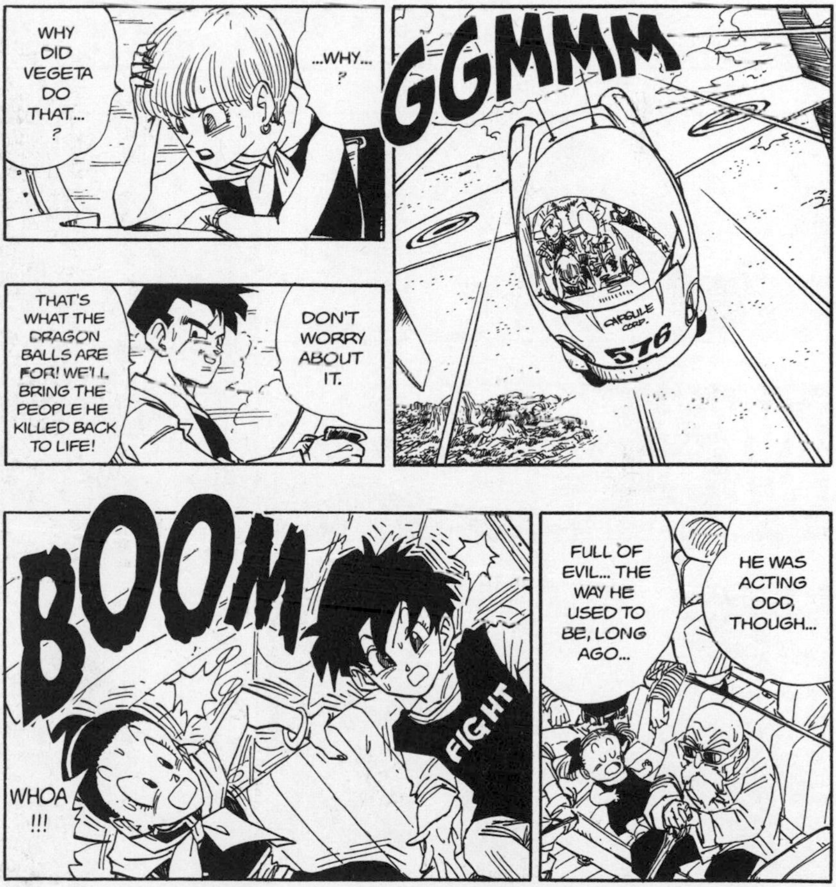

GGMMM
CAPSULE CORP.
576
...WHY...?
WHY DID VEGETA DO THAT...?
DON'T WORRY ABOUT IT.
THAT'S WHAT THE DRAGON BALLS ARE FOR! WE'LL BRING THE PEOPLE HE KILLED BACK TO LIFE!
HE WAS ACTING ODD, THOUGH...
FULL OF EVIL... THE WAY HE USED TO BE, LONG AGO...
BOOM
FIGHT
WHOA !!!

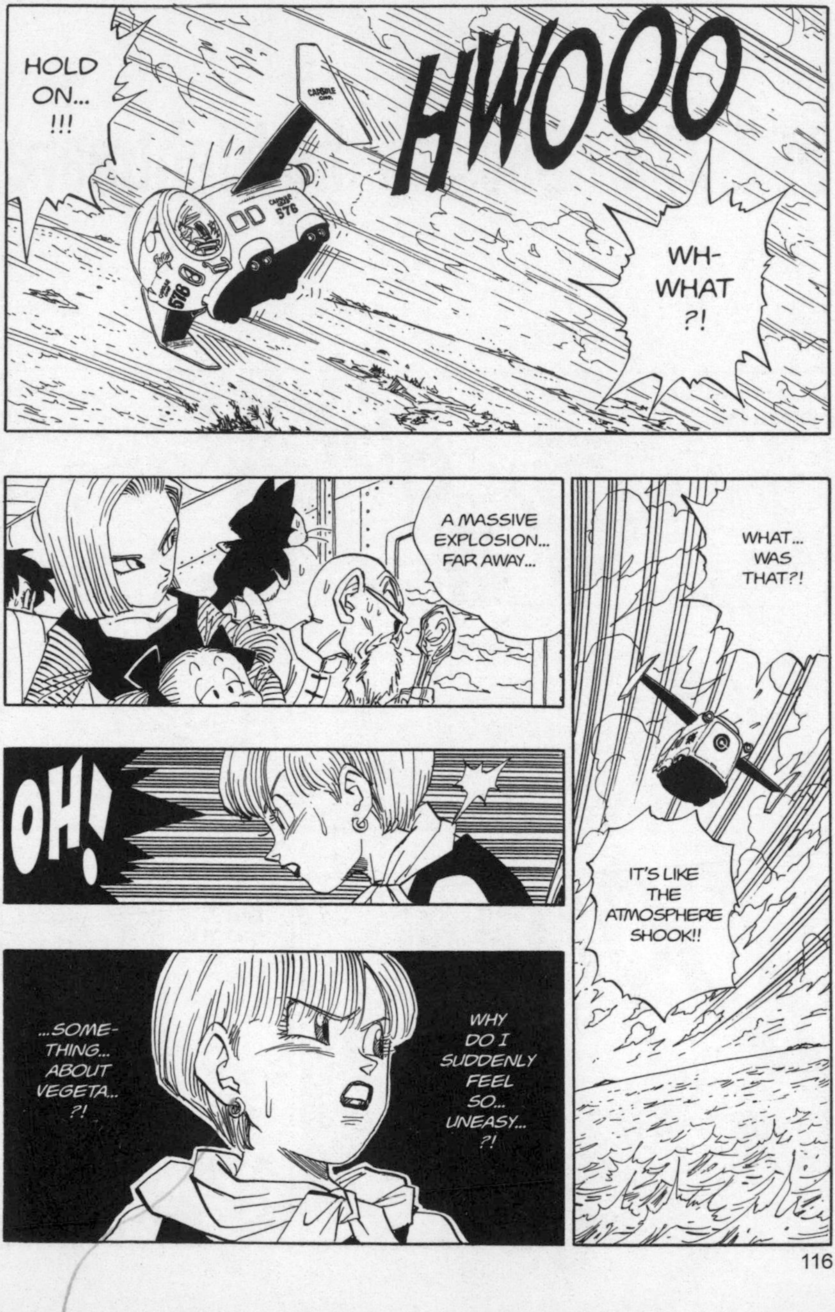
HWOOO
WH-WHAT?!
HOLD ON...!!!
WHAT... WAS THAT?!
IT'S LIKE THE ATMOSPHERE SHOOK!!
A MASSIVE EXPLOSION... FAR AWAY...
OH!
WHY DO I SUDDENLY FEEL SO... UNEASY...?!
...SOME-THING... ABOUT VEGETA...?!

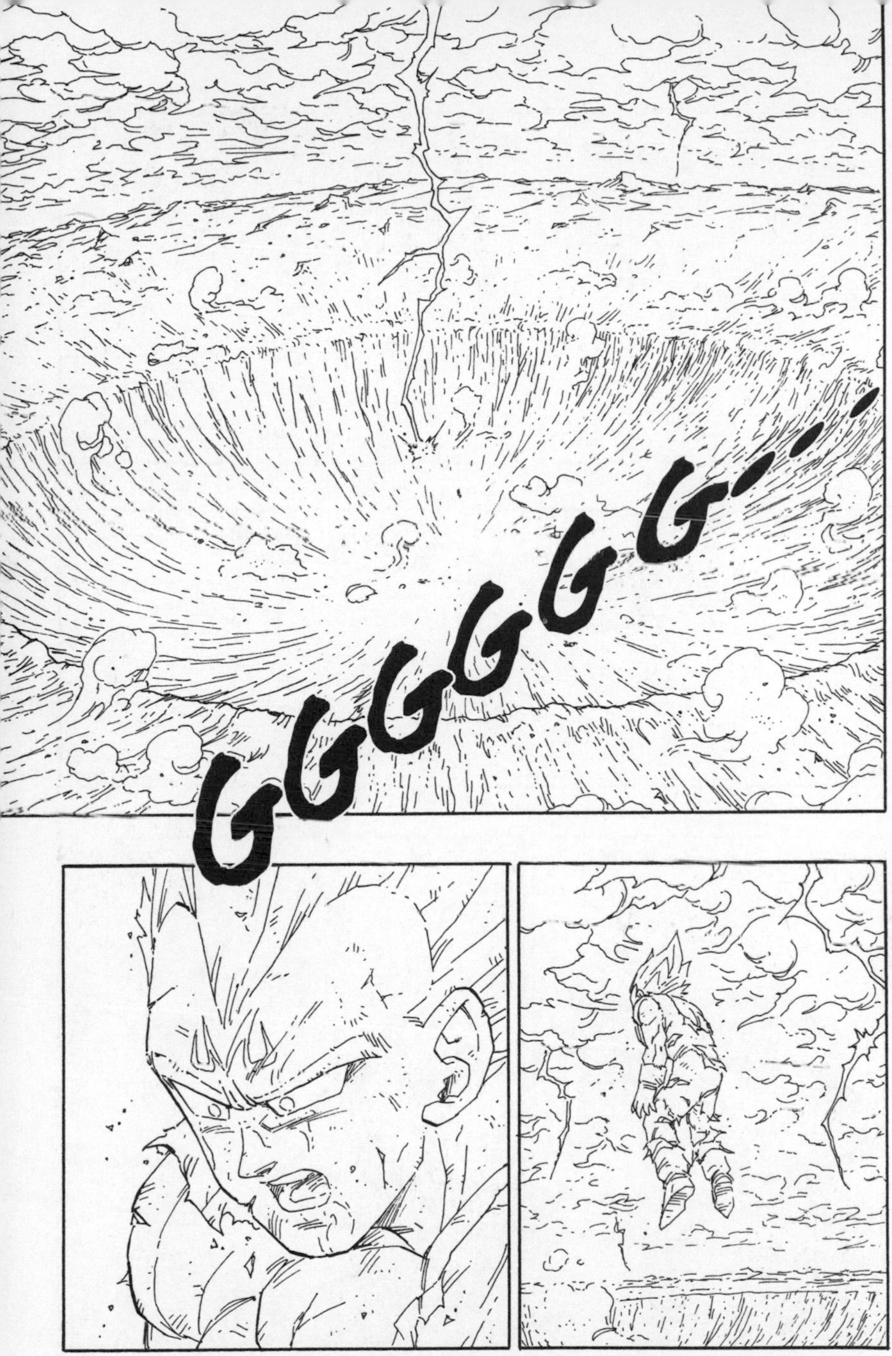
GGGGGG...

ZK
HYOOOO...

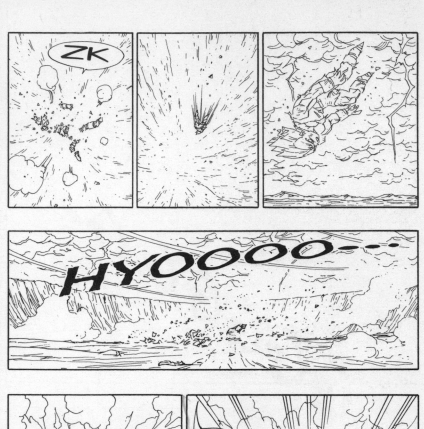

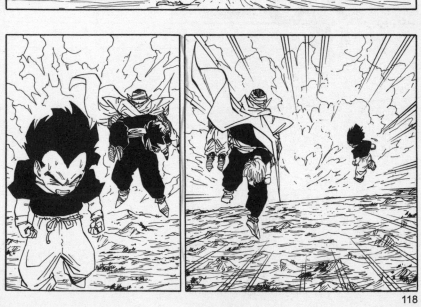

READ THIS WAY

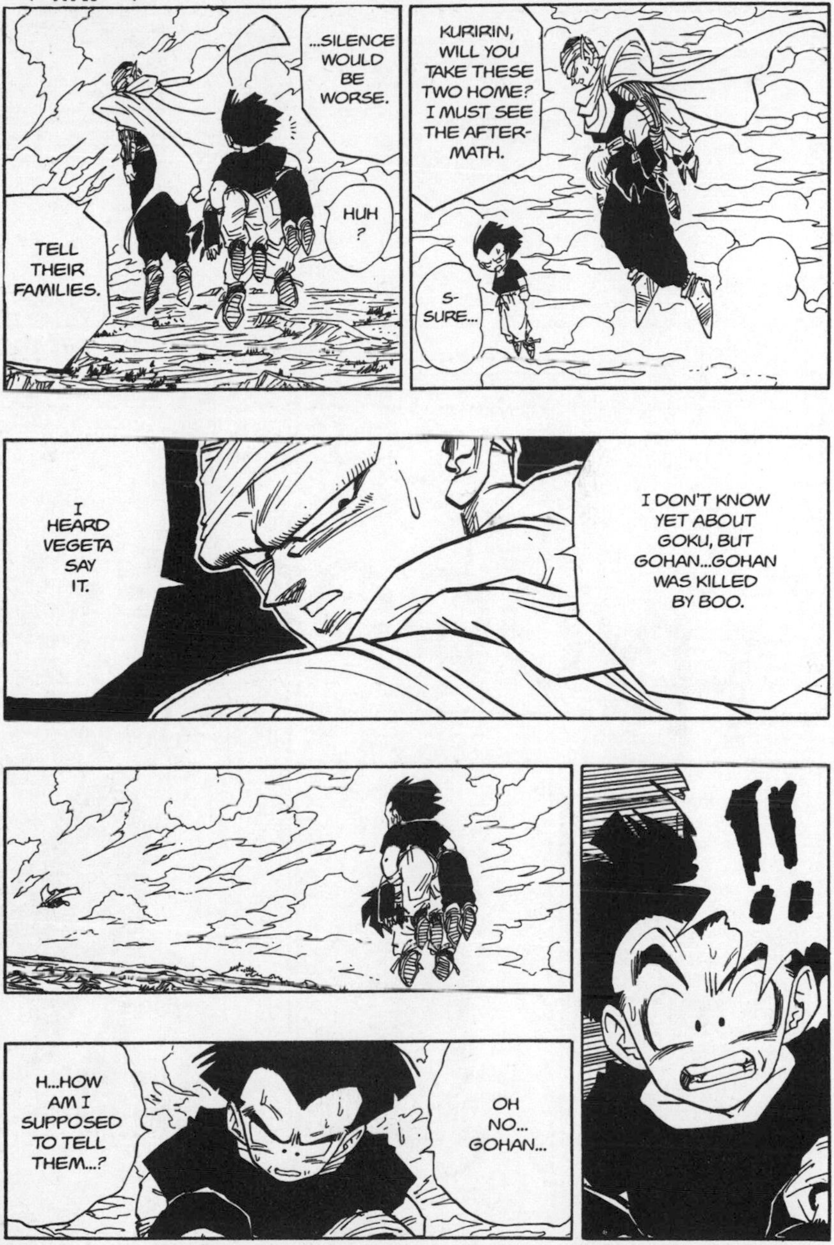
KURIRIN, WILL YOU TAKE THESE TWO HOME? I MUST SEE THE AFTER-MATH.
S-SURE...
...SILENCE WOULD BE WORSE.
HUH?
TELL THEIR FAMILIES.
I DON'T KNOW YET ABOUT GOKU, BUT GOHAN...GOHAN WAS KILLED BY BOO.
I HEARD VEGETA SAY IT.
!!
OH NO... GOHAN...
H...HOW AM I SUPPOSED TO TELL THEM...?

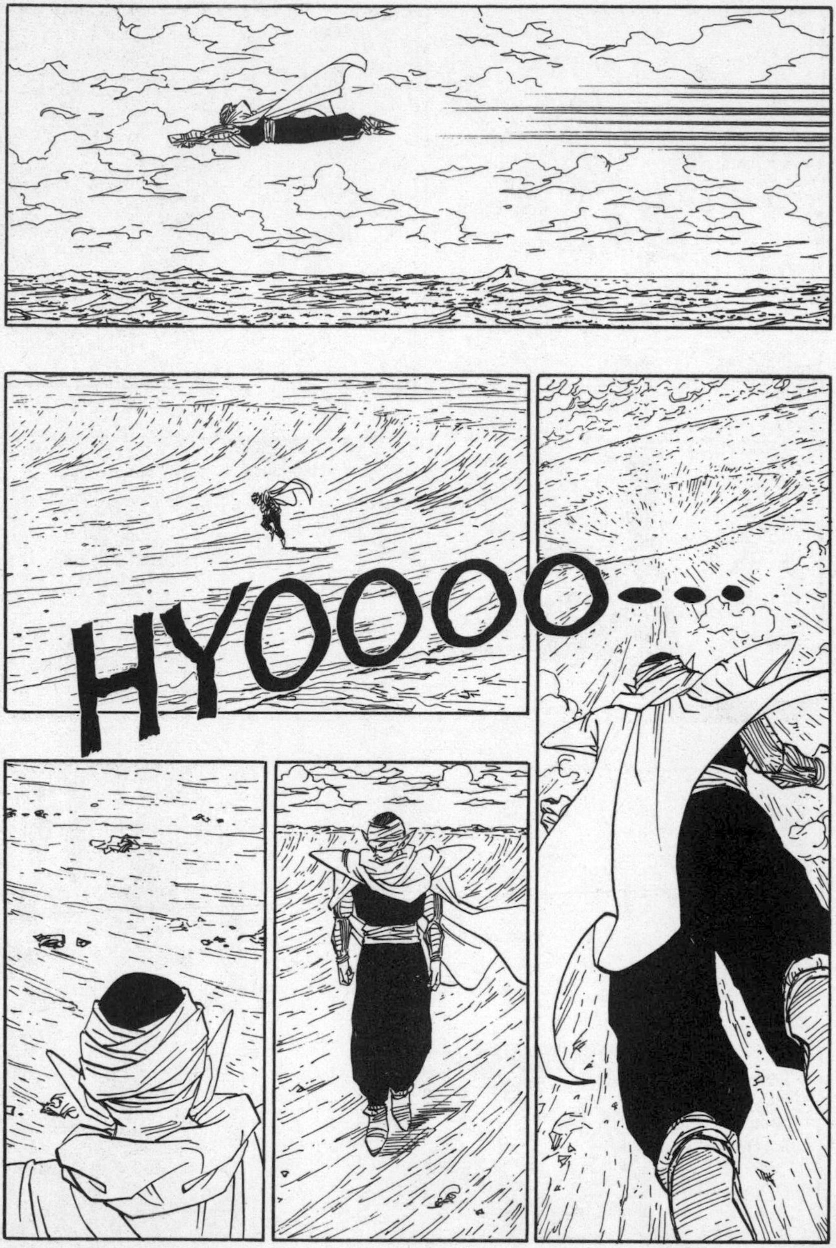
HYOOOO...

READ THIS WAY

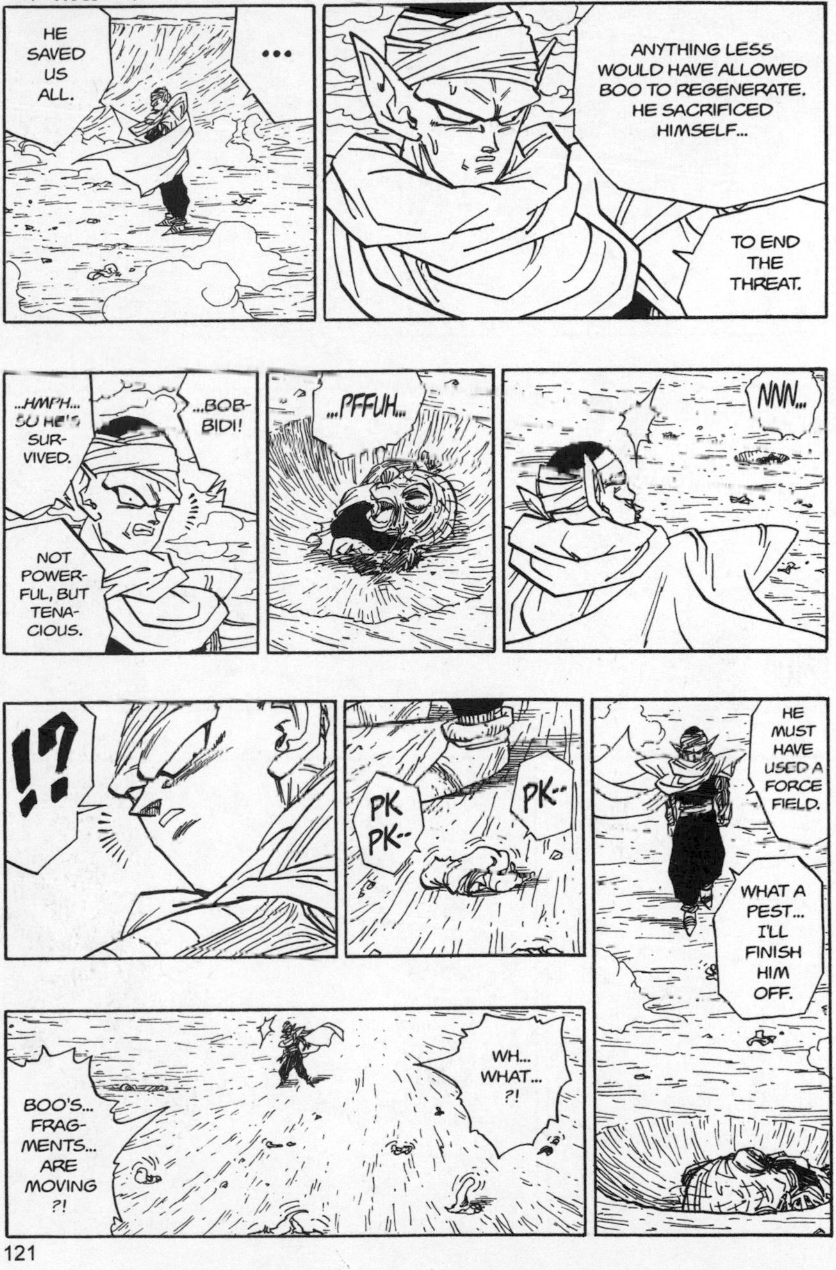
ANYTHING LESS WOULD HAVE ALLOWED BOO TO REGENERATE. HE SACRIFICED HIMSELF...
TO END THE THREAT.
...
HE SAVED US ALL.
NNN...
...PFFUH...
...BOB-BIDI!
...HMPH... SO HE'S SURVIVED.
NOT POWERFUL, BUT TENACIOUS.
HE MUST HAVE USED A FORCE FIELD.
WHAT A PEST... I'LL FINISH HIM OFF.
PK--
PK PK--
!?
WH... WHAT...?!
BOO'S... FRAGMENTS... ARE MOVING?!

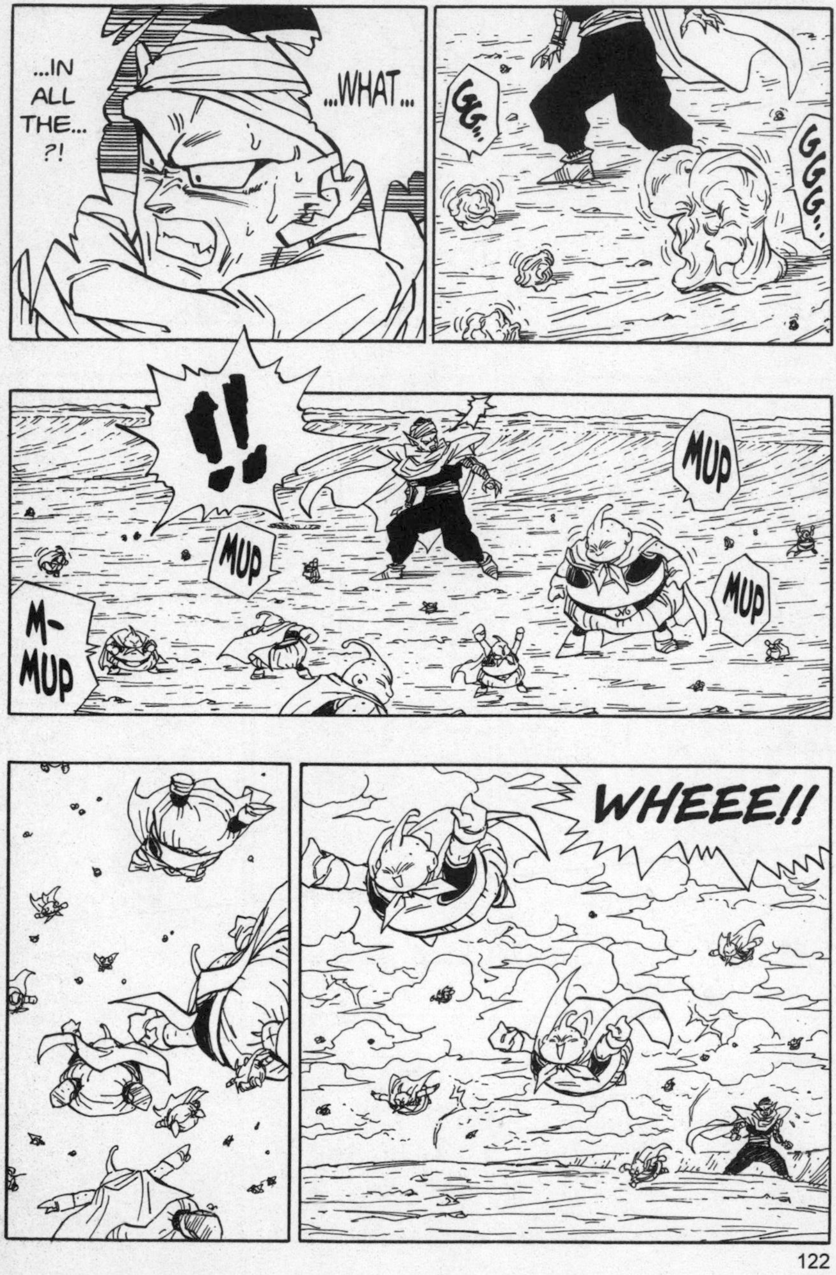
GGG...
GG...
...WHAT...
...IN ALL THE... ?!
MUP
!!
MUP
MUP
M-MUP
WHEEE!!

READ THIS WAY

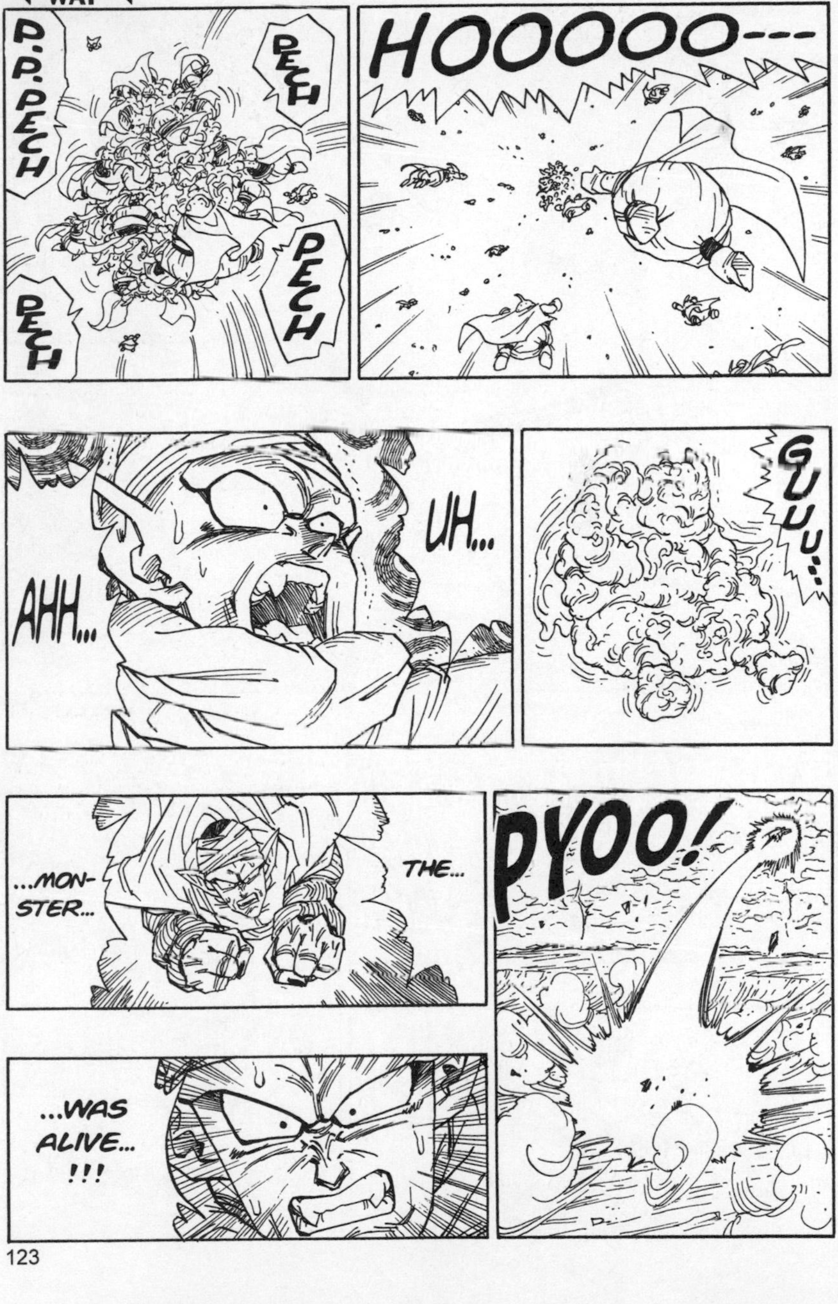
HOOOOO---
PECH
P.P.PECH
PECH
PECH
GUUU...
UH...
AHH...
PYOO!
THE...
...MON-STER...
...WAS ALIVE...!!!

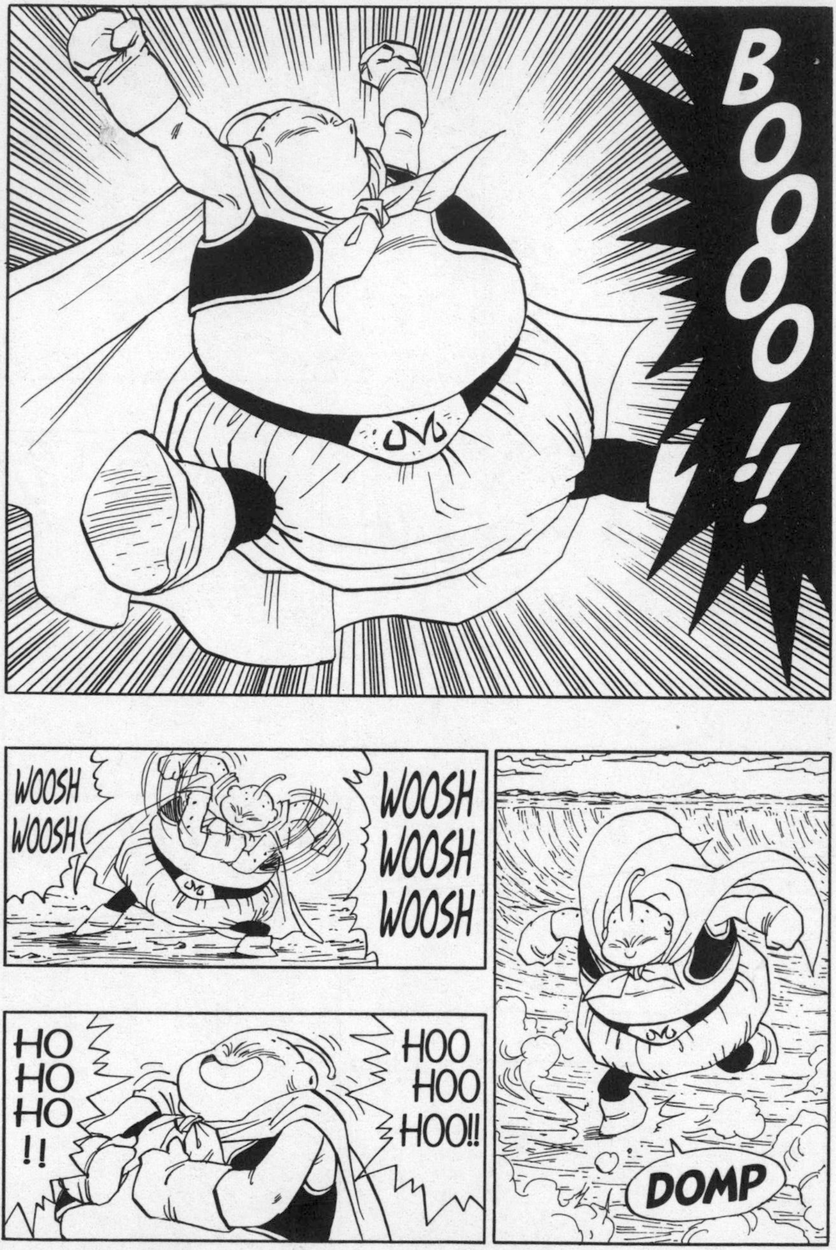
BOOOO!!!
DOMP
WOOSH
WOOSH
WOOSH
WOOSH
WOOSH
HOO
HOO
HOO!!
HO
HO
HO
!!

READ THIS WAY

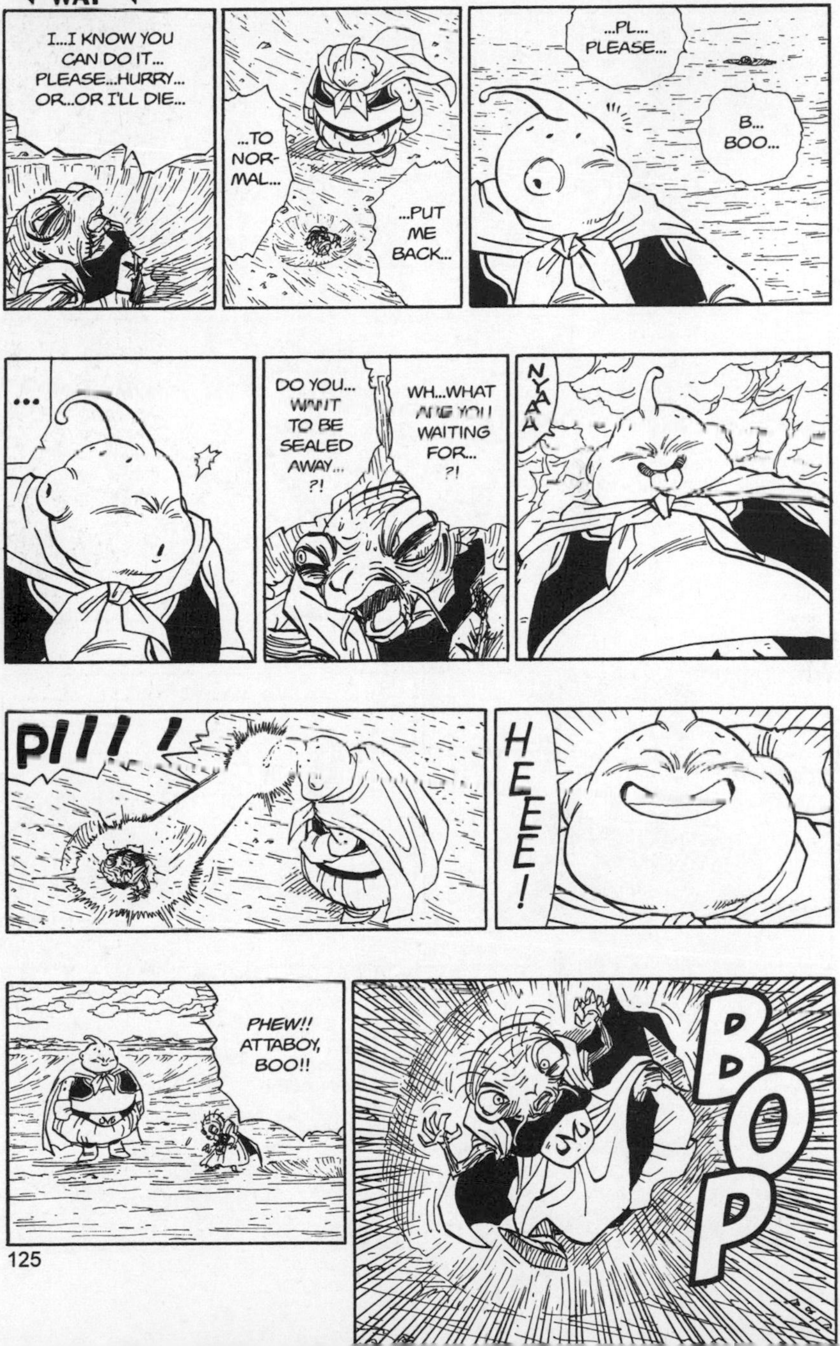
...PL... PLEASE...
B... BOO...
...PUT ME BACK...
...TO NORMAL...
I...I KNOW YOU CAN DO IT... PLEASE...HURRY... OR...OR I'LL DIE...
NYAA
WH...WHAT ARE YOU WAITING FOR... ?!
DO YOU... WANT TO BE SEALED AWAY... ?!
...
HEEEE!
PI!!!
BOP
PHEW!! ATTABOY, BOO!!

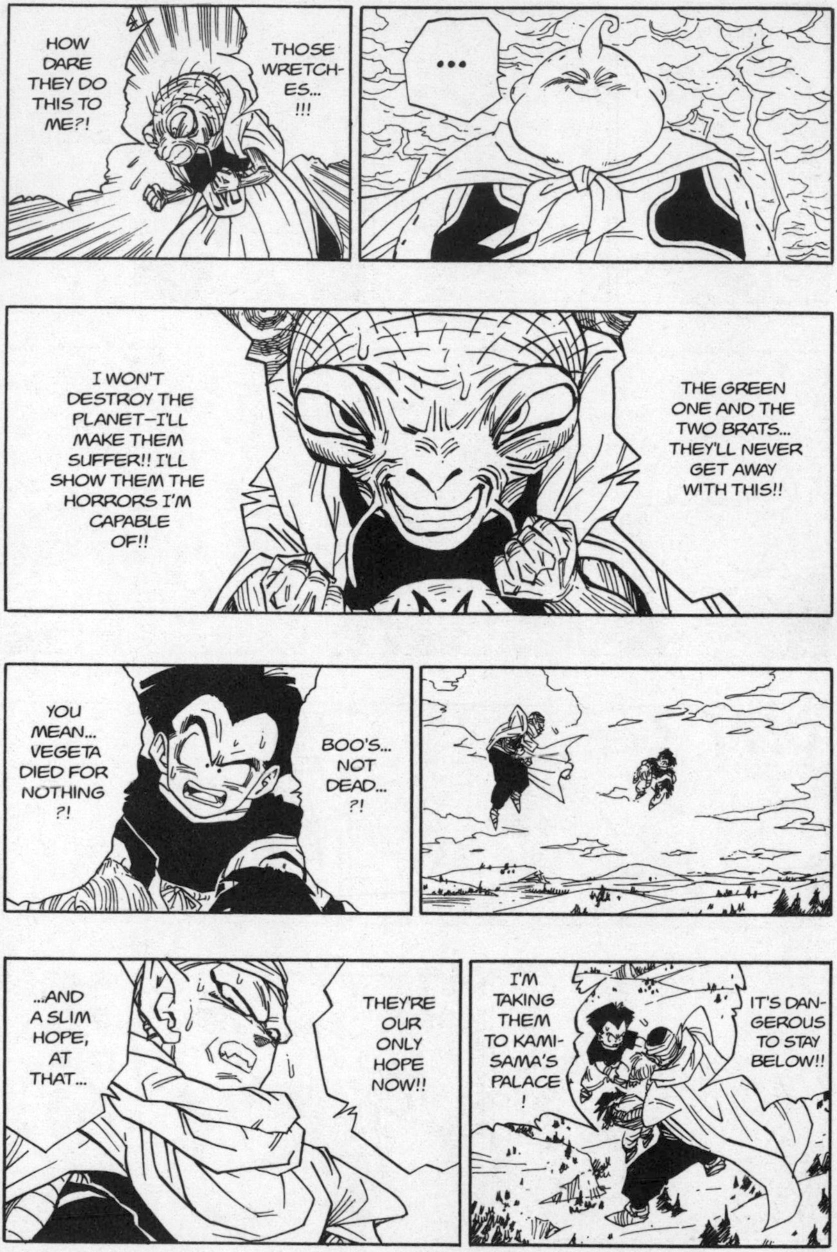
...
THOSE WRETCHES...!!!
HOW DARE THEY DO THIS TO ME?!
THE GREEN ONE AND THE TWO BRATS... THEY'LL NEVER GET AWAY WITH THIS!!
I WON'T DESTROY THE PLANET—I'LL MAKE THEM SUFFER!! I'LL SHOW THEM THE HORRORS I'M CAPABLE OF!!
BOO'S... NOT DEAD...?!
YOU MEAN... VEGETA DIED FOR NOTHING?!
IT'S DANGEROUS TO STAY BELOW!!
I'M TAKING THEM TO KAMI-SAMA'S PALACE!
THEY'RE OUR ONLY HOPE NOW!!
...AND A SLIM HOPE, AT THAT...

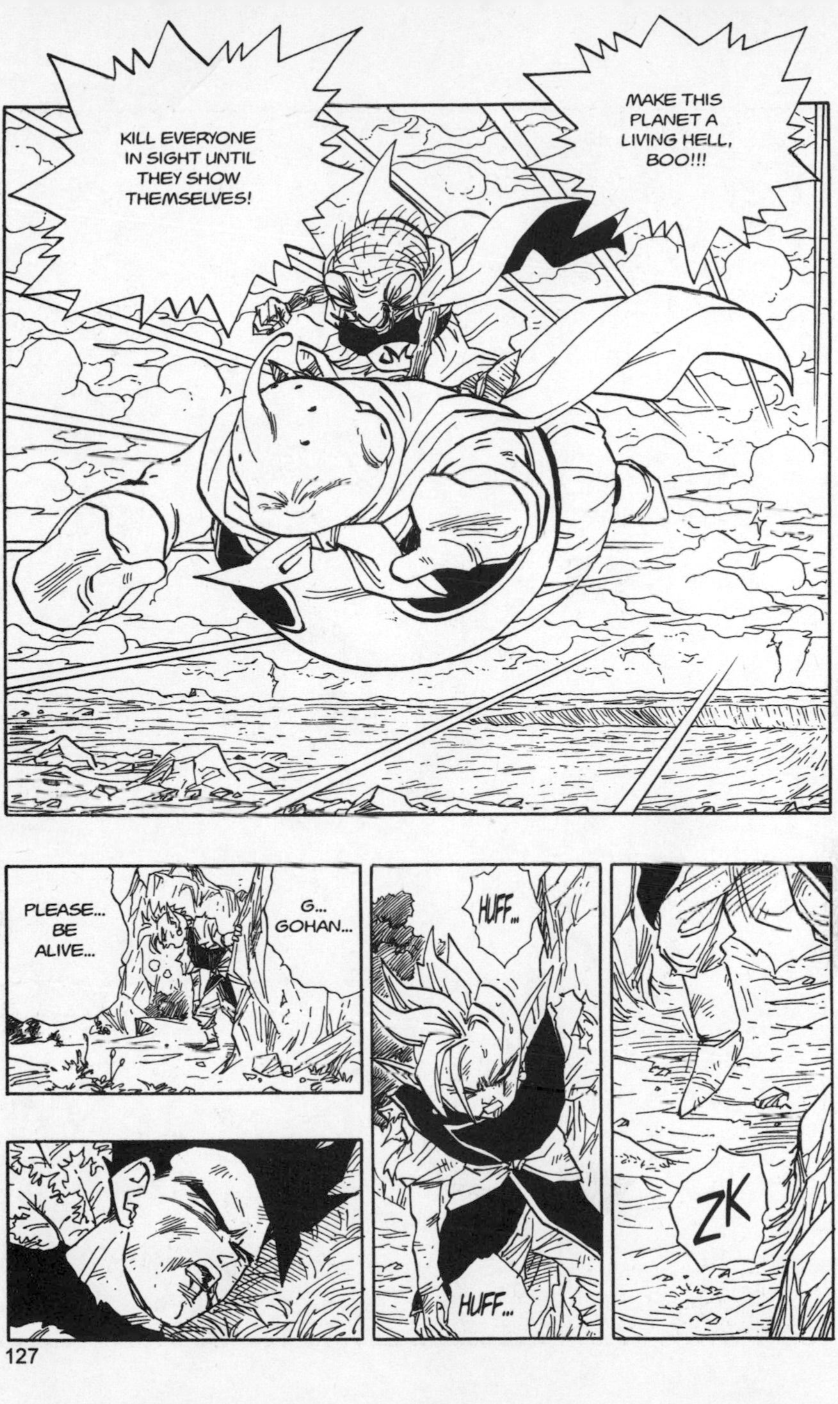
MAKE THIS PLANET A LIVING HELL, BOO!!!
KILL EVERYONE IN SIGHT UNTIL THEY SHOW THEMSELVES!
ZK
HUFF...
HUFF...
G... GOHAN...
PLEASE... BE ALIVE...

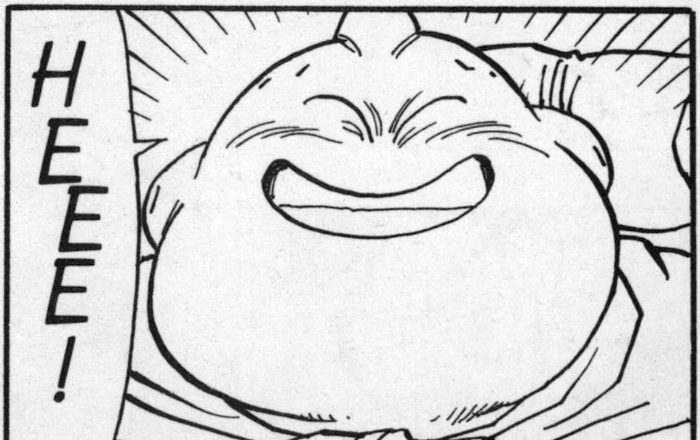
HEEEE!

DBZ:275 • A Slim Hope

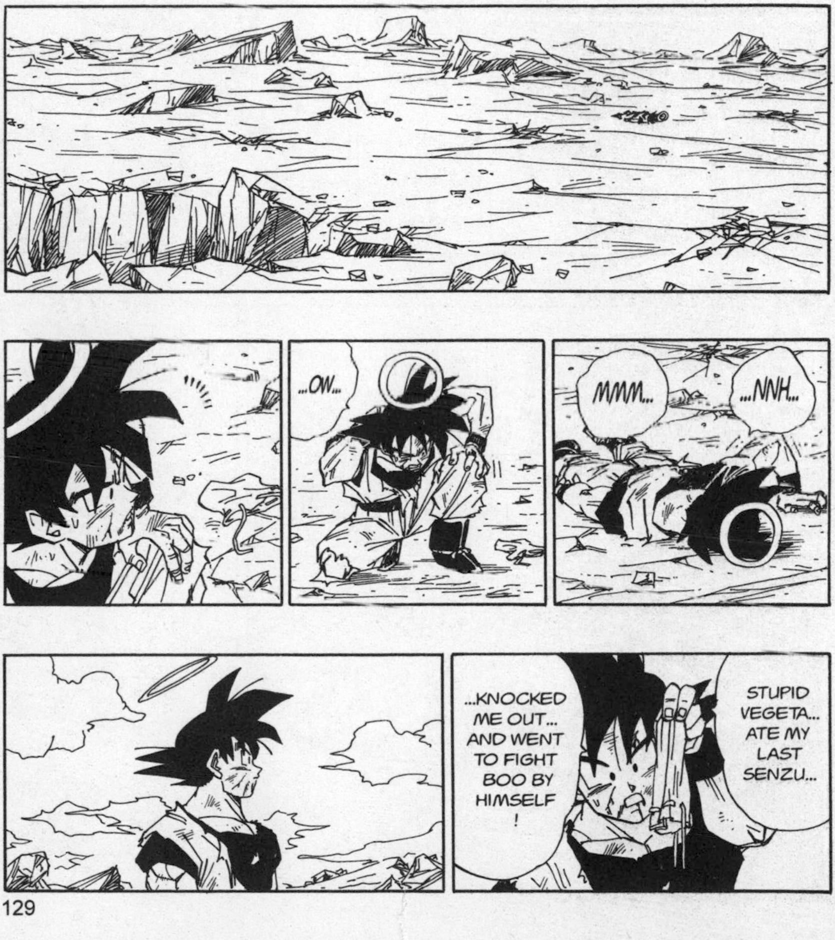
...NNH...
MMM...
...OW...
STUPID VEGETA... ATE MY LAST SENZU...
...KNOCKED ME OUT... AND WENT TO FIGHT BOO BY HIMSELF !

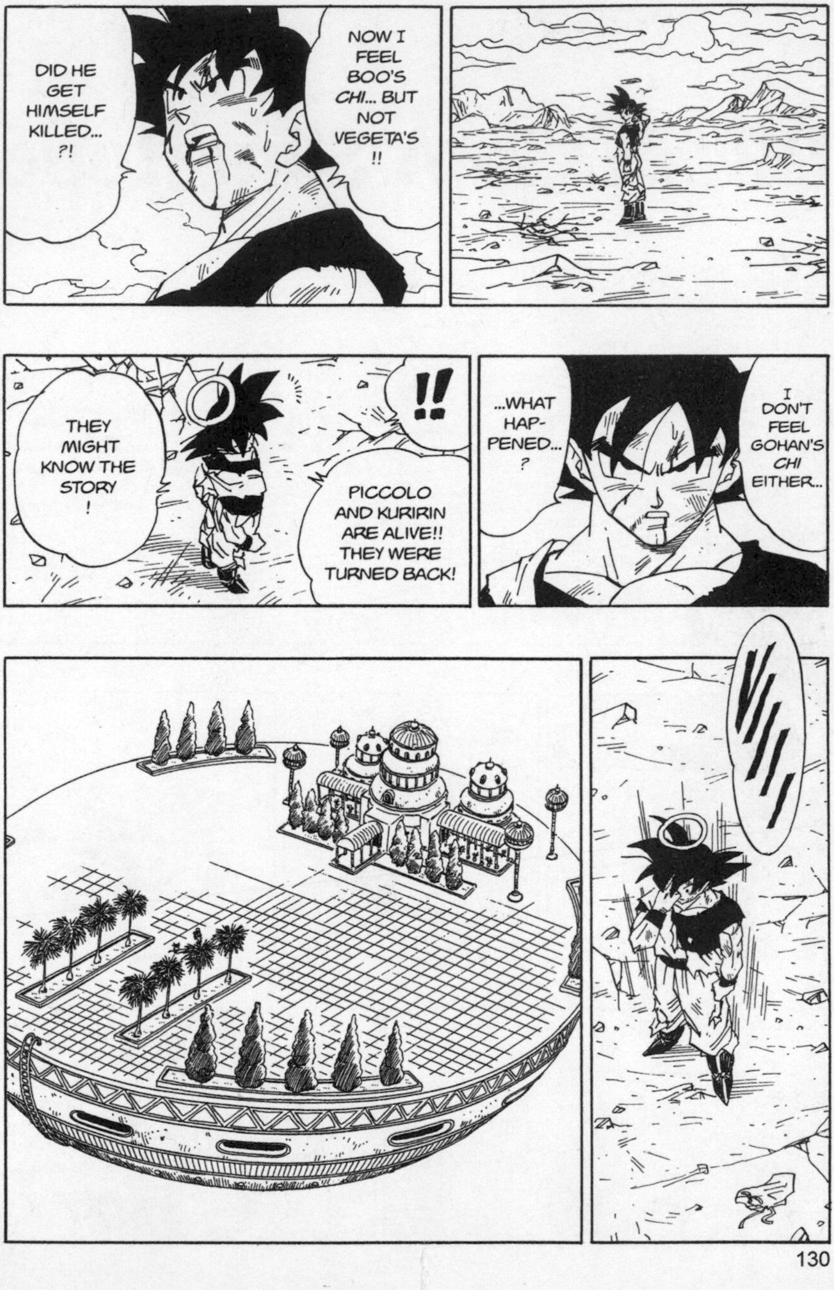
NOW I FEEL BOO'S CHI... BUT NOT VEGETA'S !!
DID HE GET HIMSELF KILLED... ?!
I DON'T FEEL GOHAN'S CHI EITHER...
...WHAT HAP-PENED... ?
!!
PICCOLO AND KURIRIN ARE ALIVE!! THEY WERE TURNED BACK!
THEY MIGHT KNOW THE STORY !

READ THIS WAY

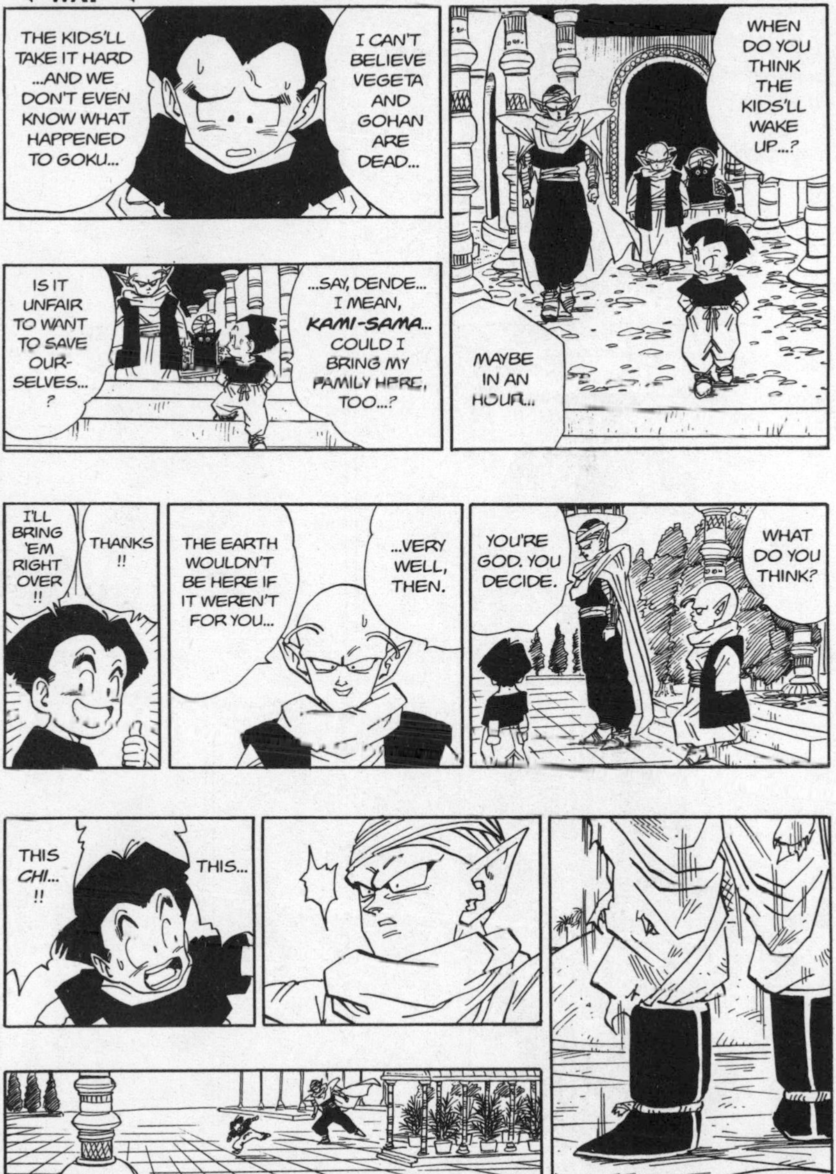
WHEN DO YOU THINK THE KIDS'LL WAKE UP...?
MAYBE IN AN HOUR...
I CAN'T BELIEVE VEGETA AND GOHAN ARE DEAD...
THE KIDS'LL TAKE IT HARD ...AND WE DON'T EVEN KNOW WHAT HAPPENED TO GOKU...
...SAY, DENDE... I MEAN, KAMI-SAMA... COULD I BRING MY FAMILY HERE, TOO...?
IS IT UNFAIR TO WANT TO SAVE OURSELVES...?
WHAT DO YOU THINK?
YOU'RE GOD. YOU DECIDE.
...VERY WELL, THEN.
THE EARTH WOULDN'T BE HERE IF IT WEREN'T FOR YOU...
THANKS!!
I'LL BRING 'EM RIGHT OVER!!
VIII
THIS...
THIS CHI...!!

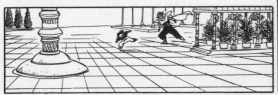

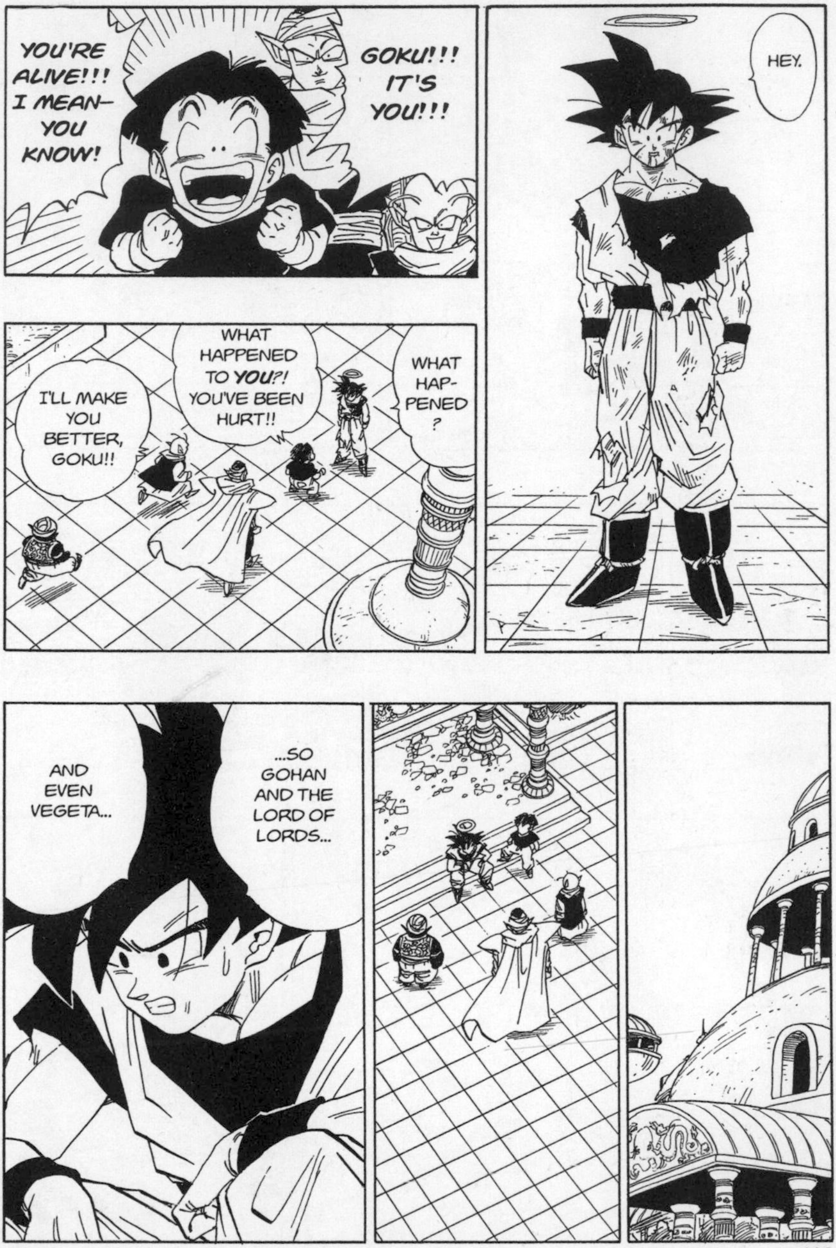
HEY.
GOKU!!! IT'S YOU!!!
YOU'RE ALIVE!!! I MEAN— YOU KNOW!
WHAT HAP- PENED ?
WHAT HAPPENED TO **YOU**?! YOU'VE BEEN HURT!!
I'LL MAKE YOU BETTER, GOKU!!
...SO GOHAN AND THE LORD OF LORDS...
AND EVEN VEGETA...

READ THIS WAY

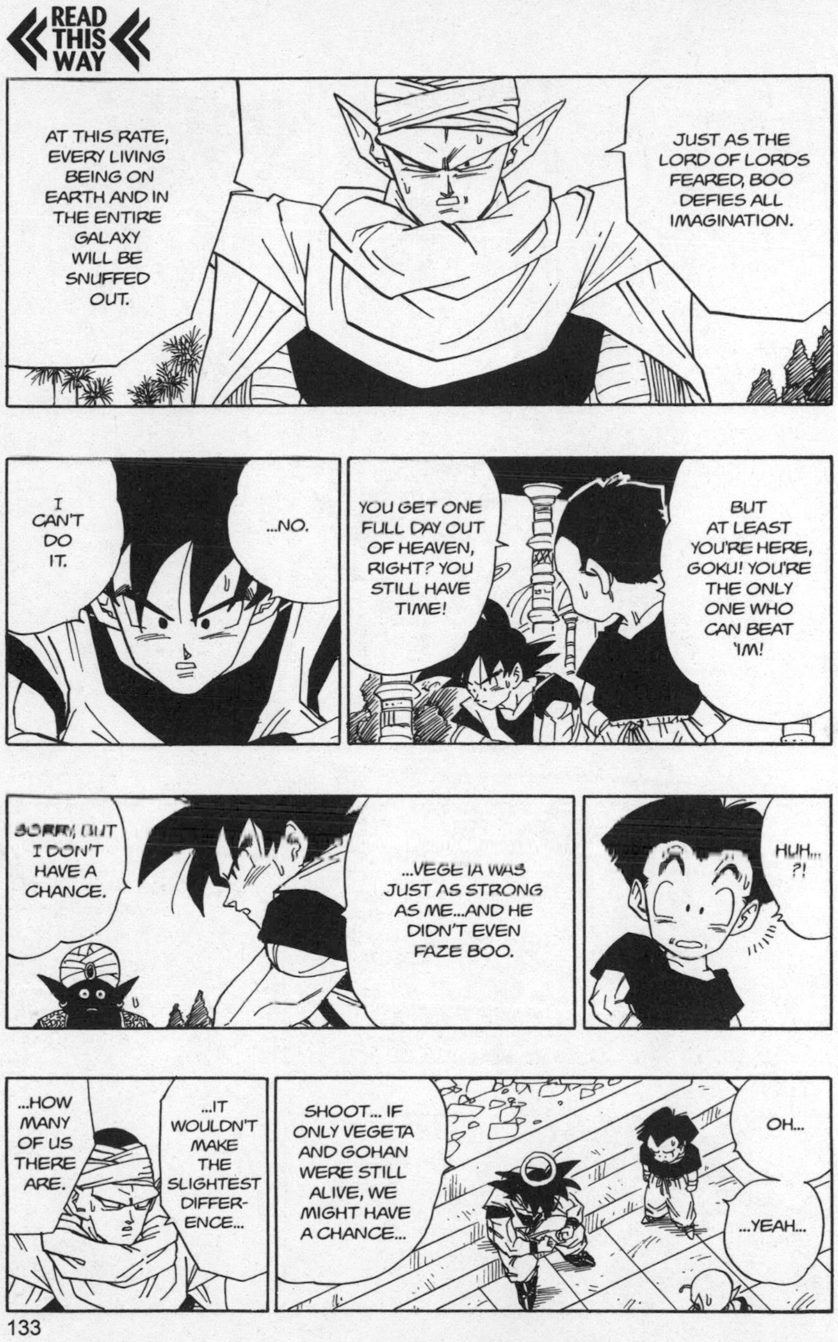
JUST AS THE LORD OF LORDS FEARED, BOO DEFIES ALL IMAGINATION.
AT THIS RATE, EVERY LIVING BEING ON EARTH AND IN THE ENTIRE GALAXY WILL BE SNUFFED OUT.
BUT AT LEAST YOU'RE HERE, GOKU! YOU'RE THE ONLY ONE WHO CAN BEAT 'IM!
YOU GET ONE FULL DAY OUT OF HEAVEN, RIGHT? YOU STILL HAVE TIME!
...NO.
I CAN'T DO IT.
HUH... ?!
...VEGETA WAS JUST AS STRONG AS ME...AND HE DIDN'T EVEN FAZE BOO.
SORRY, BUT I DON'T HAVE A CHANCE.
OH...
...YEAH...
SHOOT... IF ONLY VEGETA AND GOHAN WERE STILL ALIVE, WE MIGHT HAVE A CHANCE...
...IT WOULDN'T MAKE THE SLIGHTEST DIFFERENCE...
...HOW MANY OF US THERE ARE.

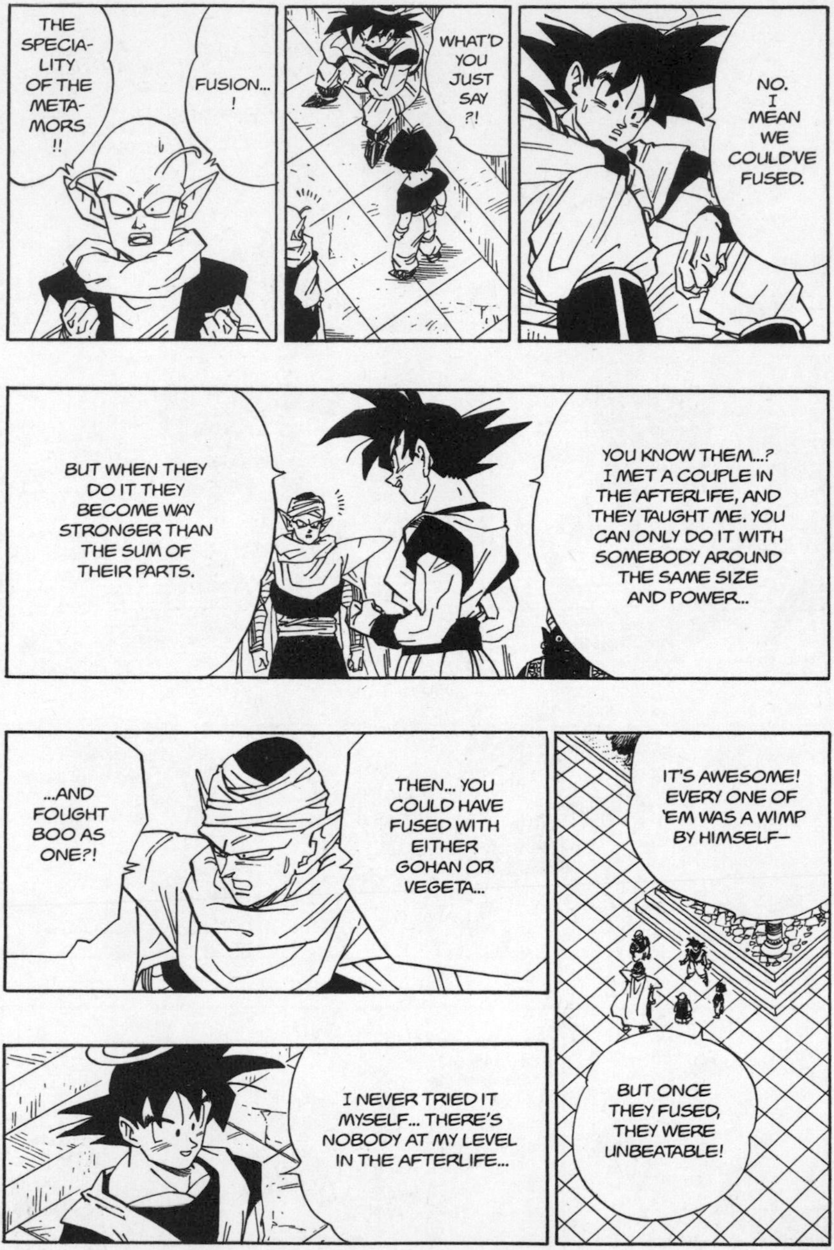
NO. I MEAN WE COULD'VE FUSED.
WHAT'D YOU JUST SAY ?!
FUSION... !
THE SPECIA-LITY OF THE METAMORS !!
YOU KNOW THEM...? I MET A COUPLE IN THE AFTERLIFE, AND THEY TAUGHT ME. YOU CAN ONLY DO IT WITH SOMEBODY AROUND THE SAME SIZE AND POWER...
BUT WHEN THEY DO IT THEY BECOME WAY STRONGER THAN THE SUM OF THEIR PARTS.
IT'S AWESOME! EVERY ONE OF 'EM WAS A WIMP BY HIMSELF—
BUT ONCE THEY FUSED, THEY WERE UNBEATABLE!
THEN... YOU COULD HAVE FUSED WITH EITHER GOHAN OR VEGETA...
...AND FOUGHT BOO AS ONE?!
I NEVER TRIED IT MYSELF... THERE'S NOBODY AT MY LEVEL IN THE AFTERLIFE...

READ THIS WAY

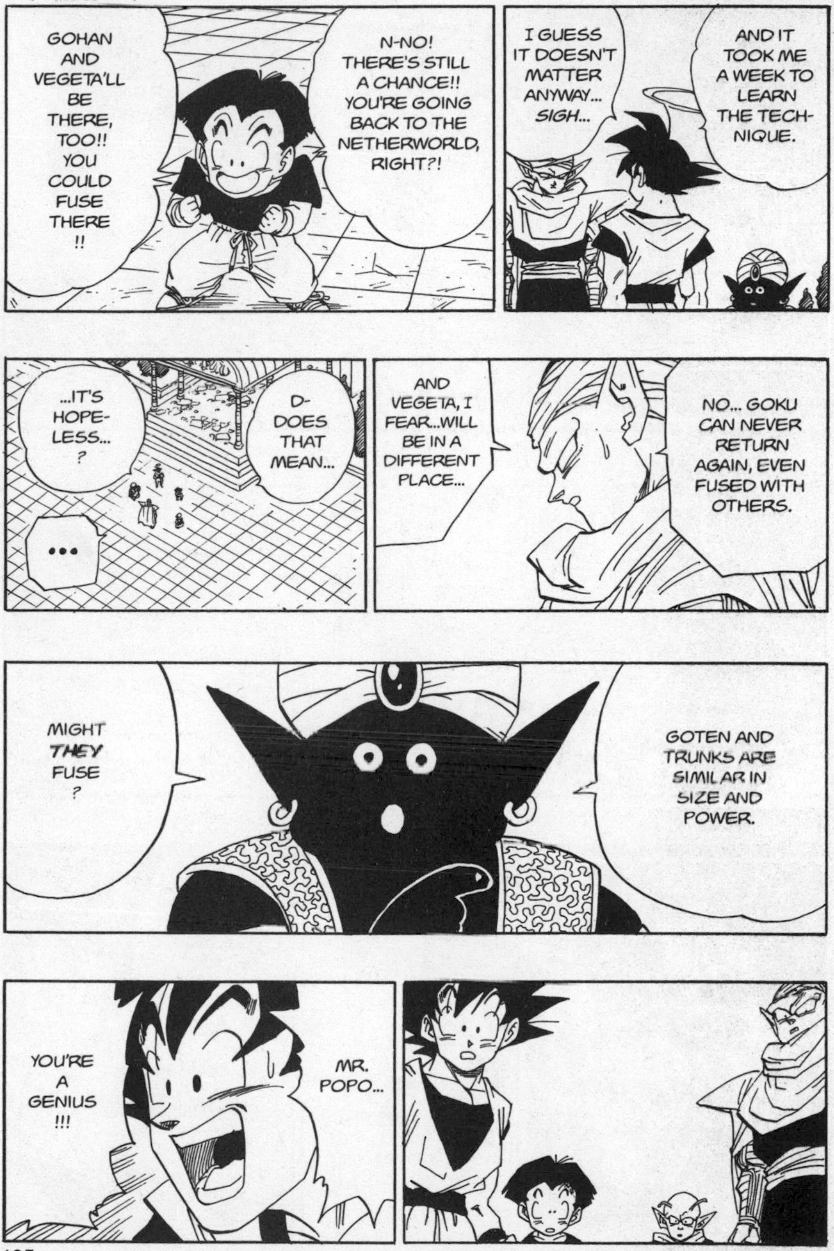
AND IT TOOK ME A WEEK TO LEARN THE TECHNIQUE.
I GUESS IT DOESN'T MATTER ANYWAY... SIGH...
N-NO! THERE'S STILL A CHANCE!! YOU'RE GOING BACK TO THE NETHERWORLD, RIGHT?!
GOHAN AND VEGETA'LL BE THERE, TOO!! YOU COULD FUSE THERE!!
NO... GOKU CAN NEVER RETURN AGAIN, EVEN FUSED WITH OTHERS.
AND VEGETA, I FEAR...WILL BE IN A DIFFERENT PLACE...
D-DOES THAT MEAN...
...IT'S HOPELESS...?
...
GOTEN AND TRUNKS ARE SIMILAR IN SIZE AND POWER.
MIGHT THEY FUSE?
MR. POPO...
YOU'RE A GENIUS!!!

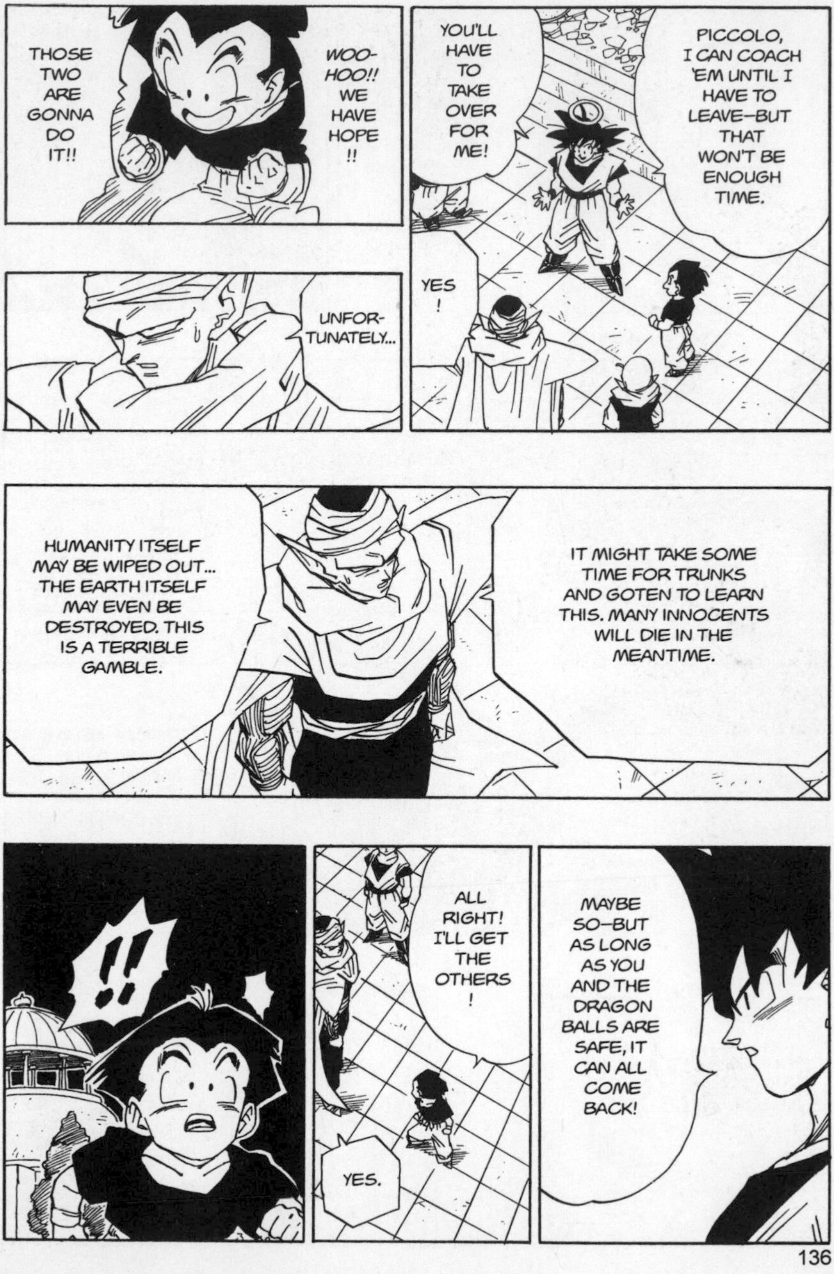
PICCOLO, I CAN COACH 'EM UNTIL I HAVE TO LEAVE—BUT THAT WON'T BE ENOUGH TIME.
YOU'LL HAVE TO TAKE OVER FOR ME!
YES!
WOO-HOO!! WE HAVE HOPE!!
THOSE TWO ARE GONNA DO IT!!
UNFORTUNATELY...
IT MIGHT TAKE SOME TIME FOR TRUNKS AND GOTEN TO LEARN THIS. MANY INNOCENTS WILL DIE IN THE MEANTIME.
HUMANITY ITSELF MAY BE WIPED OUT... THE EARTH ITSELF MAY EVEN BE DESTROYED. THIS IS A TERRIBLE GAMBLE.
MAYBE SO—BUT AS LONG AS YOU AND THE DRAGON BALLS ARE SAFE, IT CAN ALL COME BACK!
ALL RIGHT! I'LL GET THE OTHERS!
YES.
!!

READ THIS WAY

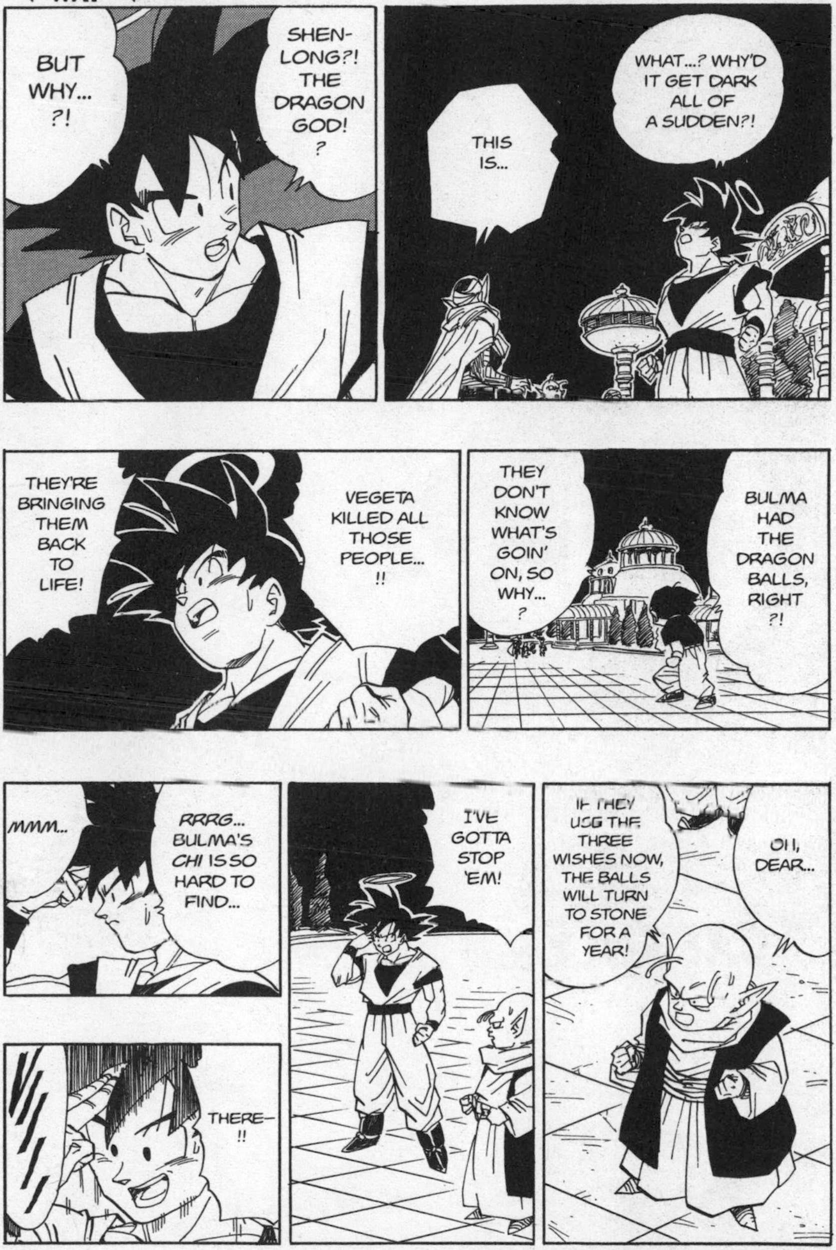

WHAT...? WHY'D IT GET DARK ALL OF A SUDDEN?!
THIS IS...
SHEN-LONG?! THE DRAGON GOD!?
BUT WHY...?!
BULMA HAD THE DRAGON BALLS, RIGHT?!
THEY DON'T KNOW WHAT'S GOIN' ON, SO WHY...?
VEGETA KILLED ALL THOSE PEOPLE...!!
THEY'RE BRINGING THEM BACK TO LIFE!
OH, DEAR...
IF THEY USE THE THREE WISHES NOW, THE BALLS WILL TURN TO STONE FOR A YEAR!
I'VE GOTTA STOP 'EM!
RRRG... BULMA'S CHI IS SO HARD TO FIND...
MMM...
THERE—!!

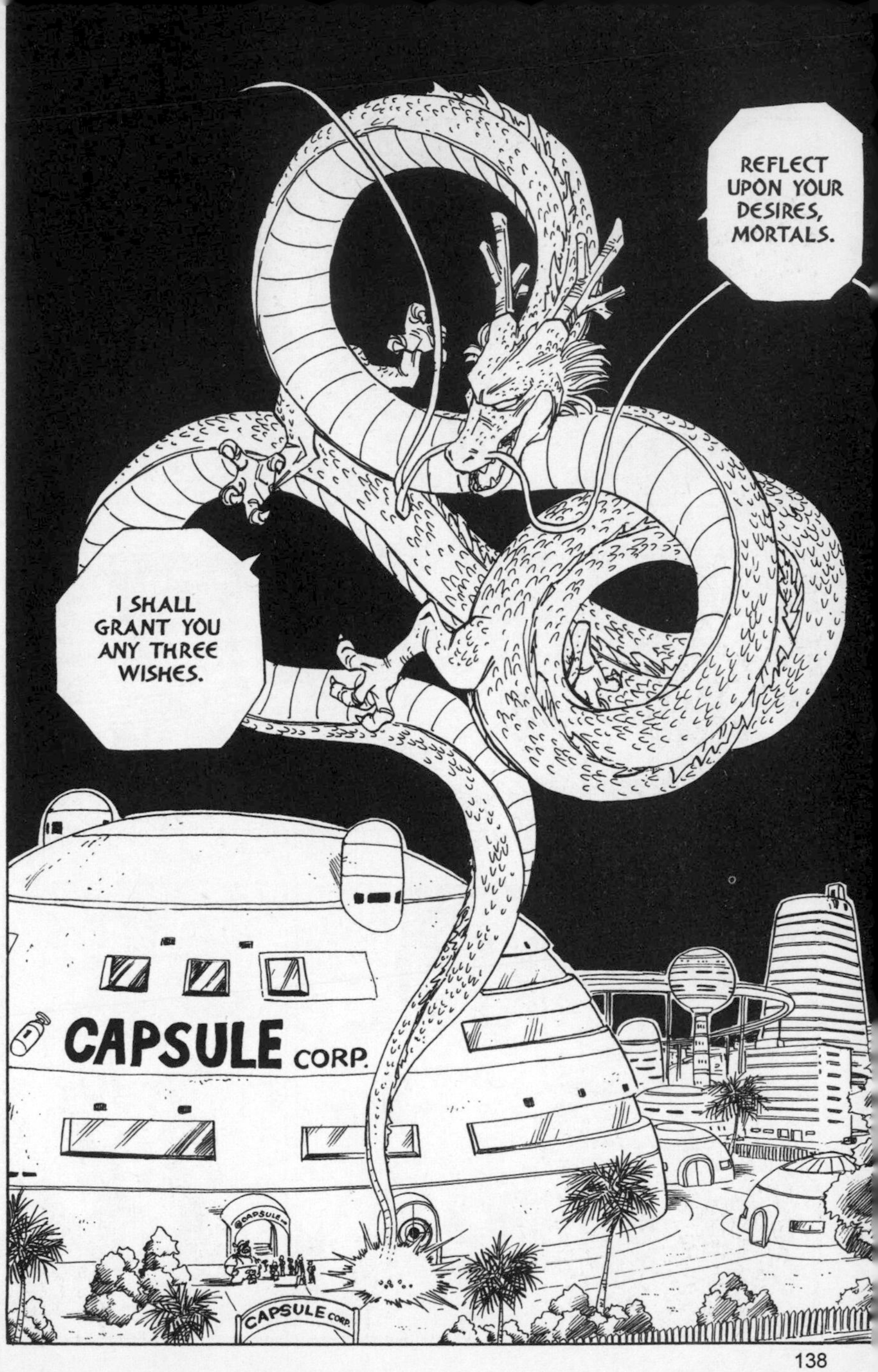
REFLECT UPON YOUR DESIRES, MORTALS.
I SHALL GRANT YOU ANY THREE WISHES.
CAPSULE CORP.
CAPSULE CORP.

READ THIS WAY

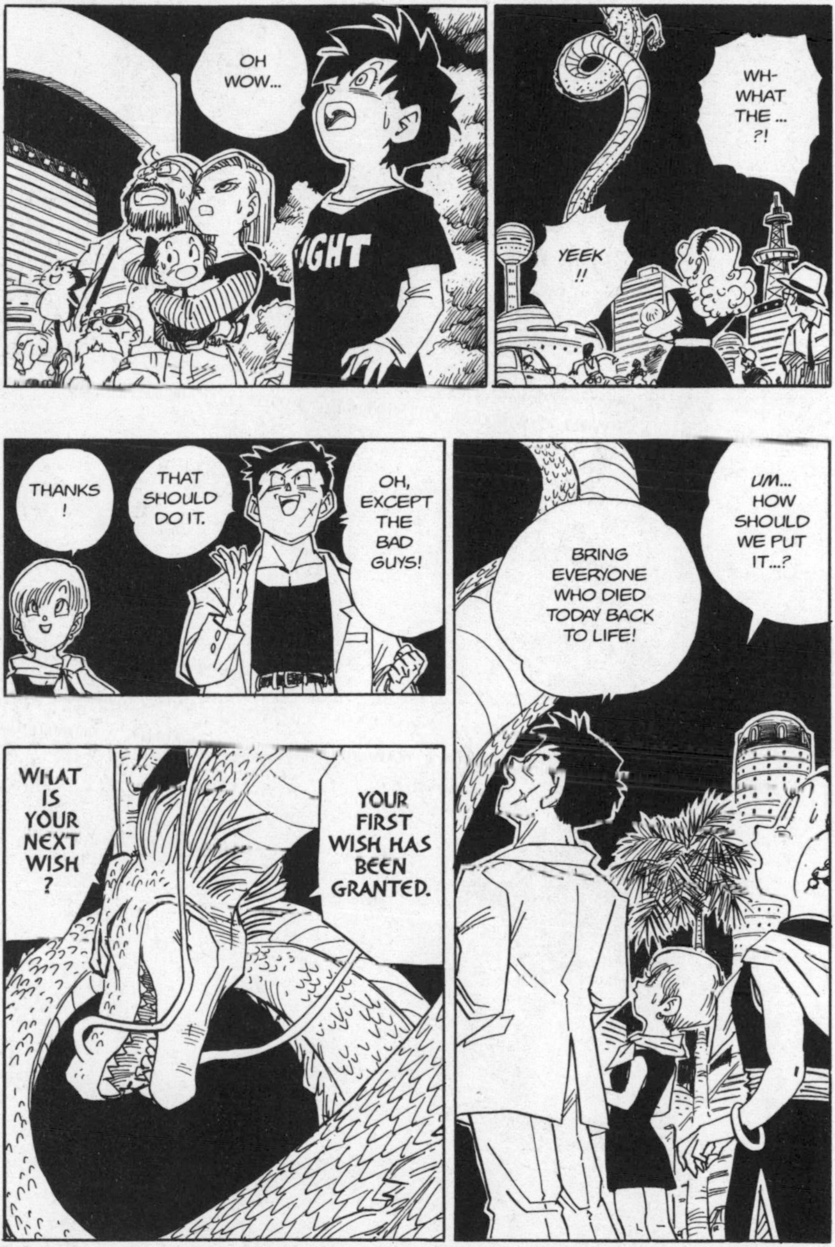

WH- WHAT THE ... ?!
YEEK !!
OH WOW...
UM... HOW SHOULD WE PUT IT...?
BRING EVERYONE WHO DIED TODAY BACK TO LIFE!
OH, EXCEPT THE BAD GUYS!
THAT SHOULD DO IT.
THANKS!
YOUR FIRST WISH HAS BEEN GRANTED.
WHAT IS YOUR NEXT WISH?

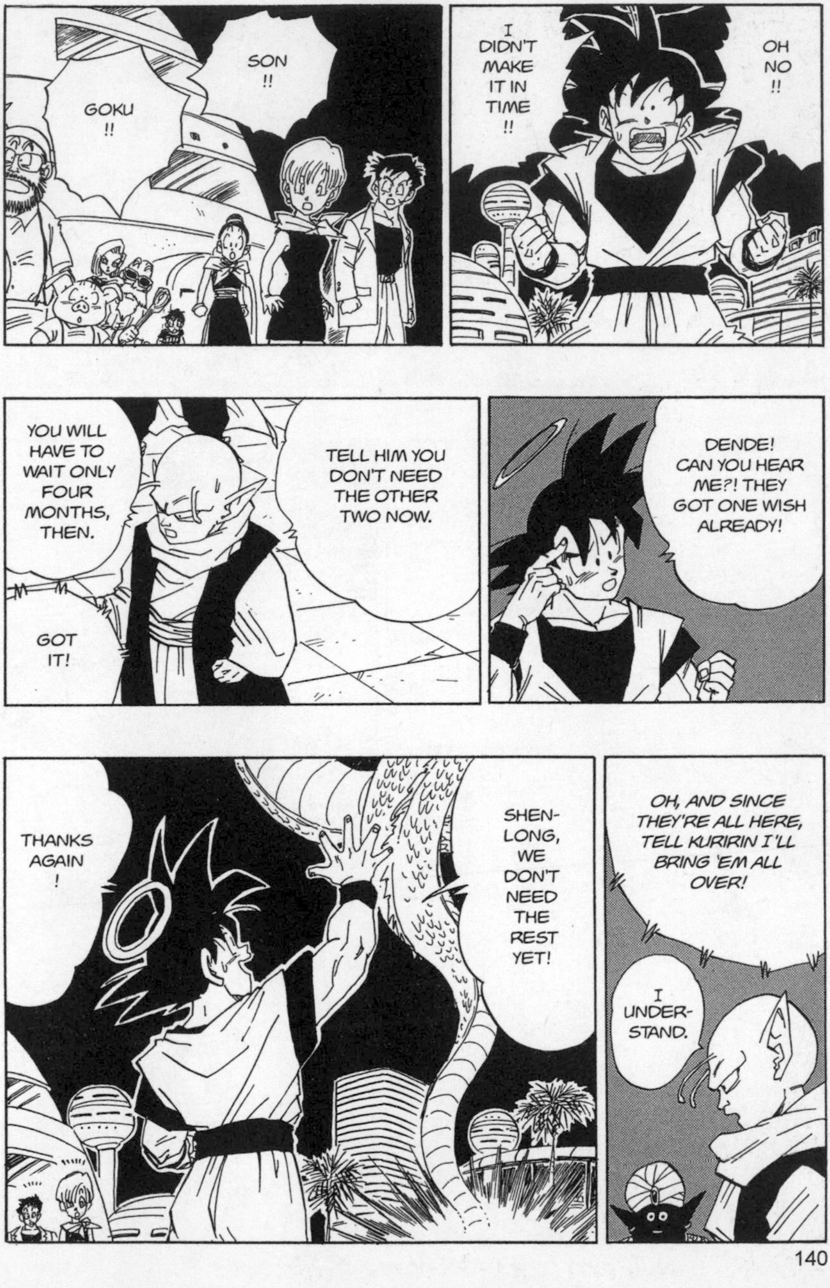
OH NO !!
I DIDN'T MAKE IT IN TIME !!
SON !!
GOKU !!
DENDE! CAN YOU HEAR ME?! THEY GOT ONE WISH ALREADY!
TELL HIM YOU DON'T NEED THE OTHER TWO NOW.
YOU WILL HAVE TO WAIT ONLY FOUR MONTHS, THEN.
GOT IT!
OH, AND SINCE THEY'RE ALL HERE, TELL KURIRIN I'LL BRING 'EM ALL OVER!
I UNDERSTAND.
SHENLONG, WE DON'T NEED THE REST YET!
THANKS AGAIN !

READ THIS WAY

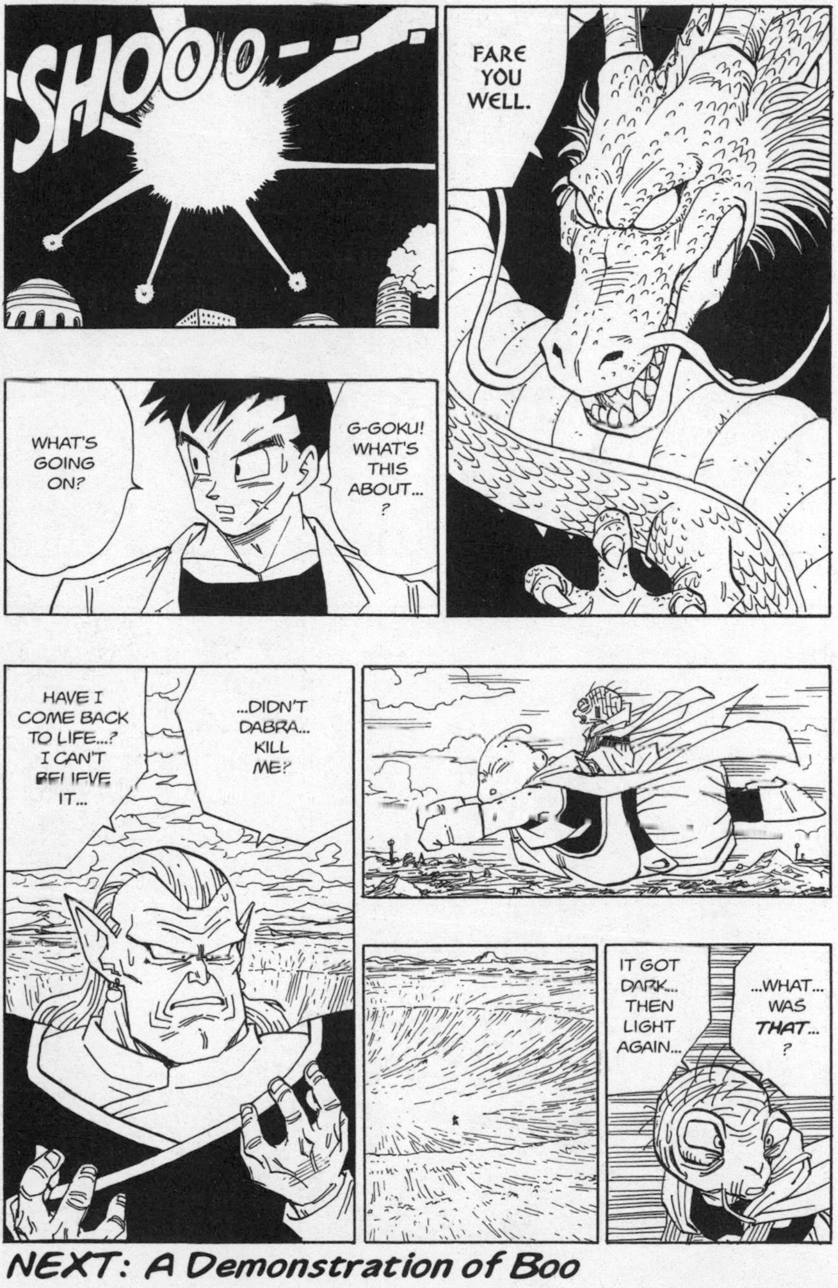
FARE YOU WELL.
SHOOO---
G-GOKU! WHAT'S THIS ABOUT...?
WHAT'S GOING ON?
...WHAT... WAS THAT...?
IT GOT DARK... THEN LIGHT AGAIN...
...DIDN'T DABRA... KILL ME?
HAVE I COME BACK TO LIFE...? I CAN'T BELIEVE IT...

NEXT: A Demonstration of Boo

DBZ:276 • Bobbidi's Revenge!!

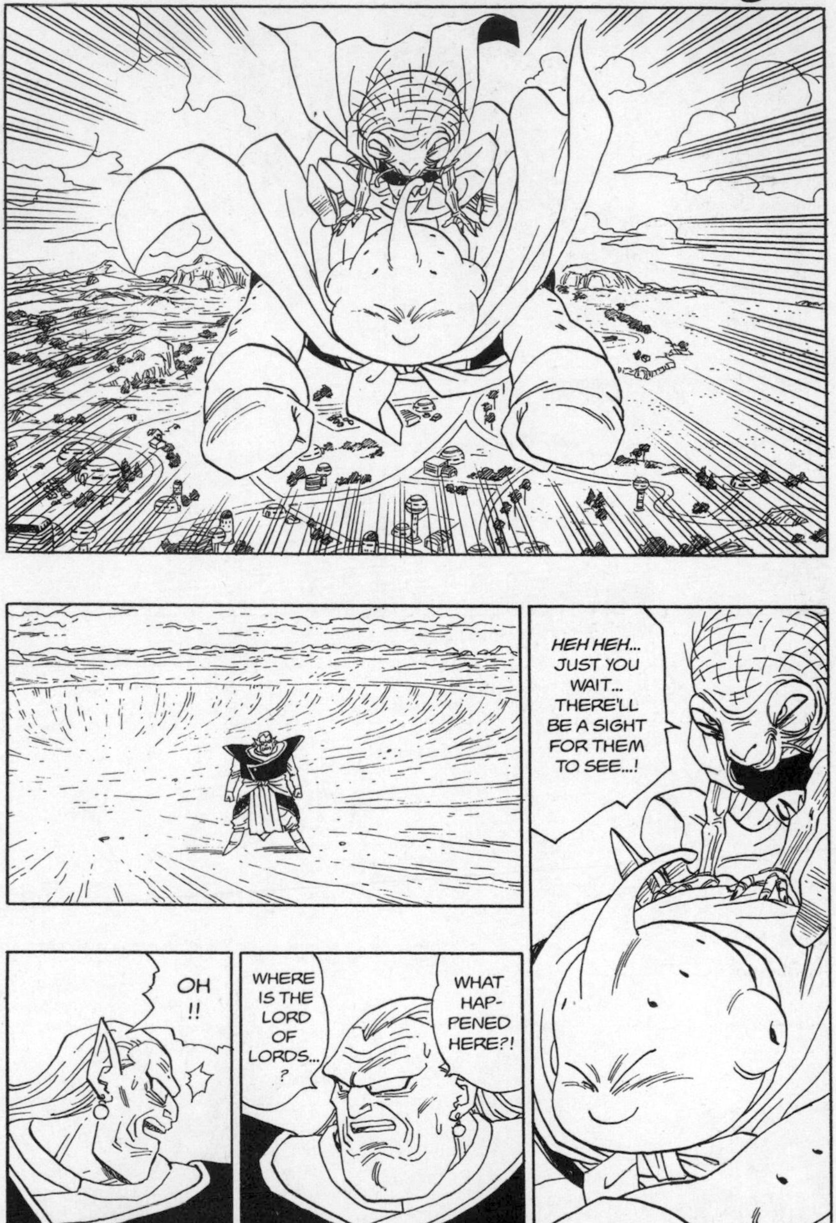
HEH HEH... JUST YOU WAIT... THERE'LL BE A SIGHT FOR THEM TO SEE...!
WHAT HAP-PENED HERE?!
WHERE IS THE LORD OF LORDS...?
OH !!

READ THIS WAY

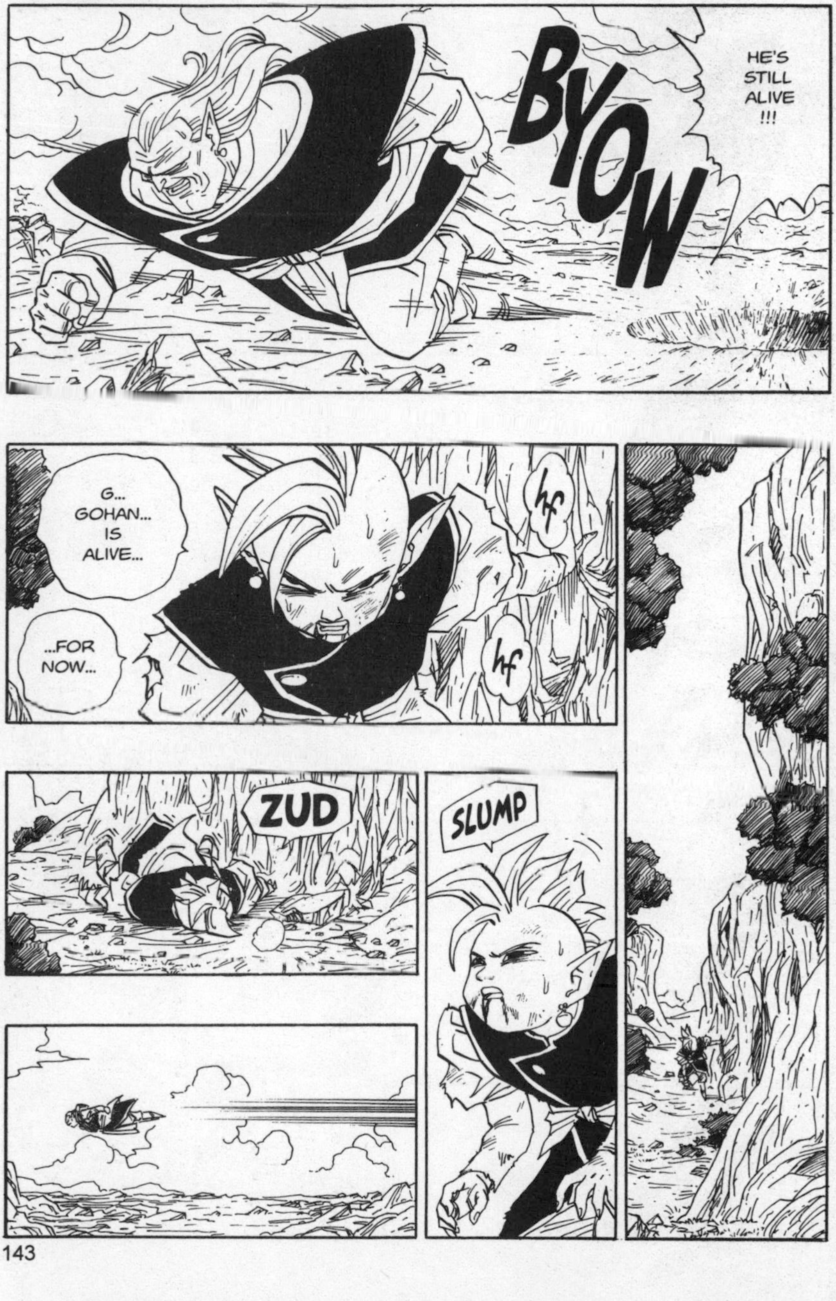
HE'S STILL ALIVE!!!
BYOW
hf
G... GOHAN... IS ALIVE...
hf
...FOR NOW...
SLUMP
ZUD

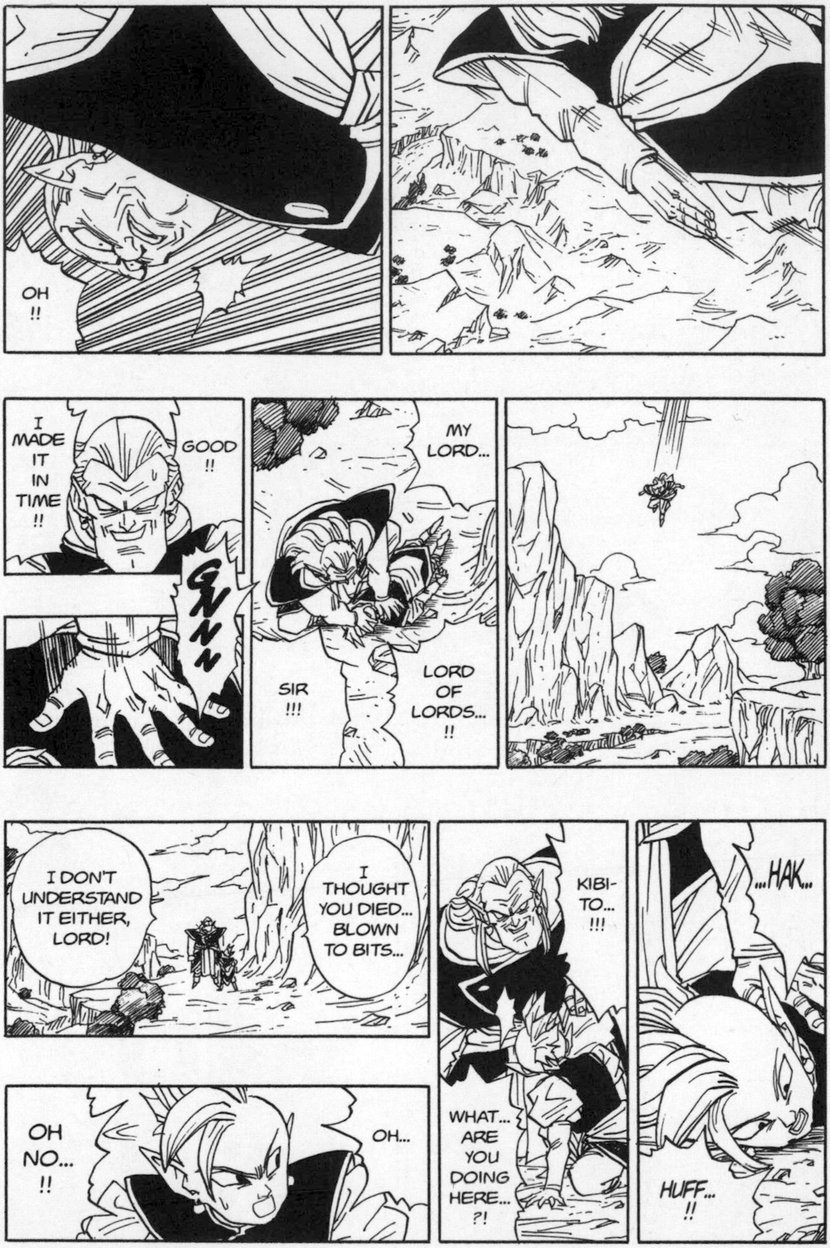
OH !!
MY LORD...
LORD OF LORDS... !!
SIR !!!
GOOD !!
I MADE IT IN TIME !!
GNNN
...HAK...
HUFF... !!
KIBI-TO... !!!
WHAT... ARE YOU DOING HERE... ?!
I THOUGHT YOU DIED... BLOWN TO BITS...
I DON'T UNDERSTAND IT EITHER, LORD!
OH...
OH NO... !!

READ THIS WAY

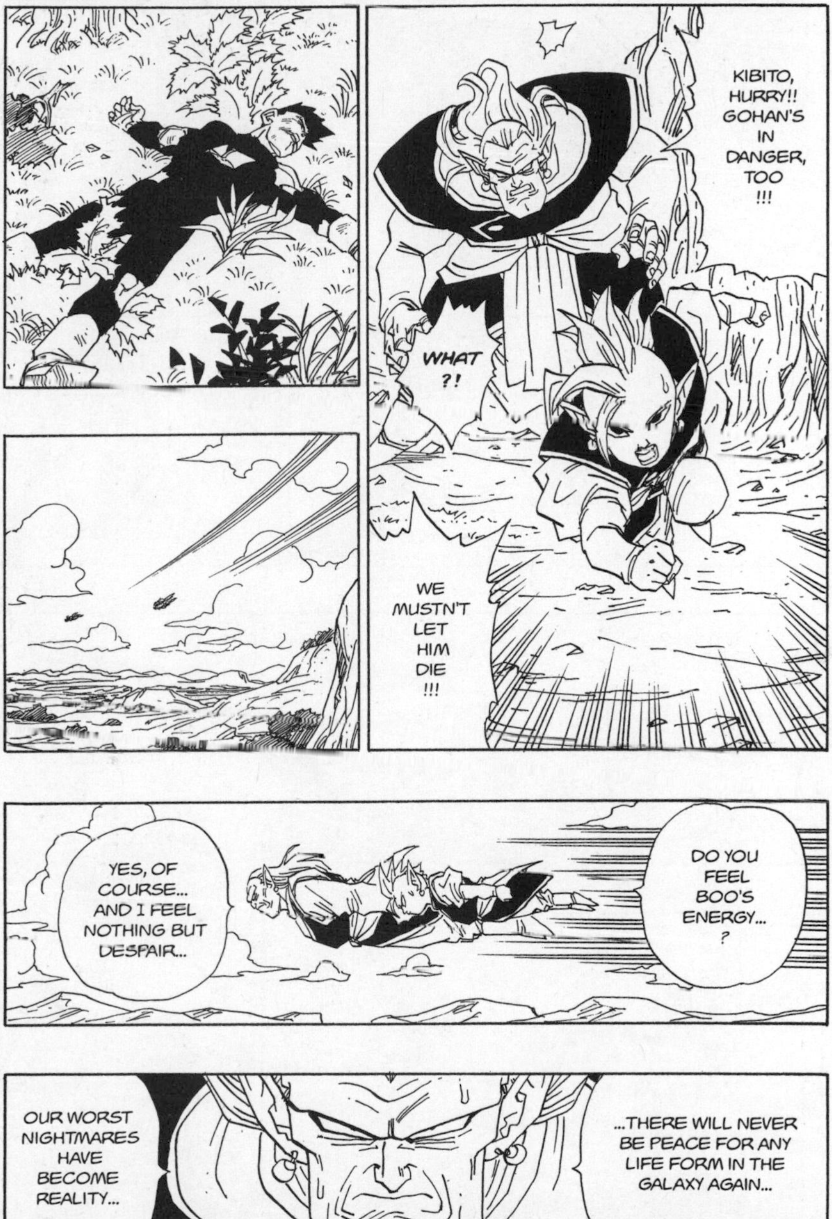
KIBITO, HURRY!! GOHAN'S IN DANGER, TOO!!!
WHAT?!
WE MUSTN'T LET HIM DIE!!!
DO YOU FEEL BOO'S ENERGY...?
YES, OF COURSE... AND I FEEL NOTHING BUT DESPAIR...
OUR WORST NIGHTMARES HAVE BECOME REALITY...
...THERE WILL NEVER BE PEACE FOR ANY LIFE FORM IN THE GALAXY AGAIN...

I CAN STILL SEE... A FAINT GLIMMER OF HOPE...

NO... DON'T SURRENDER TO DESPAIR...

...HIS POWER SURPASSES ALL IMAGINATION, AND MAY EVEN SURPASS BOO'S...

YES...

DOES THIS HAVE SOME- THING TO DO WITH SON GOHAN?

WHAT...?!

WHAT?! BUT HOW COULD THAT BE?!

YOU HAVEN'T SEEN WHAT THOSE THREE SAIYANS CAN DO...

OVER THERE!!

THERE HE IS!!

I FEEL HIM AROUND HERE...

146

KIBITO. LET'S TAKE HIM TO MY REALM FIRST.

YES... THIS WAS A CLOSE CALL...

HMM...

I'M SO GLAD!

NOT EVEN THE GREAT LORD OF THE WORLDS IS ALLOWED THERE!

Y-YOU'RE GOING TO LET A HUMAN BEING SET FOOT ON THAT SACRED GROUND?!

WHAT ?!

NOW HURRY— BEFORE HE DIES !!

THAT'S RIGHT.

VNNN

KAIKAI !!

YES SIR !

· · ·

147

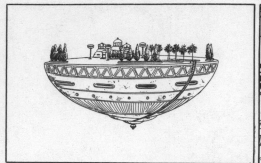

IF ONLY WE KNEW WHERE TEN-SHINHAN WAS TOO...

THEY DIDN'T WANT TO LEAVE THE PETS.

THEY TOLD ME TO JUST BRING THEM BACK TO LIFE LATER IF ANYTHING HAPPENS.

WHERE'RE YOUR PARENTS, BULMA?

...AND TRUNKS... AND VEGETA...?

SAY... WHERE ARE GOHAN AND GOTEN?

GOTEN AND TRUNKS ARE SAFE. BUT GOHAN AND VEGETA ARE DEAD.

WE HAVE TO TELL THEM SOONER OR LATER...

BOO KILLED THEM.

URK!

READ THIS WAY

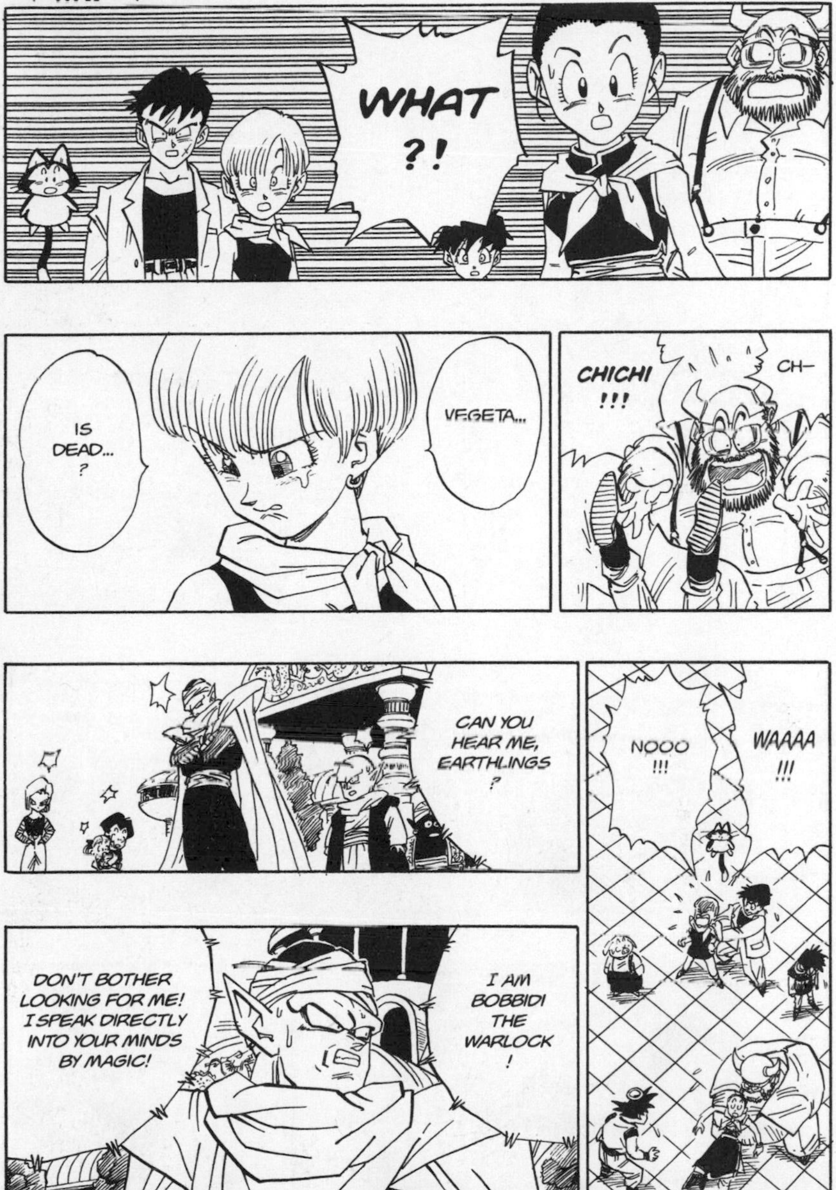
WHAT ?!
CH—
CHICHI !!!
VEGETA...
IS DEAD...?
WAAAA !!!
NOOO !!!
CAN YOU HEAR ME, EARTHLINGS?
I AM BOBBIDI THE WARLOCK!
DON'T BOTHER LOOKING FOR ME! I SPEAK DIRECTLY INTO YOUR MINDS BY MAGIC!

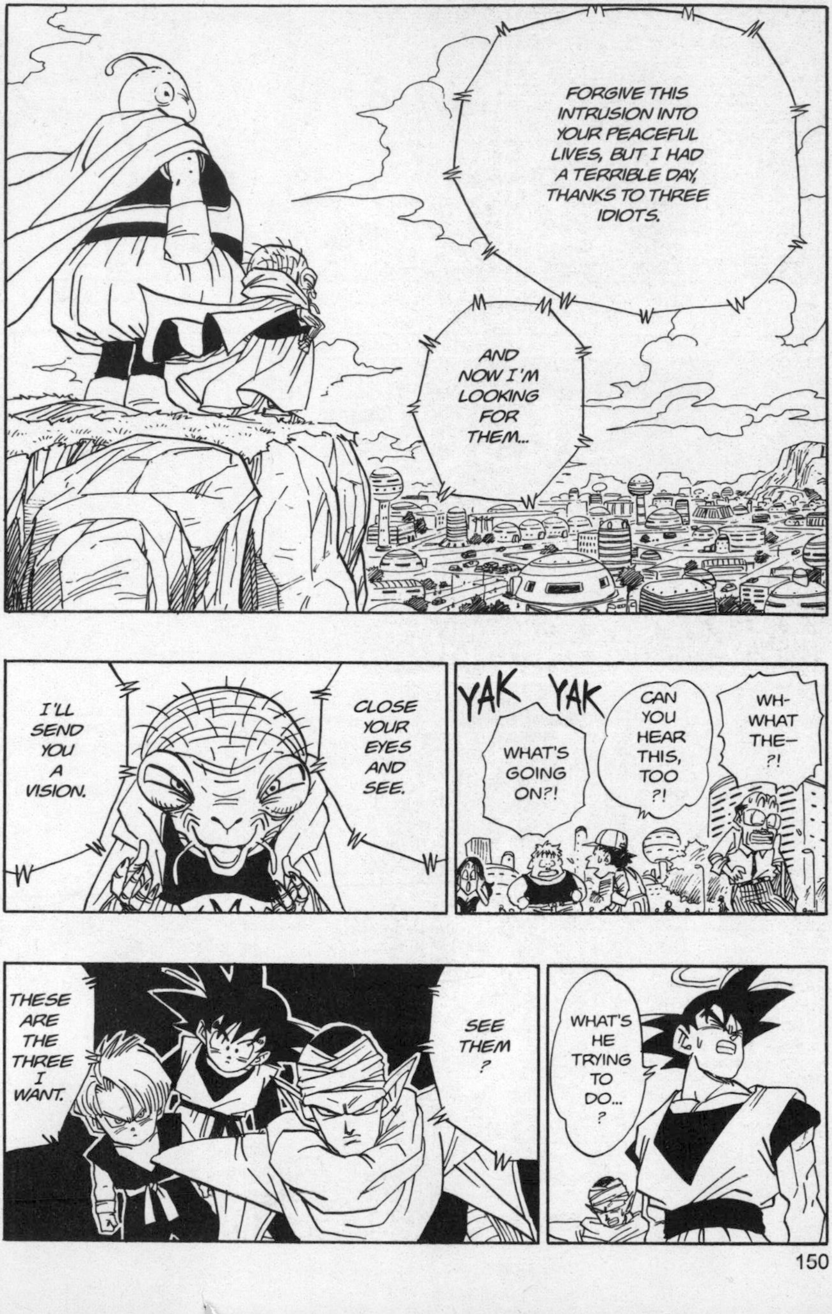
FORGIVE THIS INTRUSION INTO YOUR PEACEFUL LIVES, BUT I HAD A TERRIBLE DAY, THANKS TO THREE IDIOTS.
AND NOW I'M LOOKING FOR THEM...
WH- WHAT THE-?!
CAN YOU HEAR THIS, TOO?!
YAK YAK
WHAT'S GOING ON?!
CLOSE YOUR EYES AND SEE.
I'LL SEND YOU A VISION.
WHAT'S HE TRYING TO DO...?
SEE THEM?
THESE ARE THE THREE I WANT.

READ THIS WAY

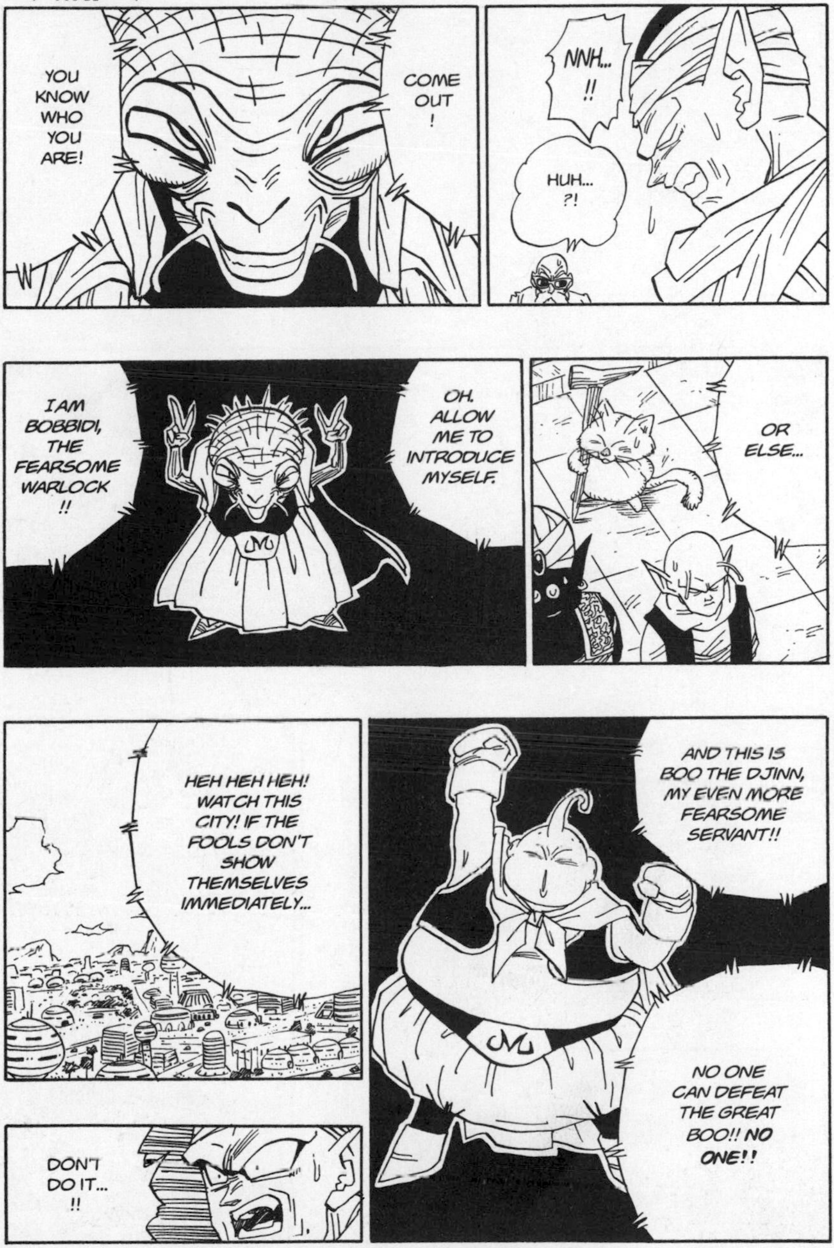
NNH... !!
HUH... ?!
COME OUT !
YOU KNOW WHO YOU ARE!
OR ELSE...
OH. ALLOW ME TO INTRODUCE MYSELF.
I AM BOBBIDI, THE FEARSOME WARLOCK !!
AND THIS IS BOO THE DJINN, MY EVEN MORE FEARSOME SERVANT!!
NO ONE CAN DEFEAT THE GREAT BOO!! NO ONE!!
HEH HEH HEH! WATCH THIS CITY! IF THE FOOLS DON'T SHOW THEMSELVES IMMEDIATELY...
DON'T DO IT... !!

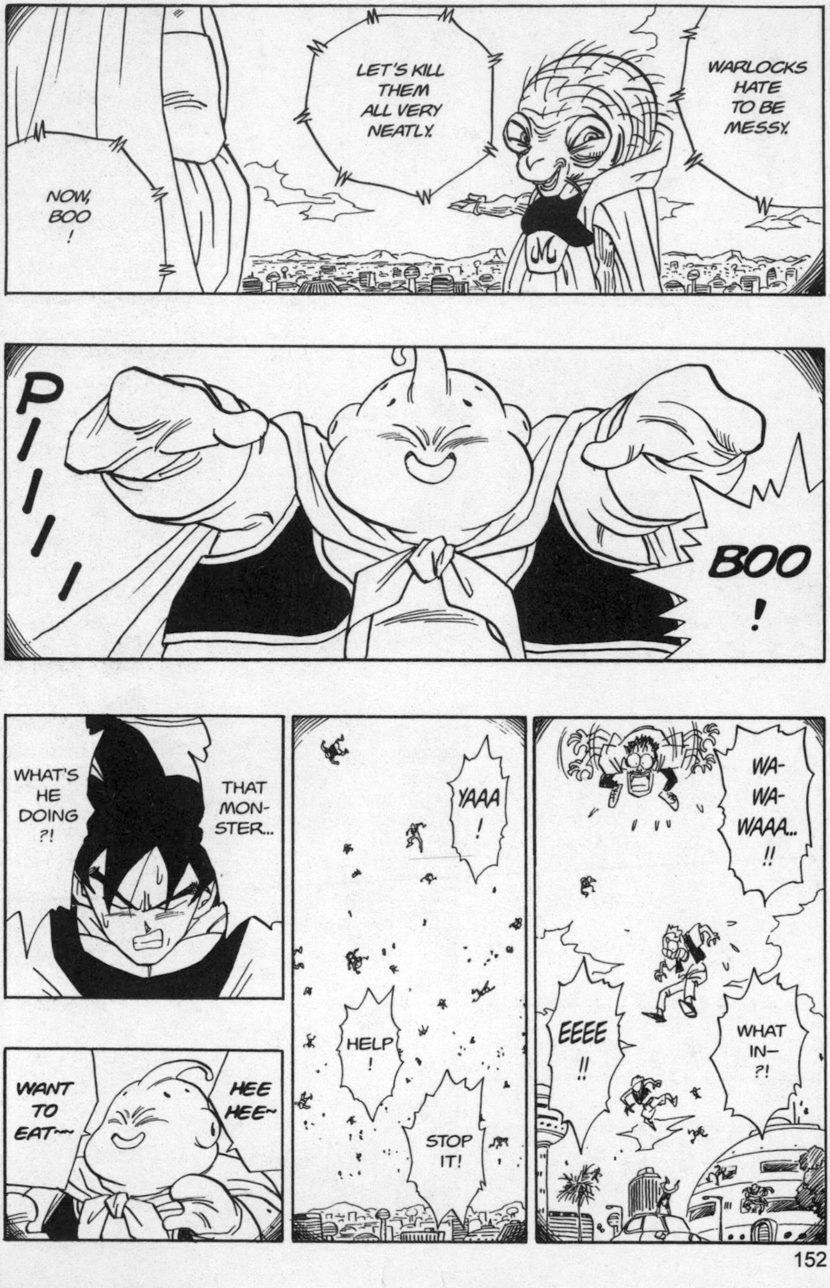
WARLOCKS HATE TO BE MESSY.
LET'S KILL THEM ALL VERY NEATLY.
NOW, BOO!
PIIII
BOO!
WA-WA-WAAA...!!
WHAT IN—?!
EEEE!!
YAAA!
HELP!
STOP IT!
THAT MONSTER...
WHAT'S HE DOING?!
HEE HEE~
WANT TO EAT~~

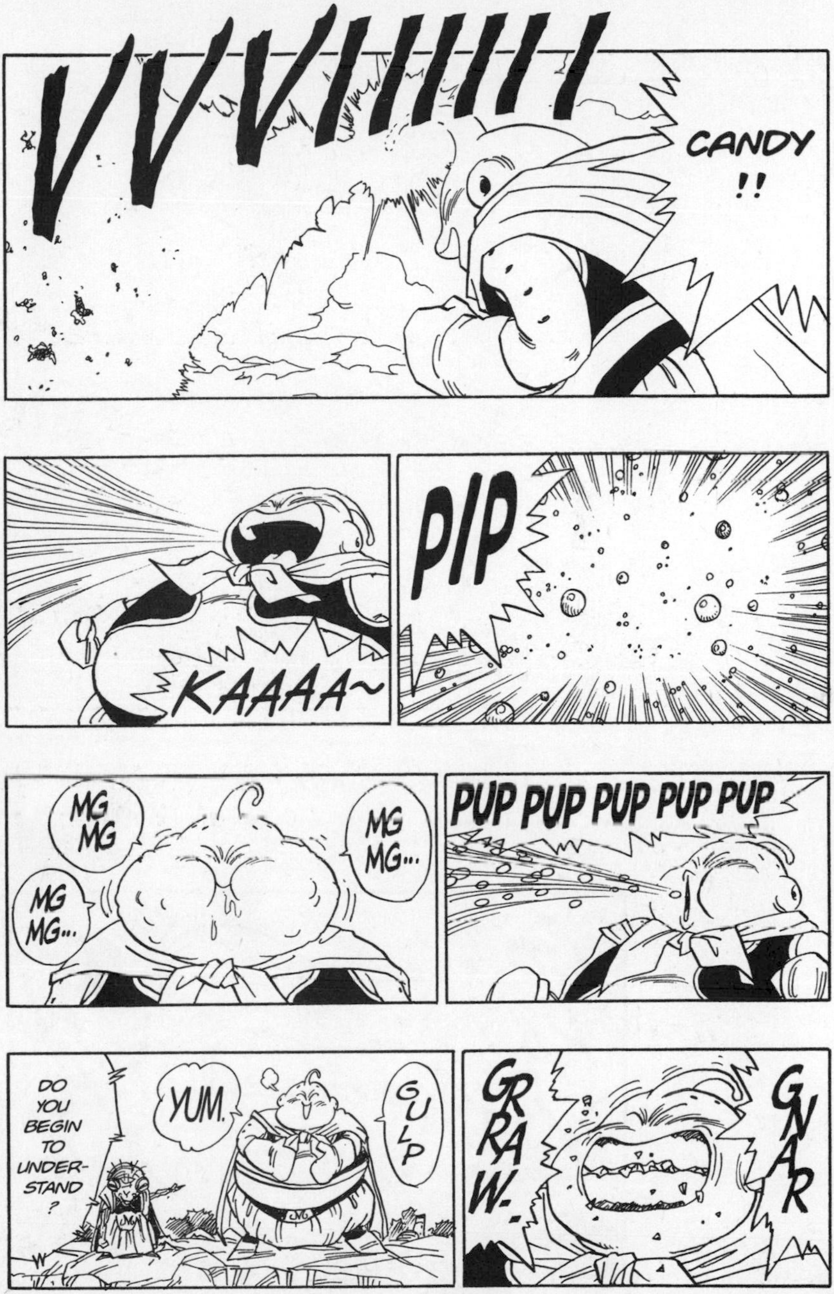

VVIIIIII
CANDY !!
PIP
KAAAA~
PUP PUP PUP PUP PUP
MG MG...
MG MG
MG MG...
GNAR
GRRAW-
GULP
YUM.
DO YOU BEGIN TO UNDER-STAND?

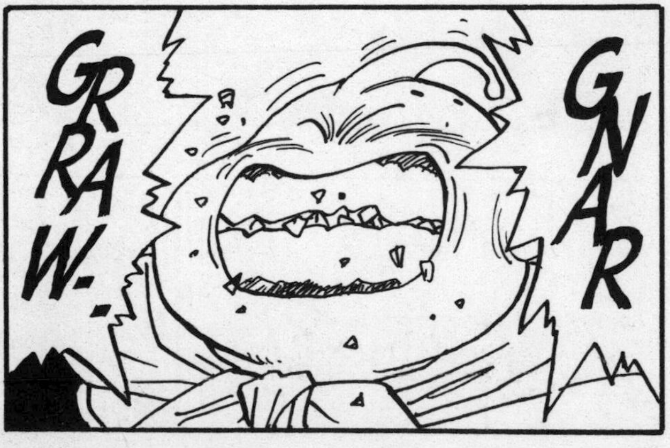
GNAR
GRRAW--

DBZ:277 • A Time of Trial

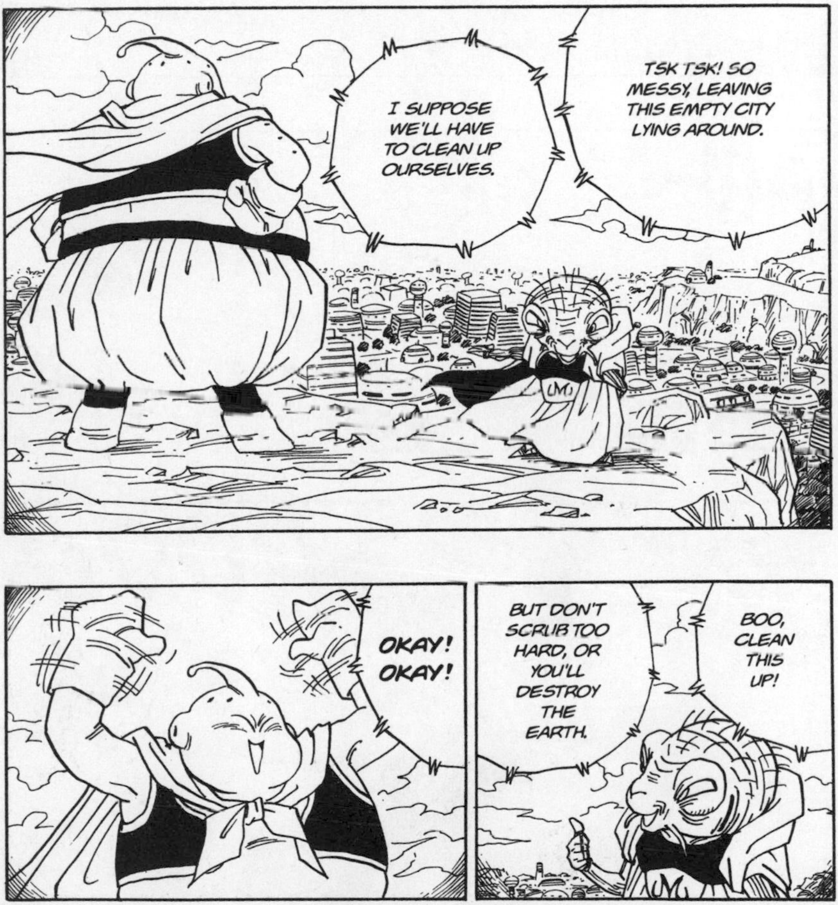

TSK TSK! SO MESSY, LEAVING THIS EMPTY CITY LYING AROUND.
I SUPPOSE WE'LL HAVE TO CLEAN UP OURSELVES.
BOO, CLEAN THIS UP!
BUT DON'T SCRUB TOO HARD, OR YOU'LL DESTROY THE EARTH.
OKAY! OKAY!

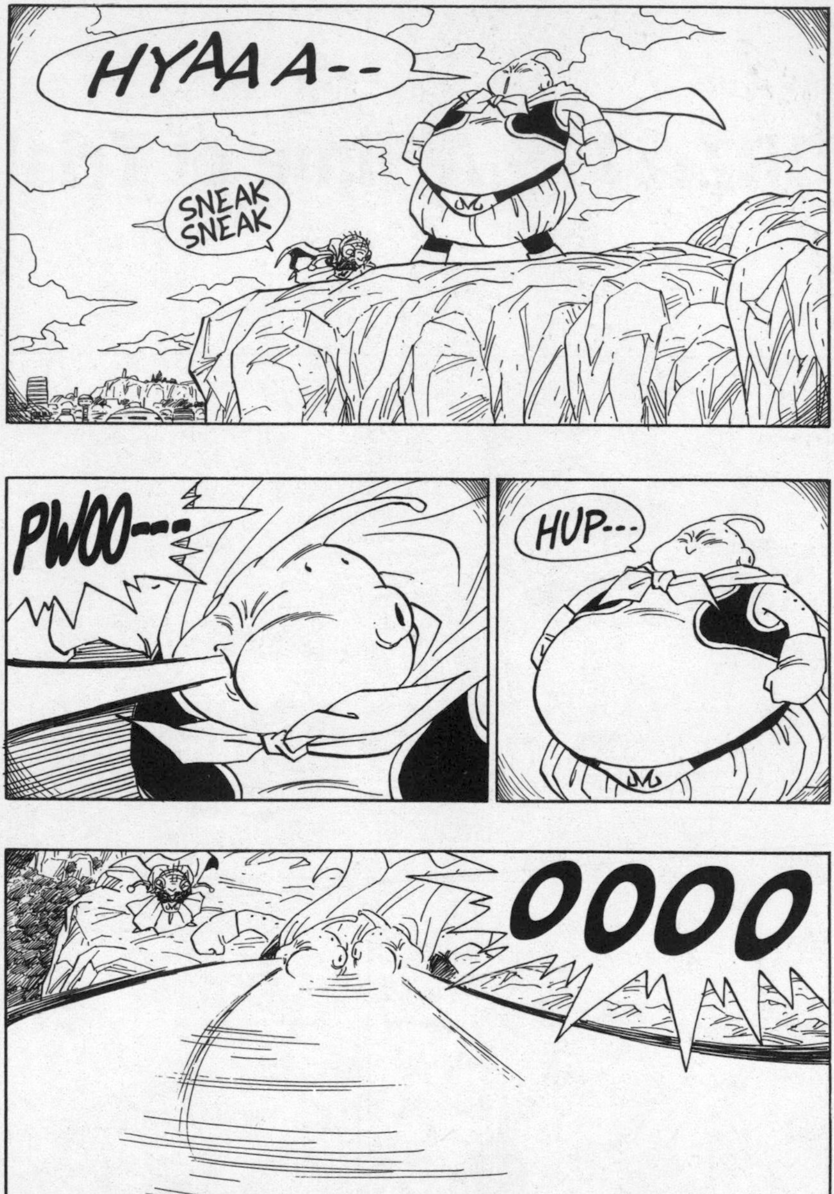

HYAAA--
SNEAK SNEAK
HUP...
PWOO---
OOOO

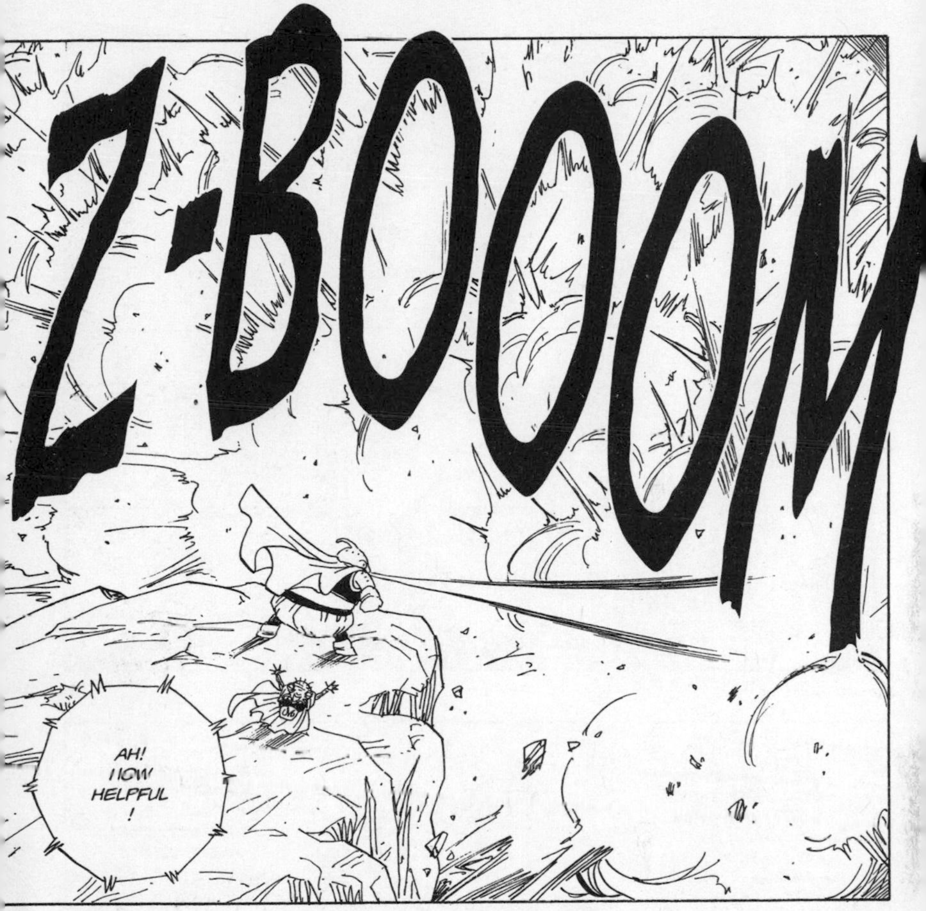
Z-BOOOM
AH! HOW HELPFUL!

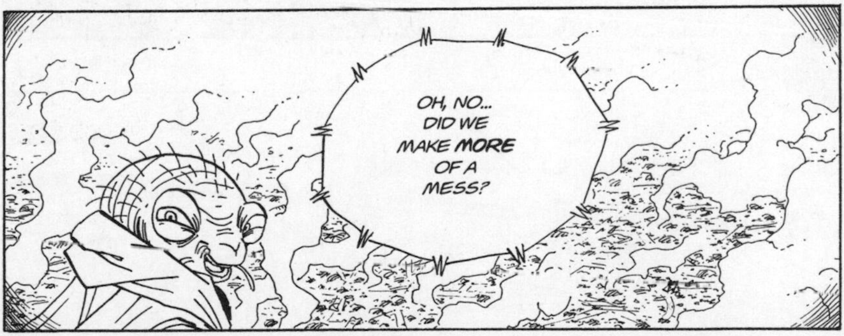
OH, NO... DID WE MAKE MORE OF A MESS?

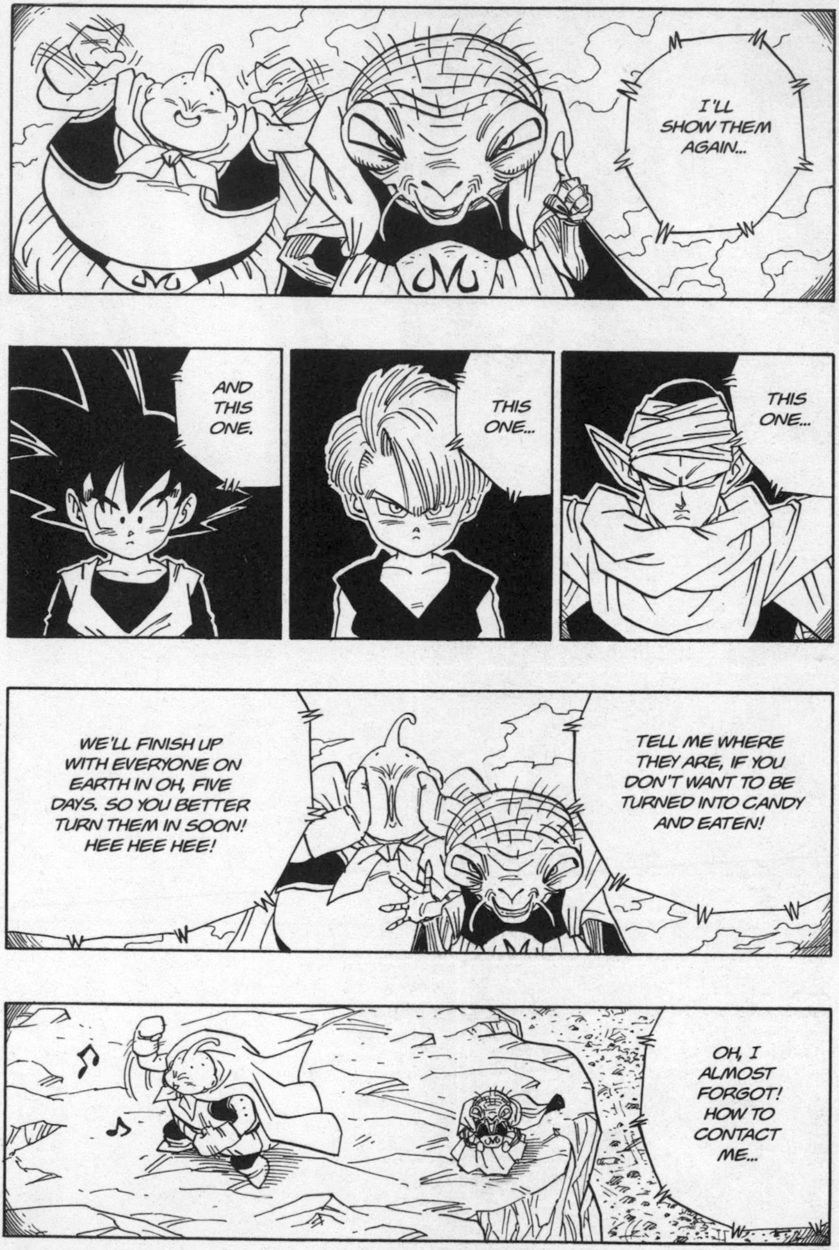
I'LL SHOW THEM AGAIN...
THIS ONE...
THIS ONE...
AND THIS ONE.
TELL ME WHERE THEY ARE, IF YOU DON'T WANT TO BE TURNED INTO CANDY AND EATEN!
WE'LL FINISH UP WITH EVERYONE ON EARTH IN OH, FIVE DAYS. SO YOU BETTER TURN THEM IN SOON! HEE HEE HEE!
OH, I ALMOST FORGOT! HOW TO CONTACT ME...

READ THIS WAY

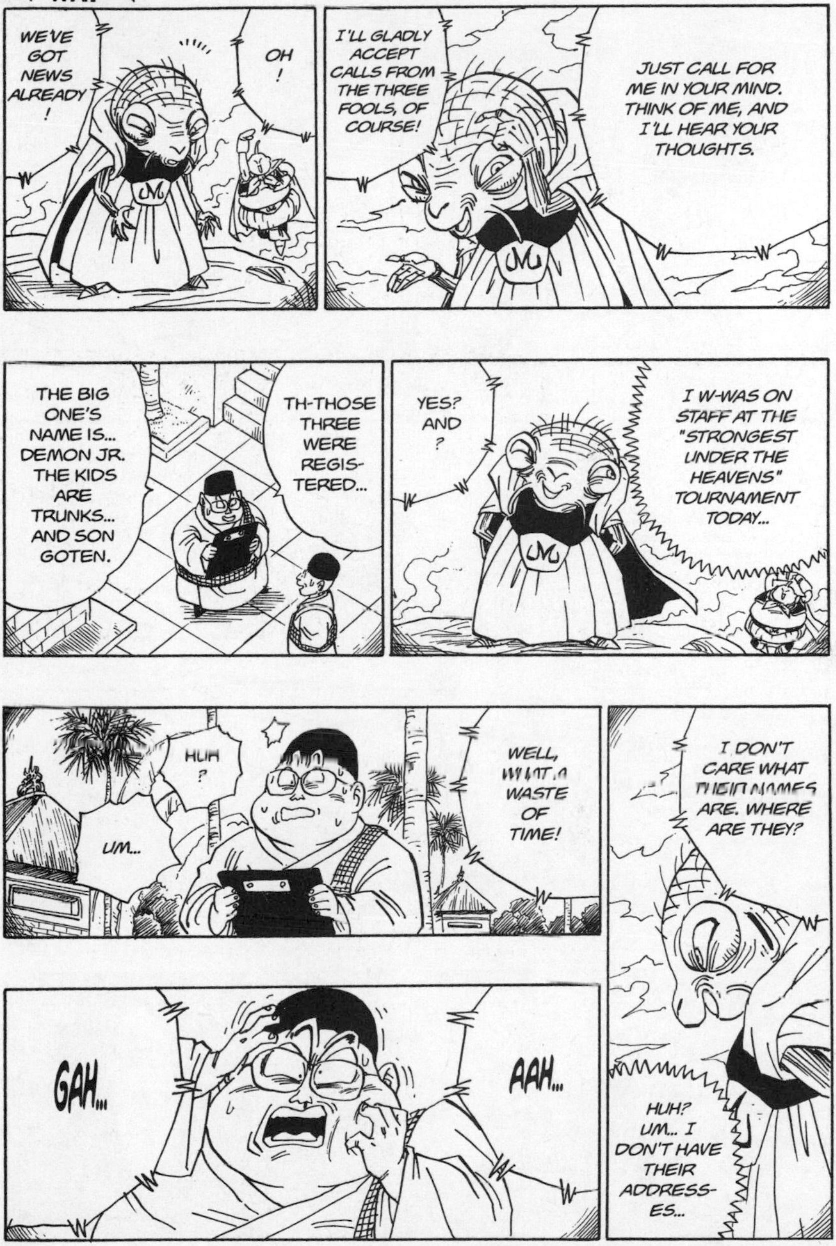
JUST CALL FOR ME IN YOUR MIND. THINK OF ME, AND I'LL HEAR YOUR THOUGHTS.
I'LL GLADLY ACCEPT CALLS FROM THE THREE FOOLS, OF COURSE!
OH!
WE'VE GOT NEWS ALREADY!
I W-WAS ON STAFF AT THE "STRONGEST UNDER THE HEAVENS" TOURNAMENT TODAY...
YES? AND?
TH-THOSE THREE WERE REGIS-TERED...
THE BIG ONE'S NAME IS... DEMON JR. THE KIDS ARE TRUNKS... AND SON GOTEN.
I DON'T CARE WHAT THEIR NAMES ARE. WHERE ARE THEY?
HUH? UM... I DON'T HAVE THEIR ADDRESS-ES...
WELL, WHAT A WASTE OF TIME!
HUH?
UM...
AAH...
GAH...

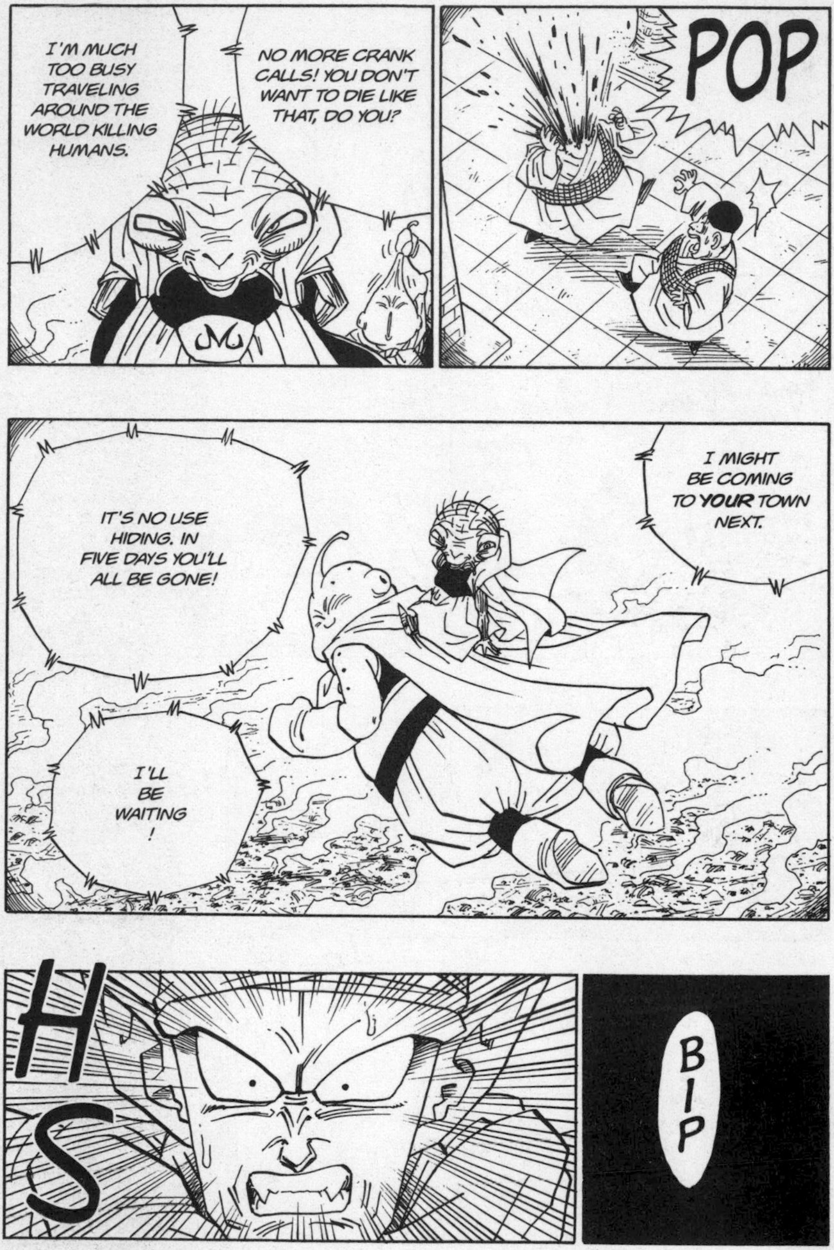
POP
NO MORE CRANK CALLS! YOU DON'T WANT TO DIE LIKE THAT, DO YOU?
I'M MUCH TOO BUSY TRAVELING AROUND THE WORLD KILLING HUMANS.
I MIGHT BE COMING TO **YOUR** TOWN NEXT.
IT'S NO USE HIDING. IN FIVE DAYS YOU'LL ALL BE GONE!
I'LL BE WAITING!
BIP
HS

READ THIS WAY

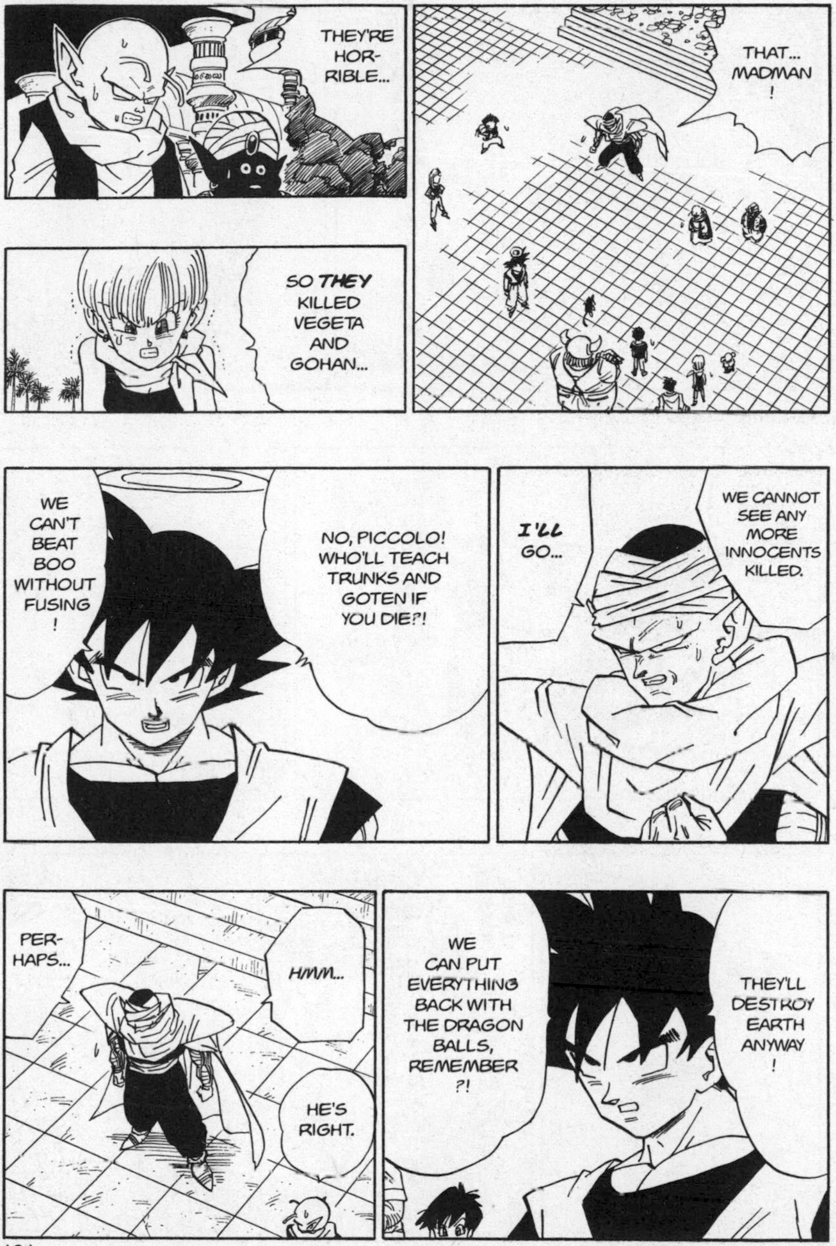
THAT... MADMAN !
THEY'RE HOR-RIBLE...
SO *THEY* KILLED VEGETA AND GOHAN...
WE CANNOT SEE ANY MORE INNOCENTS KILLED.
I'LL GO...
NO, PICCOLO! WHO'LL TEACH TRUNKS AND GOTEN IF YOU DIE?!
WE CAN'T BEAT BOO WITHOUT FUSING !
THEY'LL DESTROY EARTH ANYWAY !
WE CAN PUT EVERYTHING BACK WITH THE DRAGON BALLS, REMEMBER ?!
HMM...
PER-HAPS...
HE'S RIGHT.

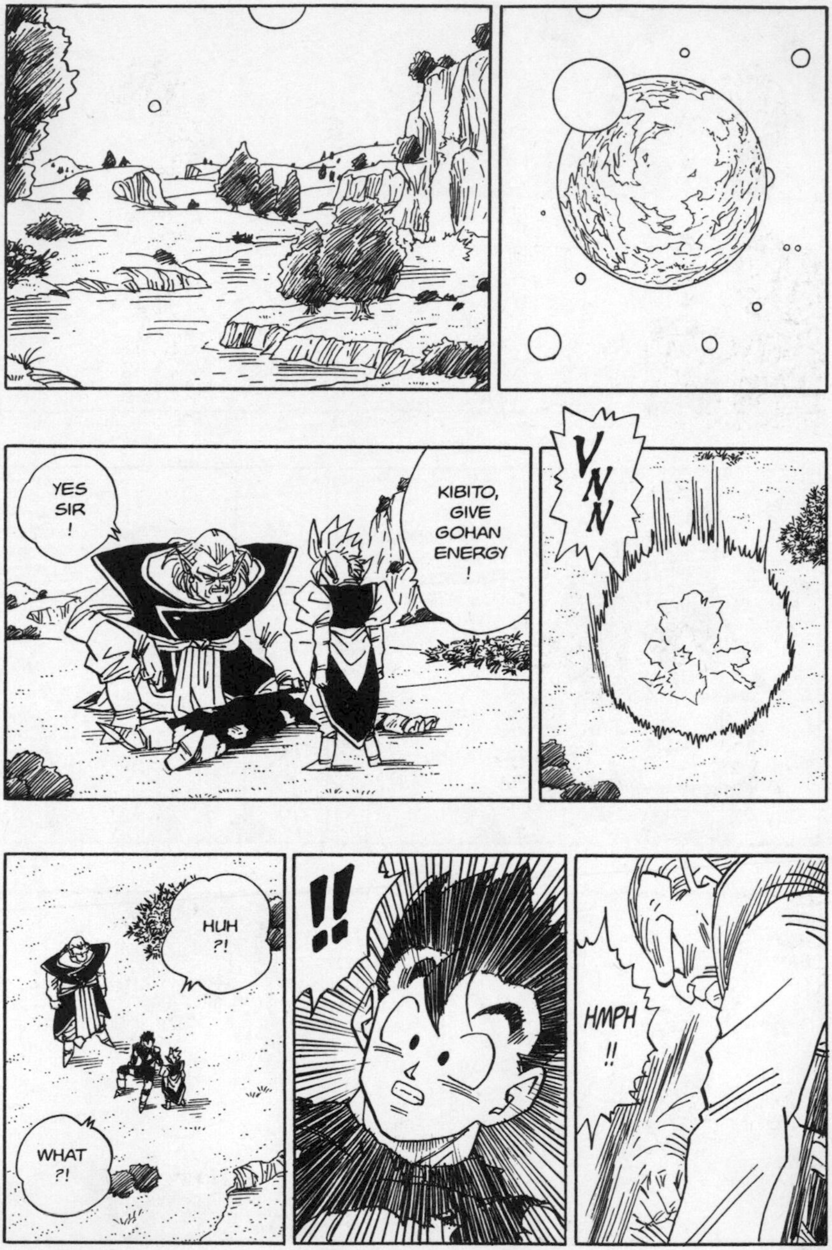
VNN
KIBITO, GIVE GOHAN ENERGY!
YES SIR!
HMPH!!
!!
HUH?!
WHAT?!

READ THIS WAY

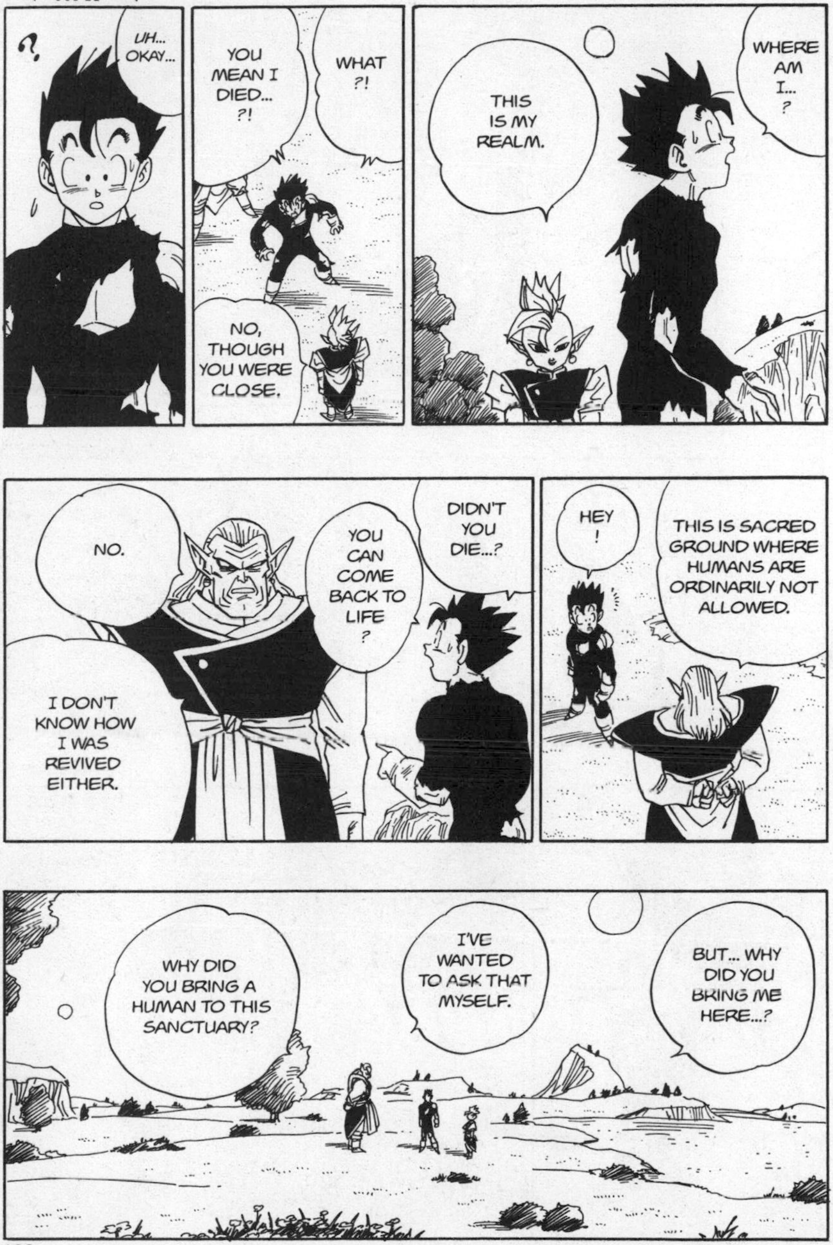

WHERE AM I...?
THIS IS MY REALM.
WHAT?!
YOU MEAN I DIED...?!
NO, THOUGH YOU WERE CLOSE.
UH... OKAY...
THIS IS SACRED GROUND WHERE HUMANS ARE ORDINARILY NOT ALLOWED.
HEY!
DIDN'T YOU DIE...?
YOU CAN COME BACK TO LIFE?
NO.
I DON'T KNOW HOW I WAS REVIVED EITHER.
BUT... WHY DID YOU BRING ME HERE...?
I'VE WANTED TO ASK THAT MYSELF.
WHY DID YOU BRING A HUMAN TO THIS SANCTUARY?

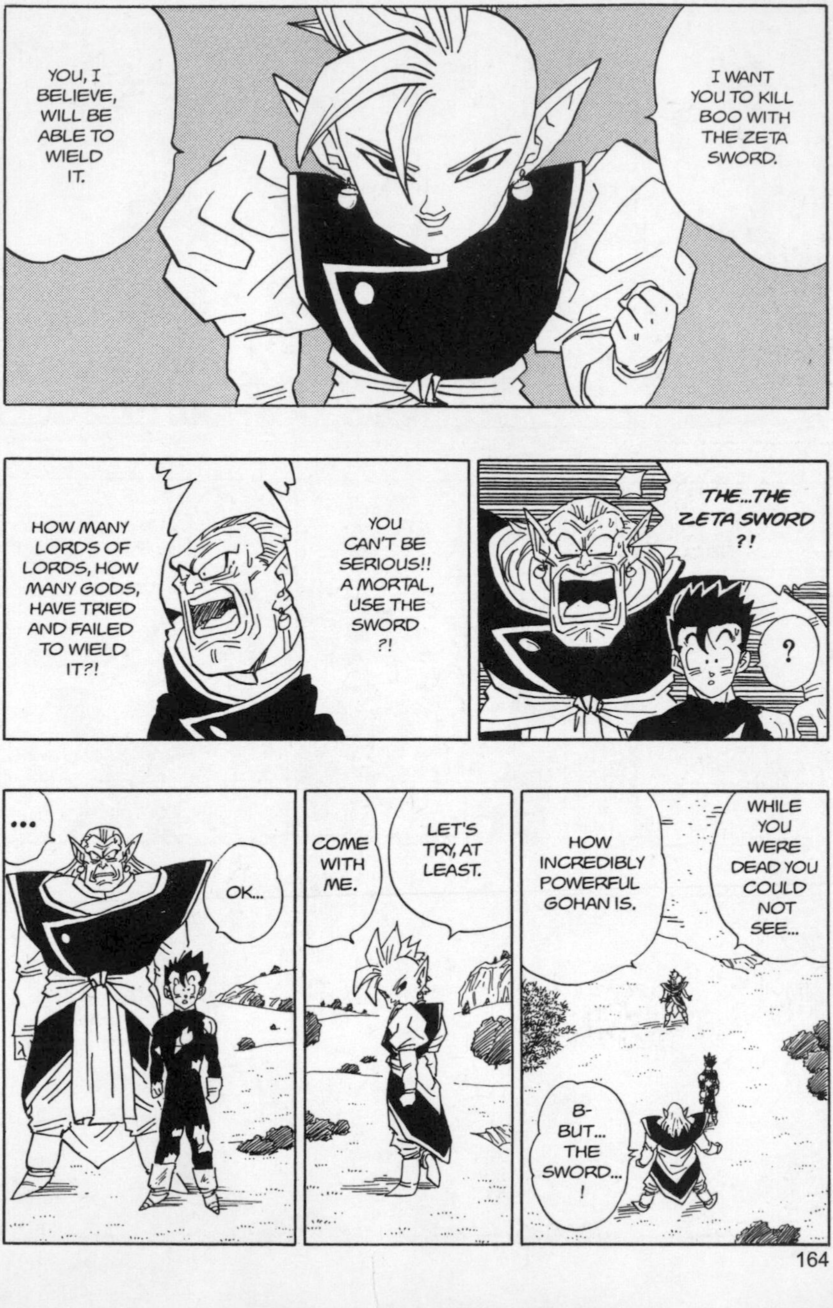
I WANT YOU TO KILL BOO WITH THE ZETA SWORD.
YOU, I BELIEVE, WILL BE ABLE TO WIELD IT.
THE...THE ZETA SWORD ?!
?
YOU CAN'T BE SERIOUS!! A MORTAL, USE THE SWORD ?!
HOW MANY LORDS OF LORDS, HOW MANY GODS, HAVE TRIED AND FAILED TO WIELD IT?!
WHILE YOU WERE DEAD YOU COULD NOT SEE...
HOW INCREDIBLY POWERFUL GOHAN IS.
B-BUT... THE SWORD... !
LET'S TRY, AT LEAST.
COME WITH ME.
OK...
...

READ THIS WAY

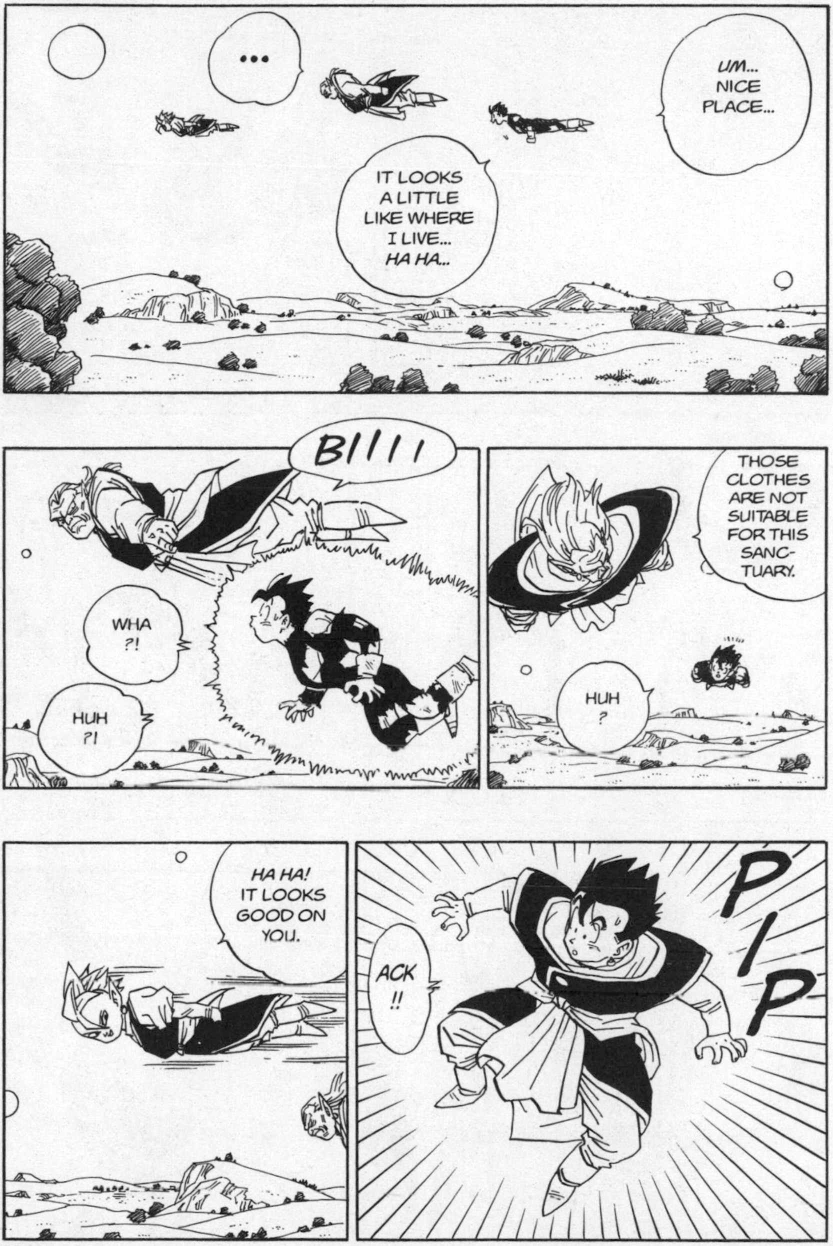

UM... NICE PLACE...
...
IT LOOKS A LITTLE LIKE WHERE I LIVE... HA HA...
THOSE CLOTHES ARE NOT SUITABLE FOR THIS SANC- TUARY.
HUH ?
BI///
WHA ?!
HUH ?!
PIP
ACK !!
HA HA! IT LOOKS GOOD ON YOU.

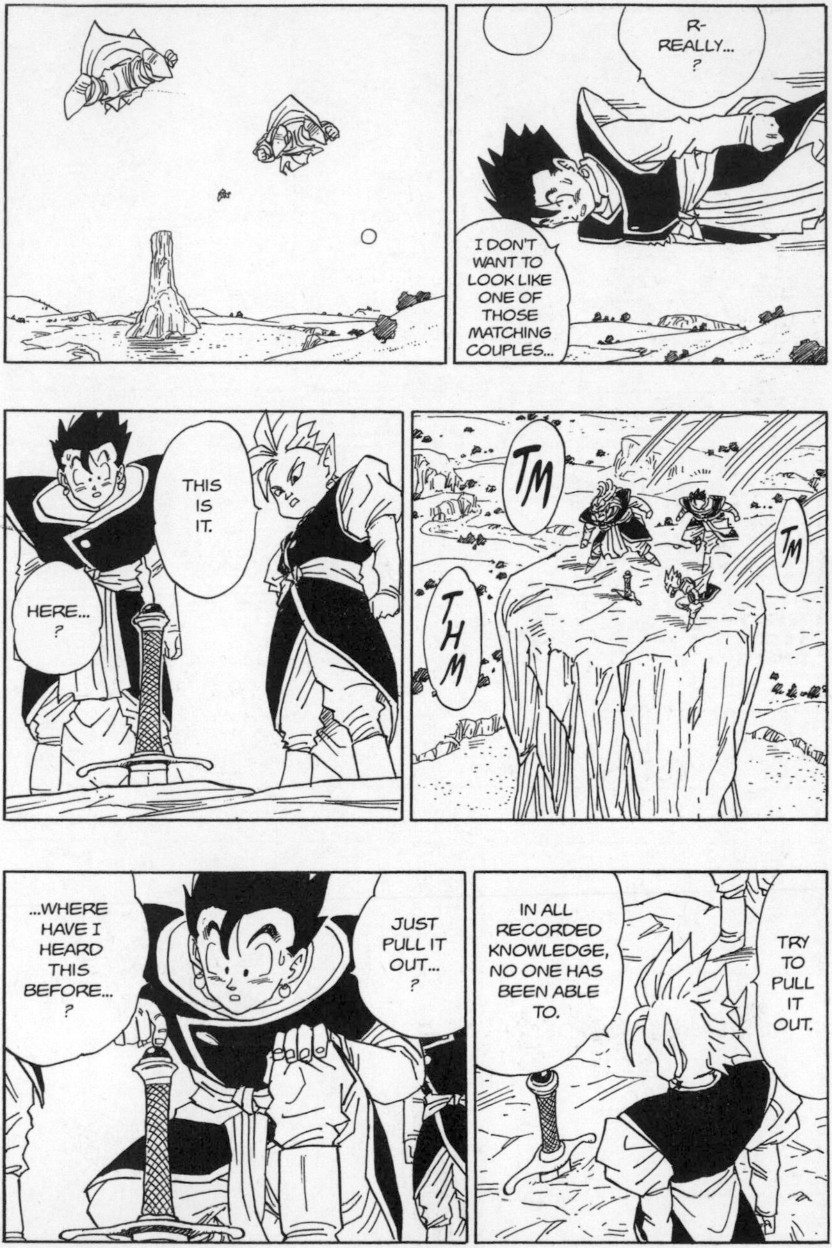
R- REALLY...?
I DON'T WANT TO LOOK LIKE ONE OF THOSE MATCHING COUPLES...
TM
TM
THM
THIS IS IT.
HERE...?
TRY TO PULL IT OUT.
IN ALL RECORDED KNOWLEDGE, NO ONE HAS BEEN ABLE TO.
JUST PULL IT OUT...?
...WHERE HAVE I HEARD THIS BEFORE...?

READ THIS WAY

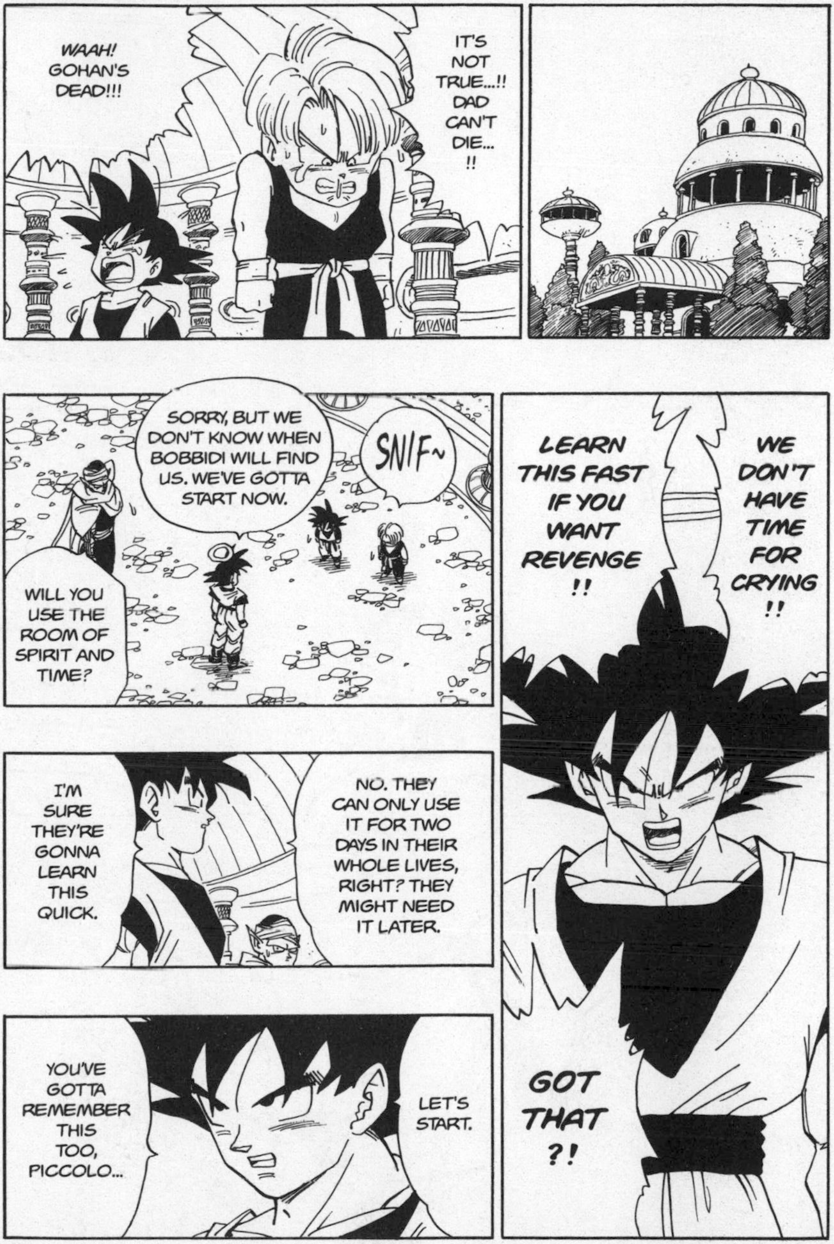

IT'S NOT TRUE...!! DAD CAN'T DIE... !!
WAAH! GOHAN'S DEAD!!!
WE DON'T HAVE TIME FOR CRYING!!
LEARN THIS FAST IF YOU WANT REVENGE!!
GOT THAT?!
SNIF~
SORRY, BUT WE DON'T KNOW WHEN BOBBIDI WILL FIND US. WE'VE GOTTA START NOW.
WILL YOU USE THE ROOM OF SPIRIT AND TIME?
NO. THEY CAN ONLY USE IT FOR TWO DAYS IN THEIR WHOLE LIVES, RIGHT? THEY MIGHT NEED IT LATER.
I'M SURE THEY'RE GONNA LEARN THIS QUICK.
LET'S START.
YOU'VE GOTTA REMEMBER THIS TOO, PICCOLO...

DBZ:278 • The Zeta Sword

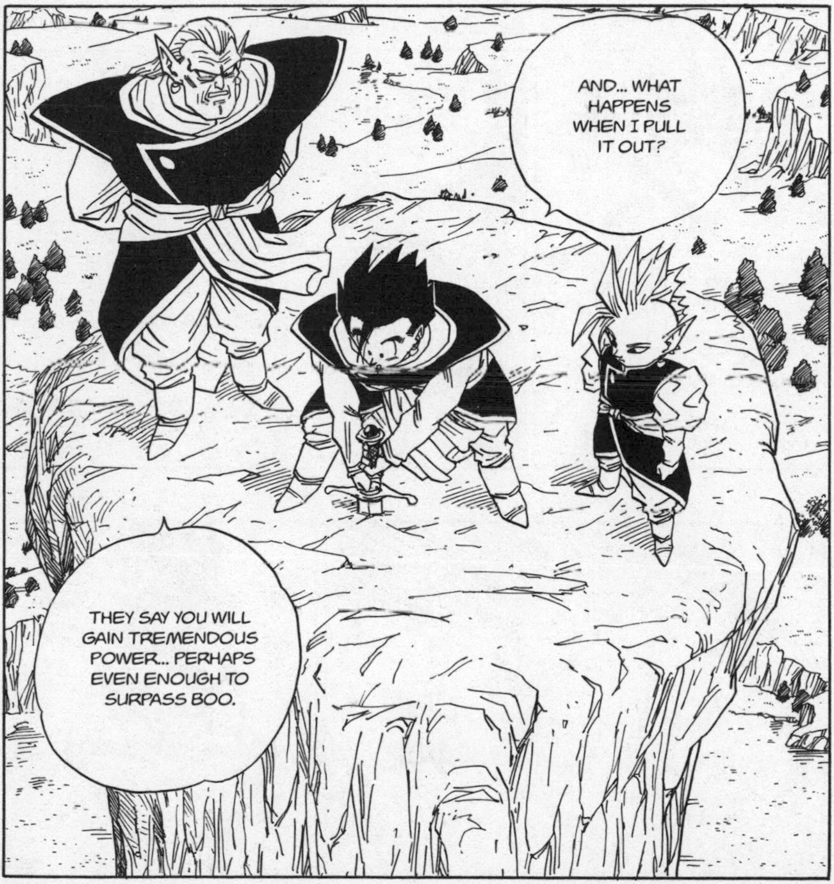
AND... WHAT HAPPENS WHEN I PULL IT OUT?
THEY SAY YOU WILL GAIN TREMENDOUS POWER... PERHAPS EVEN ENOUGH TO SURPASS BOO.

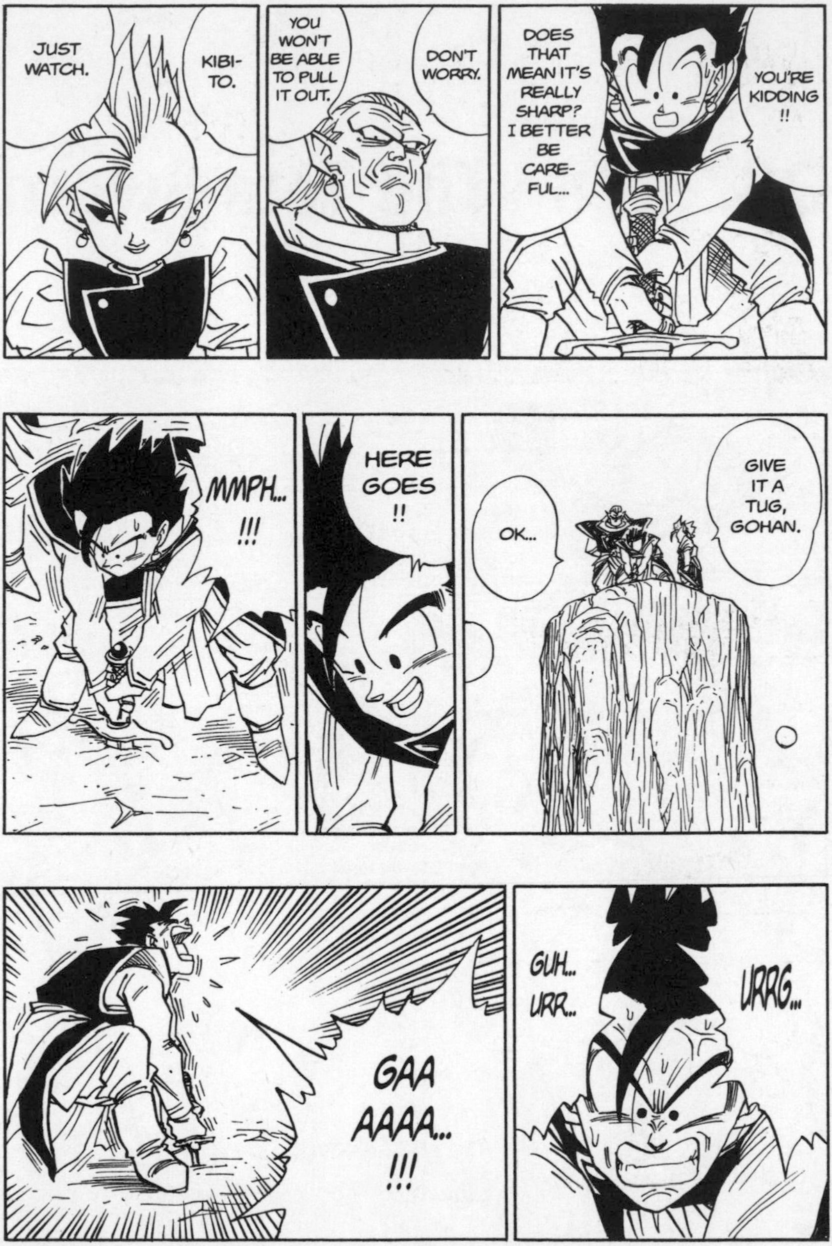
YOU'RE KIDDING!!
DOES THAT MEAN IT'S REALLY SHARP? I BETTER BE CAREFUL...
DON'T WORRY.
YOU WON'T BE ABLE TO PULL IT OUT.
KIBITO.
JUST WATCH.
GIVE IT A TUG, GOHAN.
OK...
HERE GOES!!
MMPH...!!!
URRG...
GUH... URR...
GAA AAAA...!!!

READ THIS WAY

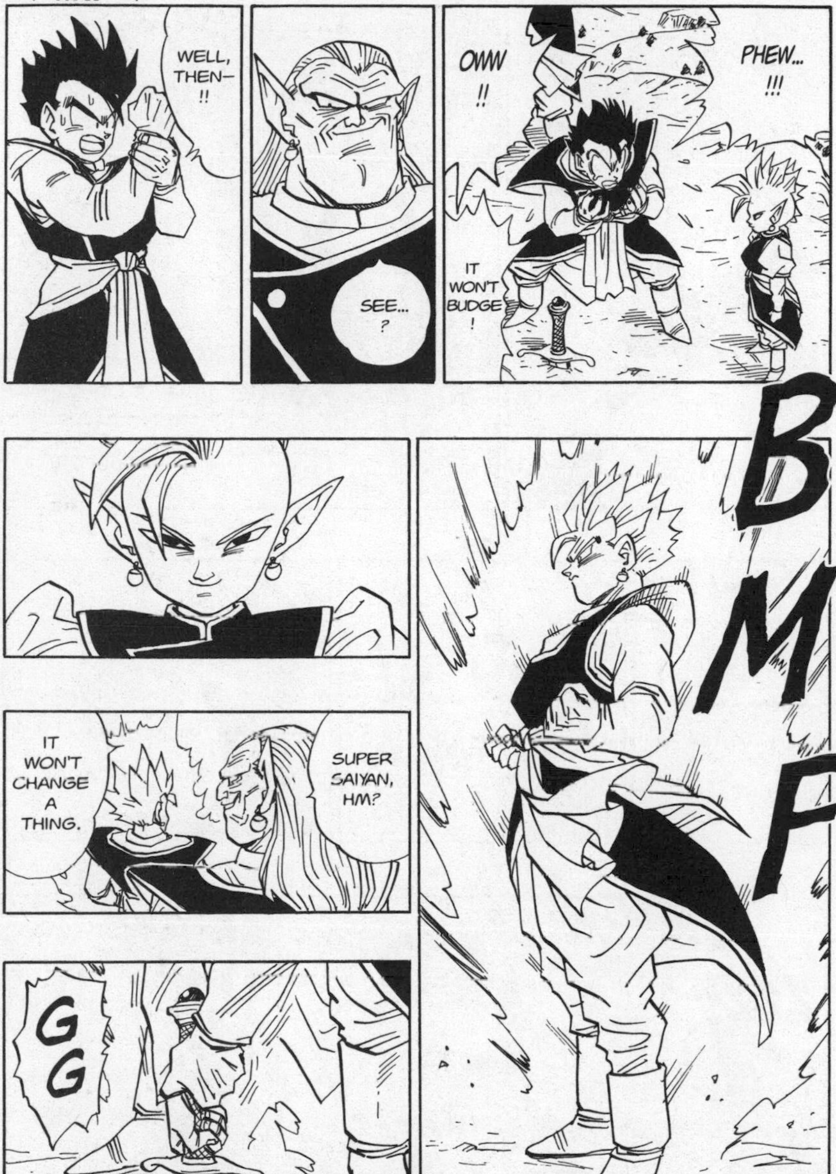

PHEW... !!!
OWW !!
IT WON'T BUDGE !
SEE... ?
WELL, THEN— !!
BMF
SUPER SAIYAN, HM?
IT WON'T CHANGE A THING.
GG

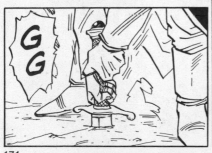

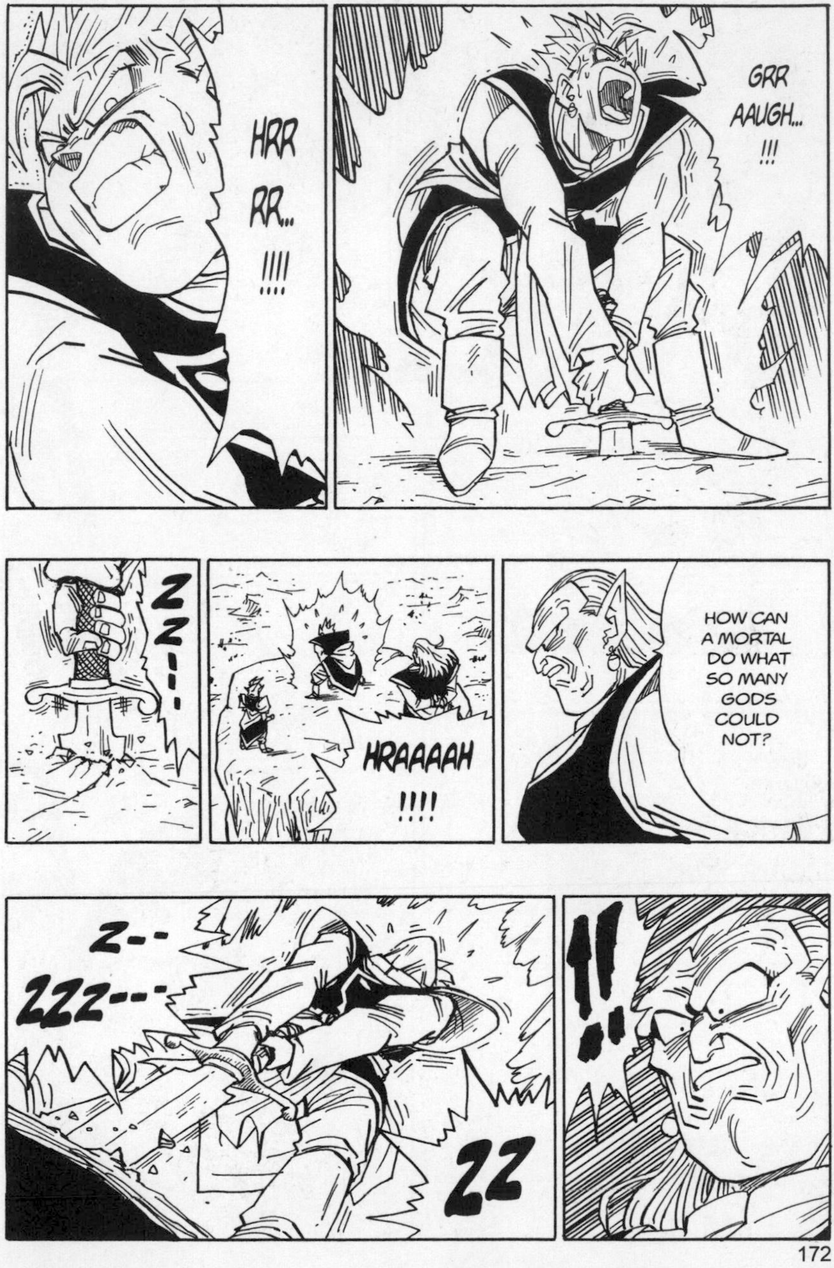
GRR AAUGH... !!!
HRR RR... !!!!
HOW CAN A MORTAL DO WHAT SO MANY GODS COULD NOT?
HRAAAAH !!!!
ZZ!!
!!
Z--
ZZZ---
ZZ

READ THIS WAY

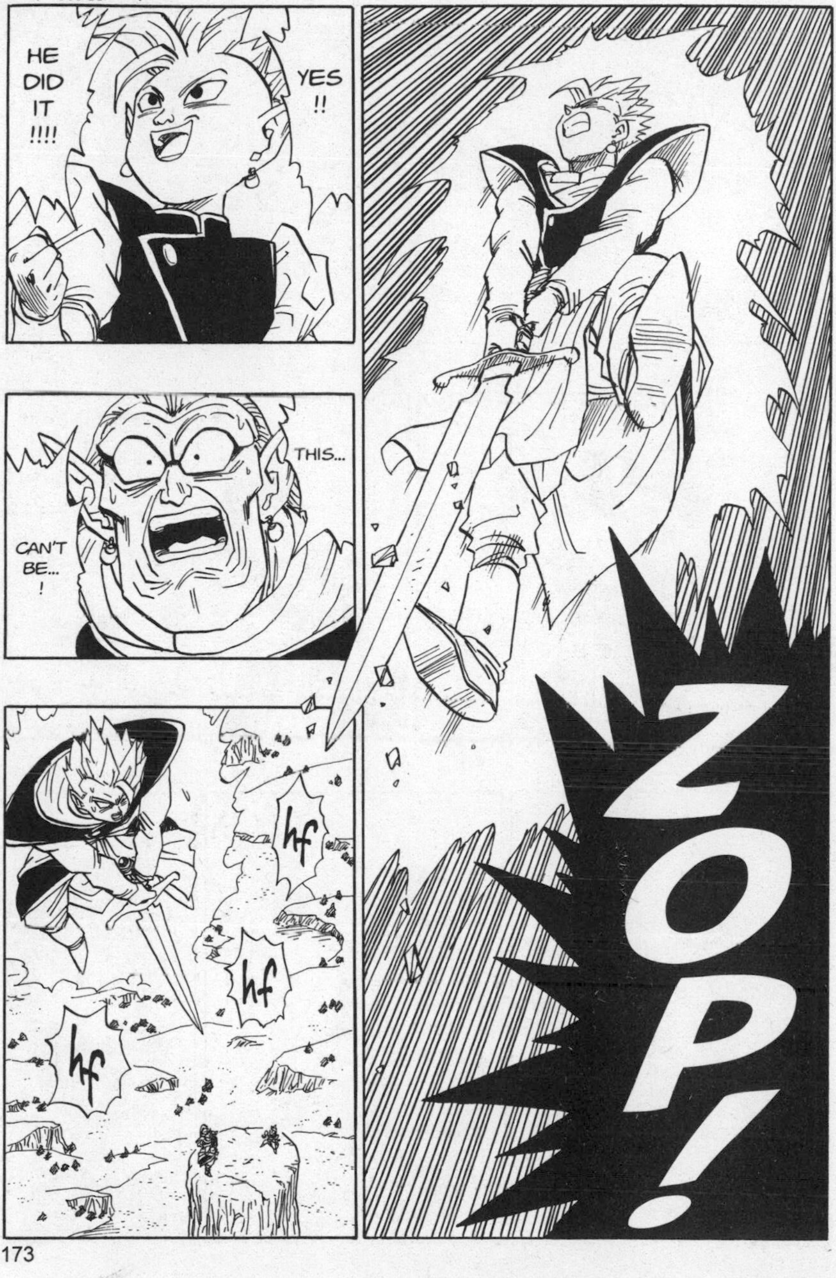
ZOP!
YES!!
HE DID IT!!!!
THIS...
CAN'T BE...!
hf
hf
hf

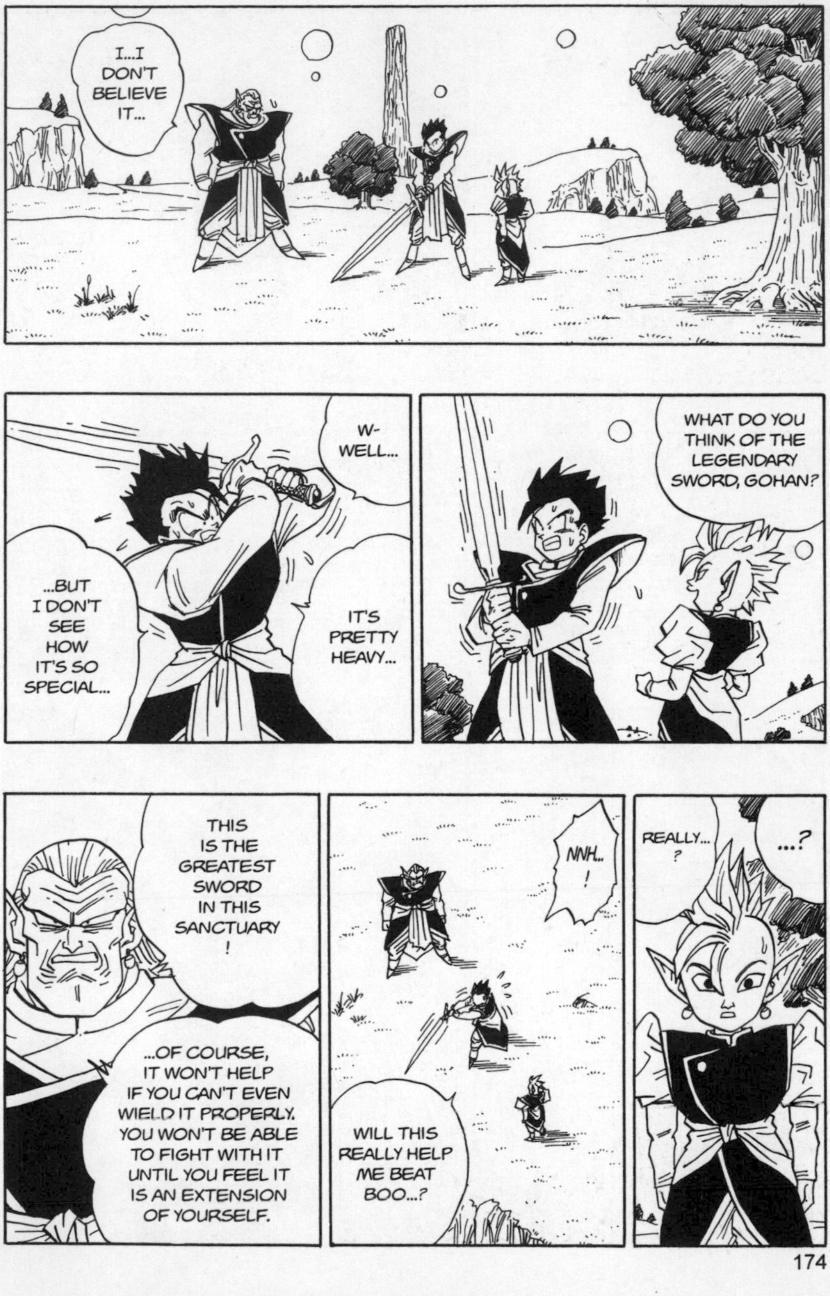
I...I DON'T BELIEVE IT...
WHAT DO YOU THINK OF THE LEGENDARY SWORD, GOHAN?
W-WELL...
IT'S PRETTY HEAVY...
...BUT I DON'T SEE HOW IT'S SO SPECIAL...
...?
REALLY...?
NNH...!
WILL THIS REALLY HELP ME BEAT BOO...?
THIS IS THE GREATEST SWORD IN THIS SANCTUARY!
...OF COURSE, IT WON'T HELP IF YOU CAN'T EVEN WIELD IT PROPERLY. YOU WON'T BE ABLE TO FIGHT WITH IT UNTIL YOU FEEL IT IS AN EXTENSION OF YOURSELF.

READ THIS WAY

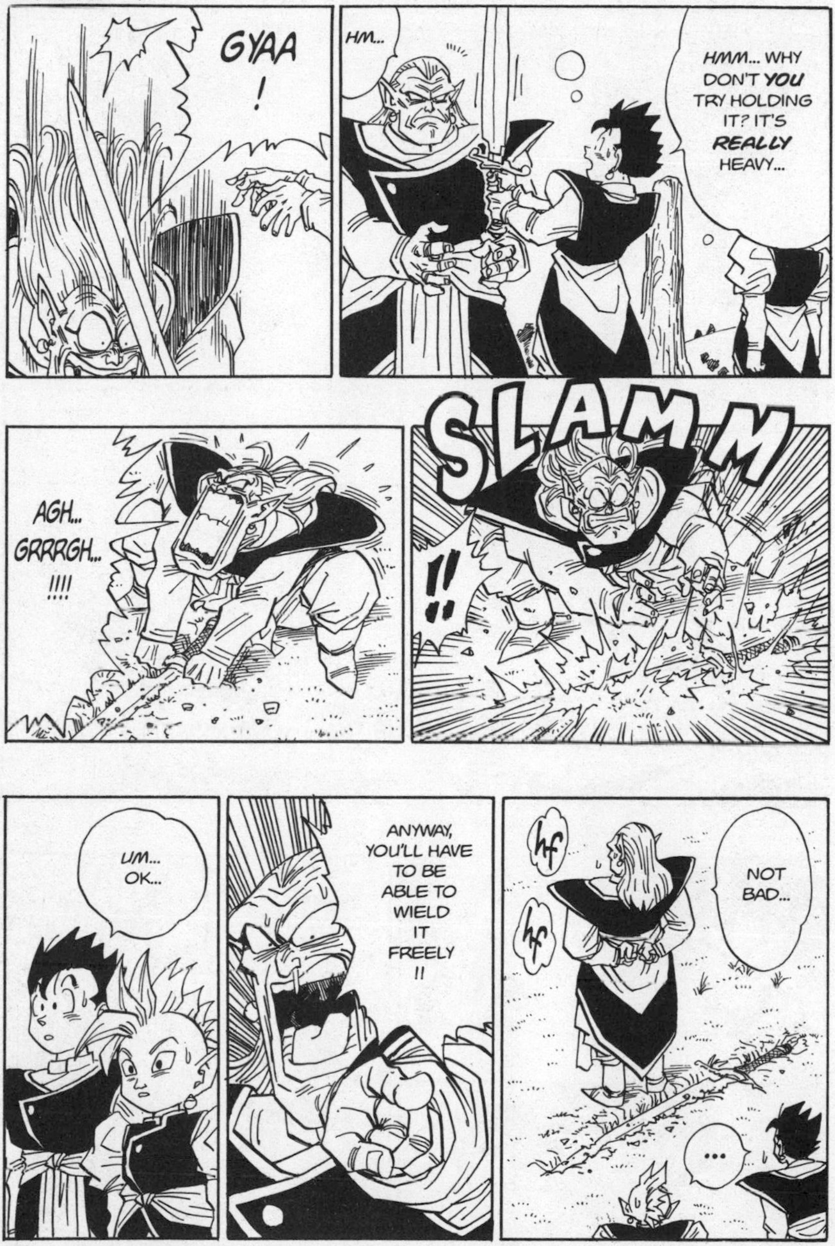

HMM... WHY DON'T **YOU** TRY HOLDING IT? IT'S **REALLY** HEAVY...
HM...
GYAA !
SLAMM
!!
AGH... GRRRGH... !!!!
NOT BAD...
hf
hf
...
ANYWAY, YOU'LL HAVE TO BE ABLE TO WIELD IT FREELY !!
UM... OK...

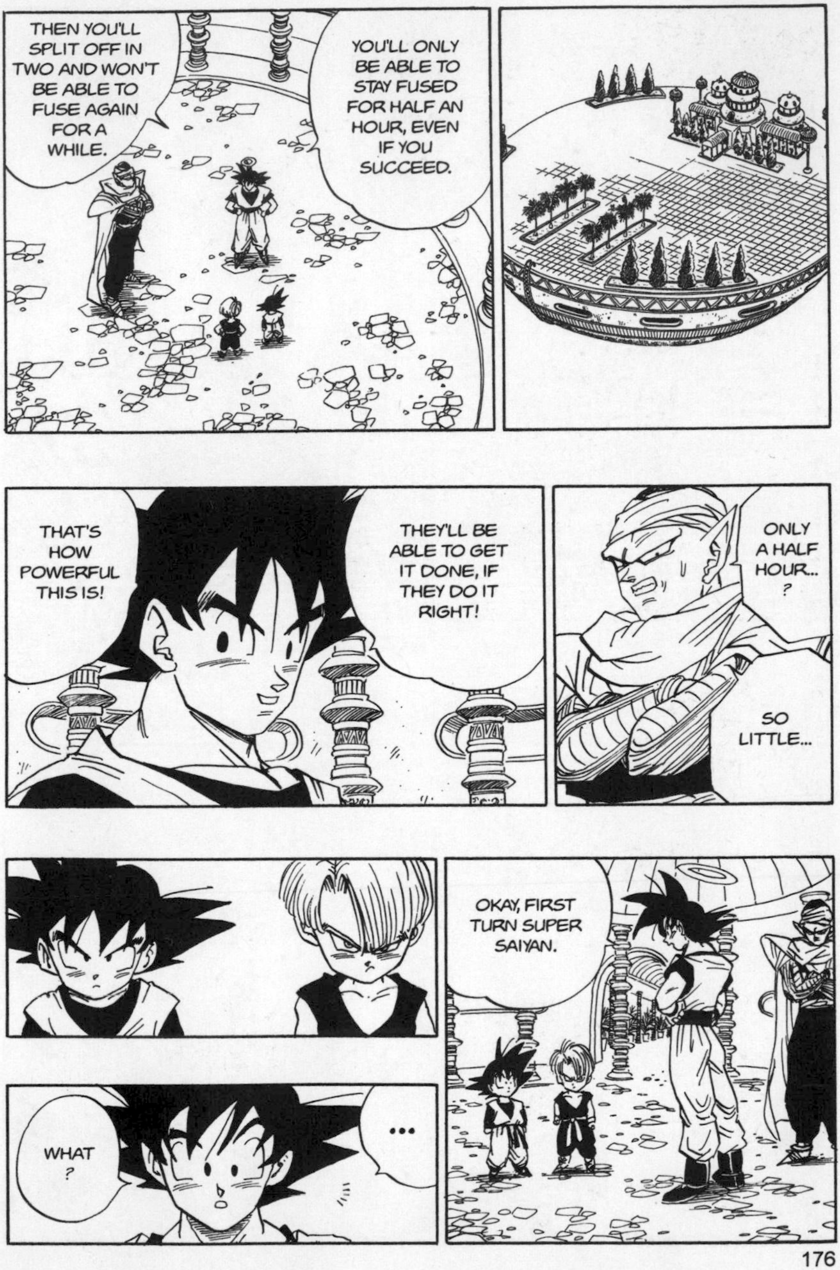
YOU'LL ONLY BE ABLE TO STAY FUSED FOR HALF AN HOUR, EVEN IF YOU SUCCEED.
THEN YOU'LL SPLIT OFF IN TWO AND WON'T BE ABLE TO FUSE AGAIN FOR A WHILE.
ONLY A HALF HOUR...?
SO LITTLE...
THEY'LL BE ABLE TO GET IT DONE, IF THEY DO IT RIGHT!
THAT'S HOW POWERFUL THIS IS!
OKAY, FIRST TURN SUPER SAIYAN.
...
WHAT?

READ THIS WAY

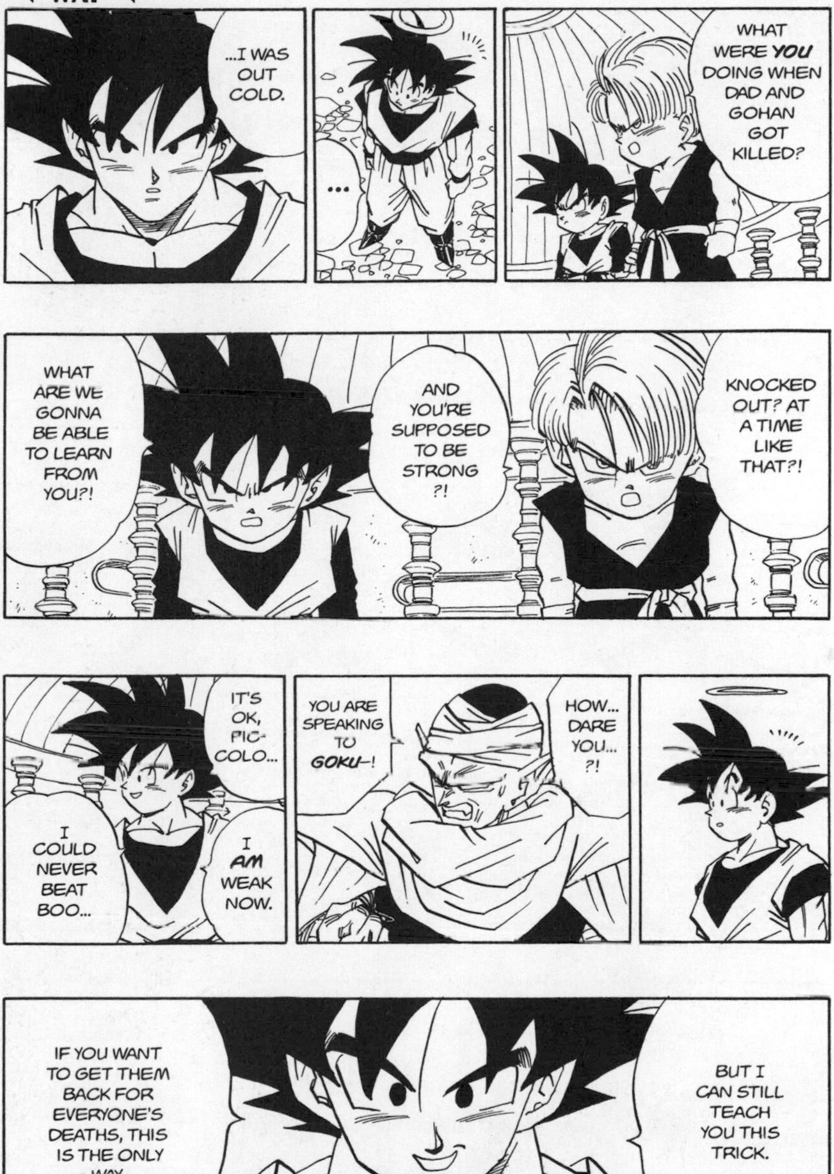

WHAT WERE **YOU** DOING WHEN DAD AND GOHAN GOT KILLED?
...
...I WAS OUT COLD.
KNOCKED OUT? AT A TIME LIKE THAT?!
AND YOU'RE SUPPOSED TO BE STRONG ?!
WHAT ARE WE GONNA BE ABLE TO LEARN FROM YOU?!
HOW... DARE YOU... ?!
YOU ARE SPEAKING TO **GOKU**–!
IT'S OK, PIC-COLO...
I **AM** WEAK NOW.
I COULD NEVER BEAT BOO...
BUT I CAN STILL TEACH YOU THIS TRICK.
IF YOU WANT TO GET THEM BACK FOR EVERYONE'S DEATHS, THIS IS THE ONLY WAY.

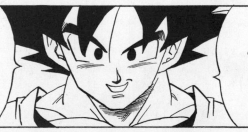

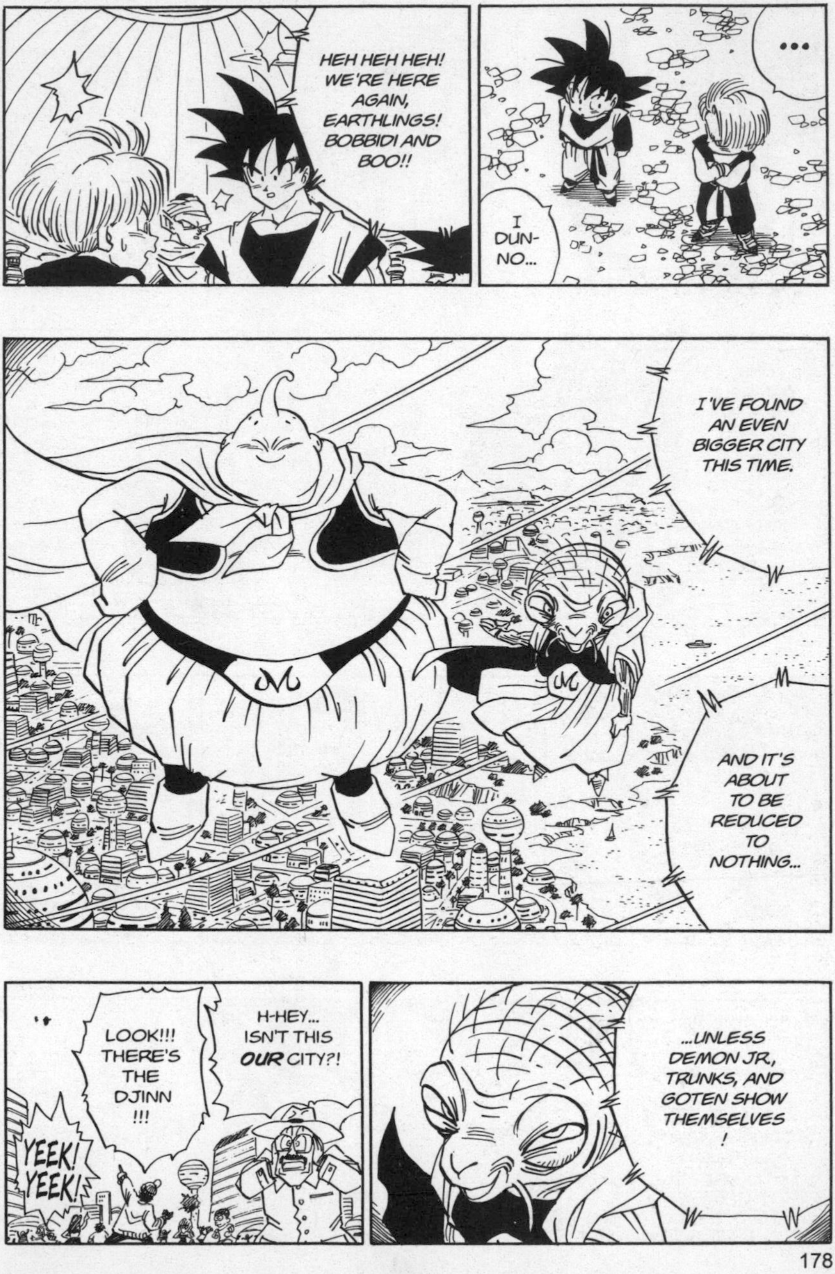
...
I DUN-NO...
HEH HEH HEH! WE'RE HERE AGAIN, EARTHLINGS! BOBBIDI AND BOO!!
I'VE FOUND AN EVEN BIGGER CITY THIS TIME.
AND IT'S ABOUT TO BE REDUCED TO NOTHING...
...UNLESS DEMON JR, TRUNKS, AND GOTEN SHOW THEMSELVES!
H-HEY... ISN'T THIS **OUR** CITY?!
LOOK!!! THERE'S THE DJINN!!!
YEEK! YEEK!

READ THIS WAY

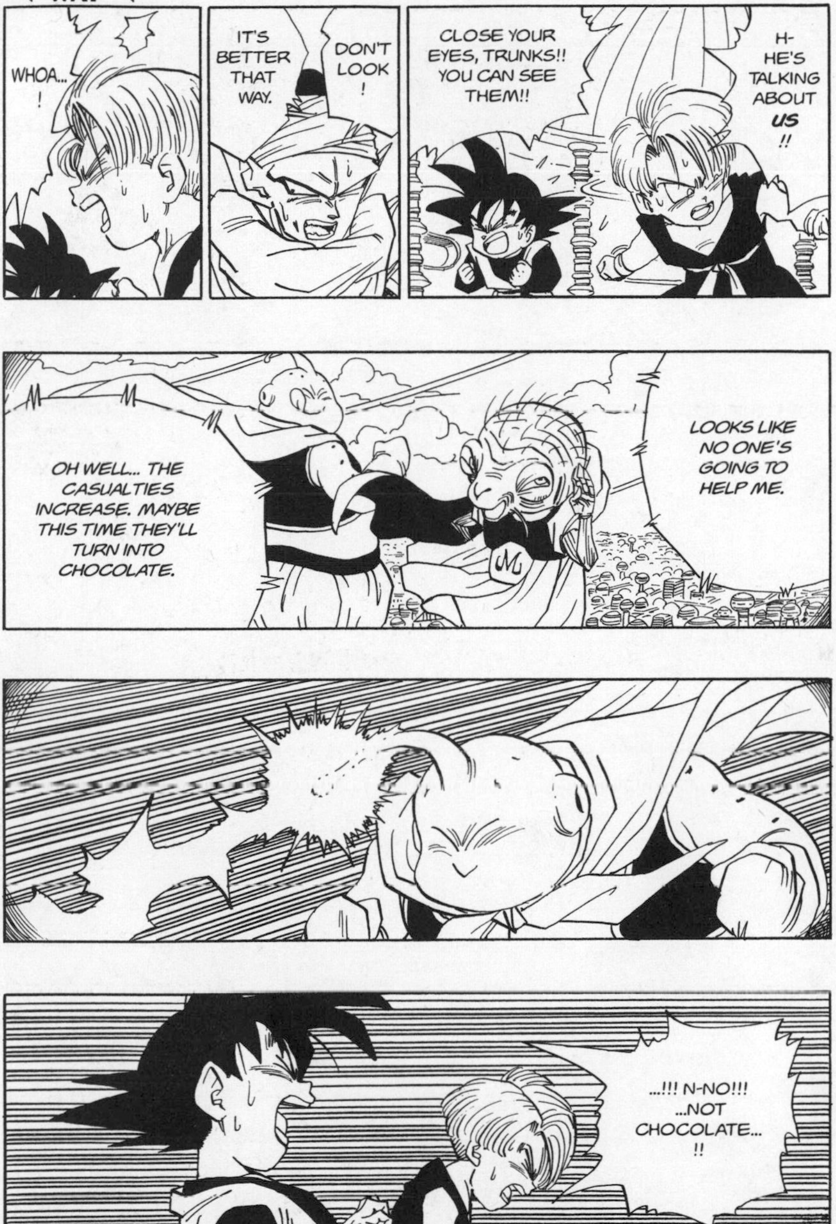
H- HE'S TALKING ABOUT US !!
CLOSE YOUR EYES, TRUNKS!! YOU CAN SEE THEM!!
DON'T LOOK !
IT'S BETTER THAT WAY.
WHOA... !
LOOKS LIKE NO ONE'S GOING TO HELP ME.
OH WELL... THE CASUALTIES INCREASE. MAYBE THIS TIME THEY'LL TURN INTO CHOCOLATE.
...!!! N-NO!!! ...NOT CHOCOLATE... !!

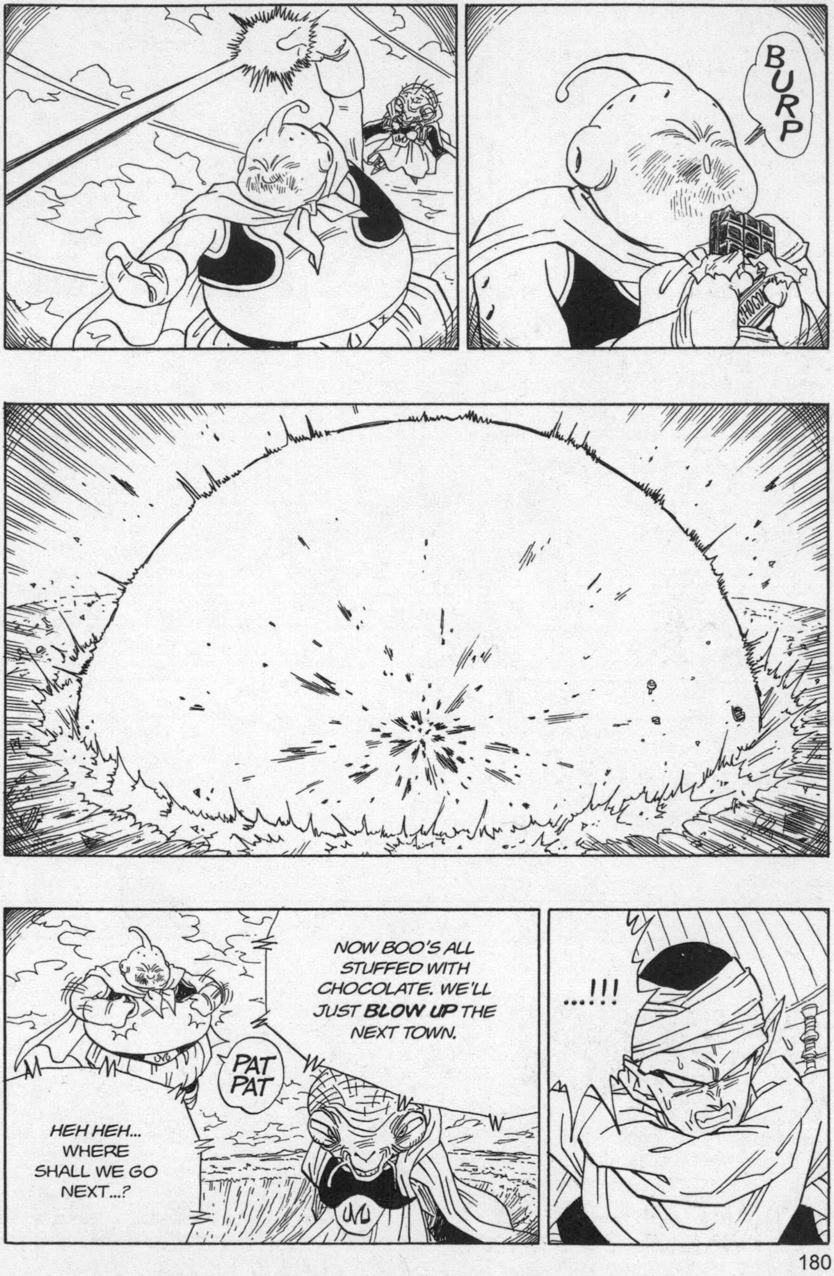
BURP
...!!!
NOW BOO'S ALL STUFFED WITH CHOCOLATE. WE'LL JUST BLOW UP THE NEXT TOWN.
PAT PAT
HEH HEH... WHERE SHALL WE GO NEXT...?

READ THIS WAY

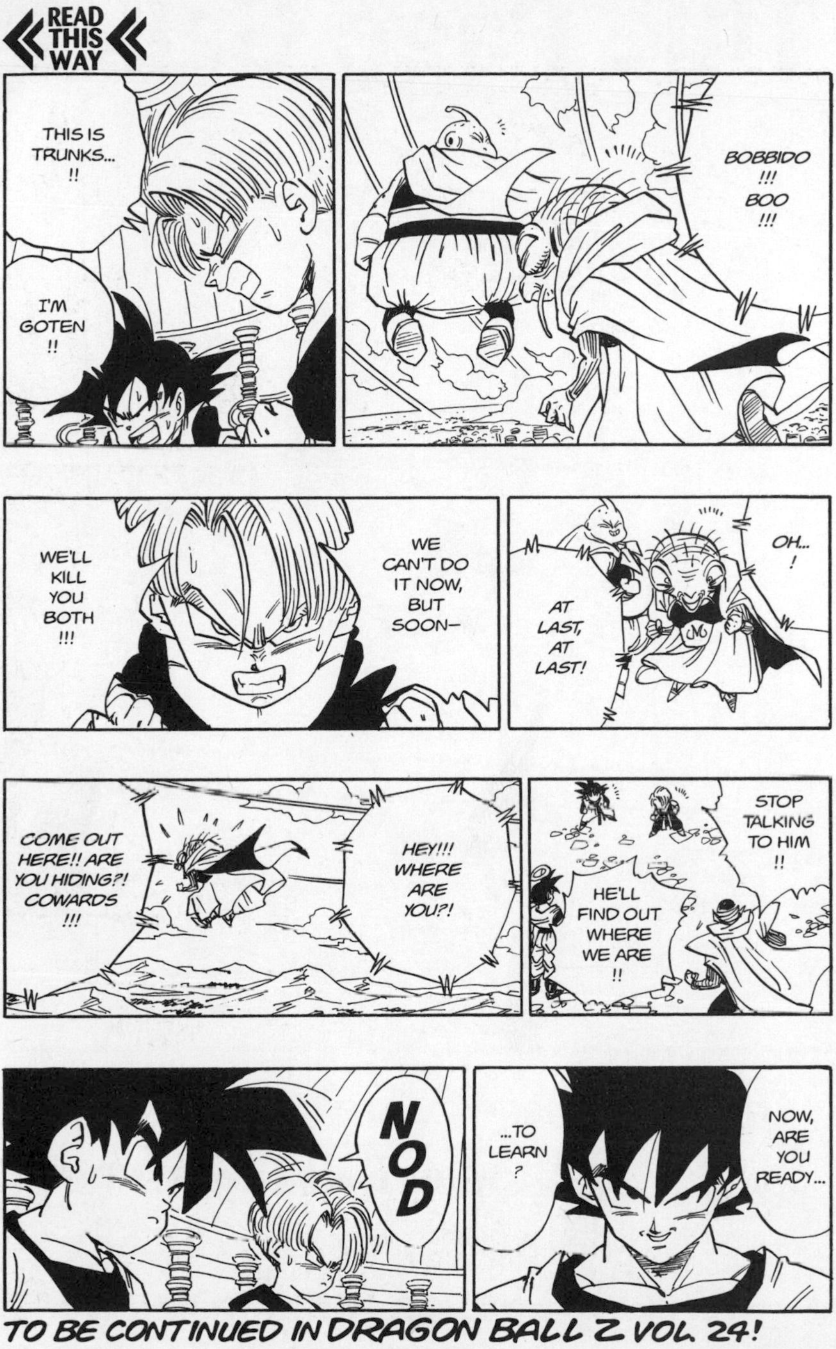
BOBBIDO!!! BOO!!!
THIS IS TRUNKS...!!
I'M GOTEN!!
OH...!
AT LAST, AT LAST!
WE CAN'T DO IT NOW, BUT SOON—
WE'LL KILL YOU BOTH!!!
STOP TALKING TO HIM!!
HE'LL FIND OUT WHERE WE ARE!!
HEY!!! WHERE ARE YOU?!
COME OUT HERE!! ARE YOU HIDING?! COWARDS!!!
NOW, ARE YOU READY...
...TO LEARN?
NOD

TO BE CONTINUED IN DRAGON BALL Z VOL. 24!

Title Page Gallery

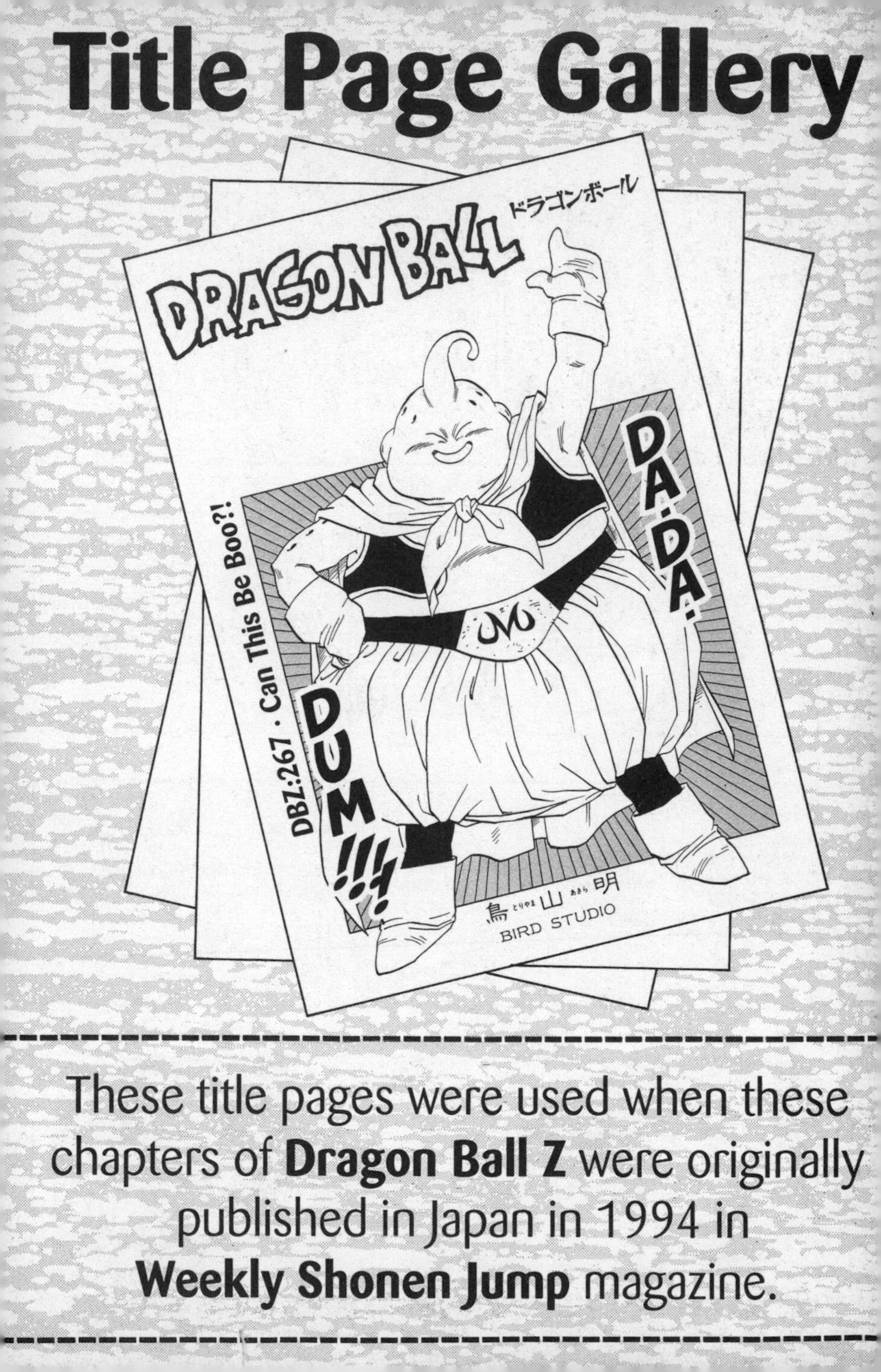
DRAGON BALL
ドラゴンボール
DBZ:267 · Can This Be Boo?!
DA DA
DUM!!!
鳥山明
BIRD STUDIO

These title pages were used when these chapters of **Dragon Ball Z** were originally published in Japan in 1994 in **Weekly Shonen Jump** magazine.

DRAGON BALL

鳥山明 とりやま あきら

BIRD STUDIO

DBZ:273 · Farewell, Proud Warrior

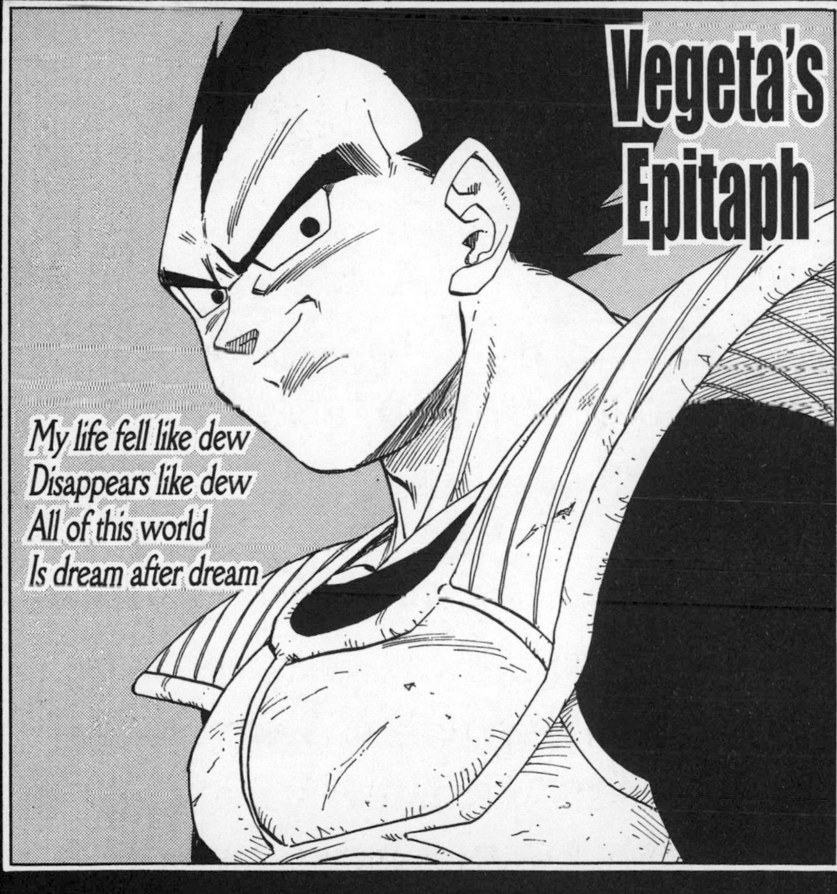
Vegeta's Epitaph
My life fell like dew
Disappears like dew
All of this world
Is dream after dream

DRAGON BALL ドラゴンボール

DBZ:276
Bobbidi's Revenge!!

とりやまあきら
鳥山明
BIRD STUDIO

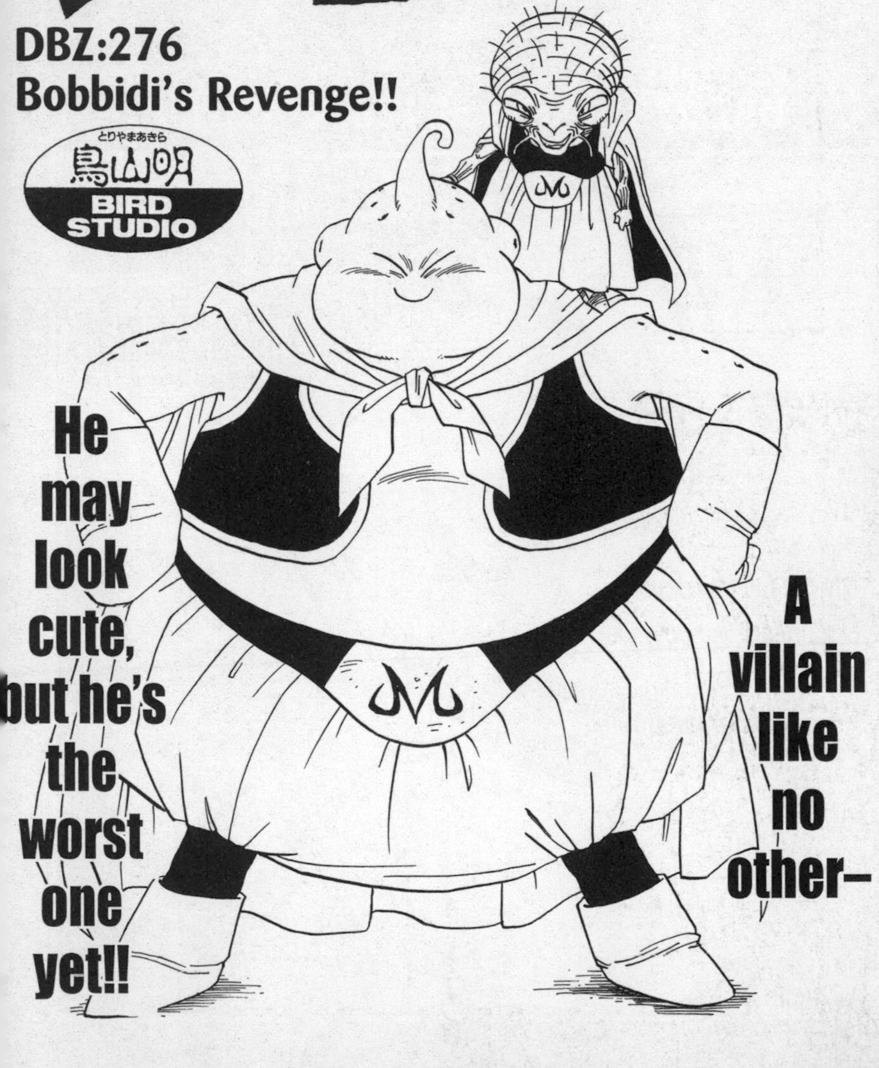
A villain like no other—
He may look cute, but he's the worst one yet!!

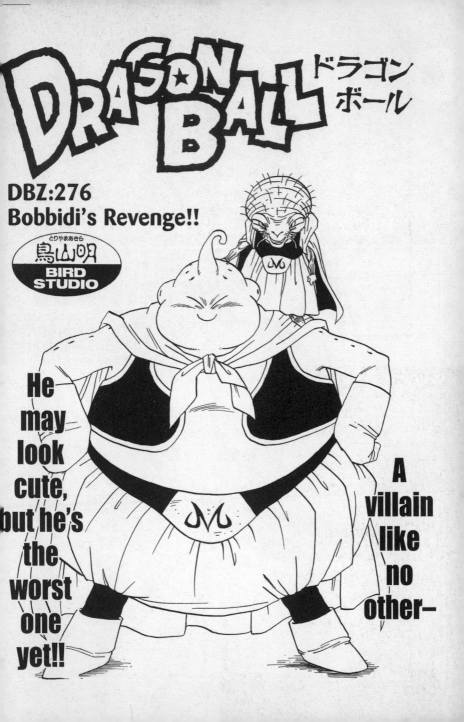

IN THE NEXT VOLUME…

The rampaging Boo turns the entire world into his candy store! To fight back, Goku transforms into his most powerful form yet, but the world's only hope may lie in Trunks and Goten, the world's youngest and most promising fighters. Can the two young Saiyans use the alien fusion technique to merge together and form a single, even stronger hero? Meanwhile, as Boo destroys city after city, the people of Earth call forth their secret weapon…Hercule!

AVAILABLE NOW!

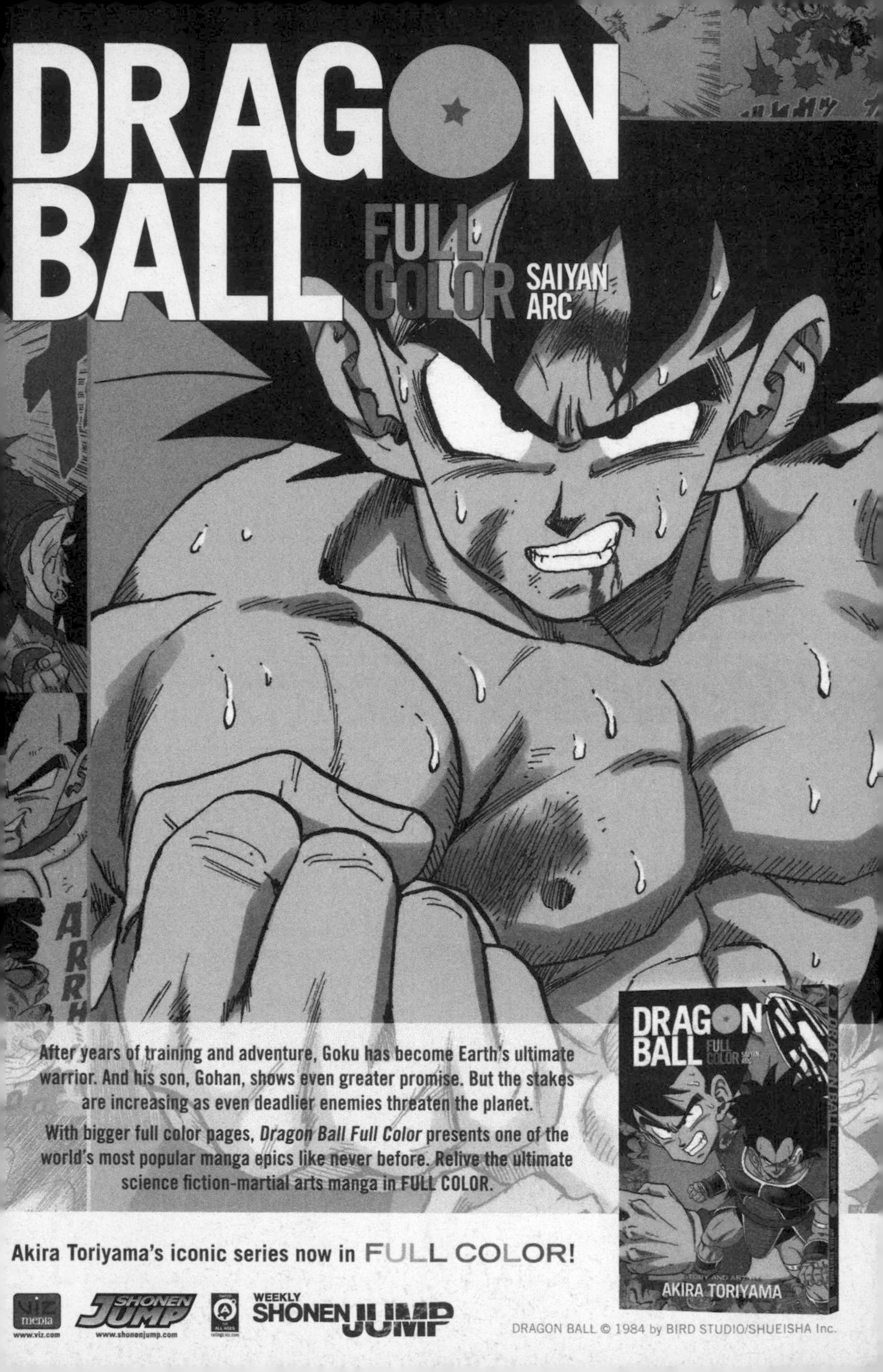
DRAGON BALL
FULL COLOR
SAIYAN ARC
ARRH
After years of training and adventure, Goku has become Earth's ultimate warrior. And his son, Gohan, shows even greater promise. But the stakes are increasing as even deadlier enemies threaten the planet.
With bigger full color pages, *Dragon Ball Full Color* presents one of the world's most popular manga epics like never before. Relive the ultimate science fiction-martial arts manga in FULL COLOR.
DRAGON BALL FULL COLOR SAIYAN ARC
AKIRA TORIYAMA
Akira Toriyama's iconic series now in FULL COLOR!
www.viz.com
SHONEN JUMP
www.shonenjump.com
WEEKLY SHONEN JUMP
DRAGON BALL © 1984 by BIRD STUDIO/SHUEISHA Inc.

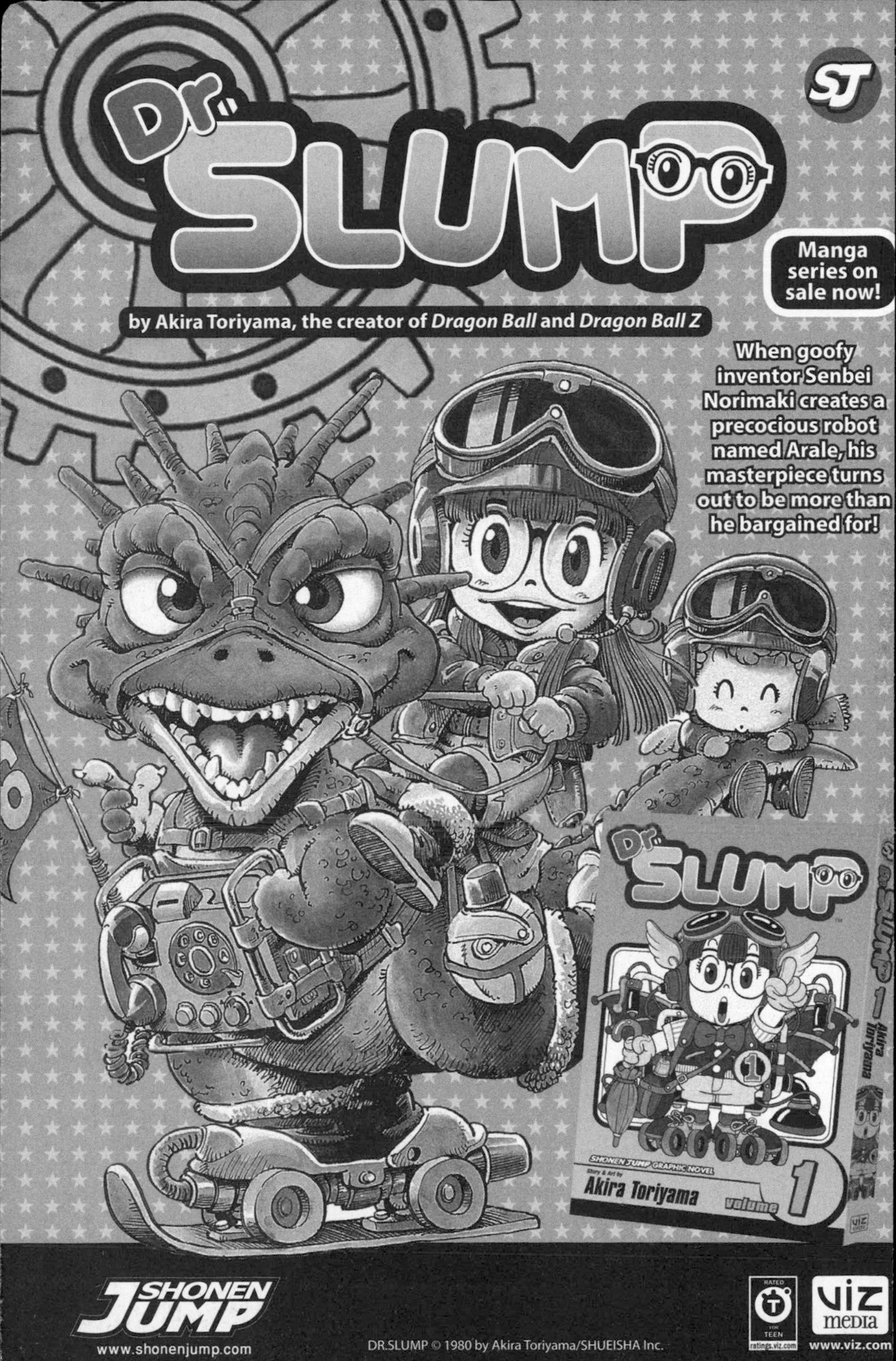

SJ
Dr. SLUMP
Manga series on sale now!
by Akira Toriyama, the creator of *Dragon Ball* and *Dragon Ball Z*
When goofy inventor Senbei Norimaki creates a precocious robot named Arale, his masterpiece turns out to be more than he bargained for!
Dr. SLUMP
SHONEN JUMP GRAPHIC NOVEL
Story & Art by
Akira Toriyama
volume 1
SHONEN JUMP
www.shonenjump.com
DR.SLUMP © 1980 by Akira Toriyama/SHUEISHA Inc.
RATED T FOR TEEN
ratings.viz.com
VIZ media
www.viz.com

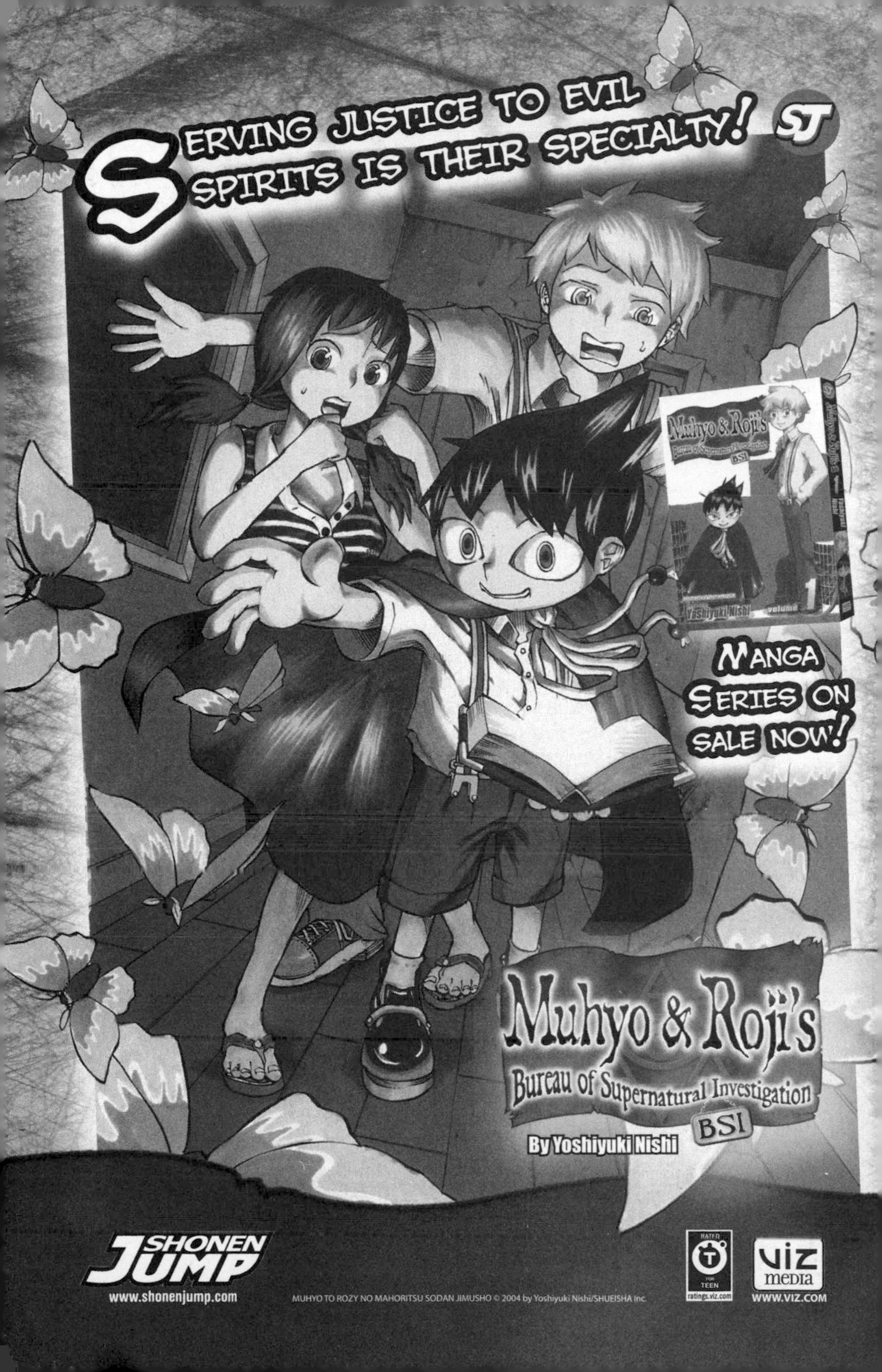
SERVING JUSTICE TO EVIL SPIRITS IS THEIR SPECIALTY!
SJ
Muhyo & Roji's Bureau of Supernatural Investigation BSI
Yoshiyuki Nishi
volume 1
MANGA SERIES ON SALE NOW!
Muhyo & Roji's
Bureau of Supernatural Investigation
BSI
By Yoshiyuki Nishi
SHONEN JUMP
www.shonenjump.com
MUHYO TO ROZY NO MAHORITSU SODAN JIMUSHO © 2004 by Yoshiyuki Nishi/SHUEISHA Inc.
RATED T FOR TEEN
ratings.viz.com
VIZ media
WWW.VIZ.COM

You're Reading in the Wrong Direction!!

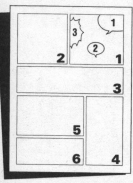

Whoops! Guess what? You're starting at the wrong end of the comic!

...It's true! In keeping with the original Japanese format, Akira Toriyama's world-famous **Dragon Ball Z** series is meant to be read from right to left, starting in the upper-right corner.

Unlike English which is read from left to right, Japanese is read from right to left, meaning that action, sound effects and word-balloon order are completely reversed... something which can make readers unfamiliar with Japanese feel pretty backwards themselves. For this reason, manga or Japanese comics published in the U.S. in English have traditionally been published "flopped"—that is, printed in exact reverse order, as though seen from the other side of a mirror.

By flopping pages, U.S. publishers can avoid confusing readers, but the compromise is not without its downside. For one thing, a character in a flopped manga series who, in the original Japanese version, wore a T-shirt emblazoned with "M A Y" (as in "the merry month of") now wears one which reads "Y A M"! Additionally, many manga creators in Japan are themselves unhappy with the process, as some feel the mirror-imaging of their art skews their original intentions.

In recognition of the importance and popularity of **Dragon Ball Z**, we are proud to bring it to you in the original unflopped format.

For now, though, turn to the other side of the book and let the adventure begin...!

—Editor

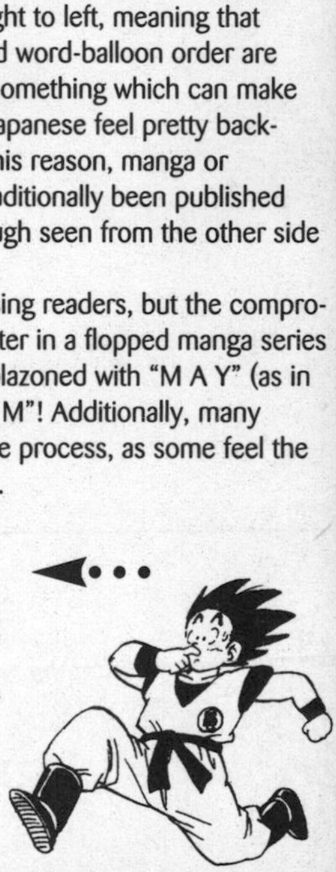